Islamophobia

ISLAMOPHOBIA

What Christians Should Know (and Do)
about Anti-Muslim Discrimination

JORDAN DENARI DUFFNER

ORBIS BOOKS
Maryknoll, New York 10545

ORBIS ✦ BOOKS
Maryknoll, New York 10545

Fathers and Brothers
MARYKNOLL.

Founded in 1970, Orbis Books endeavors to publish works that enlighten the mind, nourish the spirit, and challenge the conscience. The publishing arm of the Maryknoll Fathers and Brothers, Orbis seeks to explore the global dimensions of the Christian faith and mission, to invite dialogue with diverse cultures and religious traditions, and to serve the cause of reconciliation and peace. The books published reflect the views of their authors and do not represent the official position of the Maryknoll Society. To learn more about Orbis Books, please visit our website at www.orbisbooks.com.

Unless otherwise noted, Scripture quotations are from the *New Revised Standard Version* of the Bible, copyright © 1989 by the Division of Christian Education of the National Council of the Churches of Christ in the USA.

Manufactured in the United States of America

Library of Congress Cataloging-in-Publication Data

Names: Duffner, Jordan Denari, author.
Title: Islamophobia : what Christians should know (and do) about anti-Muslim discrimination / Jordan Denari Duffner.
Description: Maryknoll : Orbis Books, 2021. | Includes bibliographical references and index. | Summary: "This book discusses the international and historical roots of Islamophobia and its connection to Christianity and lays out a proposed Christian response"—Provided by publisher.
Identifiers: LCCN 2020046419 (print) | LCCN 2020046420 (ebook) | ISBN 9781626984103 (trade paperback) | ISBN 9781608338740 (epub)
Subjects: LCSH: Islamophobia. | Christianity and other religions—Islam. | Islam—Relations—Christianity. | Islam—21st century.
Classification: LCC BP52 .D84 2021 (print) | LCC BP52 (ebook) | DDC 305.6/97—dc23
LC record available at https://lccn.loc.gov/2020046419
LC ebook record available at https://lccn.loc.gov/20200464208

There is no fear in love,
but perfect love casts out fear . . .
Whoever fears has not reached
perfection in love.

1 John 4:18

For my husband Chris,
who has always understood.

CONTENTS

Acknowledgments

Looking back over the years during which I wrote this book, I want to first thank my husband, Chris. I am grateful to have him as a partner not only in our shared vocation of marriage, but also in our common calling to accompany and advocate for those whom our society often demonizes. Chris works as a public defender, a defense attorney representing clients who are charged with crimes and cannot afford a lawyer. His clients are often society's scapegoats, seen solely for the wrong they've been accused of and, as such, worthy only of exclusion from society. Muslims are often viewed in the same way: as dangerous, as outsiders we would rather do without. Because of these parallels, Chris understands from personal experience the skepticism I sometimes face about my own work, including disapproving comments and questions that seem to really be asking, "Why would you ever want to help *those* people?"

Chris never needed an explanation. From the first days I knew him, he could see that my concern about Islamophobia was not in contradiction to our shared Catholic Christian faith, but rather a natural outgrowth of it. For Chris, seeing the dignity and value in the victims of the "throwaway culture"—as Pope Francis calls it—is what Christianity is all about. By his daily persistence and quiet cheerfulness, Chris teaches me how to play the long game in the quest for a more compassionate and just society, and how to cultivate joy and gratitude amid the reality of grave suffering. As a skilled communicator and writer, he provided comments and edits on this book that made it infinitely better than it would have been otherwise. I am so blessed.

I also owe great thanks to Jim Keane, who no longer works at Orbis but who first approached me about working with Orbis on a book for Christians about Islamophobia. Elements of this book were percolating inside my brain for years, and fragments of it were saved in disparate Word documents on my computer, but it took Jim's email to me in the summer of 2017 to allow it to materialize. I am honored to have had the opportunity to publish with Orbis, which is well known for its books that push the universal church to live up to its highest ideals and mission. I am grateful for the support and guidance of my editor, Jill Brennan O'Brien, publisher Robert Ellsberg, and many other staff members at Orbis for all they did to make this book a reality.

I also want to thank my parents, Maggie and Tom Denari, who have always supported my writing generally and my work on Islamophobia in particular. Even before our public discourse had a word for Islamophobia, my dad encouraged my writing about it. My mom urged me on as well, both of them often reminding me to "jot it down" when I would have conversations, experiences, or ideas that would be worth revisiting one day. Many of those notes did not fit into my first book, *Finding Jesus among Muslims*, but they have found a home in the pages of this one. My parents, along with my brother, Nick, and sister-in-law, Alyssa Duffner, read drafts and served as sounding boards for ideas.

I am especially grateful to those friends and colleagues who gave their feedback on the coming pages and talked me through periods of frustration, confusion, and feelings of inadequacy. Nazir Harb Michel deserves special thanks. A dear friend and colleague, he was a supporter and cheerleader when I needed one, and without his wise insights this book would be a far different one. Mobashra Tazamal, Nena Beecham, Halla Atallah, and Asad Dandia also devoted considerable time to reading portions of the book and offering expert feedback. Michael Calabria, OFM, Edward E. Curtis IV, Catherine Orsborn, Alyssa Huberts, Kevin Sullivan, Kristin Garrity, Joan Braune, and Patrick Rogers, SJ, provided insight at critical moments in the writing process. I am also grateful to those who allowed me to recount their personal experiences and perspectives in this book, including Asad Dandia, Simran Jeet Singh, Asima and Yasiyn Silva, Nazir Harb Michel, Judy Westrate, the Reverend Bob Sims, and a friend who has wished to remain anonymous.

I owe much to my many professors at Georgetown University, who have guided me through my undergraduate and doctoral programs, as well as to my colleagues at the Bridge Initiative, where I worked for three years as a research fellow and where I am still affiliated as an associate. I have learned so much from the current and former Bridge staff, and I am grateful to the directors, especially Dr. John Esposito and Dr. Tamara Sonn, for the opportunity to contribute to the mission of such a necessary and groundbreaking initiative, especially in its formative years. Even before we worked at Bridge together, Nathan Lean gave me a leg up and was a supportive mentor in my writing on Islamophobia.

There are so many others whom I have encountered in my work on Muslim-Christian relations and who have shaped it in indelible ways. Some I came to know through college internships and academic conferences, and others I met through interfaith *iftars*, Catholic "theology on tap" events, and social media exchanges. To list them all would take up dozens of pages of this book, but their collective wisdom has informed much of what I say here. I also want to acknowledge the many Christian leaders—clergy, scholars, and laypeople from various denominations—who speak and act in prophetic ways to defend our Muslim siblings in faith. I feel a deep kinship with them, and I am grateful for their example of interreligious solidarity. Many of their names appear in this book.

While this book seeks to offer new ways of thinking about and addressing Islamophobia, it draws upon the work of countless scholars and activists—living and dead, Muslim and not—whom I reference throughout the text. I have learned so much from their expertise, and even more so from the personal experiences of Muslims and others who have been impacted by Islamophobia.

Though Muslims are not the primary audience for this book, I have ultimately written it for them. My Muslim friends have been companions, both along the spiritual journey and in the quest to make our world a more just place. For both Christians and Muslims, these two aspects of our lives are not separate; how we treat one another is intrinsically tied to our relationship with the divine. My Muslim friends have demonstrated to me and to so many others around them how to strive after what God wants and how to put one's gifts at the service of family and those marginalized by racism, sexism, and other forces of oppression.

In the United States and elsewhere, and for far too long, Muslims have been at the receiving end of suspicion, prejudice, and discrimination—and increasingly so in recent years. I hope this book can contribute to the dismantling of this problem, and to the building up of a world where people of all faiths are treated with the love and respect that reflects their God-given dignity.

Alhamdulillah
Praise be to God, always,
in good times and in bad.

NOTES TO READERS

A Warning on Troubling and Traumatic Accounts

It will be no surprise that a book on anti-Muslim prejudice and discrimination includes troubling stories and traumatic accounts. Because Christians and others who are not Muslim often lack exposure to the harsh reality of Islamophobia, I have included accounts that shine a light on the range of ways that Muslims have experienced Islamophobia. (All accounts in this book have been drawn from publicly available news reports or from the personal experiences of friends and acquaintances who have given their permission and reviewed what I have written.) These stories make for unpleasant reading at many points. I ask that teachers and reading-group leaders who guide others through the book be mindful that this material may be very distressing for some readers, especially those who are Muslim or who have their own histories of experiencing prejudice and discrimination. I recommend that teachers and guides alert their students to these troubling portions ahead of reading assignments, potentially giving them the option to skip over these sections if necessary.

Basic Facts and Clarifying Terms on Islam and Muslims

Some readers of this book will have Muslims as personal friends or acquaintances, and some will have much knowledge about the religion of Islam. Others will have had little prior exposure to Muslim people or their faith. Given that readers come to the book with different levels of knowledge and familiarity, here at the beginning of the book I provide some background information. The most important thing for readers to grasp at the outset is the distinction between three categories that non-Muslims often confuse or conflate: Muslims (a religious group), Arabic and Arabs (a linguistic and an ethnic category), and the Middle East (a geographical region).

Muslims, whose religious tradition is called Islam, make up roughly a quarter of the world's population.[1] They number 1.8 billion out of about 7.3 billion people worldwide. They are second to Christians, who number 2.3 billion around the globe, yet Muslims are predicted to outnumber Christians by 2035. There are about 1.3 billion Catholics globally, making them the largest Christian denomination.[2]

Contrary to many readers' expectations, most of the world's Muslims do not live in the region commonly known as the Middle East—only 20 percent do. Most live in South and East Asia. The six countries with the largest Muslim populations are Indonesia, India, Pakistan, Bangladesh, Nigeria, and Egypt.[3] Only the last of these is in the Middle East and is a country where people primarily speak the Arabic language, and in both India and Nigeria Muslims are not the majority religious group. Countries with majority-Muslim populations include Morocco, Iran, Sudan, Turkey, Malaysia, Burkina Faso, Maldives, and Albania—just to name a few spread around the globe. Muslims are not the majority but constitute a significant portion of the population in countries like Ethiopia, Bulgaria, Tanzania, Singapore, and France. Muslims can be found in every corner of the world—from Greenland to Argentina, South Africa to China. Though often associated in the Western imagination with the Middle East and the Arabic language, Muslims are as diverse a religious community as can be found.

In my own country, the United States, Muslims make up a very small share of the population, yet they are still incredibly diverse. The first Muslims in what is now the United States were forcibly brought to the Americas from West Africa. Though it is difficult to know what percentage of these enslaved women, men, and children were Muslims, scholars estimate that about 5 to 10 percent of those brought to the North American colonies were Muslim—a number in the tens of thousands.[4] In the Caribbean, the number of Muslims was possibly much higher, in the hundreds of thousands.[5]

Today, there are approximately 3.5 million Muslims living in the United States, constituting about 1 percent of the total U.S. population.[6] Demographers believe that by 2040, the number of Muslims in the United States will be equivalent to that of American Jews, and that by 2050, Muslims will constitute 2 percent of the total U.S. population. Black, Latinx, Arab, White, South Asian, and more—Muslims of nearly every ethnicity and background call the United States home.[7]

Arabic is a language spoken by about 274 million people around the world.[8] It is the sixth-most-spoken language in the world, though the differences among local dialects are very significant. Having originated in the Arabian Peninsula alongside other Middle Eastern languages, Arabic is considered a Semitic language due to its similarities with languages like Hebrew, Aramaic (the language Jesus spoke), and Amharic (which is spoken in Ethiopia). Arabic is written from right to left, and many of the letters link together in a cursive style when joined together in words. Just as the Spanish, French, and English languages all use the Latin/Roman alphabet in writing, a range of languages make use of the Arabic script, including Persian, Urdu, Uighur, and Pashto.

The term "the Middle East" denotes a geographic region, though there is no consensus on what expanse this term includes. It is usually used to refer to the wide swath of territory that extends from Egypt in Africa to the lands east of the Mediterranean Sea, down through the Arabian Peninsula and across to Iran (but usually not as far as Afghanistan and Pakistan, which are typically considered "South Asia," along with India and its neighbors). Sometimes North and East African countries are included in "the Middle East," as is Turkey. (If you're having trouble picturing this, pull up a world map online.) Arabic is spoken in much but not all of the Middle East; dozens of languages are spoken in this vast area, which also has tremendous geographical and environmental diversity. In Iran, for example, you will find rolling green hills that give way to snow-topped mountains, barren deserts, and lush waterfalls. There, Persian, not Arabic, is primarily spoken. Written with the Arabic alphabet, right to left, it has numerous Arabic loan words, but is linguistically closer to many European languages.

Many religions, not just Islam, are practiced throughout the Middle East and among Arabic speakers. For example, when I lived in Amman, Jordan—an Arabic-speaking country sandwiched between Iraq, Syria, Israel-Palestine, and Saudi Arabia—I stayed with a Catholic Christian host family whose native language is Arabic. They trace their family lineage to Bethlehem, the town of Jesus's birth, and have carried on the faith in the Middle East since the earliest days of Christianity.

The words *Islam* and *Muslim* come from the Arabic language. *Islam* is used to describe the religious tradition, while a *Muslim* is a person who ascribes to that faith.[9] The word *Islamic*, an adjective, is used in English to describe inanimate or impersonal things related to Islam. (It should not be used for people, who are to be referred to as *Muslims*.) The root of all these words—the Arabic letters *s-l-m*—conveys in Arabic notions of calm, tranquility, peace, and wholeness. *Muslims*, then, are people who freely devote themselves to God and experience comfort and security in doing that. Linguistically, *Islam* can be understood as the ongoing act of giving oneself over to God, whom Muslims sometimes refer to as *Al-Salaam*, the Source of Peace. To Christians, this understanding of faith as a giving of oneself over to God should feel familiar and relatable. As a Catholic, I find that it resonates with the Ignatian spirituality of the Jesuit order, which recognizes that freedom and fulfillment accompany a person's choice to live in accordance with God's desires and will for them.

As mentioned above, the Arabic language is not unique to Muslims. But it is central to Islam as a religious tradition because it was the language of the

Prophet Muhammad and his community. Arabic is also the language of the Qur'an, which Muslims believe is God's Word, or revelation, communicated to and through a man named Muhammad in seventh-century Arabia. *Qur'an* in Arabic means "recitation." According to the Islamic tradition, Muhammad initially recited the divine revelations orally in Arabic to his community over a period of twenty-plus years, and this Qur'an was then written down and compiled into book form. Because the Islamic religious tradition emerged from this Arabic-speaking context, much of the vocabulary commonly used to describe Islamic beliefs and practices comes from Arabic. When Muslims recite portions of the Qur'an in the context of prayer, for the most part they do so in the original Arabic rather than a translation. Thus, Muslims around the world often know at least some Arabic words or how to recite some Qur'anic passages. But despite its centrality in the tradition, the Arabic language is not the only "Islamic" language; in fact, any language that comes into contact with the religious tradition could be said to be Islamic.

As for Islam as a religion, giving just a brief overview is nearly impossible. A tradition going back fourteen hundred years, it is vast and diverse, characterized by the lived experiences of countless people who believe in God and Muhammad as God's final messenger. But for those unfamiliar with the religion, a few points are worth mentioning here. (This book does not purport to be an Islam 101 book, and takes the perspective that one does not need to know much about Islam to understand Islamophobia.) Muslims understand their faith to be the faith of Abraham, as Christians and Jews also do. Muslims are monotheists who see their community as a continuation of believers that stretches all the way back to Adam and Eve, who expressed belief in the one God. Many characters in the Bible are mentioned, referenced, or alluded to in the Qur'an, including Moses, Jesus, Mary his mother, Sarah, Isaac, Ishmael, Hagar, Joseph (son of Jacob), David, Solomon, and John (the Baptist). The book also includes moral commandments; reminders to be grateful to God; words of divine comfort and chastisement, wisdom and warning; divine guidance to the prophet in navigating the situations of his life and community; and other lessons for life. For Muslims, the Qur'an is more than a book to be interpreted; it is God's speech in the world. Consequently, recitation of the Qur'an is a holy art form that puts both the speaker and listener in touch with the divine.

Muslims share many points of belief and practice with Jews and Christians—too many to name here—as well as moral values, like caring for the vulnerable. There are also theological differences, as well as divergences in social and ritual norms, both among these religious communities and within Islam itself. Even with this internal diversity, Muslims often foreground God's attribute of *rahma*—mercy or compassionate love—which they invoke every time they pray. Muhammad, who is considered God's final prophet, is not worshipped but rather is considered a holy and venerable role model. Muslims remember him as a generous and caring person who had a deep connection with God and did all he could to bring forth God's will on earth. They strive to follow his example (*sunna*) and sometimes invoke him as an intercessor. Sayings attributed to the Prophet (the *hadith*) are also a source of moral and spiritual guidance for Muslims.

There are two major branches of Muslims: Sunnis and Shias, with the former constituting about 80 percent of the global Muslim population. Like Christians of different denominations, they share the basics of faith, but because of historical and political occurrences and differences of belief on certain matters, they became distinct groups.

In the minds of many of us, the religion of Islam, the language of Arabic, and the region of the Middle East are often conflated. We assume that people who claim one of these also possess the other two qualities. This assumption must be resisted, due to the fact that these aspects (religious, linguistic, and geographic) are unique, even though in some cases they overlap.

Style and Terminology

This book includes a range of Arabic words that have been transliterated into Roman characters to be legible in English. I have avoided using the diacritic marks that are common in academic writing, in order to make the book accessible to a broad audience. With the exception of individual or group names, I typically render Arabic words into English in a way that will help readers accurately pronounce them.

As for other stylistic choices, when I capitalize the word "Church," I am making reference to the institutional Catholic Church, whereas when I use lowercase "church" I am referring to the global Christian community. I tend to use the terms *interreligious* and *interfaith* synonymously, though they are not always employed as synonyms by other writers.

INTRODUCTION

In the dark of night, outside a small mosque in Nashville, Tennessee, an unknown vandal shook a canister of spray paint, the clacking sound bouncing off the white brick walls. The person cast a blood-red stream across the building, spraying its exterior and windows with a hostile message that would greet the congregants of the Al-Farooq Mosque when they arrived the next morning: "MUSLIMS GO HOME." The vandal committed the act just days after a local news program had aired a sensationalist film about the dangers of "homegrown jihad,"[1] putting a spotlight on a nearby Muslim community and making unfounded claims that they had connections to terrorist groups.

When congregants of Al-Farooq pulled up to the mosque the next day for their morning prayers, they found more: a series of interlocking crosses, undoubtedly a Christian symbol, spray-painted on the side of the building. A letter was also left there, which reportedly referred to Muslims as "friends of Satan" and as a "threat" to the United States.[2] The community was shaken up, but fortunately their neighbors sprang into action to help. An administrator at Belmont University, a nearby Christian college, quickly reached out to the mosque's leadership. He said, "It was just terrible that the cross, a sign of God's love for us, was used to terrorize, once again, a minority community here in Tennessee"—it had not been the first time.[3] The administrator offered to have Belmont pay for the materials to remove the graffiti, and he and others from the area quickly scrubbed it away and repainted the walls a crisp white. Thanking the community for their support, the mosque leadership noted that while the vandal had tried to drive a wedge between Christians and Muslims, the act had ultimately brought them closer together.

This story reflects much of what this book is about: the prejudice and discrimination that Muslims have faced, the way Christians have contributed to it, and the moral and faith-filled duty that Christians are called to play in upending Islamophobia.

A Christian Calling

Throughout the twenty-first century, in the United States, Europe, and beyond, Muslims have arrived at their houses of worship to find them vandalized or destroyed. Attackers with racist views have opened fire on Muslims while they were gathered for worship. Politicians have made anti-Muslim fearmongering the centerpiece of their election campaigns, drumming up bigotry to justify war or military spending. Muslim mothers and fathers have been verbally or physically assaulted while going about their daily lives, and Muslim children bullied by classmates. Governments and law enforcement agencies have put Muslims under special scrutiny, in some cases effectively criminalizing their religious practice and stripping them of their human and civil rights. Muslims have faced these forms of Islamophobia for a long time, but for many Christians—especially those like me who are American and White—the tragic reality of anti-Muslim prejudice and discrimination has often gone unnoticed, or has only recently appeared on our radar.

Islamophobia is not aimed at Christians.[4] Yet because it inflicts harm upon members of the human family, it is something that we are called by God and our faith to address. Religious discrimination, in whatever form it takes and whomever it targets, is a grave injustice. We know this not just as human beings, but because of our faith as Christians. It goes against our most basic Christian value of love of neighbor, and our conviction that each and every person is equally beloved by God, possessing a dignity that cannot be taken away and must be respected in all realms of life. Mistreating people because of their religion is an affront to that dignity and the image of God that they bear. As the Catholic Church declared at its Second Vatican Council, "there is no basis"[5] for discrimination or harassment against individuals or groups due to their religious affiliation; it is "foreign to the mind of Christ."[6] Muslims are by no means the only group to face religious bigotry. In a range of contexts both in the United States and abroad, Christians, Jews, Sikhs, and many other groups have been subjected to this kind of mistreatment. No matter who is targeted, prejudice and discrimination based on religious affiliation are wrong.

Despite this, Christians have contributed to anti-Muslim prejudice and discrimination, even justifying it through the language of our faith. Pastors and ministers make false and uncharitable claims about Muslims. Christian politicians and social media personalities advocate for policies that would discriminate against Muslims. Vandals target mosques and mark their destruction with Christian symbols. Sometimes Christians even advocate for or carry out violence against Muslims. Islamophobia is perpetuated by Christians in more subtle ways, too—by our offhanded comments, by negative assumptions we may have about Muslims in our midst, by our voting habits and the donations we give (or don't give) to political interest groups, and by closing off our hearts to the humanity and suffering of our Muslim siblings in faith. Most often, we contribute to Islamophobia unintentionally, thanks to the untrue ideas and latent biases about Muslims that we hold. We are often unaware that we hold these, and the fact that we have them is not entirely our fault, as they are ingrained in many aspects of society. Still, they negatively impact the way we think and even the way we act.

In my own personal circles of Christian family and friends, I have witnessed this range of Islamophobia. Family members have expressed support for discriminatory or harmful measures toward Muslims, relatives have mocked Muslims and spoken of them as if they are of lesser value than we are, priests have sowed suspicion and fear rather than love and fraternity, and friends have echoed stereotypical views without realizing it. I myself struggle with my own biases about Muslims and the way that my day-to-day actions and position in society contribute to Islamophobia, both in its interpersonal and systemic forms.

These realities in our Christian communities give rise to a second reason why we are called to care about Islamophobia—because Christian communities have often built it up in the first place. Islamophobia, as both a prejudicial ideology and a discriminatory state of affairs, is very often generated and perpetuated by Christian individuals and communities.[7] Because we are caught up in this problem, we have a responsibility to learn about Islamophobia and to work to break it down.[8] We must always look to Muslims for guidance in this endeavor, learning from their expertise and experiences—yet the task of addressing Islamophobia ultimately falls to us. As people on the receiving end of bigotry, Muslims should not have to advocate for themselves alone, nor spend their time educating us about why we should not fear them. Instead, we are the ones with the work to do. Combating Islamophobia is not "Muslims' problem," but rather our calling. Fortunately, many of us are coming to realize the harm of Islamophobia, to reckon with the fact that our Christian communities have contributed to it, and to respond to it. Drawing on the best of our faith tradition, countless Christians are already harnessing the core Christian values of love of God and love of neighbor to break down prejudice and discrimination and build up communities of hospitality and love.

Purpose and Structure of the Book

Written for a Christian audience, this book provides an introduction to the problem of Islamophobia, highlights its manifestations in Christian contexts, and offers ways for Christians to address it through the lens of our faith. In the last several years, numerous books about Islamophobia have been published, some written for academics and others for a more public audience. I draw on many of them here and am indebted to them for shaping my thinking. But this is the first book written specifically for Christians that seeks to comprehensively address Islamophobia.

In Part I, I give an overview of the issue, drawing on academic literature, media reports, and personal stories to offer a general picture of Islamophobia. Though this overview primarily focuses on the United States, where I live, it is not limited to the United States, since Islamophobia crosses national borders and is a globalized issue. In chapter 1, I give a definition of the word *Islamophobia*, which I understand as the *prejudice and discrimination that targets people based on their perceived association with Islam and Muslims*. I discuss the history of the word, the need for a term to name anti-Muslim prejudice and discrimination, and the stereotypes that fuel it. The term *Islamophobia* has only gained wide currency in recent years, but the phenomenon and its impact on individuals and communities long precede the word's use in popular discourse. In chapter 2, I look at the recent history of Islamophobia in the United States, showing how it has become more blatant and concerted, and offering a range of examples of how it has impacted the daily lives of Muslims. Chapter 3 looks at how—contrary to many people's expectations—Islamophobia is perpetuated on both the right and left of the American political spectrum. That chapter also explores the way Islamophobia extends around the world, beyond the bounds of what we call "the West." Chapter 4 examines how people who are not Muslim often get caught in the crosshairs of Islamophobia, how Islamophobia overlaps with and connects to other forms of discrimination, and how Muslims and other groups have been similarly scapegoated. In chapter 5, I shed light on manifestations of Islamophobia that often go unrecognized. Like other forms of racism, Islamophobia is not just overt or apparent bigotry. It is also systemic and subtle—sometimes elaborately orchestrated and other times completely unintentional. In the sixth and final chapter of Part I, I address many of the common stereotypes about Muslims and the questions often asked of them. I also consider some of the broader problems in our public discourse on Islam, as well as the faulty understandings about religion in general that contribute to prejudicial thinking toward Muslims.

I hope these several chapters can be a strong foundation for understanding Islamophobia, allowing readers to come away not only knowing names and events, but also having tools and frameworks for identifying Islamophobia, regardless of its purveyor or setting. Readers will also see how Islamophobia is not a new phenomenon. Though many people first started recognizing the reality of Islamophobia during the 2016 U.S. presidential election or amid the rise of anti-immigrant political parties in Europe, it stretches back long before that, even prior to the attacks of September 11, 2001. Part I is intended to be accessible to readers approaching this topic for the first time, while still relevant for academic contexts. This portion of the book could be read on its own by both Christians and non-Christians as an introduction to Islamophobia.

In Part II, I look at the role Christian communities specifically have played in contributing to Islamophobia. In recent years, more and more books about Islamophobia have been published, a number of them discussing Islamophobia among Christians. But these have primarily focused on Evangelical Protestant communities, often leaving out discussion of other Christian denominations. Because I am Catholic and have focused much of my work on Catholic-Muslim relations, I dedicate considerable space in chapter 7 to Islamophobia in Catholic communities, seeking to fill the gap left by the existing material. In chapter 8, I dig into the long history of Muslim-Christian relations to shed light on the roots of contemporary Islamophobia, looking at how Muslims were treated in Christian-majority contexts, as well as how Christians throughout history have viewed Muslims and thought about Islam. In both chapters of Part II, I demonstrate how Christian religious discourse has been used to justify prejudice and discrimination against Muslims, as well as how Christian identity has often been constructed over and against Muslims. While many Christians are familiar with ways that Muslims have mistreated us throughout history and in the present day,[9] we often have less exposure to the ways we have brought harm upon them.

Despite the Part II focus on Christians, Islamophobia is, of course, not solely a Christian issue. The problem of Islamophobia does indeed have a unique relationship with European Christian communities, which we explore later. But Islamophobia is a problem in other faith communities and among nonreligious people as well, including Jews, Buddhists, Hindus, and atheists. As a systemic issue and a phenomenon that is woven into society more broadly, Islamophobia spans religious traditions, even while there are indeed unique manifestations of it that arise in some communities more than others. (For example, the Islamophobic ideas circulated by many in the New Atheist movement are in some respects different from anti-Muslim views held by Evangelical Christians.) This book should not be read as blaming Christianity for Islamophobia. There is not something baked into Christianity as a religion that would necessarily make Christians more Islamophobic than nonreligious people or people of other faiths. Though Islamophobia is often engendered and upheld by Christians, and some Christians do put forth interpretations that attempt to justify Islamophobia, it does not have to be that way. We can tread a different path, and many Christians are already doing so.

Few existing books on Islamophobia view it through the lens of Christian faith,[10] so this book seeks to do that in Part III. Much can be drawn from the Christian tradition to craft a concerted response to Islamophobia today: stories in the Bible, examples of interreligious solidarity throughout history, Catholic social teaching, and our highest values of love of God and neighbor. In chapter 9, I highlight the principles and teachings from our Christian faith that can be harnessed to forge a positive way forward in our personal and collective relationships with Muslims. In chapter 10, I offer guidance on how we can wed our religious convictions with effective methods to address Islamophobia, highlighting the numerous ways that Christians from a range of denominations are already doing so inside the church and beyond it. I draw on wisdom from Muslim activists and scholars, as well as insights from the social sciences, particularly behavioral economics. Bringing these latter perspectives to bear on the Christian conversation about Islamophobia is one of the things that makes this book unique. I hope that this combination of approaches can allow our response to Islamophobia to be not only principled and faith-filled, but also effective and lasting.

Overall, this book attempts to give a bird's-eye view of Islamophobia, while also putting forward a Christian response to it and providing concrete ways to live out that mission. I hope readers come away from the book not only having learned something, but also better equipped to challenge Islamophobia and to build up a more loving world.

Why Me?

For the broader reasons outlined above, Islamophobia is something I have felt called to address through scholarship, dialogue, and education. But my own personal calling to address Islamophobia occurred in the spring of 2008, on a Sunday afternoon in Indianapolis, when a chain email arrived in my inbox. The message had been circulated by many kind and well-respected individuals in my Catholic parish community. But the email was an Islamophobic one, portraying Muslims as a group not to be trusted, saying that they were becoming "our enemy" for their supposed failure to speak up against "fanatics." Ordinary Muslims, the anonymous author wrote, are "irrelevant"; instead, "we must pay attention to the only group that counts . . . the fanatics who threaten our way of life." The author then urged readers to send the email to as many people as they could, claiming that not forwarding it meant complicity in this problem.

As I read the email, a sinking feeling grew in my stomach. The suspicion and blame the email cast on Muslims was unfair and untrue, and it sought to engender fear toward people like my Muslim classmates at the local Catholic high school I attended at the time. My concern and distress over the contents of the email itself were compounded by the fact that it was circulated by good, faithful Catholics. The people who sent around the email, including close family friends, were well-intentioned people active in my parish. In sending the email along, they were not in any way meaning to cause harm. They likely thought that sharing the message with others was helping to solve a problem of ignorance, rather than furthering bigotry.

That email was not the first manifestation of Islamophobia I had encountered. As I watched the presidential election campaigns playing out that year, I had begun to recognize the ways that politicians—even back then in 2008— were sowing misunderstanding and fear of Muslims. It was a problem that already concerned me, at least in an abstract way. But receiving that chain email brought the troubling reality of Islamophobia—which I didn't even have a word for at the time—into clear and present relief. Though I only knew a few Muslims and had yet to study Islam or Islamophobia formally, I felt the impact of the email in a deeply personal way. The email not only said something about Muslims, it also said something about *us*—the Catholic Christian community that approved of the message enough to forward it along. It demonstrated a deep disconnect between the values we professed and the way we sometimes failed to live them out.

The experience of receiving this anti-Muslim chain email was a moment of personal calling for me, and it engendered a vocation that has since been nurtured by my Christian faith and my friendships with Muslims. This book is an outgrowth of those experiences, as well over as a decade of study and work on Muslim-Christian relations. After attending Catholic schools in Indiana, I obtained my undergraduate degree at Georgetown's Walsh School of Foreign Service in Washington, DC, where I studied Arabic, the Middle East, and both Islam and Christianity. I was very involved with the Muslim student group on campus, participated in numerous Catholic ministries, and led an interfaith group. During that time, I also gained professional experience interning at the Council on American-Islamic Relations and at the U.S. Conference of Catholic Bishops, both in Washington. After studying abroad in Amman, Jordan, during my undergraduate years, I returned to the country (which, perhaps providentially, shares my name) a year later on a Fulbright scholarship. Funded by a yearlong State Department research grant, I studied how everyday interactions between Christians and Muslims in Jordan were impacted by Christian television media, particularly by the rise of American-funded Christian stations and their (often negative) portrayal of Islam. Back in the United States, I worked as a researcher for three years at the Georgetown-based Bridge Initiative, where I studied Islamophobia, writing on the range of manifestations of anti-Muslim prejudice and discrimination. I devoted particular attention to Christian (especially Catholic) views of Islam and Muslims, and to how Islamophobia had become normalized in some Christian contexts. Currently, I am pursuing a doctorate in theology and religious studies at Georgetown, having received an M.A. in the same program. (These experiences have afforded me a unique and informed perspective on Islamophobia, but as a White, Christian female living in the United States, I am not directly impacted by Islamophobia or other related forms of discrimination—a fact that surely limits what I can know and convey to others about the phenomenon.)

Some of my fellow Christians are puzzled by my career trajectory, but its motivations are not too different from my peers who devote their energies in other realms. Christian faith informs countless other personal vocations that Christians live out; I have friends and family members who work to remedy problems like climate change, mass incarceration, and healthcare inequality, or who serve others through professions like medicine, physical therapy, and teaching. Similarly, the need to break down Islamophobia is not unrelated or tangential to our faith commitments as Christians. As the Catholic Church has affirmed in its Vatican II statement on other religious communities, "We cannot truly pray to God the Father of all if we treat any people as other than sisters and brothers, for all are created in God's image."[11] The temptation to overlook Muslims' inherent human dignity is damaging to Christian faith and its authentic expression in our daily lives. Yet the work of dismantling Islamophobia affords us the opportunity to live out the gospel message we profess with even greater integrity. At my church growing up, we would often sing a song with the refrain,

> *And they'll know we are Christians by our love, by our love*
> *Yes they'll know we are Christians by our love!*

I have written this book in the hope that my Christian faith community can better live out this ideal.

Threats, Harassment, and Fear

Unfolding a piece of paper left in her school cubby, a ten-year-old girl found a sinister accusation scrawled inside—"You're a terrorist," it said. The next week, this young Muslim girl living in the Boston suburbs found a second note in the same place. This time it was a threat—"I will kill you."[12] Reduced to a dehumanizing caricature that did not resemble her nor anyone she knew, the usually upbeat girl felt a justified sense of terror.

Her family was understandably stunned at this threat of mortal violence, and her fifth-grade teacher was heartbroken, too, that a classmate (or, even worse, a teacher) would do such a thing. In the eyes of the anonymous person who left the note, the girl was seen not for who she is—caring, funny, and smart—but instead as someone defined by the heinous actions of a few who claim to share her Muslim faith. On these crumpled pieces of note paper, the girl's humanity and individuality were written off in a few words. And the fact that her fellow Muslims in the United States and throughout the world live out their faith in widely diverse yet ordinary ways was overlooked, too.

Nearly two decades earlier, on a fall morning in 2001, teenager Nazir Harb Michel was combing his hair in front of his bedroom mirror, listening to an oldies station before heading off to his high school. Before he could finish, the music was interrupted by a breaking news update. A feeling of shock overcame him as the journalist reported on commercial airliners crashing into New York City's two tallest towers and into the Pentagon building just outside Washington, DC—centers of U.S. financial and military power. Eventually, Americans would come to learn that the perpetrators were Arab Muslims who were part of a terrorist group called Al-Qaeda, which killed close to three thousand Americans on September 11, 2001.

In the days and weeks that followed, Nazir—a Muslim who is Arab and Latino—found himself made fun of, ostracized, and with fewer friends. Classmates he had socialized with before the attacks no longer sat with him at lunch, and a Christian friend he had had since childhood gave him a sneering look that said, *How could you?*, as if Nazir had committed the horrific crime. His social studies teacher, who had previously fostered Nazir's learning about Islam, openly asked him, "How could you belong to a community that would do this?" Nazir had grown up in a mixed Muslim-Christian household, but had only formally accepted his Muslim faith a few months prior to 9/11. Now he was constantly expected to speak on behalf of his entire faith tradition, as the representative of over 1.7 billion people. That pressure, and the suspicion he felt from others, has not dissipated in the almost two decades since 9/11. And it would come to have more devastating impacts on his family—in 2005, his uncle was killed in a hate crime.[13]

As these stories convey, it is deeply unfair and unjust to define Muslims by their religion's worst adherents. The young girl outside Boston and Nazir, like their fellow Muslims everywhere, are not less deserving of fair treatment because of the horrible actions of a few of those who share their religious identity. Yet this troubling and false logic often underpins the way that many people think about Muslims today, and it leads to threats, harassment, hate crimes, and institutionalized discrimination. As Christians, we know that when some of our fellow Christians do something wrong and immoral—even if they claim to do it out of their religious convictions—it does not warrant treating our entire community as if we have committed the same crime. In our own Christian tradition, many of us look at groups like the Westboro Baptist Church, the Ku Klux Klan, or the White Christian supremacist groups that have proliferated in recent years and see interpretations of the faith that are radically at odds with our own.

Yet we often fail to carry over this perspective when we think about Muslims. Even among Christians who recognize that religious bigotry is morally wrong, questions still linger: *Isn't Islamophobia justified? Don't we have good reason to fear Islam, and to treat Muslims differently? Aren't Muslims more dangerous and utterly different from the rest of us?* The fact that these questions arise in us is understandable. Many of us do not know Muslims personally, and the news media often show us militants rather than ordinary people trying to live their lives. On top of that, we constantly hear from best-selling authors and well-paid pundits that "they," Muslims, are nothing like "us."

But what we know from our experience as Christians is also true of Muslims. Though some Muslims invoke or express their faith tradition in harmful ways—and they are the ones who often make headlines—many others do so in ways that contribute positively to the human family. Muslims are a large religious community, second only to Christians globally in size. They are not a uniform or monolithic bloc, but rather just as diverse as Christians around the world. Muslims interpret and live out their faith in a range of ways, so much so that two people who call themselves Muslim might have widely divergent practices and nearly opposite views on some matters. The militants we hear about in the news do not represent or reflect the vast majority of Muslims, who live quiet lives amid struggles common to all human beings.

In some places and contexts, Muslim militant groups or individuals have indeed harmed and mistreated Christians and other religious groups—not to mention their fellow Muslims, who are by far the largest share of their victims.[14] In the mid- to late 2010s, the self-styled "Islamic State," also known as ISIS, committed atrocities against Christian communities and other groups in areas of Iraq and Syria where ISIS had taken power. During this period, individuals claiming affiliation with ISIS also targeted Christians in places like Nigeria and France, while scores of Christian worshippers in Egypt and Sri Lanka have been killed during church services in bombing attacks by other militants who were Muslim.[15] The fact of these tragic and brutal events does not mean, however, that all or most Muslims are committing acts of violence or are intent on doing something similar. Only a tiny sliver of the Muslim population globally has been involved in militant activities—statistically speaking, only a small fraction of a single percentage point of the global Muslim community. Far too often, we wrongly assume that most Muslims share the same motives and intentions as the militants covered in news programs. But this erroneous thinking can have dangerous consequences, leading to tangible forms of anti-Muslim discrimination and collective blaming, such as the harassment, threats, and even violence endured by Muslims like Nazir, his late uncle, and the anonymous fifth-grader in Massachusetts.

The egregious actions and ideas of militant groups like ISIS or Al-Qaeda stand in stark contrast to the views and values of the vast majority of Muslims worldwide. Muslim theologians and religious leaders around the globe have strongly condemned the brutality and ideology of these groups, though their vocal outcry is not often covered by mainstream media outlets. One such condemnation came in the form of an open letter to Abu Bakr al-Baghdadi, the leader of ISIS. Over two hundred senior Muslim scholars and leaders around the world signed the letter, which outlined how ISIS violated Islamic norms and values.[16] This letter was only one of myriad condemnations of terrorist groups that Muslims have issued in the last two decades. Friends and colleagues of mine who are Muslim have also expressed their sadness and frustration that Christians often presume they would agree with the actions of militant groups like ISIS and Al-Qaeda. On the contrary, their faith motivates them to enact justice and goodness in the world.

Oftentimes, both in popular media and public discourse, harmful acts committed by Muslims are explained as being motivated "by religion." Boiling these events down to solely "religious" motivations is inaccurate, as I discuss in more depth later in this book. A host of other factors related to political, social, and economic power, as well as human psychology, play into conflicts, even those that sometimes break down across lines of religious identity. The idea that "Islam is the problem" is not only a flawed way of diagnosing the issue, but it also wrongly leads us to view Muslims as a whole with suspicion.

To reiterate, the fact that some Muslims do harmful, condemnable things to Christians and others gives us no license to treat Muslims as a group—or those we come into contact with—poorly or differently than we would treat anyone else. Nor does it give us permission to brush off the seriousness of the prejudice and discrimination that Muslims face. In fact, the concern we have about the mistreatment of Christians by Muslims should be part and parcel of our concern about Islamophobia. No matter whom is targeted, discrimination and violence are unacceptable.

Living Out the Golden Rule

On a hot summer afternoon in 2018 in central Nigeria, Muslims sat shoulder to shoulder in the local mosque, concluding their afternoon prayer. Knees pressed to the floor and sitting back on their feet, they followed the prayer leader's movements, turning their heads to the right, and then to the left, and whispering, *Peace be with you*, the concluding gesture of *salat*, the brief prayer ritual many Muslims complete five times a day. As the congregation rose and began to disperse, the leader, Imam Abubakar Abdullahi, heard shots fired in the next town over. Increasingly concerned as the gunfire grew louder, Imam Abdullahi opened the doors to his mosque and adjacent home, urging those in the town center to enter quickly to hide. Over two hundred people—mostly Christians—huddled on the ground to avoid stray bullets, while the imam locked the doors and stood guard outside.[17]

Gun-toting militants, with their faces covered so that he could not recognize them, approached Imam Abdullahi. Relations between Muslims and Christians had, up until the year before, been good in central Nigeria, but conflicts between herders, who are predominantly Muslim, and farmers, who are predominantly Christian, had led to violence and communal reprisals in the area. In a later interview, Imam Abdullahi said, "We [Christians and Muslims] never had a problem with each other. We have lived in peace until suddenly these attackers came to destroy the village and kill people. I wouldn't let that happen."[18]

He found himself prostrating on the ground, pleading with the attackers to spare the people inside.[19] After some time, and to the imam's great relief, the militants left. Those sheltering inside shared a meal together before they were moved to a safer location. But the ordeal was traumatizing for the imam, who had trouble sleeping for over a week after the incident, which could have turned out very differently. Imam Abdullahi cited his faith as his reason for protecting the Christians in his care. After winning the 2019 International Religious Freedom Award from the U.S. government for his courage and bravery, he told an interviewer, "Our religion as taught by the Prophet Muhammad showed that he lived in peace and harmony with diverse ethnic groups and people of different faiths. . . . We follow his teachings and footsteps." Paraphrasing a passage of the Qur'an, he called on all people to remember that God created the diversity of humanity for a reason, and that we must respect that diversity and work for peace among our God-given differences.[20]

This story is just one of myriad ways that Muslims around the world have stood with and defended Christians, both amid the usual struggles of daily life and in precarious situations of life and death. They do this not just as individuals of goodwill, but as an expression of their Islamic religious faith. In Mosul, Iraq, after ISIS was pushed out, Muslim residents of the city advocated that two historic Catholic churches be included in the UNESCO rebuilding project, stating that the city would not be itself without them.[21] In Pakistan, Muslims of a small town financially supported the rebuilding of the local Catholic church used by their Christian neighbors,[22] and leaders like Maulana Syed Muhammad, the head of a mosque in the city of Lahore, work to promote interfaith harmony.[23] In Morocco, Muslim clergy from around the world gathered in 2016 to advocate for improved protection of minority religious communities in Muslim-majority countries.[24] In Lebanon, Muslim theologians like Nayla Tabbara draw on religious texts and centuries of tradition to construct robust theologies of interfaith hospitality and welcome.[25] On the U.S.-Mexico border, American Muslim imam Omar Suleiman advocates for the rights of detained migrants, many of whom are Christian. In Tennessee, Georgetown's Muslim student association spent a Thanksgiving break restoring a run-down church. In Jordan, a Muslim family orchestrated a surprise Christmas celebration—complete with gifts and a tree—for a family who could not celebrate that year. And in Australia, for over a decade, a group of Muslims have attended Catholic Easter services to show solidarity with their Christian friends in faith, despite the fact that their religious beliefs about Jesus differ.[26]

It is a shame that we rarely hear about these positive stories, and it is worth pondering why our media does not cover them more often. Because we hardly hear about them, many Christians I know have the false perception that Muslims do not care about Christians or anyone else beyond their own religious fold. But these accounts are a reminder of the countless ways that Muslims support Christians and defend our rights, just as Christians in so many places and contexts support Muslims. For those of us who are fortunate to have Muslim friends, colleagues, or neighbors, we know this firsthand. In my own life, Muslims have been steadfast friends, offering up prayers for me and supporting me in tangible ways in work and life. When I lived in Amman, Jordan, Muslim acquaintances and strangers took care of me, shuttling me safely across the city in cabs, welcoming me in for tea, and displaying the compassion that is central to their faith.

Of course, there is still much more to be done; Christians and Muslims both have a long way to go in how we treat the religious "other." Anti-Christian attitudes and actions exist among Muslims in some places, and the inverse is true of Christians. Recognizing the failures of both groups helps us to resist falling into the false dichotomy of comparing an idealized yet untrue image of ourselves with the worst, imagined view of Muslims. As we lament the shortcomings and biases of our two faith communities, we can also celebrate the successes and seek to build upon them in our own lives. As Christians, we are grateful for all that Muslims do for us, knowing that—regardless of any reciprocation—we are called to address Islamophobia in whatever ways we can.

Them *and* Us

I hope readers come away from this book understanding what Islamophobia is and how it works—that it is interpersonal, institutional, and implicit, and that it is generated and propped up by industry and imperialism.[27] But most importantly, I hope readers get a glimpse into the *impact* that Islamophobia has, how it deeply affects the lives of parents and children, teachers and students, siblings and grandparents who strive to devote themselves to God and neighbor. In my own circle of Muslim friends alone, I know individuals whose mosques have been targeted by anti-Muslim protests and arson, who have experienced harassment on the street or in public places, who have tolerated offensive comments made toward them by colleagues and college professors, and whose relatives have been killed in hate crimes or unjustly imprisoned. And many of them have faced the range of subtle suspicion to outright hostility from people who call themselves Christian.

Though it is less obvious and more indirect, Islamophobia also has an impact on *us* as Christians. Indeed, some Christians have been on the receiving end of bigotry intended for Muslims. But even beyond that, Islamophobia is harmful to us. When we fail to address our own prejudice and to do our small part to combat Islamophobia in our communities and society, we fall short of living up to our Christian calling. The goal of this book is that we may better live up to the melodic refrain sung in so many of our churches: *that they'll know we are Christians by our love.*

Part I

WHAT IS ISLAMOPHOBIA?
An Overview

1

MORE THAN FEAR

Defining Islamophobia

It was supposed to be a quiet evening. Like she did most days, Zeynep[1] sat outside the café she co-owned with her husband in Bloomington, Indiana, a college town bordered by forests and farmland. In the evening light she sipped tea alongside her nine-year-old daughter. Suddenly, she felt her head being forced downward, toward the table, a man's hand around her neck. A male college student began to strangle her and pull off her headscarf, or hijab, as those in the vicinity heard him shout, "White power!" Thanks to the intervention of a passerby and the woman's husband, the perpetrator was subdued.[2]

Most readers of this book were probably not very familiar with the word *Islamophobia* before 2015, when this attack occurred, but now it is commonly used in the news media and everyday conversation to describe troubling incidents like the attack on Zeynep. In this chapter, I offer a definition of Islamophobia, explaining what I mean by it and what I do not. I also outline the history of the term and make a case for why we should use it. After discussing Islamophobia as a form of scapegoating, I end by examining the stereotypes about Muslims that are at the heart of Islamophobia.

Defining the Term

By the word's etymology alone, Islamophobia would seem to simply mean "fear of Islam."[3] Though this fear is indeed part of Islamophobia, the word denotes something broader and deeper than an individual person's aversion to Muslims' religion. I use the term to describe the *prejudice and discrimination that targets people based on their perceived association with Islam and Muslims.*[4] This is the way many people in the news media and in the rapidly growing field of Islamophobia studies use the word as well.[5]

There are a few important components of this definition. First, my understanding of Islamophobia includes how people *think and feel* about Muslims, and how Muslims are actually *treated*. Many existing academic

3

definitions focus on the former (the prejudice), defining Islamophobia as anti-Muslim ideology or an "unwarranted social anxiety"[6] about Muslims. Others focus on the latter (the discrimination), considering the tangible practices of discrimination against Muslims that occur at both interpersonal and institutional levels. My definition of Islamophobia includes both. In the next chapter, when we look at the ways that Islamophobia has worsened in recent years, we consider not only how the public feels about Muslims and political speech about them, but also the prevalence of hate crimes and other forms of institutional discrimination. These two broad aspects of Islamophobia are often interdependent and influence each other. Preconceived ideas about Muslims shape the way they are treated, and those behaviors toward Muslims in turn reinforce society's ideas about them and their faith. For example, when Muslims are portrayed primarily as terrorists or "bad guys" on television, it can lead the general public and even politicians to treat them that way, too. And when Muslims are consistently treated as an inferior class by law enforcement or other institutions, it shapes public perceptions about them as well.

This definition of Islamophobia includes both overt bigotry and more subtle (or even unintentional) forms. Islamophobia is not only about the shouting of anti-Muslim slurs or the conscious and explicit demonization of Muslims in political discourse, but also things like recurring stereotypes used to characterize Muslims in the media and unpublicized law enforcement practices that actively target Muslims for increased and unwarranted scrutiny. Like other forms of racism, Islamophobia is a structural and systemic problem that goes far beyond personal bigotry. It also involves implicit biases—unconsciously held ideas we have about Muslims or visceral reactions we have that shape the way we act, even without our realizing it. These more invisible and subtle forms of Islamophobia are dealt with in depth in chapter 5.

Another facet of Islamophobia is that it can impact people who are not Muslim. South Asian, Arab, and Black individuals of other religions or no religion are often targeted in Islamophobic attacks because the popular imagination has come to associate Muslims with certain forms of appearance and with particular "foreign" regions of the world. Most notably, we conflate *Muslim* with *Arab* or *Middle Eastern*—as I discussed in the note to readers at the beginning of this book. Other images and associations that come to mind when we think of Muslims are long beards, headscarves, face veils, flowing dresses, knit caps, turbans, and checkered scarves, not to mention brown skin and countries like Pakistan (which is more accurately considered part of South Asia, not the Middle East). None of these things are exclusive to Muslims, but they have come to define them in the Western imagination. As a consequence, Islamophobia can target people who are not Muslim but who possess some of the characteristics that are thought to be markers of Islam. In the United States, men of the Sikh faith—who hail from South Asia and frequently wear turbans—are often targeted in Islamophobic attacks. Additionally, Muslims who bear these expected markers of Islam—who "look Muslim"—are more often targeted in hate crimes compared to their fellow Muslims who are White or who don't fit the common stereotypes about where Muslims are from or what they look like.

This dynamic is part of what scholars call the "racialization" of Islam. This phrasing may at first seem confusing or off-base since Islam is a religious tradition, not a race or ethnicity.[7] Indeed, Muslims are incredibly diverse, totaling 1.8 billion people who hail from every corner of the world.[8] But as described above, Western society imagines Muslims as sharing a set of physical and ethnic traits that are universal and natural to them.[9]

There is an additional facet to the racialization of Islam that goes beyond skin color, biological features, or other visible characteristics we often associate with race. It has to do with the way specific *cultural* and *behavioral* traits are ascribed to Muslims. Western society sees Muslims as inherently prone to violence, misogynistic, intolerant, backward, and untrustworthy. These negative qualities, among others, are considered natural and intrinsic to Muslims, much in the same way as physical traits or ethnic categories are passed on biologically. This set of attributes is seen as defining Muslims and as unique to them, making them inherently different from other groups and thus worthy of lesser treatment.[10] As Andrea Smith puts it, "Islam becomes the marker of inherent difference."[11] This racializing of Islam is a form of essentialism, in which seemingly permanent, unchangeable qualities serve as the supposed basis for treating a group differently.[12]

To give but one example of this cultural/behavioral racialization, Muslims are "raced" as being prone to violence and attacking civilians. This inclination to terrorism is mistakenly and unfairly considered "natural and innate" to Muslims,[13] something at their core. This belief then paves the way toward believing that mistreatment of Muslims is justified or deserved. Think back to the young girl from outside Boston who received threatening anti-Muslim notes. Because she was Muslim, she was reduced to the trope of "violent" and deemed worthy of being mortally harmed.[14] This is the troubling logic of Islamophobic discrimination, and it is taken up in many more official, government-sanctioned ways, too. In the United Kingdom, for example, teachers have reported Muslim children to government programs for "preventing violent extremism," just for ordinary and innocuous things like using the religious phrase *Alhamdulillah*, meaning "Praise be to God."[15]

Thus, as we have seen, the racialization of Islam is not just about appearance-related and ethnic traits, but also the cultural and behavioral ones alleged to be at the core of Islam and Muslims. (Later, we look more at these cultural stereotypes about Muslims, and when and why they arose in the Western imagination.) This process of racialization often occurs unconsciously in our minds and goes unacknowledged by society. But it is what informs and "justifies" anti-Muslim prejudice and discrimination. As scholars Enes Bayrakli and Farid Hafez write, "Islamophobia operates by constructing a static 'Muslim' identity, which is attributed in negative terms and generalized for all Muslims."[16]

It is for all these reasons that Islamophobia can be understood as a form of racism—not because Muslims actually constitute a race in the way we commonly use the word, but because we treat them as such. As critical theorist Leerom Medovoi writes, Islamophobia involves "making a race out of a religion,"[17] the creating and perpetuating of a social hierarchy founded on the idea that an entire group has intrinsic, negative qualities that make them worthy of mistreatment.[18] The concept of the racialization of Islam appears throughout this book, especially in chapter 4, where I share more examples of how Islamophobia impacts people who are not Muslim and how Islamophobia is connected to other forms of racism.

To reiterate, I define *Islamophobia* as *prejudice and discrimination that targets people based on their perceived association with Islam and Muslims.*[19] With all its facets, Islamophobia is far more than the term's literal, linguistic meaning—"fear of Islam." And yet Islamophobia is not unrelated to the fear and apprehension that many people have about Islam. When Muslims and their faith are defined as violent, oppressive, intolerant, and backward—as they so often are in global discourse and public imagination—it is no wonder that the rest of us come to fear them and see them as deserving of differential and inferior social status. Islamophobia includes (1) the fear that people have about Muslims and Islam, (2) the things that *feed* that fear, and (3) the *outcomes and results* of that fear. As we see throughout the rest of the book, Islamophobia is not just about fear; it is also about power—the political, economic, and social forces that subject Muslims to unequal treatment.[20] As synonyms for *Islamophobia*, I often use *anti-Muslim bigotry, anti-Muslim prejudice and discrimination*, and *anti-Muslim racism*. I do this to avoid being repetitive and because these phrases help communicate the meaning of the term *Islamophobia*.[21]

"The Right Word for a Real Problem"

Some readers may be wondering: Why should we use the word "Islamophobia" to describe a form of bigotry and racism that is much more than simple "fear of Islam"?[22] The answer is in part practical: Islamophobia is the word that has come to the fore in our public discourse. Since 2015, usage of the word has become much more widespread in news media, politics, and common conversation around the world to describe anti-Muslim views, activities, and structures. This is despite the fact that the word is not linguistically perfect. Islamophobia is a bit like the term *anti-Semitism* in this way. If taken literally, anti-Semitism would refer to antipathy toward anyone who speaks a Semitic language, including those who speak Arabic, which is a Semitic language. But, as we know, the term *anti-Semitism* is used today to refer to bigotry against Jewish people specifically.[23] With both "Islamophobia" and "anti-Semitism," the words' etymological components do not exactly reflect the way we use them—and that is okay. The public still understands their meaning, and they serve an important purpose in putting a name to a reality that very much needs to be acknowledged and reckoned with. This is a second reason to use the word: we do need a term. We can only hope to dismantle Islamophobia once we have brought it into the light by giving it a name. Having a fairly succinct, single-worded term helps us do this.

Though the word *Islamophobia* has only entered common parlance in the last decade, its history is about a hundred years old.[24] It first appeared in French as *Islamophobie* in the 1910s and 1920s, where it was used by Europeans who wrote about French colonial policy and activities in North Africa. Some of these writers used it not simply to talk about ignorance-based "fear of Islam" but rather to identify a concerted, negative motivation on the part of Europeans who subjugated North African Muslim populations and sought to justify their actions.[25] The word eventually entered the English language, but was used quite sparingly and mostly in scholarly and specialized contexts.[26] In the decade following the September 11, 2001, attacks, the term appeared occasionally in headlines of newspaper articles reporting on hate crimes that were being committed against American Muslims. It wasn't until 2010, amid a national controversy about a Muslim community center being built in New York City not far from the site of the 9/11 attacks, that I and many others first heard the word *Islamophobia*. In a cover story that year, *Time* magazine asked, "Is America Islamophobic?"[27]

But the term truly did not become mainstream in the United States until the end of 2015, amid the political campaigning ahead of the U.S. presidential election that was held the following year.[28] Before that time, when I would meet new people at social gatherings or professional functions and tell them I studied Islamophobia at the Georgetown University–based Bridge Initiative, they would look at me with puzzlement. Even if they did not ask what the word meant, it was clear from their vague expressions that they had never heard of "Islamophobia" before. All of that changed by early 2016. By then, presidential candidate Donald Trump had called for a "complete and total shutdown of Muslims" entering the United States, numerous other politicians had campaigned on anti-Muslim talking points, and hate crimes against Muslims had spiked across the United States—trends to be discussed more in the next chapter. After those events, people I met had very different reactions to my use of the word. Their nodding along indicated that they had heard the term, understood what Islamophobia was, and were fairly concerned about it. "I can't believe what he is saying about Muslims," they would tell me about then-candidate Trump. In such a short period of time, virtually overnight, our public discourse shifted drastically, with Islamophobia becoming a widely used and understood term. Journalists and Democratic political candidates began using the word to describe both the anti-Muslim rhetoric and policy proposals voiced by Republican candidates and the rise in anti-Muslim hate crimes that accelerated along with the bigoted language.[29]

But despite this documented history of the word *Islamophobia* and its present-day usage, there are some who claim that the term has a different origin. Activists and commentators affiliated with anti-Muslim hate groups claim the word was made up by Muslim extremists in recent decades to distract from instances of violence committed by Muslims, to silence any and all critique of Islam and Muslims, and to serve as cover for a supposed "Muslim takeover" of the West.[30] (These same anti-Muslim activists also downplay reports of prejudice and discrimination against Muslims, alleging that the incidences are all hoaxes.) These false claims have gained considerable traction among some on both the left and right of the political spectrum. I bring them up not only because readers may have encountered this narrative, but also to make clear that critiques of Muslim persons or Islam as a religious tradition are not inherently Islamophobic. This is an obvious point. In both scholarly contexts and in everyday conversation, we can and should discuss our disagreements and differences, making our assessments and preferences known. And no doubt there are things that some Muslims do or have done that readers will not (and should not) approve of, just as there are things Christians and others do that are worthy of strident condemnation as well.

That being said, there are ways that critiques of Muslims and Islam (even when well-intentioned) can be bound up with Islamophobia. In our public discourse, criticisms of Islam and Muslims are often based on untrue generalizations that make those criticisms inaccurate and unfair. Criticism is valid when it is based on factual realities, but not when it is built on sweeping stereotypes and imagined injustices. Thus, it is important that we educate ourselves, but even more crucial that we do not make grandiose statements without having all of the information, and that we avoid setting up false dichotomies between *us* and *them*.

More Than Ignorance and Unfamiliarity

When I first started out in this field over a decade ago, studying and researching Islamophobia while getting to know Muslims, a survey came out that found that a majority of Americans said they did not personally know anyone who was Muslim. At the time, this statistic seemed to me a simple explanation for why Islamophobia existed. *If every non-Muslim met a Muslim,* I thought, *Islamophobia would no longer be a problem. If everyone had a Muslim friend or coworker or classmate, we could overcome this prejudice and discrimination.* But now, I realize that the issue is not simply ignorance, and that getting to know Muslims personally and learning about Islam are not its only remedies.[31] As we will see, Islamophobia is a systemic problem that is deeply embedded in the structures of our society. Like other forms of discrimination, it does not just exist and operate at the level of consciously held biases and person-to-person interactions. It is also a problem that is built into and pervades societal institutions. Even if every non-Muslim person got to know someone who is Muslim, or learned a lot about Islam, we still would not be rid of Islamophobia. That is not to say that personal relationships and interreligious understanding are not eminently important, but what it does mean is that Islamophobia is not simply a problem of benign ignorance or lack of awareness. We have to tackle the ignorance, but also the nefarious forces that both feed and capitalize on it. We need to learn about the dynamics of anti-Muslim racism and see how it operates. This book seeks to be an aid in that mission.

Seeing Muslims as the "Scapegoat"

Islamophobia can also be understood as a form of scapegoating, with Muslims as the target.[32] Scapegoating is "a process by which blame for an in-group's misfortunes is transferred to a 'goat': a person, animal, inanimate object, or an out-group, which is then eliminated. Through [that expulsion] the in-group 'escapes' from its woes and is rejuvenated."[33] In other words, when things are going wrong in society, people look for a reason why and for someone to blame. They often find the answer in a perceived outsider or "other"—perhaps racial minorities, recent immigrants, or those who are seen as different or inferior. Perceiving this scapegoat as the source of their troubles, the broader society will heap blame onto them, even though the scapegoat may have little to do with the issues plaguing them. The scapegoat is eventually "expelled" from the society—either exiled or killed.

This "scapegoating mechanism" is as old as society itself. Anthropologist and literary scholar René Girard, who popularized the notion, argued that societies cannot endure without a scapegoat.[34] This targeted "other" serves as a distraction from society's deeper problems and rivalries, which, if left unchecked, would devolve into all-out conflict and chaos.

Today, in the United States, Europe, and elsewhere, Muslims have become a convenient scapegoat. Even though the vast majority of Muslims have nothing to do with acts of terrorism, we often ascribe collective blame to them. When Muslims are in the spotlight, it is easier for the rest of us to overlook deeper societal issues and our own role in them. (As we see in chapter 3, both the political right and left often come together around a "Muslim enemy," finding common ground by scapegoating Muslims.) Whether in the political realm or elsewhere, this scapegoating can have devastating consequences, with Muslims being excluded from a range of settings, expelled from the country, and worse.

The key to the scapegoat mechanism is its invisibility. Totally unaware of what they are doing, the broader society perceives their targeting of the scapegoat to be entirely justified. As Girard wrote, "A scapegoat remains effective as long as we believe in its guilt. Having a scapegoat means not knowing that we have one."[35] This is why it is so crucial, as Girard puts it, to reveal the scapegoat mechanism: to bring it into the light so that society members can come to grips with the injustice they are committing.[36] Thus, much of the work of combating Islamophobia involves helping people to see this scapegoating for what it is, to realize how and why it is going on, and then to stop it before it claims more lives.

Stereotypes We Cannot Shake

Once images are firmly rooted in the collective
memory of a community, they die hard.

—Samir Khalaf[37]

As the next chapter shows, Islamophobia in the United States and beyond has become more blatant and concerted in recent years, both in the realms of government and everyday life. But some things have remained fairly constant, going back several decades if not more. One of these more constant factors is the set of racialized stereotypes[38] that has long been used in the United States, Europe, and elsewhere to characterize Muslims as a group. In chapter 6, I revisit these stereotypes to unpack why they are not accurate representations of Muslims and their religion. But here it is beneficial to outline what they are, to shed light on how and why they emerged, and to trace their role in shaping attitudes and justifying discriminatory treatment of Muslims both before and after 9/11.

The common stereotypes we hold about Muslims today did not simply arise organically, as natural reactions to who Muslims are or out of our own ignorance. Rather they are connected to power, competition, and scapegoating. The most widespread stereotypes about Muslims and their religion are that they are *violent, oppressive to women, intolerant of other religious groups, foreign, backwards, untrustworthy, licentious,* and *tyrannical.*[39] These tropes are so ingrained in how Western, non-Muslim people think about Muslims that we take them to be truisms; we do not recognize how they govern our perceptions of Muslims or act as frames that shape our interpretation of world events. Of course, individual Muslims, Muslim communities, and the Islamic religious tradition are not immune from some of these issues. Episodes of violence, problems of persecution, and trends of gender inequality have plagued Muslim communities and predominantly Muslim societies, just as they do everywhere. In some cases, Muslims have used religious language to sanction these things or believe that God's will calls for them. The trouble is when these characterizations become the basis for gross generalizations about Muslims; when they are deemed essential to Muslims and invoked to distinguish Muslims as a whole from other groups; or when we engage in reductionism, boiling down the diversity of Islam to these things and asserting or implying that these issues do not exist elsewhere. The function of stereotypes is to set up an "us versus them" dichotomy, wherein "they" are defined by things that "we" are not. This function comes into clearer relief when we think, for example, about the stereotypes of foreignness and backwardness; throughout human history and in a range of contexts, these tropes have frequently been ascribed to one's enemies.

Many of the stereotypes about Muslims first emerged in the Middle Ages and onward as Christian peoples and empires were trying to distinguish themselves from Muslims, who in many contexts were their political, societal, and theological rivals. Later, in the nineteenth and twentieth centuries, as European and American powers were seizing and colonizing large swaths of territory with predominantly Muslim populations, claims that Muslims were uniquely violent, backward, and oppressive to women and religious minorities served to justify Europeans' taking control and maintaining it through force.[40] As discussed more in later chapters, this period also saw the genesis of the idea of "the West," which was defined in contradistinction to the negative attributes that Euro-American powers ascribed to Islam and "the Orient." This Western perspective maintained that "*They* are violent, intolerant, oppressive to women, and stuck in the past, whereas *we* are peaceful, welcoming, the picture of equality and progress." This narrative, which was fueled in part by Orientalist scholarship in academia, was reinforced in popular media of the time. Poems, plays, novels, sermons, and the travel diaries of missionaries to "the East" helped to cement these ideas in the popular imagination,[41] just as movies and television shows do today.

Undoubtedly, these stereotypes were and continue to be bolstered by acts of aggression and other wrongs that some Muslims have undertaken.[42] Yet these stereotypes originated and persist in large part because they serve the interests of powerful governmental, economic, and social entities, which often benefit from the subjugation or scapegoating of entire groups of people.

In the wake of the Islamic revolution in Iran in 1979, when the plight of American hostages there was covered on the news every night, these stereotypes about Muslims became more salient and widely held among Americans. Islam remained on Americans' radar, albeit in a subtle way, throughout the rest of the twentieth century, as the United States and coalition forces later invaded Iraq[43] in the 1990s and was engaged militarily in the Middle East.[44] Thus, as historian of American religion Edward E. Curtis IV has written, "By the time of the 9/11 attacks, the association of all Muslims and Islamic religion with violence, misogyny, and general backwardness had already become an entrenched form of conventional wisdom."[45]

To be sure, these charges and the other stereotypes listed above have not only been leveled against Muslims. They have been used in many times and places throughout world history, cited as reasons for mistreating certain populations. In the United States in particular, many of these stereotypes have been used to characterize groups like Catholics, Jews, and Mormons, in addition to other non-White or non-Christian groups, which were cast as internal threats and opponents of American freedom and values.[46] The world over, it is common for an in-group to make claims about an out-group's inherent violence, and about their supposed threat to "our" women and girls. These claims are hallmarks of what is called "dangerous speech"—rhetoric that galvanizes one population to feel justified in harming another.[47] In many cases, this dangerous rhetoric has served as a precursor to ethnic cleansing and genocide.

Despite the fact that many of these stereotypes have been used to speak of other groups, the particular set I outlined above has become quite sticky, so to speak, when it comes to Muslims. In modern times, these tropes of violence, misogyny, intolerance, and so on have come to define our expectations about Muslims and their faith. Islam is perceived to be these things innately and permanently, and all Muslims—as people who practice the faith—are, too. In 2017, when issuing the first version of its Muslim ban (which is discussed more in the next chapter), the Trump administration employed this set of racialized, anti-Muslim stereotypes to indicate to Customs and Border Patrol who should be targeted upon entry into the United States. Strikingly, the administration's list closely mirrors my list above. The order reads,

The United States must be vigilant during the visa-issuance process to ensure that those approved for admission do not intend to *harm* Americans and that they have no ties to *terrorism*. In order to protect Americans, the United States must ensure that those admitted to this country do not *bear hostile attitudes toward it and its founding principles*. The United States cannot, and should not, admit those who do not support the *Constitution*, or those who would place *violent ideologies* over American *law*. In addition, the United States should not admit those who engage in acts of *bigotry or hatred* (including *"honor" killings*, other forms of *violence against women*, or the *persecution* of those who practice *religions different from their own*) or those who would *oppress* Americans of any race, gender, or *sexual orientation*. (Emphasis mine)[48]

The list hits upon nearly all of the typical anti-Muslim stereotypes. Violence and terrorism—check. Anti-freedom—check. Intolerant of other religions—check. Anti-women—check. Honor killings—check. (In Western discourse, the phenomenon of honor killings is almost exclusively linked to Muslims—thus, another nod.) Anti-gay—check. (This ascription has become more common in recent years.) Though the executive order did not use the word "Muslims," it did not have to. The intended target was clear.

Now that we have seen the racism, scapegoating, and stereotypes undergirding Islamophobia, we turn to a broader view of the historical trajectory of anti-Muslim prejudice and discrimination.

2

THE NOT-SO-RECENT HISTORY OF ISLAMOPHOBIA IN THE UNITED STATES

"I felt like a million bees were stinging my face. I was bleeding so badly and I felt I was dying."[1]

A young Muslim man in his twenties, Rais Bhuiyan was working a shift at a convenience store in Dallas, Texas. He had recently moved there from Bangladesh, where he had grown up and trained as an Air Force pilot. Although starting a new life and career in the United States had been a challenge, Rais was optimistic, hoping to work in the technology sector. But on September 21, 2001, his life was shattered, quite literally. Ten days after 9/11, when members of Al-Qaeda flew planes into the World Trade Center towers in New York and the Pentagon in Washington, DC, a man named Mark Stroman charged into the convenience store with a shotgun. At first, Rais thought the man was using the gun as a threat to rob him, so he opened the cash register to hand over the money. But Stroman, an avowed White supremacist, wanted "revenge" for what happened on 9/11. He asked Rais where he was from, and before he knew it, a spray of shotgun pellets erupted into Rais's face.

Stroman left, and somehow Rais managed to pick himself off the floor and call for help. He was taken to the local hospital and treated for his injuries, but the physical and emotional traumas he endured are lasting. He lost sight in one eye, and to this day the pellets from Stroman's weapon remain lodged in his head. Anxiety about being shot again followed Rais everywhere. But he was luckier than two other men in the area who became Stroman's victims. Days before shooting Rais, Stroman had killed Waraq Hasan, a Pakistani American Muslim, at a different Dallas convenience store. Stroman was not apprehended and went on to shoot Rais, and then to kill a Hindu man, Vasudev Patel, days after that.

Even though Islam was not top of mind for many Americans before September 11, 2001, they were already primed with the negative sentiments and stereotypes we explored in the last chapter, leading some, like Stroman, to lash out against Muslims (and those they perceived to be Muslims) in the immediate aftermath of 9/11.

14

Islamophobia is a fairly new word in our public discourse—it was hardly if ever used after 9/11 to describe the spate of attacks that occurred then. Yet, as this story attests, the existence of Islamophobia is not as recent as our familiarity with the term. Its beginning is by no means marked by the rhetoric or policies of candidate or President Donald Trump, even though these are what finally convinced many U.S. Christians that it was a problem. This chapter looks at the last two decades in the United States, from the attacks and aftermath of September 11, 2001, onward. Islamophobia did not begin on 9/11, but that tragic event and its fallout marked the start of its most defining epoch. During the twenty-first century, especially in the last ten years, anti-Muslim speech and acts have become *more blatant*, and the campaign to scapegoat Muslims for political, economic, and social gain has become *more concerted and organized*. Only in a few small ways have we seen Islamophobia lessen or improve. I trace this recent history of Islamophobia in the United States by weaving together data and trends on anti-Muslim hate crimes and Americans' attitudes toward Muslims, political rhetoric and government policies, violent events like military incursions and attacks on civilians, and anti-Muslim conspiracy theories and controversies that thrust Muslims into the national spotlight. There are other dynamics at play as well, which I explore in later chapters. Here, I also shine a light on the toll that these forms of Islamophobia take on American Muslim individuals and communities.

A Timeline of Islamophobia in Twenty-First-Century America

The shootings in Texas were just a few of the hundreds of acts of anti-Muslim violence that were recorded in 2001 in the aftermath of 9/11. During those days, people were murdered and assaulted, houses of worship were attacked, and Muslims, who lived their lives in relative anonymity before then, found that a spotlight now focused on them wherever they went. In the news media, politicians and commentators implied or outright declared that Muslims' religion was the reason for these acts of terrorism and that Muslims as a whole were responsible. This became the common perception in the United States, despite the fact that the 9/11 hijackers were just nineteen men and that Al-Qaeda possessed political motives, albeit couched in religious language, for their heinous assault on civilians.[2] Yet the false perception of broad Muslim complicity—coupled with existing notions of Muslims as threatening and "other"—led some Americans to engage in "retaliation" on the community they felt was responsible. Often conflating Muslim with Arab, Middle Easterner, and South Asian, they targeted those they thought fit that bill. In the days and weeks following 9/11, anti-Muslim hate crimes across the United States skyrocketed.[3]

The FBI first started collecting data on anti-Muslim hate crimes in 1996. From then through the turn of the millennium, the number of crimes hovered around 20 or 30 per year nationwide, a meager number compared to what would come later. In 2001, the numbers spiked to 481 incidents in one year. Since then, the annual number of confirmed anti-Muslim hate crimes has not reached that peak again, but it has also never fallen back below 100 per year. 9/11 marked a clear turning point in anti-Muslim discrimination in the United States.[4]

In the immediate wake of September 11, the U.S. military invaded the Central Asian country of Afghanistan, where the Al-Qaeda group behind the 9/11 attacks had found a safe haven under the Taliban regime that controlled much of the country. Shortly thereafter, in 2003, the United States invaded Iraq, another predominantly Muslim country, under false pretenses. From 2002 to 2006, as the United States waged its "war on terror" in Iraq and Afghanistan, and as Americans saw Muslims as an enemy every night on television, the number of yearly anti-Muslim hate crimes hovered around 150, remaining higher than they had been before 9/11. In the latter part of the decade, the numbers started to trend downward, as the ongoing wars receded from view.

But anti-Muslim hate crimes saw a renewed rise in 2010. In August of that year, a young blonde-haired man named Michael Enright hopped into a yellow taxicab in downtown Manhattan. Glancing up at the driver of the car and noticing his brown skin and trimmed beard, Enright asked him where he was from and if he was Muslim. A father of four, Ahmed Sharif answered that yes, he was a Muslim, and Enright proceeded to ask other questions, including a few about Ramadan, the Islamic holy month that Sharif was in the midst of observing. As Enright began to make fun of the month's observances, Sharif fell quiet, sensing a rising tension. Then, suddenly, Enright began shouting. He pulled out a knife and stabbed Sharif several times, in his neck, face, arm, and hands.[5] Amazingly, Sharif survived. Enright was charged with a hate crime and attempted murder and assault.[6]

This incident occurred during the height of a national controversy in 2010 that erupted over the building of an Islamic center in New York City. In Manhattan, a local Muslim organization had sought to build what was effectively a Muslim YMCA, a community center called Cordoba House (and later Park51) that would bring together people of different faiths around recreational and cultural activities, and that would house a prayer space for Muslims. But pundits and bloggers who opposed it dubbed the building project the "Ground Zero Mosque," claiming it was offensive for Muslims to build an Islamic house of worship blocks away from where the 9/11 attacks had taken place. The main organizers of this opposition were Pamela Geller and Robert Spencer,[7] who lead the anti-Muslim hate groups Stop the Islamization of America and the American Freedom Defense Initiative. These voices and many who attended their New York City rallies blamed Islam for the 9/11 attacks and spoke of American Muslims as an internal threat to the country's security.[8] In their appearances on cable news channels, Geller and Spencer cast doubt on the motives of the Park51 center, calling its leader a "radical"[9] and the building a "monument" to terrorism and a symbol of Muslim conquest.[10] What should have been a non-issue was stirred up into a controversy so large that President Barack Obama felt he had to weigh in to defend the right of the Muslim community to build the center.[11]

But the damage was already done. Ultimately, the anti-Muslim campaign succeeded in shuttering the building project. Even more significantly, it had succeeded in shaping American public opinion toward Muslims ahead of the midterm elections coming later that year. After weeks of headlines and nightly news segments about the Ground Zero Mosque that normalized the voices of its opponents, polling data showed that a majority of Americans opposed the construction of the community center,[12] and that the American public viewed Muslims much more negatively than other religious groups.[13] Republican politicians capitalized on the controversy and the sentiment it engendered, largely opposing the Park51 center and pulling it into their political campaign talking points.[14] The opposition included both the new wave of Tea Party GOP candidates, as well as more mainstream Republican politicians like John McCain, Mitt Romney, and Michael Bloomberg.[15] Other mosques around the country came under increasing scrutiny too, like in Murfreesboro, Tennessee, where local and national activists tried to shut down a local mosque-building project. As part of her election strategy, local Republican Lou Ann Zelenik opposed the Murfreesboro mosque and called it a "training center" for Muslims to commit violence.[16]

After spending a summer largely dedicated to generating fear about America's Muslim population—with politicians like Newt Gingrich even going so far as to compare Muslims to Nazis[17]—Republicans ultimately succeeded in taking back the Senate and House of Representatives from Democrats in the November 2010 midterm elections. The Ground Zero Mosque controversy cannot be understood outside of this political context; it was an example of scapegoating a religious minority for political gain. Anti-Muslim hate crimes that year ticked back up to their earlier war-on-terror levels.

Hate crimes against Muslims remained high the next year, as anti-Muslim sentiment became increasingly normalized in political discourse. New York Republican representative Peter King held hearings in Congress with the stated aim of investigating "radicalization" in American Muslim communities, bringing in leaders of anti-Muslim hate groups who testified to Congress that Muslim organizations were trying to undermine American freedoms. The hearings looked frighteningly similar to those held by Senator Joseph McCarthy in 1954 during the height of the Red Scare, when outsized concerns about Communists in government and public life led to the scape-goating of many Americans. As politicians and commentators promoted a "Green Scare" in 2011—green being a color often associated with Islam—they also sought to convince the public that *sharia*,[18] Islamic religious law, was poised to erode citizens' rights and liberties. They claimed that virtually every American Muslim civil organization and public figure was secretly part of a conspiracy to upend the U.S. Constitution and impose barbaric rule upon non-Muslims.[19] As these pundits advocated for sharia to be outlawed, the public began to feel the same way. Throughout the 2012 election season and beyond, numerous states began passing "anti–foreign law" bills that appealed to a voter base increasingly fearful of Muslims.[20]

For the next few years, anti-Muslim hate crimes lessened slightly, though again not falling as far as their pre–Ground Zero Mosque levels. But then in 2015, they shot up even more radically than they had in 2010—to 257 for the year. That year began with the high-profile massacre of eleven journal-ists working for a French satirical newspaper, *Charlie Hebdo*, by two brothers claiming an affiliation to Al-Qaeda, an event that was followed by many anti-Muslim hate crimes in the United States and Europe. Then a new U.S. presidential election campaign season began, with candidates in the Repub-lican field employing Islamophobic rhetoric while vying for their party's nomination. This coincided with a large exodus of refugees from war-torn places like Syria and Iraq, who sought safety in the United States and Europe.[21] GOP politicians often sowed fear about refugees, most of whom were Muslim, claiming they were a threat to U.S. security and social norms. A large portion of the anti-Muslim hate crimes that year occurred in the last two months of 2015 alone. During that short period, attackers claiming an affiliation with ISIS killed over one hundred people in Paris, France; in San Bernardino, California, a Muslim husband and wife, whose motives remain unclear, killed several people;[22] and presidential candidate Donald Trump subsequently proposed a "total and complete shutdown of Muslims entering the United States." In 2015, attacks against mosques were three times higher than they had been the year previous,[23] and assaults—violent or physical attacks—against Muslims were on par with what they were in 2001, after 9/11.

In 2016, hate crime numbers climbed even higher, to 307, as anti-Muslim rhetoric on the presidential campaign continued and as other highly publi-cized acts of violence committed by Muslims occurred in the United States and Europe. After the November election of Donald Trump to the U.S. presidency, some Americans pleased with his victory took it as license to attack Muslims, immigrants, and people of color. It was a new post-9/11 record for anti-Muslim hate crimes. Though the total number that year remained lower than they had been in 2001, violent attacks climbed even higher, with the number of assaults against Muslims in 2016 surpassing the post-9/11 numbers.[24] From 2017 to 2019, anti-Muslim hate crimes dipped but remained relatively high (273, 188, and 176 annually), never dropping below their pre-2015 levels.[25] As of this writing, the FBI has not yet released the data from 2020.

Looking at these long-term trends in hate crimes, we see ebbs and flows, but overall waves of worsening Islamophobia after 2001. Anti-Muslim hate crimes are now five times more common than they were before 9/11. The periodic spikes track with a range of events. In the case of 9/11, there was a jump after a major incident of violence committed by Muslims; those who had nothing to do with the attack were wrongly targeted in "retaliation." But spikes in anti-Muslim hate crimes are not just reactionary; they do not always correlate with attacks committed by Muslims. In fact, in 2013, the year that two brothers who were Muslim set off bombs at the Boston Marathon—a high-profile crime—anti-Muslim hate crime numbers remained steady. They did rise, however, alongside the contrived controversies and political scape-goating of Muslims in 2010–11 and 2015–16. This correlation between anti-Muslim political rhetoric and increased hate crimes remains a major concern for Muslim communities—as it should for all of us.

The Impact of Interpersonal Islamophobia

In the abstract, these trends are easy to dismiss, but they take a human toll. Particularly during the 2016 election campaign, when hate crimes were at a fever pitch, the fear among my Muslim friends and colleagues for their physical safety was palpable. It seemed like every day on my social media feed, I would read stories about mosque arsons, violent assaults, anti-Muslim bullying in schools, and harassment online and in public. My peers warned their parents not to attend the mosque, and their parents in turn expressed concern for them going out and about. Many Muslim individuals and fami-lies—even lifelong American citizens—contemplated leaving the country if things got much worse. As I write this book in the summer of 2020, anti-Muslim incidents in the United States are not making national headlines, but they are still occurring, even amid the COVID-19 pandemic.

Praying in Peace?

The mosque, or *masjid*, is supposed to be a place of prayer, respite, and community, but in the twenty-first century mosques have become magnets for anti-Muslim animus. To give just one snapshot of the extent of this problem, from January to July 2017 alone, an average of nine mosques per month—at least two per week—were targeted across the United States.[26] Islamophobic incidents at mosques go from offensive and intimidating to outright violent and destructive. Vandals have left torn up Qur'ans, sometimes smeared with feces, on mosque doorsteps and inside prayer spaces they've ransacked.[27] (The seriousness of desecrating a Qur'an in this way is comparable to the seriousness of desecrating the Eucharist—the Body of Christ—for Catholics.) Vandals have also left rotting pigs' heads and strips of bacon outside mosques, as if—because Muslims generally do not eat pork—it will serve as a "Muslim kryptonite" of sorts. In Plainfield, Indiana, attackers have repeatedly targeted the headquarters of the Islamic Society of North America, spray-painting vulgar graffiti on the exterior and riddling its signage with bullet holes. Arson is common, too. In New Haven, Connecticut, in 2019, a mosque was set ablaze, meaning that its congregants—including a friend of mine from college and her family—were prevented from observing the Ramadan traditions in their mosque.

As Christmastime is for many Christians, Ramadan for Muslims is a time of prayerful gatherings and meaningful moments. Yet the holy month in recent years has been accompanied by an uptick in attacks on mosques.[28] This seems to be an unfortunate consequence of increased media coverage of Muslims' holidays and prayer practices. Even when this media coverage is intended to be positive and to improve viewers' understanding, it sometimes has the impact of drawing the negative attention of those with anti-Muslim hostilities. As a Muslim family in New York was leaving Ramadan prayers from their mosque in 2016, two sons were brutally attacked.[29] Outside Houston, Texas, that same summer, a man was shot and stabbed as he walked from the mosque parking lot to perform his early morning prayers.[30] In 2020, someone shot bullets into the prayer hall of Masjid al-Noor, a mosque in Indianapolis, Indiana, on one of the days of Eid al-Fitr, the concluding celebratory days at the end of Ramadan. Fortunately, due to the otherwise devastating COVID-19 pandemic, few people were in the mosque and so no one was killed or injured. Witnesses attested, however, that if the mosque's entire congregation had been present—as would typically be the case for Eid—there would have undoubtedly been many casualties.[31]

Even when direct violence is not involved, the threat of it is often felt at mosques.[32] Across the United States, demonstrators have set up "protests" outside of mosques and Islam-related conferences, with some demonstrators carrying automatic weapons, holding signs, and wearing military fatigues. Anonymous perpetrators have also left sinister messages on mosque answering machines and Facebook pages. A few weeks after Donald Trump's election to the U.S. presidency in November 2016, a letter threatening genocide was sent to numerous mosques around the United States. It spoke of how the new president would "cleanse" the country, and "do to you Muslims what Hitler did to the Jews."[33] Deadly plots against mosques have also been foiled before taking place.[34]

Going to pray at one's house of worship is supposed to be an experience that brings peace and tranquility. But because of myriad cases like those described above, Muslims in the United States sometimes bring trepidation and concern through the door with them. When I, a White Christian, go to church, I rarely if ever have these kinds of worries. But my Muslim neighbors do, as many religious communities do in different parts of the world.

Strollers and Sports Teams

Undoubtedly, Muslims experience Islamophobia outside the mosque, too. In 2007, a Muslim woman who owned a nail salon in Southern California was assaulted and robbed by people who also left anti-Muslim graffiti on the walls of her establishment.[35] In northern California in 2015, a Muslim man was playing volleyball with friends in a local park when a woman came up to him and started ranting about religion. After he took out his phone and started filming her, she struck him and threw a cup of coffee at him.[36] Later that year, in Brooklyn, a woman assaulted two Muslim mothers who were walking with their babies in strollers. The perpetrator yelled obscenities and toppled over one of the strollers.[37] In 2020, a woman wearing a headscarf picked up her coffee order at a Starbucks counter to find that the barista had written "ISIS" on the label instead of her name.[38]

According to a number of surveys from the last decade, Muslims, more than any other major American religious groups, report experiencing religious discrimination in their daily lives.[39] In 2019, 62 percent of Muslims said they had experienced discrimination, with Muslim women experiencing it more than men.[40] Schools have also become sites of Islamophobic discrimination and threats; bullying of Muslim students is a pervasive problem.[41] In the context of sports, Muslim young people have also dealt with religious discrimination or double standards when it comes to dress and uniforms. In 2019, Ohio high schooler Noor Abukaram ran her personal best at a cross-country meet, but afterward was informed she had been disqualified because of her hijab.[42] She had run in her athletic headscarf for years without issue or resistance. Muslims also face issues of hiring discrimination or mistreatment in the workplace, and undergo particular scrutiny at airports. Muslims have been removed from planes because of other passengers' discomfort with their presence,[43] and report receiving (supposedly random) secondary screening much of the time they fly.[44]

Islamophobia Comes Home

Even at home, Muslims cannot escape Islamophobic targeting. In early 2015, a Muslim family in Charlotte, North Carolina, awoke to gunshots being fired into their home, striking the mother in her bed.[45] During the spike in hate crimes later that year, someone threw large rocks into the home of a Muslim family in Plano, Texas.[46] In 2017, a Muslim family in Virginia came home to find their green cards and valuables taken, their Qur'an ripped up, and slurs written on the walls.[47] There have also been plots of mass killings against housing complexes or towns with large Muslim populations. In 2015, Robert Doggart—a former congressional candidate from Tennessee— plotted to recruit a militia and carry out a violent massacre against the town of Islamberg in rural New York.[48] According to the statement of charges, he reportedly said, "I don't want to have to kill children, but there's always collateral damage," during a wiretapped phone call.

This overall climate of Islamophobia has had a significant and detrimental impact on Muslims' health. "Physical wounds can heal but the emotional wound and the loss of sense of safety and security is a permanent scar," Mohamed Omar, the executive director of a mosque in Bloomington, Minnesota, told reporters in 2020 after his colleague was assaulted and left with a broken shoulder outside their mosque.[49] The fear Muslims have to live with, of being attacked, he said, is a public health issue. Psychologists have found that even for Muslims who have not been the direct victim of a violent hate crime, Islamophobia is a serious burden to bear.[50] In 2017, half of American Muslims reported that it had become harder in recent years to be Muslim in the United States.[51] When Muslims hear about an attack on someone who looks like them, or that a mosque in another town or even another country has been targeted, they worry that they might be next, because they indeed could be.[52] Security cameras and armed guards have become familiar sites at mosques, especially during Ramadan.[53] Some young Muslim women have been afraid to wear headscarves for fear of sticking out, being met with suspicious or hostile stares, or being targeted in more violent ways.[54] Whether in its interpersonal forms or in the more structural manifestations we will explore throughout this book, Islamophobia harms bodies and weighs on minds and hearts in ways that cannot be quantified.

The Trump Effect

"We have a problem in this country. It's called Muslims. Our current president [Obama] is one. . . . We have training camps growing where they want to kill us. . . . My question is, when can we get rid of them?"[55] Smiling and chuckling as a voter asked this question at a 2015 New Hampshire town hall, Donald Trump replied, "We need this question" and vowed to "look at that."[56] Trump did not challenge the question's anti-Muslim premise or implications, but rather let them stand. Overtly Islamophobic rhetoric was a winning political strategy among Republican candidates, particularly during the 2016 cycle. Shortly before the New Hampshire event, Trump's competitor Ben Carson had seen his polling numbers rise after he asserted that a Muslim should not be eligible to run for president.[57] When Trump's campaign tried the same tactic, his numbers surged, and he ultimately clinched the nomination after a series of increasingly shameless anti-Muslim comments and policy proposals.

But Trump was not simply a beneficiary of the blatant anti-Muslim turn within the party. In many ways, Trump had helped inaugurate it several years before. During 2011 and his first run for the U.S. presidency, he was one of the leading advocates of what became known as the "birther conspiracy" about President Barack Obama.[58] He cast doubt on whether Obama was born in the United States, and wondered aloud if his foreign birth certificate would reveal that he was a Muslim. "Maybe it says he is a Muslim," Trump said in a 2011 interview on FOX News.[59] Obama was and remains a Protestant Christian, but Trump continued to fuel the idea that Obama was Muslim during his campaign run, and other Republican candidates contributed to the notion's proliferation as well.[60] By 2015, nearly a third of Americans believed that Obama was Muslim, along with 43 percent of Republicans and 54 percent of those who supported Donald Trump's presidential bid.[61] Of course, Obama's supposed Muslim-ness was not seen as an innocuous quality.[62] In the eyes of many voters and the politicians who promoted the idea, it made Obama an enemy to America and its Christian character.[63] Obama was not the first American president to be smeared with this Muslim label; it was also leveled against Thomas Jefferson during his 1800 presidential run against John Adams.[64]

During his own presidential runs, Trump frequently resorted to anti-Muslim rhetoric. He insisted that there is a "Muslim problem in the world;" falsely claimed that a quarter of all Muslims are "very militant;" entertained the idea of shutting down mosques as a supposed solution to terrorist violence; and refused to disavow the idea of a Muslim registry, even when it was compared to Nazi practices against Jews in Europe.[65] As president, his anti-Muslim rhetoric continued, often on Twitter.[66] In one example, he amplified concerns that Muslim prayer rugs had been found along the U.S.-Mexico border.[67] Prayer rugs are an item almost-universally used by Muslims in their worship, and thus Trump's concern about their presence reveals his underlying assumption that Muslims as a group are inherently dangerous. This kind of anti-Muslim rhetoric has tangible consequences. Researchers

Karsten Müller and Carlo Schwarz found that, since his presidential run, "Trump's tweets about Islam-related topics predict increases in . . . hate crimes on the following days."[68]

Ted Cruz, a Republican frontrunner in the 2016 presidential election, also traded in blatant anti-Muslim rhetoric during the campaign. After an attack in Nice, France, in which a Muslim man with ISIS sympathies deliberately drove a van into a crowd of people, killing many, Cruz announced that police should "patrol and secure Muslim neighborhoods" and praised a New York City law enforcement practice of spying on Muslims going about their everyday activities.[69] Rick Santorum, Scott Walker, and Marco Rubio also took up the strategy. Santorum endorsed the idea of religious profiling of Muslims[70] and cast suspicion on the entire community with comments like, "There are serious questions about Islam and the spread of Islam and how it spreads."[71] Walker falsely claimed that there are "only a handful of reasonable and moderate followers of Islam."[72] Rubio compared Muslims to members of the Nazi Party,[73] and also cast doubt on the existence of Islamophobia.[74]

Few candidates running for the Republican nomination in 2016 refrained from this kind of anti-Muslim fearmongering. It also resurfaced during the 2018 midterm elections. One prime example of this was the rhetoric of Republican Roy Moore, who ran for a Senate seat in Alabama. Despite his Islamophobic comments—that Islam is a "false religion,"[75] that Muslims and other religious groups do not deserve religious protections, and that the Qur'an is comparable to Adolf Hilter's *Mein Kampf*—he received little pushback or condemnation from his Republican counterparts.[76] During their campaigns and after Ilhan Omar and Rashida Tlaib became the first Muslim women to serve in the House of Representatives, they faced considerable Islamophobic targeting from GOP politicians[77] and interest groups, as well as death threats,[78] with relatively little reaction from their Democratic counterparts.[79]

The rhetoric among Republicans was not as blatant during the earlier 2012 race, but it laid the foundation for what came later. Presidential candidate Herman Cain said he would not be comfortable appointing a Muslim as a federal judge or to a cabinet position because of "this creeping attempt, there is this attempt to gradually ease Sharia law and the Muslim faith into our government."[80] Candidate Michele Bachmann made headlines for her claim that Hillary Clinton's top aide, Huma Abedin, had ties to Muslim terrorism.[81]

Over time, the anti-Muslim rhetoric among Republicans became more and more brazen, with Bachmann declaring that "it is about Islam"[82] and others, like Florida representative Allen West, calling American Muslims a "fifth column"—a phrase used to refer to a supposed internal enemy that will undermine the nation.[83] Thus, when then-candidate Trump finally called for a "ban" on Muslims entering the United States in a campaign press conference in December 2015,[84] it was simply the logical conclusion of the racialized claims about Muslims that had characterized Republican rhetoric for years. Republicans had claimed or insinuated that Muslims were not to be trusted, that they were a foreign threat to the security and freedom of "the rest of us." If Muslims were indeed these things inherently and universally, then keeping them out of the United States would seem like a reasonable option—hence, a Muslim ban.

The campaign proposal to ban Muslims received support from a majority of Republican voters.[85] Exit polling showed that, during the primaries, around two-thirds of GOP voters approved of the idea.[86] Other surveys showed that substantial segments of the broader U.S. population also did, especially when they could hide behind the anonymity of an online survey rather than speak to an actual person administering the poll.[87] But others were quite open about their support of the idea. When a CNN journalist asked a voter, on camera, about his opinion as he waited in line to enter a Trump campaign rally, the young man said, "Yes, I do [support a ban]. I don't want 'em here. Who knows what they're going to bring into this country. Bombs, ISIS. Gotta go." After speaking to numerous others, the journalist reported that "No one here we spoke with had a problem with the plan."[88]

In government and beyond, a kind of "proud Islamophobia" has emerged. Shop owners have advertised their stores as "Muslim-free zones," and a dangerous campaign called "Punish a Muslim Day" was publicized in the United States and United Kingdom.[89] Some anti-Muslim activists, who downplay the very real prejudice and discrimination that Muslims face, happily declare themselves to be "Islamophobes."[90] In politics and public life, many are no longer concerned with hiding their bigotry.

Government policies under Trump also became more blatantly Islamophobic. Prior to his presidency, for decades the U.S. federal government had indeed singled out Muslims,[91] who found themselves targeted by discriminatory policies and court rulings. Troubling examples of this, as well as cases on a more local level, appear throughout this book. But the Trump administration's so-called travel ban—with its "extreme vetting" components and alongside the administration's severe restrictions on refugee resettlement—has been one of the most wide reaching in its impact and overt in its focus on Muslims as a whole.

After Trump's election, his team looked to adjust his initial position on banning Muslims,[92] focusing instead on banning people coming from specific countries, rather than an entire religious community.[93] As Trump's colleagues even admitted, this was more for cosmetic and practical reasons than for moral ones. They pivoted not because they suddenly realized it was wrong to discriminate against an entire religious community, but because they were concerned about making the policy more appealing to a broad swath of the public and ensuring that it would not be struck down by the courts.[94] Banning Muslims as an entire religious group would violate the U.S. Constitution, so they focused instead on banning entry to people from a range of predominantly Muslim countries. This policy would satisfy the anti-Muslim views of Trump's base, while seeking to avoid legal pitfalls related to religious discrimination.[95]

In January 2017, just a week into his presidency, the Trump administration finally issued what it euphemistically called the "travel ban," fulfilling one of his key campaign promises. The executive order barred entry to people from Iran, Iraq, Libya, Somalia, Sudan, Syria, and Yemen (all Muslim-majority countries); indefinitely banned all Syrian refugees; and temporarily blocked all other refugees.[96] Opponents of the ban filed lawsuits seeking to halt its implementation, leading the administration to roll out three different versions of the ban, with some countries swapped onto and off of the list.[97] The third iteration, issued in September 2017, barred people from Iran, Libya, Somalia, Syria, and Yemen, as well as North Korea and Venezuela, but these last two only in a very limited way. From Venezuela, only some government officials and their families were barred, and at the time of the ban visitors to the United States from North Korea were already quite rare.[98]

This third version of the ban was brought before the Supreme Court, where it was ultimately upheld. The majority of the justices based their ruling on the fact that the U.S. president has the prerogative to temporarily restrict entry into the United States from other countries to protect national security. The justices argued that the ban's waiver program (which would allow individuals from banned countries to apply to still come to the United States) prevented the order from being overly unjust, and they hinged their decision to uphold it on this aspect of the policy. But the dissenting justices and other critics pointed to the ban's original and underlying Islamophobic premise[99]—which the media and many politicians downplayed after Trump's election[100]—as well as its actual outcomes.

In all of its iterations, the ban had a devastating impact on Muslims, both in the United States and abroad. When the first version of the ban was announced, it left many Muslims stranded, deported, and waiting for ages in airports, including American citizens and longtime U.S. residents.[101] The directives in the order had been vague and sweeping, leaving Customs and Border Patrol (CBP) officials with little guidance on how to implement an already prejudiced policy. And even though the administration had stripped from it any explicit reference to "Islam" or "Muslims," it was not free of its Islamophobic insinuations and intent. As seen in the last chapter, the order listed several undesirable qualities and attitudes and said that anyone exhibiting these should be barred from entry into the United States. This list was made up of the most common and blatant anti-Muslim stereotypes.[102] The order itself was titled "Protecting the Nation from Foreign Terrorist Entry into the United States," employing the stereotypical anti-Muslim dog whistle "foreign terrorist."[103]

A short time after the ban was enacted and thousands of Americans protested against it at airports around the country, a Georgetown University undergraduate student named Sikander[104] came into my office at the Bridge Initiative, where I was working at the time. As we chatted, he told me he had planned to visit Pakistan, where he grew up, over the coming summer break, but that now, because of the ban, he did not think he would be able to. "Pakistan is not on the list of banned countries," Sikander recognized as we talked, "but I am afraid that, as a Muslim, if I leave the U.S., I won't be able to get back in to finish out my studies at Georgetown." But choosing this option and staying in D.C. meant that Sikander would not be able to see his family for quite awhile. This was a dilemma that countless Muslims—both U.S. citizens and not—faced in those days.

Fortunately, Sikander was able to return home to Pakistan and then come back to Georgetown. Many others were not so lucky. The ban separated mothers from their dying children, adult children from their ailing parents, spouses and engaged couples, and so many others.[105] In its final iteration upheld by the Supreme Court, the ban included a waiver policy that was supposed to allow select individuals from banned countries to still enter, provided they meet strict vetting procedures. But the waiver process was rarely implemented, leaving many stranded in limbo.[106]

Data also shows that Muslim refugees have been disproportionately targeted by both the ban and other limits that the Trump administration has put on refugee resettlement.[107] From 2016 to 2019, the resettlement of refugees who are Muslim decreased by 90 percent. In 2019, Christians made up the vast majority of the refugees allowed into the United States, despite the fact that the majority of refugees globally are Muslim.[108]

In 2020, the Trump administration added six more countries to the banned list: Eritrea, Kyrgyzstan, Myanmar, Nigeria, Sudan, and Tanzania.[109] All of them have sizable Muslim populations, save Myanmar, where the small minority of Rohingya Muslims has fled genocide. Many of the newly banned countries are on the African continent, making Black people some of the primary targets of the ban. The administration planned to announce the updated ban on the third anniversary of the previous one—a clear sign that this policy was not aimed at fixing a real national security issue. Instead, the timing speaks to the kind of U.S. citizenry the Trump administration wanted to see—one with fewer numbers of Muslim, Black, and poor people.[110]

Islamophobia as an Industry

Islamophobia was not an ignorant reaction to the public
presence of Muslims in America. It was manufactured.

—Edward E. Curtis IV[111]

One reason why Islamophobic speech and policies have worsened in recent years is due to a network of individuals and organizations that actively promote it. Made up of a cadre of bloggers, activists, speakers, and think-tank heads, this "Islamophobia network"—as it is often called—has succeeded in shaping public sentiment, discourse, and policy and in mainstreaming Islamophobia over the last ten-plus years.[112] A decade ago, many of the anti-Muslim activists and writers whom I studied were fringe figures. But by early 2017, some of them had become household names, not to mention familiar faces in the White House. Their views had gained entrance to the highest halls of power in the U.S. government; they had managed to orchestrate numerous anti-Muslim controversies that captured national and international attention; and the organizations that they ran had gained more support throughout towns and cities across the United States. They achieved all this, in large part, due to how organized and well funded they were. These figures and hate groups work together closely, along with political, corporate, and philanthropic entities that benefit financially or otherwise from the existence of anti-Muslim prejudice and discrimination. Fueling and sustaining Islamophobia has become a well-coordinated "industry,"[113] and a lucrative one at that.[114]

The Ground Zero Mosque controversy and the hysteria around sharia are only two of the most memorable anti-Muslim campaigns for which the Islamophobia network has been responsible. Over the last decade, this cohort of individuals and organizations has also been behind anti-Muslim advertisements on New York City buses and in Washington, DC, metro stations; protests outside local mosques and Muslim conferences; and anti-refugee initiatives. They have also launched campaigns to foment concern about so-called Islamic "indoctrination" in schools and the increase in halal food options at local grocery stores.[115]

The individuals responsible for these efforts run think-tank-style organizations, nonprofit activist groups,[116] or widely read blogs, and many of them have published best-selling books. They give frequent media interviews and organize speaking engagements around the country. In some cases, these individuals mobilize people at the grassroots level, who then take directives from email blasts on how to implement these groups' anti-Muslim agenda in their local setting. Readers might recognize some of their names: Pamela Geller and Robert Spencer (whom I have already mentioned), Frank Gaffney, Brigitte Gabriel, and Ayaan Hirsi Ali, among numerous others.[117] Scholars and journalists have traced the connections between these groups[118] and the way they work together, especially online, to promote common messaging and misinformation about Muslims.[119] Some of the most significant groups are Gabriel's ACT! for America, Gaffney's Center for Security Policy, the Clarion Project, the Gatestone Institute, and the David Horowitz Freedom Center, along with Spencer's and Geller's organizations. Many of these have been labeled anti-Muslim hate groups by the Southern Poverty Law Center, which tracks hate groups in the United States.[120]

This network of individuals first started getting organized during the early years of the second Iraq War during the presidency of George W. Bush.[121] Over time, they have worked more closely with Republican politicians in Washington and around the country, shaping their views and policy positions. The Islamophobia network has also found a home at FOX News, where they are not only brought on as "expert" commentators, but also where hosts like Glenn Beck, Laura Ingraham, Bill O'Reilly, and Jeanine Pirro themselves had echoed and given credence to their conspiracy theories and anti-Muslim claims.[122]

In 2015, when he announced his plan for a ban on Muslims, Donald Trump cited a survey that had been issued by an organization few Americans had heard of: the Center for Security Policy (CSP). Despite its generic name, my colleagues and I were eminently familiar with the DC-based group, the work of its head, Frank Gaffney, and their long history of anti-Muslim fearmongering in right-wing outlets like FOX News and Breitbart. Six months prior, we had penned an article pointing out the flaws of this survey and its findings, which cast American Muslims as an existential threat to the United States. At his press conference, Trump used this anti-Muslim "report" to justify his policy proposal and he praised CSP's work.[123]

Ultimately, Trump brought into his campaign and administration numerous advisers and officials who had either worked directly for or alongside anti-Muslim groups prior to joining his team. They include now-well-known names: Jeff Sessions, John Bolton, Steve Bannon, Stephen Miller, Michael Flynn, Mike Pompeo, Sebastian Gorka, and Kellyanne Conway, whose consulting firm happened to be involved with the CSP poll.[124] Several of these individuals have won awards from these anti-Muslim groups, given talks at their events, or parroted their talking points. Steve Bannon, for example, when he was head of Breitbart, frequently featured the voices of his favorite "experts" on Islam—Geller, Spencer, and Gaffney.[125] Though some of these Trump officials left or were fired from their White House jobs, others with anti-Muslim agendas were brought in, and their views still informed the administration's activities.[126] None of these individuals had to renounce anti-Muslim views and associations with hate groups but rather were given the opportunity to funnel anti-Muslim agendas into U.S. government policy. Figures who had been on the fringes just a decade ago have ended up working in the U.S. presidential administration or were just a friendly phone call away. After Trump was elected, Brigitte Gabriel celebrated the "direct line" that her group, ACT! for America, had to the White House. Shortly after his inauguration, she was invited there to speak with staff.[127] Ted Cruz's and Ben Carson's campaigns had also hired and consulted with Gaffney and other figures in the Islamophobia network, as have politicians working and running at the level of state and local government.[128] Longtime congressional politicians have also worked closely with anti-Muslim groups. For example, Rep. Peter King appeared on ACT! for America's web show right before holding the first of his "Muslim radicalization" hearings, which elevated more anti-Muslim voices.[129]

It is not the case that the Trump administration, GOP politicians, and other political and governmental entities have simply been duped into working with the Islamophobia network. While they may genuinely believe the conspiracy theories and anti-Muslim ideas the Islamophobia industry feeds them, political campaigns and government and military entities often have need of these anti-Muslim activists in order to make their own goals a reality. As Namira Islam, a human rights educator and attorney, writes, "The prevalence of these narratives leads to buy-in for the enactment of policies . . . [that] have collectively had a devastating impact on American Muslims and Muslims abroad."[130] Fear helps win elections at home, and dehumanization of people "over there" helps sell weapons and normalize the idea of war against Muslims abroad. Ahead of the 2008 presidential election, more than 28 million American voters in swing states opened their mailboxes to find a copy of a film titled *Obsession: Radical Islam's War on the West*. Distributed by the Clarion Fund/Project, an anti-Muslim group, it featured many of these anti-Muslim commentators and sought to sow fear about a Muslim takeover of the West.[131] A similar film, *The Third Jihad*, was later produced by Clarion and ultimately screened in NYPD and other law enforcement trainings.[132]

The Islamophobia network's writers and activists themselves also benefit considerably from their activities. From the high salaries they receive from generous donors who fund their organizations, to speaking fees and royalties from their best-selling books, they receive significant financial payoffs from their work, not to mention significant social and political influence.[133] The relationship between anti-Muslim activists and the governmental and corporate entities that work with them is a symbiotic one—but it leaves Muslims increasingly scapegoated and targeted by both interpersonal and more institutional forms of Islamophobia.

The organized nature of Islamophobia is also witnessed online. Ahead of the 2016 election, Russian-based social media campaigns stirred up anti-Muslim sentiment in the United States,[134] and other entities have generated false or misleading stories about Muslims with the intention that they go viral.[135] There are also coordinated efforts to lift up negative content about Muslims in search results, and to suppress truthful or positive information. Cadres of readers or bots "click" on content they want to appear first in search engine results, and they give negative ratings to content they find undesirable in order to drive them downward. One place this occurs is on Amazon, where customer ratings of books play an important role in determining which books get recommended to other potential buyers. Colleagues of mine who are academics in the field of Islamic studies or Islamophobia often find that their well-researched books have been targeted with a slew of one-star ratings, which shove their books toward the bottom of search results. (I have seen a similar tactic used to target the posts on my personal website.) Oftentimes, it appears that these negative reviewers have not even read the book or the post. Their reviews are not substantive, and they echo or even quote directly from talking points found on anti-Muslim websites.

Silver Linings amid Gathering Clouds: Public Attitudes toward Muslims

Interestingly, negative views of Muslims and Islam among the American public often do not follow the same trajectory as anti-Muslim hate crimes. Perhaps surprisingly, the Pew Research Center found that American public opinion toward Muslims as a religious community actually improved in the immediate aftermath of 9/11, as hate crimes were at their all-time high.[136] This is because many in the public rightly recognized that Muslims as a group should not be judged based on the actions of the worst of their fellow Muslims, an opinion bolstered by leaders and politicians who hoped to protect Muslims from unjust backlash.

A similar pattern occurred in 2015 and 2016. Survey data shows that Americans' stated attitudes toward Muslims showed a dramatic improvement between November 2015 and October 2016, regardless of political affiliation.[137] As pollster Shibley Telhami wrote in the *Washington Post* in early 2017, one might have expected the opposite, given the prevalence of negative political rhetoric about Muslims from Republicans, as well as the occurrence of deadly attacks committed by Muslim perpetrators in San Bernardino, California, and at an LGBTQ nightclub in Orlando, Florida. As Telhami put it,

"Attitudes of most Americans toward Islam and Muslims improved overall precisely because Trump the candidate was seen to have the opposite view."[138] Many voters, especially Democrats and independents, latched onto the counternarrative offered by Bernie Sanders, Hillary Clinton, and Martin O'Malley, who spoke far more positively of Muslims, at least in part to distinguish themselves from their Republican competitors. As the American public's awareness of and concern for Islamophobia increased, positive gestures and statements of solidarity with Muslims also became more common. Religious congregations, public officials, and ordinary people expressed support for Muslims, placing posters in their storefronts and banners in their yards. Many also took concrete actions, including protesting against Islamophobia at the January 2017 Women's March or at the airports where Muslims were being detained due to the Trump administration's Muslim ban.

But despite these bright spots, in the last two decades overall, Americans' views of Muslims have been relatively negative. In Pew polls, Americans consistently admit to feeling the "coldest" toward Muslims compared to other major religious groups in the United States.[139] In Gallup surveys, at least up until 2015, over 40 percent of Americans admitted to "harboring at least some prejudice" toward the group.[140] And concerns about Islam being "more violent" than other religions doubled from 2002 to 2014.[141] Especially at heightened moments of national conversation about Muslims, a large number of Americans have said that they would not want Muslims holding public offices like that of a Supreme Court justice or U.S. president.[142] And as noted above, significant minorities of Americans have also supported Donald Trump's plan to ban Muslims from the United States, as well as his later enactments of this proposal.

Responding with Resilience

Amid worsening Islamophobia throughout the twenty-first century, the strength and resilience that Muslim Americans have demonstrated is admirable and inspiring. Even with the toll that Islamophobia takes, they refuse to let it define them. Muslim friends and colleagues in my own circles continue to live lives of generosity and service, dedicating themselves to their families, communities, and causes that matter to them. According to one recent survey, though Muslims' satisfaction with the trajectory of the country's future has diminished, they are still more likely than other Americans to express optimism about the future of the country.[143]

They include people like Rais Bhuiyan, the man shot in the convenience store after 9/11. Twenty years after his life was shattered by that hate crime, Rais is striving to upend the kind of attitudes that prompted his maiming after 9/11, trying to prevent more loss of life. Rais even worked to save the life of his attacker, Mark Stroman, who had been sentenced to death for his murderous rampage. When Rais went on an Islamic pilgrimage to Mecca in 2009, he asked God why he had survived and what he should do with his life. He left with a mission, encouraged by the Qur'anic teaching that "saving [one] life is like saving the entirety of mankind." In addition to founding a nonprofit to teach about hate crimes and his experience of mercy and forgiveness, he did all he could to stay Mark's execution, even appealing to the Supreme Court. "I saw him as a victim, too," Rais has said of Mark. "I deeply felt by executing him we would simply lose a human life without dealing with the root cause."[144] Ultimately, Rais did not succeed in saving Mark's life, but they did reconcile. One of the last phone calls Mark made before he died was to Rais. He told him, "I love you, bro."[145]

3

Both Sides

How Islamophobia Spans the Political Spectrum
and Circles the Globe

In an elementary school bathroom, a fourth-grade boy bent over the toilet and threw up. The school office called his mother to tell him, and when she picked him up shortly thereafter, she learned why.

The woman, Asima, and her son, Yasiyn, are Muslim.[1] It was the morning after the 2016 elections, when Donald Trump had been elected president. Yasiyn had felt fine when he woke up that morning, but upon hearing about the election results, he started to feel unwell. "Do we have to move?" he asked. Even though he was only nine years old, Yasiyn, like many Muslim kids across the United States, was well aware of the Trump campaign's prejudicial rhetoric and discriminatory policy ideas about Muslims. On the drive to school, Yasiyn had expressed to his mother how nervous and scared he was, telling her the election made him feel a little sick.

When he arrived at school, Yasiyn talked to one of his good friends. As Asima recounted in a Facebook post, the young boy told Yasiyn that he was happy that Trump had won, and then proceeded to list groups of people he "secretly hated," including Muslims, whom he hoped would be dealt with differently by the new president. Yasiyn was at a loss for words, not knowing how to respond as his friend's words sunk in. A few minutes later, he rushed to the bathroom to throw up.

In the wake of the 2016 election, stories like this splashed onto my social media newsfeed. Yasiyn was not the only Muslim child in America whose classmates had expressed their dislike of them more openly in the days after the election. Other Muslim kids, wanting to preempt potential ill treatment by the new president, told their parents they wanted to move out of the country, where the American government could not harm them.[2]

Because of stories like this, and the trends we saw in the last chapter, many people perceive Islamophobia to be something limited to the right side of the American political spectrum. The political right has indeed embraced Islam-

34

ophobia more openly and explicitly in recent years. In reaction, Democrats came out more strongly and forcefully against Islamophobia, taking it up as an explicit political issue for the first time in 2016. But Republicans are not alone in their Islamophobia problem. It plagues the political left, too. Though it is often less apparent, many on the left—both those who serve in government and those who shape culture through media—have furthered Islamophobia through policies and discourse. As this chapter shows, Islamophobia often brings the right and left together and allows them to unify around a common Muslim enemy. Islamophobia is a system that creates inequality and affords benefits to some people at the expense of others—and individuals and institutions on both the right and left have contributed to that, whether they are in the realm of government, journalism, academia, or the general public. Both sides also draw on the racialized stereotypes about Muslims already discussed.

Fortunately, many people across the American political spectrum have actively resisted anti-Muslim scapegoating and policies, but much more must be done. Indeed, both sides of the political spectrum need to seriously interrogate the ways that Islamophobia is a feature, not a bug, of Western liberalism, construed broadly.[3]

Islamophobia is by no means exclusively a North American or even European problem. Contrary to the assumptions of many, Islamophobia also exists beyond those regions of the world that we typically think of as "the West." In our globalized world of social media, Islamophobia is not bounded by borders. Though the internet has facilitated more learning and knowledge among many populations, it has also allowed stereotypes and misunderstandings to cross national boundaries effortlessly, and has enabled many of the anti-Muslim activists we met in the last chapter to organize and work together more effectively with their counterparts around the world. Another way that Islamophobia is a transnational phenomenon is that many governmental regimes either stoke fears of Muslims to achieve political gain or implement policies that target their Muslim populations, all the while employing the same anti-Muslim tropes that circulate in the West. In this chapter, I examine these varied facets, highlighting cases that illustrate larger trends.

Actions Speak Louder Than Words

Beneath archways decorated in blue floral patterns and under the heat of news camera lightbulbs, the U.S. president walked up to a podium. It had been set up hastily on the carpets of the Islamic Center of Washington in the District of Columbia, and Muslim leaders flanked the commander in chief, all of them in stocking feet. With Americans still reeling from the September 11, 2001, attacks the week prior, and hate crimes against Muslim Americans accelerating at a rapid pace, George W. Bush knew he must speak out—both to Muslims and to the American people at large. "Like the good folks standing with me," he said, "the American people were appalled and outraged at last Tuesday's attacks, and so were Muslims all around the world."[4] After quoting from the Qur'an, he told Americans that the carnage they saw and experienced on 9/11 is not an accurate reflection of Islam. "The face of terror is not the true faith of Islam. . . . When we think of Islam, we think of a faith that brings comfort to a billion people around the world," he said. He went on to highlight the positive role and contributions that Muslims make to American society, and to express concern that Muslims—especially women who wear headscarves—felt intimidated to go about their daily lives in public. Speaking of those targeting Muslims in acts of hate, he said, "Those who feel like they can intimidate our fellow citizens to take out their anger don't represent the best of America," he said. "They represent the worst of humankind. And they should be ashamed of that kind of behavior."

A Republican, President Bush was praised back then for his speech at the mosque, a gesture that signaled to Americans that they should not conflate Islam with terrorism, and that their Muslim fellow citizens should be respected. The Muslim leaders who stood with him hoped his speech would help curb hate crimes,[5] and though it is hard to measure the impact, the positive public opinion toward Muslims in the immediate aftermath of 9/11 is likely due in part to Bush's efforts. The content and tone of his speech—and the reassurances he gave to American Muslims on that fall day—stood in stark contrast to the negativity that has characterized the GOP rhetoric on Islam and policy toward Muslims since then.

In the wake of 9/11, the Bush administration inaugurated its open-ended "war on terror". This war was not waged against a single enemy like Al-Qaeda, but rather against "terror"—a feeling, an idea, a tactic. Though Bush insisted that the United States' enemy was not Muslims or Arabs,[6] he called it a "crusade," invoking the memory of the Christian aggression toward Muslims during the Middle Ages.[7] Moreover, the conflation between Islam and terrorism had already become so entrenched in the public imagination that to many Americans it was hard to tell the difference. Because the label of "terror" was such a vague one, it could be applied anywhere, thus giving license to open-ended conflict, justifying virtually any U.S. military action that involved Muslims.

Despite the fact that the government of Iraq had nothing to do with the 9/11 attacks, the amorphous war on terror expanded to include it. To justify their military actions against Iraq, the Bush administration utilized false claims that Saddam Hussein's government there had weapons of mass destruction (WMD) and could imminently harm the United States, its allies, and interests if the regime was not toppled. Many Democrats, including then-senator Joe Biden, helped normalize the Bush administration's claims and supported the case for invading. "I do not believe it is a rush to war but a march to peace and security," Biden said in 2003.[8] After an intense media campaign to get the American people to buy the administration's untrue claims about WMD, Congress voted to approve war against Iraq, and in March 2003, the U.S. military dropped bombs on Iraq's capital, Baghdad. It has been nearly two decades, and ever since then the United States has exerted considerable geopolitical power in that strategically-located and oil-rich region.

In Iraq's fertile crescent, in the hills of Afghanistan, and in the American heartland, the war on terror began to look more and more like the war on Muslims that Bush had promised it would not be. In the post-9/11 fervor, Congress passed the USA PATRIOT Act in 2001, which increased the ability of the government to spy on U.S. citizens and search their personal records without their knowledge and with little to no judicial oversight.[9] It allowed for the indefinite detention of noncitizens, led to serious infringements on civil liberties, and most seriously impacted Muslims and Arabs.[10] In the wake of 9/11, the Department of Homeland Security was created to carry out the mission of the PATRIOT Act,[11] as was the program called NSEERS, which was a "special registration" program intended to prevent future terrorist attacks.[12] More than eighty thousand noncitizen men, most of them from Muslim-majority countries, were required to register with the program. It resulted in thousands being interrogated and detained on American soil, and in some cases deported, yet the program did not lead to one terrorism conviction. Other measures, like the no-fly list, terrorist watch list, and secondary screening procedures at airports, have also been used to racially and religiously profile Muslims, Arabs, South Asians, and others.[13]

Abroad, staggering numbers of Afghan, Pakistani, and Iraqi civilians were killed, either directly by the United States or by the violent situation the invasions had inaugurated. A 2015 report found that the total body count among these three countries during the war on terror years was 1.3 million, with a million of those in Iraq alone.[14] To put that in perspective, just under three thousand American civilians were killed on 9/11; about forty-four hundred U.S. troops have died in Iraq; and about twenty-four hundred U.S. troops have died in Afghanistan, as of August 2020.[15]

During the war on terror, many people were also detained in secret U.S. prisons abroad, referred to as CIA blacksites, without due process and often facing torture tactics allowed by the Bush administration.[16] In 2003, photos emerged of atrocities committed by U.S. military officials at Abu Ghraib prison in Iraq, where soldiers sexually abused and inflicted serious bodily

harm on prisoners who lacked any recourse to a fair hearing.[17] At Guantánamo Bay, on foreign soil in Cuba, the United States has indefinitely held
hundreds of adults and children—all of them Muslim—the vast majority
of whom have never been charged or convicted of a crime.[18] One of them
was Mohamedou Slahi from Mauritania, who was held for fourteen years at
Guantánamo without charges. While there, he penned a memoir detailing his
experiences and the torture he faced, and after a legal battle, the best seller
was published while he was still imprisoned.[19] Slahi was not alone in his experience of torture at Guantánamo. Gruesome reports of mistreatment and
torture have been widespread.[20] Since the prison at Guantánamo opened in
2002, most of the detainees have now been released—including Slahi—but
forty individuals remain held there, twenty-three of them without trial in
indefinite detention.[21]

When the Bush administration wanted U.S. power to be felt by others
but not the American people, it used bombing campaigns, also known more
euphemistically as "drone strikes," to engage in its war on terror. Under
George W. Bush, the United States bombed Pakistan, Somalia, and Yemen, in
addition to its wars in Afghanistan and Iraq.[22]

Republican politicians put up little resistance to the Bush administration's actions or policies that primarily targeted Muslim populations. A few,
however, sought to oppose the overt anti-Muslim campaign rhetoric that
came to characterize the party. When Barack Obama was first accused of
being a Muslim during his run for president in 2008, Colin Powell, who had
worked in Bush's Republican administration, spoke out:

> He is not a Muslim, he's a Christian. He's always been a Christian.
> But the really right answer is, what if he is? Is there something
> wrong with being a Muslim in this country? The answer's no, that's
> not America. Is there something wrong with some seven-year-old
> Muslim-American kid believing that he or she could be president?
> Yet, I have heard senior members of my own party drop the sugges-
> tion, "He's a Muslim and he might be associated with terrorists." This
> is not the way we should be doing it in America.[23]

Whereas Obama's competitor, John McCain, had simply refuted the claim
and insisted that Obama was "a good man,"[24] Powell refused to reproduce
the false and racist logic that a Muslim cannot be a good person. To this day,
Powell's response remains one of the most principled and accurate responses
to Islamophobia, not just in his party but across the political spectrum.

In reaction to the most blatant anti-Muslim propositions of the 2016
campaign, some other Republicans did speak out. Then-senator Jeff Flake of
Arizona visited a mosque in his home state and said,

There can be no religious test for those who serve in public office. We do not tolerate religious discrimination in the workplace, or in the neighborhood. The slogan on the Statue of Liberty—give us your poor, your tired and your huddled masses yearning to breathe free—contemplates no religious test for those who reach our shores.[25]

Then–Indiana governor Mike Pence, who would later become Trump's vice president and support his policies, wrote on Twitter of the Muslim ban: "Calls to ban Muslims from entering the U.S. are offensive and unconstitutional."[26]

But many GOP reactions were lukewarm and failed to identify the clearly discriminatory nature of this policy proposal.[27] Ted Cruz, who was among the frontrunners in the 2016 Republican primary race, told reporters,

I do not agree with his proposal. I do not think it is the right solution. . . . The broader solution is a commander in chief willing to speak the truth, willing to name the enemy—radical Islamic terrorism—and willing to do whatever it takes to utterly destroy radical Islamic terrorism and to defeat ISIS.[28]

Republicans like Cruz who were running for office continued to trade in anti-Muslim rhetoric, bringing up "radical *Islamic* terrorism" anytime they could. They were all playing the same game—fearmongering about Muslims to win political points. Their supporters either did not recognize it, condoned it, or liked them more for it.[29]

What makes the Bush administration and the Republican Party's embrace of anti-Muslim rhetoric and policies particularly ironic is that, before September 11, 2001, many Muslims identified with the Republican Party and its conservative social and economic positions.[30] In 2000, Bush had campaigned hard to win the Muslim vote.[31] Today, there is a joke sometimes made in Muslim circles in Washington, DC, that Muslims are to take credit—or to blame, depending on one's point of view—for George W. Bush being elected president in 2000. But in the wake of the Bush administration's devastating war on terror and the damage it inflicted on Muslim families in the United States and abroad, Muslim Americans today overwhelmingly favor the Democratic Party and support its candidates in elections.[32] In recent years, increasing numbers of Muslims are running for political office as Democrats. Rep. Keith Ellison from Minnesota and Rep. André Carson from Indiana were the first Muslims elected to Congress in 2006 and 2008, respectively, and in 2018 Rashida Tlaib from Michigan and Ilhan Omar from Minnesota became the first Muslim women to serve as House representatives. At the state and local level, more and more Muslims are running for office, too—many of them motivated to run after Trump's victory.[33]

Hope and Change?
Democrats and Islamophobia

Striding across a burgundy carpet, another president in stocking feet approached a podium and began to speak. Large windows etched with Arabic script, and a cherry-wood wall carved with a pattern of interlocking stars, framed his silhouette. President Barack Obama's audience, made up of school-children and congregants of the Islamic Society of Baltimore, Maryland, was eager to hear his speech on that afternoon in February 2016. It was Obama's first and only visit to a U.S. mosque during his eight years as president, and it happened at the tail end of his second term. His reason for not going sooner likely had to do with the fact that charges of being a Muslim had dogged him for his entire presidency. But amid the rise in anti-Muslim hate crimes and rhetoric, he sought to reassure Muslim Americans of their integral place in American society, and he spoke out against the bigoted attacks that many were facing. "When any part of our family starts to feel separate or second-class or targeted," he says, "it tears at the very fabric of our nation."[34]

President Obama's mosque visit is just one of the ways that Democrats sought to combat the Islamophobic rhetoric that had become so normalized in the American political sphere, not to mention the hate crimes that were occurring simultaneously. Running to be Obama's successor, Bernie Sanders and Martin O'Malley made public visits to mosques, and along with the even-tual Democratic nominee, Hillary Clinton, they spoke out forcefully against Trump's Muslim ban proposal.[35] Helping to set the tone on the Democratic side, Martin O'Malley was the first candidate to use the term "Islamophobia" to describe what the country was witnessing, and Sanders and Clinton followed suit.[36] O'Malley was the only 2016 presidential candidate to call out the Islamophobia industry specifically—in a speech at the Arab American Institute, he criticized the "shadowy network of hateful" organizations bent on "scapegoating and marginalizing Arab and Muslim Americans."[37]

Inclusion of Muslims became a core part of Democrats' messaging strategy during that campaign cycle, and individuals who were visibly Muslim (like women who wear headscarves) were often featured conspicuously at rallies, in campaign ads, and on the stage at the Democratic National Conven-tion. Many readers will remember the DNC speech by Khizr Khan, the father of a Muslim American soldier killed in Iraq. Looking into the camera and with his wife, Ghazala, at his side, he reached into the breast pocket of his suit and pulled out a small booklet. Holding it up for all to see, and speaking directly to Donald Trump, he declared, "Have you even read the United States' Constitution? I will gladly lend you my copy!"[38] The audience in the arena cheered, and across the country, eyes teared up as people watched this moment of hopeful defiance on television.

Many Americans were deeply moved by the speech and troubled by the reports of rising hate crimes they were seeing in their communities and around the country. But the left's rejection of Islamophobia was not only about the inherent injustice of the problem. Much of it has had to do with their general opposition to Donald Trump. Many liberals, both candidates and voters, latched on to whatever Trump was against.[39] No doubt there was and is sincerity on the part of many, but the left's acknowledgment of the extent of Islamophobia has been lacking. When commentators refer to the litany of President Trump's sins when it comes to bigotry—his misogyny, bigotry toward LGBTQ people, anti-Blackness, mockery of disabled people, anti-Latinx and anti-Asian stances and comments—Islamophobia often does not make the list. When the slate of main speakers was announced for the Democratic National Convention in 2020, there were no Muslims on the list,[40] and Trump's anti-Muslim policies were hardly mentioned as reasons voters should oppose his winning a second term. The fact that Islamophobia is not top of mind demonstrates how normalized it still is, especially in its more subtle and systemic forms.

That being said, many Democratic politicians have become more responsive to their Muslim constituents, who are an increasing (albeit still small) share of the electorate. Muslim political advocacy groups and grassroots efforts have succeeded in pushing Democratic politicians to put issues that affect Muslims on their platforms. For example, during the 2020 election season, Joe Biden became the first presumptive Democratic nominee to speak at a large Muslim PAC event. He vowed to upend the Trump administration's Muslim ban policy on his first day in office.[41]

Yet Democrats and the political left are not immune from Islamophobia, both in speech and action. Despite the fact that many non-Muslim Democrats have adopted a nominally anti-Islamophobia stance since the 2016 campaign, it is still a problem among liberals, both in the realm of government and in the U.S. culture at large.

Subtle but Serious: Islamophobia on the Political Left

Islamophobia coming from the left (and center) is often more latent and harder to detect than that which emanates from the right.

—Khaled Beydoun[42]

The day before Khizr Khan gave his rousing speech at the 2016 DNC, Bill Clinton—husband to presumptive nominee, Hillary Clinton—offered his own words about Muslims. "If you're a Muslim and you love America and freedom and you hate terror," he said, "stay here and help us win and make a future together." As analyst Tuqa Nusairat wrote, "Muslim Americans from Virginia to California collectively cringed and groaned."[43] I did, too. The former president's line might have been well intentioned and meant to be a jab at Trump, but embedded in his comment is the same flawed logic that underpinned Trump's Muslim ban proposal. By effectively calling for a loyalty test for Muslims, Clinton was assuming that Muslims as a rule or by default are a threat—violent, seditious, and tyrannical. Only when they prove they are not would they be considered welcome and deserving of the rights afforded to Americans.

Hillary Clinton, the Democratic nominee for president, also fell into similar, problematic ways of talking about Muslims during the election. At a town hall debate between her and Trump, a Muslim woman posed a question about Islamophobia, and how each candidate would work against it from the Oval Office. As she had in numerous other campaign settings already, Clinton quickly pivoted from condemning Islamophobia to talking about the urgency of needing Muslims as "eyes and ears" "on the front lines" in the war against the Islamic State militant group (ISIS).[44] This implies that violence and terrorism are a given in Muslim communities, and that many ordinary Muslims are bound to encounter sentiments from their more "extreme" counterparts that need reporting to law enforcement. As attorney and educator Namira Islam also points out, this approach "continues to frame terrorism as a distinctly Muslim problem, one that needs to be resolved within the community, instead of a geopolitical problem that requires a more nuanced analysis."[45] It also gives the false impression that Muslims have not intervened when they are concerned that someone they know is planning to cause harm to others—which in fact they have, often getting law enforcement involved. In response to Clinton's remarks, journalist Ismat Sarah Mangla wrote, "American Muslims don't possess some special knowledge of terror attacks. They are simply trying to live unsensational lives, serving as doctors, engineers, lawyers, teachers, artists and journalists. Their citizenship shouldn't come with conditions—it's not contingent on how 'useful' they are in the war on terror."[46]

Clinton's way of speaking of Muslims during the campaign had also implied this conditional worth, that Muslims' only value to the United States is through their ability to help the rest of America fight terrorism. Clinton often seemed less concerned about the inherent immorality of Islamophobia—which should have been reason enough to oppose it—and more concerned with how it was "dangerous." By this she did not so much mean that it was dangerous for America's Muslims (who, as we have seen, were facing high numbers of hate crimes), but rather how it was a threat to U.S. national security and interests.[47] Donald Trump's rhetoric was "dangerous,"

Clinton said, because it would anger and alienate potential Muslim allies in the fight against ISIS, both governments abroad and in Muslim communities in the United States. It could cause distrust between Muslims and law enforcement, and could be a "recruiting tool" for ISIS. (Republican Marco Rubio made an identical point when he was campaigning against Trump in the primary.[48]) Though it may not be immediately apparent, this idea is based on the (racialized) premise that Muslims are inherently violent—or at least more so than other groups. The underlying idea is that Islamophobia is bad because it will make Muslims mad, and that Muslims' natural response to mistreatment is lashing out violently. Clinton's logic (which is shared by many across the political spectrum) also casts Muslims as a disposable "other," whose needs and rights do not matter except in how they relate to those of *us*.[49] At their core, the basis of the Clintons' ideas about Muslims was not all that different from Trump's; assumptions of Muslims' inherent violence, foreignness, and lesser humanity are present in both.

Even as President Obama was on the receiving end of Islamophobic sentiment and was maligned for supposedly being Muslim, he and his administration (which included Hillary Clinton as secretary of state) contributed to Islamophobia in ways big and small. At the mosque in Baltimore and in other settings, he echoed Clinton's ideas expressed above. His personnel at times distanced the president from Muslim Americans in photo ops. At a campaign rally in 2008, his staff removed a hijab-wearing woman from the area behind the podium, so that she would not be seen directly behind the president as he spoke.[50] This stands in stark contrast to the ways that, in 2016, Democratic candidates actively sought to put women in hijabs front and center at rallies and in ads, to drive home their pro-Muslim stance. (Muslims in large part appreciated this focus on Muslim representation, but many also felt wary that it was done more for political gain than actually inaugurating real change.)

During the Ground Zero Mosque controversy in 2010, Obama affirmed that the Muslim group had the constitutionally protected "right" to build the community center, but later walked back his support, calling into question the "wisdom" of their choice to build it so close to the site of the September 11 attacks.[51] Other Democrats outright opposed the building project, including Democratic majority leader in the House, Harry Reid.[52] Some called it "insensitive," an argument that implies that all Muslims and Islam as a religion bear responsibility for what happened on 9/11.

These issues with Democratic discourse on Muslims may seem less significant when compared to the examples from Donald Trump, Ben Carson, Ted Cruz, and others. But, as we have seen, they operate out of a similar racialized logic about Muslims. And Democrats' problem with Islamophobia does not end at rhetoric and viewpoints; it also extends to actions and policies. Indeed, many of their rhetorical positions are secondary outgrowths of the concrete (and unequal) state of affairs that both Democratic and Republican politicians want to create or maintain when it comes to Muslims.

Dashing Hopes: The Obama Administration

> *Neoconservatives invented the War on Terror,*
> *but Obama liberals normalized it.*
>
> —Arun Kundnani[53]

The positive change that Barack Obama promised to bring when he was elected president was not reflected in the ways his administration dealt with Muslims. A number of the problems that George W. Bush inaugurated were continued or expanded under Obama's watch. At home, he repeatedly signed into law the National Defense Authorization Act, which included measures that permitted the unconstitutional practice (started under the Bush administration) of detaining American citizens indefinitely and without charges. The president also broke his promise to close the prison at Guantánamo Bay and to address the injustices that transpired there. Only at the end of his presidency did he formally dismantle the NSEERS program, a move many believed was done out of concern that the Trump administration would revive it.[54] Overseas, the Obama administration ramped up the drone attacks that were started under Bush, dropping far more bombs than Bush had. Obama also bombed more countries, a total of seven Muslim-majority countries, during his tenure—Afghanistan, Iraq, Pakistan, Somalia, Yemen, Libya, and Syria. The U.S. military killed many noncombatants and civilians in these drone strikes, somewhere between 380 and 800 (though the government tried to claim that only a fraction of these deaths were civilians).[55] Under Obama, the military also used drone strikes to assassinate American citizens abroad, including children, who were murdered before they could stand trial for their alleged crimes.[56] In places like Iraq and Yemen, U.S. military bombing campaigns contributed to the entrenchment of the Al-Qaeda terrorist group there, as people became justifiably angry with the United States over its aggressive campaigns and the civilian deaths that ensued.[57]

Back at home, the Obama administration in 2014 inaugurated a program called Countering Violent Extremism (CVE),[58] intended to prevent terrorism in the United States. Though its name makes it sound neutral and uncontroversial, it focused primarily on Muslim communities, despite the fact that, as legal scholar Faiza Patel writes, "in the U.S., right-wing violence is at least as much of a problem as that carried out in the name of Al-Qaeda or ISIS."[59]

CVE operates out of a flawed theory of "radicalization," which asserts that it is possible to predict who will commit acts of violence based on the content and strength of their convictions.[60] According to this model, one of the indicators of radicalization is if a young Muslim has started to engage in more practices connected to their religion—like praying more or growing a beard. Underlying this "religious conveyor belt" idea is the Islamophobic assumption that becoming "more Muslim" will make a person more violent. According to the radicalization model, other indicators of extremism include a person's political or social views, such as their concern about the mistreatment of Muslims abroad at the hands of the U.S. military. (Mental health issues and feelings of loneliness are also to be flagged.)

Despite the fact that these religious practices and political views are to be protected by the First Amendment, CVE programs encourage local community leaders to report youth who exhibit these qualities to law enforcement.[61] CVE programs want teachers, parents, religious leaders, and mental health professionals to be the "eyes and ears" in communities and to turn to law enforcement *before* any crime has been committed. As the Brennan Center for Justice's Emmanuel Mauleón has written, this is effectively about "coopting community leaders and institutions to spy on their own communities."[62] The result is the quashing of the human and civil rights of those (Muslims) targeted, not to mention a breakdown in community cohesion. The first federally funded CVE programs focused on Muslim communities in Boston, Los Angeles, Minneapolis, and a Maryland suburb of Washington, DC,[63] and others were added later. Black Muslim youth have been particularly targeted by CVE.[64] Even when White supremacist and neo-Nazi groups were temporarily added to CVE's focus later during the Obama administration, Muslims were still the primary target.[65] Under the Trump administration, CVE activities persisted.[66] For a time, the administration even considered renaming it "Countering *Islamic* Extremism,"[67] a move that would have made explicit the program's initial Islamophobic impetus.

Islamophobia in Liberal Culture:
The Case of Bill Maher

Though Bill Maher has been a fervent critic of many of President Trump's positions and policies, the liberal comedian and commentator sounds quite similar to Trump and other Republicans when he talks about Muslims. In his monologues on his HBO show, *Real Time*, and conversations with guests, he has a penchant for making sweeping generalizations about Muslims, founded more in the typical stereotypes than in reality.[68] A self-avowed atheist and critic of religion across the board, he insists that Islam is unique among the religions for its supposedly inherent endorsement of violence, misogyny, backwardness, and intolerance.[69] "It's been one culture that has been blowing shit up over and over again," he said of Muslims in 2015, ignoring or unaware of the incessant bombing campaigns of Muslim-majority countries that the U.S. military has been involved in for the last many decades.

Having voiced support for the idea of religious profiling of Muslims,[70] Maher takes pride in eschewing "political correctness" and asserts that problems among Muslims are not an extreme or fringe issue but rather go to the core of the religion, making statements like "the more you know [about Islam], the more you would be afraid,"[71] and "the Muslim world has too much in common with [ISIS]."[72] Maher sets up false dichotomies between Western liberalism and a supposedly monolithic Muslim "culture"[73] and downplays the existence of Islamophobia, claiming the word is only used to censor people like him who purport to speak the truth about Islam.[74] Maher is not alone— other well-known New Atheists share his Islamophobic views,[75] including Richard Dawkins, the late Christopher Hitchens, and Sam Harris, who believes there is an existential clash between Islam and the West and states plainly his view that "we are at war with Islam."[76] Though they often share the hawkish foreign policy views of neo-conservatives, Maher and others seek to defend these positions by trying to appeal to values that are shared by his fellow liberals.[77] "I'm not anti-Muslim; I'm anti-misogyny," he said in 2018. "I thought feminism was a thing with liberals."[78]

Concerns about women's rights are indeed top of mind for self-identified liberals, who may take pride in their opposition to misogyny. Many also see themselves as above the overt bigotry toward Muslims and others exhibited by Republicans like Trump. Because of this, liberals who share Maher's sentiments may be unaware of the way that they (like those on the political right) have absorbed and then replicate stereotypes about Muslims, including the trope of Islamic oppression of women.

Undoubtedly, there are instances and trends the world over where Muslim women are at the receiving end of mistreatment or do not have the same rights or privileges that men do. Religious norms, interpretations, and institutions can and do play into these dynamics. But the perception that oppression of women is a universal feature of Islam, and is mandated in all Muslim-majority countries, is not a reflection of reality. The experiences of Muslim women vary widely around the world, something I discuss more in chapter 6, along with the role of religion in these matters. But this stereotype does have sticking power, for at least a few reasons. For one, the trope of "the oppressed Muslim woman and the oppressive Muslim man" contributes to a strong (if unwarranted) sense of Western people's own enlightenment, progressivism, and superiority; it plays strongly into our sense of self. In fact, the accusation that "*they* mistreat (*our*) women" has long been leveled against one's perceived enemies, and is often coupled with a lack of recognition of the same problems in one's own group.

Additionally, the idea serves to justify Western military intervention abroad. The notion that "Muslim women need saving"[79] has been invoked to spur and prolong U.S. military engagement around the world, most notably in Afghanistan (though there are other examples in U.S. history, too).[80] First Lady Laura Bush made this argument, and the notion was emblazoned on a *Time* magazine cover from 2010 featuring the image of a young Afghan woman, Bibi Aisha, whose nose had been cut off by her husband. The headline read, "What Happens When We Leave Afghanistan."[81] Despite the fact that they come off as well-intentioned—and indeed may be in some cases—these views about Muslims often serve as a cover for U.S. militarism.

In my own experience, I have heard the trope about women come up often among Democrats and "coastal elites." They make offhanded comments about the oppression of Muslim women, as if it is totally self-evident and universal, or they talk about not wanting their daughters to be in close proximity to Muslim men, as if they would naturally cause harm to them. Concerns about the treatment of LGBTQ people[82] and religious minorities in Muslim-majority contexts also sometimes cross a line into blatant Islamophobia when they are founded on stereotypes rather than facts, and when they cast Muslims as having a unique problem with homophobia (which is an issue in a range of religious communities). In these cases, liberals (including many journalists[83]) often do not recognize the stereotypical nature of these statements; the fact that these notions do not reflect the nuances of reality; and that these ideas can sometimes be harnessed to enact discriminatory or harmful measures against Muslim individuals and communities.[84] These stereotypes are also used to deflect critical reflection on the ways that liberal societies struggle with these same injustices.[85]

Drawing Together the Right and the Left:
The Case of Ayaan Hirsi Ali

Though the U.S. electorate is deeply polarized, Islamophobia forges bonds across party lines and the political spectrum. An example of this is one of Bill Maher's frequent guests, Ayaan Hirsi Ali. Having endured traumatic experiences as a child and young woman—including female genital cutting/mutilation—the Somalia-born Ali fled to the Netherlands. There she served as a politician and became well-known for her advocacy for women and her criticism of Islam, the faith she had left behind. As a public figure, she has not been shy about her views. She has called Islam "a destructive, nihilistic cult of death" and has advocated that the religion as a whole be defeated "militarily."[86]

Ali also claims that violence[87] and women's mistreatment is "inherent"[88] to Islamic doctrines, despite the diversity of interpretations and ways of practicing Islam. Ali now resides in the United States and authors books with sensational titles like *Infidel, Heretic,* and *The Caged Virgin,* and she runs a foundation that focuses on women's rights while giving a platform to those who share her anti-Muslim views.[89] Though she and her work are praised and boosted by those on the left, like Bill Maher, she also works closely with the far right.[90] For example, she endorsed a recent book[91] by the writer and anti-Muslim hate group leader Robert Spencer, who has elevated her stature in his own sphere.[92] Appearing onstage at right-wing, anti-Muslim events while also being featured frequently in the left-leaning *New York Times* and on NPR radio shows, Ali is one of the most effective figures in the Islamophobia network,[93] traversing the political spectrum and bringing the two sides together around a common enemy.

Beyond the United States:
Islamophobia in the West

Islamophobia is not simply an American problem. Across North America, Europe,[94] and so-called Western countries, there have been similar trends in Islamophobia in recent years: sharp increases in anti-Muslim hate crimes, including violent and deadly attacks, often at mosques;[95] scapegoating during election years and the rise of blatantly anti-Muslim political parties;[96] widespread negative attitudes toward Muslims among the public; mass protests against Muslims and immigration of refugees; passage of legislation that drives Muslims out of the public sphere; and widespread surveillance and arbitrary arrests of Muslims as part of measures cast as counterterrorism.[97]

In Quebec City, Canada, in 2017, Alexandre Bissonette charged into a mosque with a gun. The young Canadian, motivated by White nationalist and anti-Muslim views, fired wildly, killing six Muslims who were praying there and injuring nineteen others. It was the deadliest attack among the anti-Muslim hate crimes that surged rapidly across Canada from 2012 to 2017.[98] Every year was worse than the previous. In 2012, there were 45 anti-Muslim hate crimes reported by police across the entire country. By 2017, there were a staggering 349, the year of the Quebec mosque rampage. At his trial, Bissonette testified about what prompted him to carry out the massacre: it was Trump's implementation of his Muslim ban policy, only two days prior, and his frustration with his own country's response of welcoming Muslim refugees who had been turned away by the United States.[99]

Similar events have been witnessed around the globe, from the United Kingdom to New Zealand. That same year, in 2017, a man rammed his car

into a group of congregants mingling outside their local mosque in Finsbury Park in London.[100] In Oslo, Norway, in 2019, a man attempted to kill
worshippers in their mosque on Eid al-Adha, a major Muslim holiday, but
fortunately worshippers pinned him down before he could carry out the
attack.[101] Perhaps the most well known of these mosque tragedies took place
in Christchurch, New Zealand, where Australian Brenton Tarrant shot and
killed fifty-one Muslims—some at point-blank range—across two mosques.
They had been gathered for their Friday congregational prayer when Tarrant,
a self-described "racist" with White nationalist and anti-Muslim motives,
stormed in and filmed his highly planned murderous rampage, simultaneously
casting it on social media. Shortly before the attack, he posted a manifesto
online that was full of conspiracy theories and racist ideas about Muslims that
have long been peddled globally by more mainstream figures.[102] In all three of
these cases, the perpetrators were apparently driven to commit these violent
acts by right-wing, anti-Muslim ideology circulating widely online.

In 2015, as predominantly Muslim refugees arrived in Europe from Syria
or other war-torn areas, dehumanizing campaigns and language became more
and more normalized, with Muslim men even cast as "rape-fugees."[103] Survey
data shows that large swaths of the public across Canada[104] and Europe hold
Islamophobic views.[105] In places where Muslims are a smaller percentage
of the population,[106] or among those who have less personal contact with
Muslims,[107] negative views toward Muslims are often higher. Though public
perception of Muslims has improved in many places—similar to the trend in
the United States—anti-Muslim views still remain strong among supporters
of far-right, populist parties in Europe.[108] These parties have proliferated
across Europe over the last decade, and anti-Muslim positions are at the
core of their ideology. As researcher Mobashra Tazamal has written, "in the
European context, anti-Muslim discourse pivots on fears of Islamization: the
perceived threat of Islamic encroachment on Europe's secular way of life."[109]
The Dutch Party for Freedom, led by Geert Wilders, describes its mission
as "de-Islamizing" the Netherlands. Wilders has advocated that the Qur'an
be banned in his country, that Muslim immigration should be stopped, and
that Muslim institutions should be shut down because Islam is an "existential threat to our survival as a free nation."[110] Similar parties have also arisen
in other European countries, including France's National Front/Rally led by
Marine Le Pen,[111] Alternative for Germany (AfD),[112] and the United Kingdom's Britain First[113] and Ukip.[114] Even when they do not succeed in winning
elections, these parties still have a large impact in shaping public perceptions
and discourse on Muslims.[115] Movements like PEGIDA, which originated in
Germany and stands for "Patriotic Europeans against the Islamization of the
West," have staged large-scale protests across European cities.[116]

Though Muslims make up a minority of the population across European countries, in nations like Germany, France, and the United Kingdom they constitute a significant portion of the population—about 5, 7, and 5 percent, respectively.[117] And despite the fact that Muslims have been part of what we now call Europe for centuries (or immigrated to Europe from countries formerly colonized by European powers), they are still often seen as foreigners and perceived as a threat to European culture. Survey data has shown that Europeans (as well as Americans) vastly overestimate the size of Muslim populations in their countries, something that perhaps contributes to—or is a result of—anti-Muslim fears.[118]

Across European and North American countries, many national and regional laws have been passed that discriminate against Muslims and infringe upon their religious expression.[119] In 2009, after a widespread anti-Muslim billboard campaign supported by far-right parties, Switzerland's citizens voted in a referendum to ban minarets, the towers built alongside mosques from which the Islamic call to prayer is traditionally broadcasted. The referendum passed, despite the fact that there were only a total of four minarets across the entire country and none of them broadcasted the call to prayer—evidence that this had been a contrived political controversy.[120]

Many of the restrictions on Muslims have had to do with women's clothing. As of 2020, eight European countries ban headscarves in government settings and four countries do not allow students to cover their heads in schools.[121] And, according to a 2018 survey of European public opinion, "most Europeans support at least some restrictions of religious dress for Muslim women."[122] When politicians and public figures campaign for these clothing bans, they often frame their efforts as liberating Muslim women from oppression and "free[ing] girls from submission."[123] Yet research into the impact of such laws has demonstrated that they may "actually hinder the economic and social integration of Muslim women" in those countries.[124] The state's policing of what Muslim women wear (which is by and large a choice these women make) also stands in stark contrast to stated Western values and discourse on women's freedom. There are other ironies, too, which betray the stereotypical and discriminatory foundations of these laws. Since 2011 in France, face veils—which are worn by a tiny minority of Muslim women there—have been illegal in public spaces. Yet that ban remained in place in 2020, even as the French government mandated masks in public to slow the spread of COVID-19.[125]

Some bans on religious clothing affect few people and are more symbolic in their impact,[126] sending a message to all that Muslims are not part of "us." But other policies have a more tangible impact. In Quebec in 2019, the government banned Canadians in that province from wearing religious symbols—like Muslim headscarves—while working in some public sector jobs.[127] The impetus for the ban was largely about the public's discomfort with Muslims and Islam,[128] but the law ended up targeting more than just Muslim women who wear headscarves in accordance with their religious convictions. Jews who wear kippahs or other head coverings and Sikhs who wear turbans are effectively banned from certain careers, like public school teacher, police officer, or government attorney.[129] Under the law, wearing Christian symbols like crosses is banned, too. Though the main target was Muslims, religious expression of all Quebecers became "collateral damage" of the law.[130]

Just as in the United States, measures framed as counterterrorism have led to the infringement of Muslims' human and civil rights in Europe. In France, after the ISIS-linked attacks that killed over one hundred people in Paris in 2015, the government instituted a state of emergency that allowed "3,600 warrantless raids and placed 400 people under house arrest," most of which targeted Muslims.[131] The measures, which were only supposed to be temporary, have since been passed into common law.[132] In 2020, after killings of two church-goers and a teacher by two Muslim perpetrators, bills were introduced in France that would have the effect not only of impinging on the rights of French Muslims but also threatening the civil liberties of all French people.[133]

Islamophobic policies also are put forward so that politicians can benefit politically from scapegoating Muslims. An example of this was the conservative campaign in Canada for the Zero Tolerance for Barbaric Cultural Practices Act. Implicitly pointing to Canada's Muslim community,[134] it focused on rooting out "polygamy, early and forced marriage and female genital mutilation" from Canada, despite these being small if not nonexistent phenomena. Rather than a sincere effort to address injustices in Canada, the act was more a political tactic, in which conservative politicians played into the public's stereotypes about Muslim oppression.[135] In this way, it was quite similar to the "anti–foreign law" bills that were passed in dozens of state legislatures across the United States. Despite their vague phrasing, those laws were a part of concerted campaigns to sow Americans' fear of sharia, or Islamic law, which was also cast as universally "barbaric." (I discuss these anti-sharia campaigns further in the next chapter.) As my colleagues at the Bridge Initiative and I wrote in 2015, the Canadian and American laws both offer "solutions to problems that don't exist, and [focus] unwarranted attention on Muslims while ignoring concerns posed by other groups."[136]

Across the Atlantic:
Viral Videos and Islamophobic Connections

Several years ago, a YouTube video made the rounds on social media in the United States. Overlaid with sinister music meant to evoke desert living, the video warned viewers that Muslims would soon take over Europe. Relying on shoddy and unsourced data on birthrates, the narrator spoke in a deep, ominous way about "Islamic immigration." The diverse flags of European countries shown on a map of the continent dissolved into red flags emblazoned with a crescent moon and star, a symbol often used nowadays to represent Islam. "In thirty-nine years," the narrator declared, with the music swelling, "France will be an Islamic republic." After lamenting this impending takeover through repopulation, the video turned to North America. "It's time to wake up . . . ," the narrator said, urging viewers to "spread the gospel message."[137]

The video is an early example of what, a decade later, we can recognize as the "Great Replacement" and "White genocide" conspiracy theories, which motivated the attacks against mosques in Quebec City, Oslo, and Christchurch. Groups who espouse far-right, White supremacist, or Christian nationalist ideas believe that people of color, Muslims, and Jews are trying to take over the West and diminish the White population, primarily through immigration and high birthrates.[138] This unfounded and racist notion first gained prominence in Europe but traveled across the Atlantic and has also taken root in the United States.[139] For years, anti-Muslim activists in Europe sought to "warn" Americans about how their continent had turned into "Eurabia,"[140] urging them to curb Muslim immigration before the United States becomes "the United States of Arabia."

The proliferation of this racist theory across the Atlantic is just one example of how Islamophobic trends in Europe are often a precursor to their appearance in the United States. Another example is a program called Prevent in the United Kingdom, which served as the model for the CVE programs in the United States. Requiring public workers to report individuals who seem to be exhibiting supposed signs of "radicalization" or "non-violent extremism"— but who committed no crime—Prevent has resulted in the stigmatizing and disproportionate targeting of Muslims.[141] According to government data, British Muslims were forty times more likely than other Brits to be referred to the program.[142] Because it leans on community members to be the "eyes and ears" of law enforcement, Prevent relies on the public's stereotypes about who could be considered an extremist, leaving Muslims to bear the brunt of the program.[143] As in the United States, Muslims in Britain have also reported feeling spied on and censored, unable to voice opinions and perspectives that should be legally protected but are deemed suspicious under the Prevent scheme.[144] Despite the fact that American activists vocally resisted the adoption of such a program in the United States, the Obama administration went along with its implementation.

The influence of Islamophobia across the Atlantic has also moved in the opposite direction. Anti-Muslim activists and pundits from the United States have had a large role in shaping attitudes toward Muslims in both European and non-European Western countries. When Anders Brevik killed over seventy people in Norway in 2011, he extensively cited the writing of Robert Spencer, in addition to other anti-Muslim activists, throughout the manifesto attempting to justify his rampage.[145]

The Islamophobia network is much more than an American phenomenon. It consists of individuals and organizations whose symbiotic bonds stretch across oceans.[146] Geert Wilders, the Dutch politician bent on excising Islam from the Netherlands, has frequently been a speaker at anti-Muslim conferences in the United States,[147] in addition to events on Capitol Hill organized by Republican congressmen Steve King[148] and Louie Gohmert,[149] who also have track records of Islamophobic views.

Going Global:
Islamophobia beyond the West

Though Islamophobic tropes emerged in large part out of European colonialism and American imperialism, they have not remained confined to Western contexts. In recent years, countries around the world employed the Western trope of the "Muslim as terrorist Other" while enacting discriminatory policies against Muslim populations.[150] In China, the government is framing their internment of Uighur Muslims—an ethnic and religious minority there—as a "war on terror."[151] The government portrays their concentration camps, where over one million people have been imprisoned, as re-education centers that will strip Uighurs of their supposedly radical views and cure them from Islam, which they treat as a kind of mental illness.[152] Having shuttered many mosques, the government rounded people up for things like attending the mosque, going on an Islamic pilgrimage, and living their lives in ways that were deemed too "religious."[153]

As Mobashra Tazamal has observed, in India, Prime Minister Narendra Modi and his government have "increasingly drawn on the same post-9/11 securitized and racist rhetoric when speaking about the country's Muslims, which make up 14 percent of India's 1.3 billion."[154] Though Muslims are the second-largest religious group in India, and they have a long and rooted history on the subcontinent, Modi's Hindu nationalist party casts them as foreigners and has implemented policies to strip some Muslims of their citizenship or prevent them from becoming citizens.[155] With Hindu nationalism normalized in the realm of government, anti-Muslim rhetoric and violence at the hands of Hindu nationalists among the public have become more common.[156]

Other religious minorities in China and India have also faced extreme repression and religious persecution. Christians in China have witnessed government closures of numerous churches, as well as bans on buying Bibles and Christmas celebrations.[157] Christians in India have also been at the receiving end of animus and violence from Hindu nationalists.[158] The reality of these other forms of persecution drives home the fact that Islamophobic rhetoric is often a tool of larger and broader political and social projects of domination that result in the marginalization of multiple groups.

In Myanmar (formerly Burma), the Rohingya, a Muslim group and ethnic minority, have long been persecuted as perceived outsiders in the Buddhist-majority country. The government has consistently denied them citizenship, and mobs have targeted them in deadly riots.[159] The year 2016 was a turning point, however, when the military razed entire Rohingya villages, killed many, and hundreds of thousands of Rohingya had to flee the country.[160] These genocidal actions were fueled by a rise in Islamophobic rhetoric among Buddhists, who make up the country's majority religious group. The Buddhist monk Ashin Wirathu is one of the main instigators; his social media posts and speaking tours have sometimes been followed by acts of communal violence against the Rohingya, whom he speaks of in dehumanizing terms.[161] Burmese Islamophobia reflects many of the trends in Western anti-Muslim discourse—scapegoating Muslims as "terrorists" or "jihadist extremists." Yet in Myanmar it is wedded with a form of Buddhist nationalism.[162] To the dismay of many, the Burmese Nobel Peace Prize winner Aung San Suu Kyi has white-washed this ethnic cleansing.[163] Though previously lauded for her opposition to the military junta there and pushing for democracy, as Myanmar's head of state Suu Kyi has been roundly criticized for her (lack of) response to the humanitarian crisis.

Contrary to many Americans' expectations, these forms of Islamophobia are also at work in many Muslim-majority contexts.[164] Whether in Egypt, Syria, Saudi Arabia, Pakistan, or elsewhere, governments often use the terrorist trope in order to quash dissent and normalize detainment of political prisoners and other forms of state violence. In the Middle East and South Asia, Islamophobic sentiment is also fomented on the level of media and popular discourse, among Christians, secular Muslims, and others.

All of this is a testament to the globalized nature of Islamophobia. As we have seen, the West, and particularly the post-9/11 United States, has exported the notion of the racialized Muslim—the terrorist, Brown, dangerous Other—and diverse regimes and political parties throughout the world have taken it up. This reality shows us that the work of breaking down Islamophobia must involve people from across the political spectrum and around the world.

4

More Than Muslims

How Islamophobia Intersects with
Other Forms of Prejudice

In Wisconsin, men wearing turbans and women in colorful headscarves and long tunics gathered to pray in a building with large, golden domes. Not long after, a neo-Nazi named Wade Michael Page stormed inside with a gun, killing six people and injuring others. His victims were not Muslim, as Page likely expected, but those who practice the Sikh faith.[1] Page attacked them in their house of worship, called a *gurdwara*, in the summer of 2012 during the Muslim holy month of Ramadan, when Muslims across the United States were being targeted in a spate of hate crimes. Since September 11, 2001, Sikhs have been victim to heinous and violent hate crimes at stunning levels, in many cases by perpetrators who thought they were attacking Muslims.[2] The first person murdered in a hate crime after 9/11 was not an Arab Muslim, but a South Asian Sikh: Balbir Singh Sodhi.[3]

A year after the massacre at Oak Creek, a young Black man named Cameron Mohammed was leaving a Florida Walmart with his girlfriend after nightfall. Cameron was raised Catholic in Tampa, by parents from Trinidad in the Caribbean. A White Christian man named Daniel Quinnell approached him in the parking lot, asked Cameron if he was Muslim and Middle Eastern, called him the n-word,[4] and shot him in the face with a pellet gun.[5] Fortunately, Cameron survived, but not without serious injuries.

In 2015, Khalid Jabara was not so lucky. An Arab American Orthodox Christian from Oklahoma, Jabara was shot and killed by his neighbor, who had already been charged for violently assaulting Khalid's mother and who called Khalid anti-Muslim and other slurs before murdering him outside his home.[6]

These stories are tragic and tangible evidence of the way that Islamophobia impacts people who are not Muslim, as well as how Islamophobia overlaps and intersects[7] with other forms of discrimination. In exploring these connections with anti-Black racism, anti-Latinx bias, and anti-Semitism in this chapter, we can also see the many similarities between how Muslims and other groups, including Catholics and Japanese Americans, have been scape-goated throughout U.S. history. This chapter also brings us back around to the notion of racialization, which I discussed in chapter 1 and which is a helpful conceptual tool in exploring the impact of Islamophobia both within and outside Muslim communities. The stories and trends examined in this chapter are also a reminder that our own Christian faith community is impacted by Islamophobia in very direct and even fatal ways. The well-being, freedom, and religious liberty of all people is in jeopardy when Muslims' rights are infringed upon.

Mistaken for Muslim?
The Racialization of Islam

After returning from a semester abroad in the country of Jordan in 2012, I was back in my hometown of Indianapolis, Indiana, visiting family. Sitting on my grandma's couch, I showed her pictures of the host family I had lived with in Amman, the capital city. Looking at a picture of one of my host sisters, whose long brown hair lay neatly over her shoulders, my grandma expressed puzzlement that she was not wearing a *hijab*, or headscarf.

"They're Christian, Grandma," I explained. "They don't wear hijabs."

"But . . . they're Arab?" she replied.

Her confused response made me realize that, in my grandmother's mind, *Arab* and *Muslim* were synonymous. If a woman is Arab, she must be Muslim, and thus must wear a headscarf—(even though not all Muslim women wear headscarves).[8] My grandmother certainly was not going through these step-by-step connections in her mind, but the implicit association between *Arab* and *Muslim* (not to mention *Muslim* and *headscarf*) was there. Her response was a reminder for me of how, in Western society, being Muslim is perceived as being integrally linked to being Arab, as well as to being from the Middle East.[9] Many people from my own background—White Christians in the United States—assume that all Arabs and people from the Middle East are Muslim, and that other Brown people who hail from other places are Middle Eastern, Arab, and thus, Muslim.

This conflation—which I also discuss in the "Notes to Readers" section at the beginning of this book—helps us to see how Islamophobia is often at play even in cases of prejudice and discrimination where Islam is not explic-itly invoked. As we have already seen, Islamophobia can be understood as a form of racism. It is prejudice and discrimination that results from Muslims being cast as a monolithic bloc, and is based on an imagined picture of what a Muslim is—what Muslims should look like and where they are from (brown-skinned, hijab-wearing if female, bearded if male, Arab, Middle Eastern) and what tendencies every Muslim is likely to have (violent, oppressive if male, oppressed if female, intolerant, foreign, and so on). These qualities are thought to define Muslims, to be "natural and innate to each member of the group."[10] In this way, anyone who fits part of this bill is "raced" as Muslim.

This explains why Sikhs are often targeted. Because South Asians with brown skin and those who wear turbans share traits associated with society's image of "the Muslim," they are faced with the violence that—by this racist logic—they are assumed to deserve. Their appearance is taken to be evidence of an internal character that is threatening and inherently "other."

In most cases, it is not that perpetrators consciously "mistake" Sikhs for Muslims and would pick a new target if they realized their error in identification. Rather, the issue is that they implicitly perceive people with certain characteristics or appearance as being part of a non-White threat. A related example is what happened in 2015 to Samson Woldemichael, an Ethiopian Christian immigrant to the United States.[11] He was driving for Uber in Charlotte, North Carolina, when his passenger verbally threatened to kill him and called him a Muslim before brutally assaulting him.

The racialization of Islam also sheds light on the dynamics of a tragic murder in Kansas in 2017. Srinivas Kuchibhotla was sitting in an Applebee's restaurant having dinner when he was shot and killed. When the perpetrator, Adam Purinton, sought to justify his actions after being arrested, he said it was because his victim was "Middle Eastern."[12] Kuchibhotla was not from the Middle East, but rather from India in South Asia. Yet, in the U.S. public imagination, brown-skinned individuals like South Asians are often mistakenly thought to be Middle Eastern, a region that is perceived to be inextricably linked to Islam—and all the negative perceptions that go with that. As such, it is impossible to separate perceived Muslim-ness from these cases. Islamophobia plays a role even when it is not explicit.

Of course, the potential of Islamophobia being at play in a hate crime does not mean that it is the only dynamic at work. In the United States, xenophobic attitudes persist alongside a concerted effort to maintain White racial dominance. This has been made especially evident since the election of Donald Trump to the U.S. presidency after which there was a jarring spike in physical and verbal attacks against Black and Brown people, not to mention LGBTQ people and others. Islamophobia is just one of numerous forms of racism and bigotry in the United States, all of which contribute to the oppression of some and the dominance of others.

The racialization of Islam also explains why people who are Muslim, but who do not "look" like it, only face Islamophobic prejudice and discrimination once people find out their religious identity. My friend Nazir—the Seattle high school student from this book's introduction—once told me a story that illustrates this well. When he was a prospective college student after 9/11, he toured a Catholic university in the United States, spending the day with several other students also nominated for a scholarship. Toward the end of the afternoon, it somehow came up that Nazir was Muslim. A young White student turned to him and said, "You don't look Muslim." There was no accusation or malice in her voice, but a matter-of-factness that revealed her expectations about what a Muslim should look like—and it wasn't like Nazir. Today in his thirties, Nazir wears trendy glasses, skinny knit ties, and a cropped beard, and will happily admit that he sometimes dresses like a hipster. Because he does not fit the expectations of what a Muslim looks like, he often does not face interpersonal Islamophobia until people find out he is Muslim, or until he speaks in Arabic or puts on clothing seen as more "Islamic."

"Double Jeopardy":
Islamophobia and Anti-Blackness

In the United States, about a quarter of Muslims are Black, making them the largest racial or ethnic group of American Muslims.[13] This group includes both African American Muslims, whose ancestors faced forced enslavement in the Americas, and African Muslims who immigrated to the United States in more recent generations. In the United States and abroad, Black Muslims face the compounded realities of anti-Black racism—which their fellow Black people of all faiths (or no faith) experience—and Islamophobia—which their fellow Muslims of other races deal with as well.[14] In a particular way, Black Muslim women who wear headscarves live at the intersection of these dual, compounding racisms.[15] In the British town of Leicester in 2017, Zaynab Hussein, a Somali British woman, suffered several broken bones and was in the hospital for five weeks after she was deliberately run over by driver Paul Moore—twice.[16] Other Black Muslim women have experienced similar violent traumas, or fear them. Minnesota college student Ahlaam Ibraahim told NPR,

> As a black woman, I'm scared of the police because I see people that look like me killed simply for being black. As a Muslim woman, I'm scared of being attacked and killed. Do they notice I'm a Muslim because of my hijab and my blackness because of my melanin?[17]

In the United States, both Muslimness and Blackness have been seen as threats to the status quo of White supremacy and Christian social dominance. This trend is illustrated well by the controversial *New Yorker* magazine cover from July 2008, where then-presidential candidate Barack Obama was depicted as a turban-wearing Muslim, and future–First Lady Michelle Obama was drawn with a large afro hairstyle, camouflage-patterned pants, and a large gun slung over her shoulder—the stereotypical Black Power activist. The drawing showed the couple standing in the Oval Office of the White House, fist-bumping, a gesture meant to represent the combined threat of Blackness and Muslimness. Whether intended as ironic or not, the cover image demonstrates that Islamophobia and anti-Black racism are deeply intertwined. This can be witnessed not only in everyday cases of violence like hate crimes, but also in how the U.S. government has treated Black (and) Muslim communities.

Anti-Black slurs and anti-Muslim slurs often blend together or are used in concert. After 9/11, hateful harassers sometimes used the epithet "sand n-gger," hurling it at Arabs and South Asians, whether they were Muslim or not. More recently, in 2018 a Muslim family in Kansas came home to find the interior of their house vandalized with the n-word and phrases like "Allah scum."[18] In 2020, it came to light that a former New Jersey town police chief, who was being prosecuted for a racially motivated attack, had said that Black people have "no value" and are "like ISIS," and that someone should "mow them down."[19]

Even though nowadays the so-called Muslim threat is usually imagined as Brown and from the Middle East, it was not always that way. From the early to the mid-twentieth century in the United States, the "Muslim threat" was Black.[20] Starting in the 1930s, the government started surveilling and prosecuting Muslims—a population that was predominantly made up of Black Americans during that period—believing they were a threat to the political and social status quo.[21] Eventually, using an unconstitutional program known as COINTELPRO, the FBI put a special focus on the Nation of Islam (NOI) movement, tapping their phones, using informants to monitor the community, and causing internal strife among those in the organization.[22] (The bureau used these tactics against the NOI's Malcolm X, Christian civil rights leader Martin Luther King Jr., and others who pushed for the rights and human flourishing of Black people in the United States.) The FBI even used the news media to "prosecute a war of disinformation about Muslim groups," creating what Edward E. Curtis IV calls the "Black Muslim Scare of the 1960s," which was the "pinnacle of pre-9/11 fears about the Muslim threat to the American nation-state."[23]

The government's concerns about Black Muslims and their supposed "foreign" connections had some of its roots in existing Orientalist tropes. As scholar Will Caldwell writes, as more and more Black Americans were converting to Islam, "their profession of Islam was itself deemed a threatening 'desire for violence,'" and thus as a bloc they "were understood to be implicitly dangerous and subversive," alleged to be connected with whatever group was deemed America's enemy at the time (the Japanese, communists, etc.).[24] Indeed, prominent Muslims like the boxer Muhammad Ali were staunch voices against the racism of the United States and the war in Vietnam. But even that kind of peaceful resistance to the status quo was deemed dangerous by the state.

Despite the unique facets of this earlier moment of institutionalized American Islamophobia—which focused on Black as opposed to Brown Muslims—it shares much in common with Islamophobia today. Today, like in the 1960s, Muslim critiques of U.S. foreign or domestic policy are punished by the state, even if, as Curtis writes, "they do not pose a direct security threat to the nation-state" and should be constitutionally protected.[25] The PATRIOT Act, passed by Congress after 9/11, facilitated the resurrection of many of the discriminatory and unconstitutional practices of the COINTELPRO era, including wiretapping without judicial oversight.[26] Not only that, but under the Trump administration there was a resurgence in government targeting of those opposing racial injustice, what the FBI now calls "Black Identity Extremists." Legal scholar Khaled Beydoun writes that this move could lead to Black Muslims being doubly targeted by law enforcement.[27] The far right, including anti-Muslim hate groups, have also taken up the 1960s playbook and sought to sow fear about a supposed red-green-black "axis" made up of communists and socialists, Muslims, and Black activists.[28] The expansion of the Muslim ban in 2020 to include a number of African countries also speaks to the intersection of anti-Black racism and Islamophobia, and their compounded impact on Black (and) Muslim people.[29]

The Ban before "the Ban":
Race, Religion, and Belonging in the United States

Membership in the 'Christian fold' served as a marker
that [people] were part of the white race.

—Jeannine Hill Fletcher[30]

Though today we conceive of race and religion as clearly distinct categories of human existence, their history shows us that they are tied together quite tightly. In chapter 8, we will see how this was the case in Christian Europe, but it has also been true in the American context. One early example is a law enacted in the late 1600s in the British colony of Virginia that specified who could and should be enslaved. It said that all of those "not being Christians" who have been "imported into this country by shipping shall be slaves"—"negroes, moors, mullatos, and others borne of and in heathenish, idolatrous, pagan and Mahometan parentage and country."[31] (*Mahometan* was a term used, often pejoratively, for Muslims during that period.) Blackness, Muslimness, general godlessness, and barbarity were all strung together, often inseparable in the Euro-American imagination.

In the United States, citizenship was long tied to Whiteness, and Whiteness was bound up with being Christian. Due to the Naturalization Act of 1790, which allowed immigrants to become U.S. citizens if they were "a free White person," from that time until 1944 few Muslims could become legal residents or citizens, because their religious identity was considered antithetical to Whiteness. As legal scholar Khalid Beydoun writes,

> The requirement meant that immigrants seeking lawful residence and citizenship were compelled to convince authorities that they fit within the statutory definition of whiteness. Arabs, along with Italians, Jews and others, were forced to litigate their identities in line with prevailing conceptions of whiteness—which fluctuated according to geographic origin, physical appearance and religion. Courts unwaveringly framed Islam as hostile to American ideals and society, casting Muslim immigrants as outside the bounds of whiteness and a threat to the identity and national security of the United States.[32]

Arab Christians were able to successfully make the case to U.S. courts for their Whiteness earlier than Arab Muslims, and thus there was large-scale Arab Christian immigration to the United States around the turn of the twentieth century. Eventually, in 1944, the U.S. courts decided that Arab Muslims met the standard of Whiteness, but due to the quota system of the 1924 Asian Exclusion Act and National Origins Act, few Arabs and Muslims from other parts of the world could immigrate to the United States. It was only after 1965, when the immigration quotas were lifted through the Immigration and Nationality Act, that non-White Muslims could finally immigrate to the United States.

This history demonstrates that the Muslim ban policy executed under the Trump administration was not an aberration in U.S. immigration history. Rather, it is of a piece with the longer trajectory of racially and religiously based immigration bans. This history also gives a glimpse into the conjoined nature of race and religion, and the way that a person's religion often determined whether or not they were considered White, an American "insider" worthy of rights and protections. For much of U.S. history, Muslims have been viewed as an "enemy race," an idea that persists among many Americans today.

Birds of a Feather:
Anti-Semitism and Islamophobia

In our popular imagination, Jews and Muslims are often seen as pitted against one another in an entrenched religious rivalry. One of the key things that this simplistic and untrue narrative ignores is the fact that both Jews and Muslims have been the targets of forms of discrimination that have been and continue to be intertwined.[33] Islamophobia and anti-Semitism have a common origin in the history of Christian-dominated Europe, where Jews and Muslims were often treated as subjected classes or foreigners worthy of expulsion. (Examples of the treatment of religious minorities in Christendom are discussed in chapter 8.) In the wake of the Enlightenment, ideas about Jews' and Muslims' innate (read, "racial") inferiority solidified further, albeit thanks to a more academic veneer. In scholarship of that period, especially during the nineteenth century, both Judaism and Islam were cast as "Semitic" religions, due to the centrality of the Hebrew and Arabic languages in religious practice and discourse.[34] European scholars viewed Christianity and Buddhism as "Aryan" religions that were more "universal," dynamic, and conducive for human flourishing. In contrast, the Semitic religions of Judaism and Islam were portrayed as ancient, stunted, and suited to people who were less civilized.[35] These ideas ultimately were harnessed in the 1940s during the Holocaust, when the Nazis murdered over six million Jews.

Despite their inherent racism and devastating implications, these ideas persist, continuing to undergird anti-Jewish and anti-Muslim discrimination. According to a 2008 Pew survey, "among the U.S. and the six European countries . . . , the correlation between unfavorable opinions of Jews and unfavorable opinions of Muslims is remarkably high."[36] In both Europe and the United States, White Christian supremacist groups openly espouse this dual bigotry, claiming that there is a Jewish-Muslim conspiracy to take political and cultural control.[37] During the coronavirus pandemic in 2020, neo-Nazi groups in Europe encouraged their followers online to "deliberately infect" Jews and Muslims with the virus.[38] In the United States in recent years, attacks against Jews have risen drastically; the total number of hate crimes against American Jews far outpaces the numbers of anti-Muslim crimes.[39]

In certain recent acts of anti-Semitic violence, the connection to Islamophobia has been clear and present. When a shooter killed eleven people at the Tree of Life synagogue outside Pittsburgh, Pennsylvania, the perpetrator's motive was in part due to the fact that Jewish congregations were helping to resettle Muslim refugees in the United States.[40] In 2019, another shooter attacked a synagogue in Poway, California, during Passover, killing one, because he had been inspired by the recent massacre of Muslims across two mosques in Christchurch, New Zealand.[41] That event had also inspired him to set fire to a mosque in Escondido, California, just weeks earlier.

In the face of rising Islamophobia and anti-Semitism, Muslims and Jews are standing together—and standing up for each other—in inspiring ways. After the Tree of Life shooting, American Muslims raised over two hundred thousand dollars for the victims' families,[42] and they undertook a similar fundraising effort after a Jewish cemetery was vandalized in 2017.[43] Jews have been some of the most consistent and outspoken voices combatting Islamophobia in American discourse, with rabbis, journalists, and Jewish human rights groups expressing their solidarity in public ways.[44] Compared to other major religious groups in the United States, Jewish Americans are the least likely to hold onto explicit anti-Muslim stereotypes, and are among those who report having warmer feelings and more favorable views toward Muslims.[45] After the Christchurch massacre, Pittsburgh-area Jews raised money for the victims' families in New Zealand, an act of reciprocation and solidarity.

Islamophobia and the Latinx Community

In the last several years in North America, Latinx persons have also been at the receiving end of anti-Muslim slurs. Juan Calero, who is not Muslim, was called a terrorist and told to leave the United States one day while walking in New York City in November 2015, at the height of the U.S. presidential campaign's anti-Muslim rhetoric.[46] It was not the first time that Calero had been targeted in this way. His brown skin and beard have led others to "race" him as an Arab Muslim and harass him as such. In Ontario, Canada, in 2017, a White man named Mark Phillips charged at Sergio Estepa—who is originally from the South American country of Colombia—and assaulted him with a baseball bat. Before the assault, he pointed at Estepa, yelling, "Terrorist! Terrorist! We've got ISIS right here!"[47]

In El Paso, Texas, in 2019, Patrick Crusius went on a shooting rampage and killed twenty-three people at a local shopping mall. Beforehand, he posted a manifesto online that began, "In general, I support the Christchurch shooter and his manifesto. This attack is a response to the Hispanic invasion of Texas."[48] He, like the Christchurch shooter and the synagogue shooters earlier, ascribed to the Great Replacement conspiracy theory and was a White supremacist who wanted to rid those in his community who threatened his vision of a White America.

We should also not overlook the fact that many Muslims are Latinx. In the United States and the Americas more broadly, more and more Latinx persons are converting to Islam, though the population remains relatively small. In the United States, Latinx Muslims likely number fewer than two hundred thousand people.[49] These individuals, like Black Muslims, often face a compounded reality of bigotry, targeted both for their religious and their ethnic identities.

Repeating History: Anti-Japanese Discrimination and the Specter of Internment Camps

Over and over throughout U.S. history, the government and dominant societal institutions have found convenient scapegoats in recent immigrant groups, especially those who were considered non-White. During the Second World War, which the United States was fighting against the Nazis, Japan, and their allies, Japanese Americans were portrayed as a "fifth column"—an internal threat who had allegiances to an outside power and would undermine the stability and safety of Americans. After the Japanese bombing attack on Pearl Harbor, Hawaii, large numbers of American citizens of Japanese descent in the western United States were rounded up and held temporarily in concentration camps. This order to round up citizens was issued by President Franklin D. Roosevelt and was upheld in the Supreme Court case *Korematsu v. United States*. In 2018, the Supreme Court expressed disapproval of that ruling, but did not formally overturn it.[50]

Today, Muslims are often cast as a fifth column and Trojan horse.[51] In media interviews, published books, and social media campaigns, the activists of the Islamophobia network incessantly claim that Muslims are seeking to "destroy Western civilization from within."[52] Despite the fact that many Muslims are born in the United States and that some—especially African American Muslims—trace their history on this continent back centuries, Muslims are still cast as intrinsically foreign and a recent immigrant group. Anti-Muslim groups often smear Muslim organizations and Muslims in political life by claiming that they are associated with foreign terrorist groups[53]—charges that, if they were true, would justify widespread measures to crack down on this fifth column. Ahead of the 2016 presidential elections, some Republican supporters of Donald Trump's run cited the history of Japanese American internment as a precedent for their own potential policy of a registration of American Muslims.[54]

Recognizing how similar today's scapegoating is to what they experienced in the 1940s, Japanese Americans have been some of the most vocal opponents of anti-Muslim fearmongering in politics. They know the harm that this language can lead to because they experienced its effects firsthand. U.S. representative Mike Honda, who was imprisoned as a child in an internment camp, wrote in 2011, "The interned four-year-old in me is crying out for a course correction so that we do not do to others what we did unjustly to countless Japanese-Americans."[55]

Recycled Smears:
How Anti-Catholic Bias Prefigured
Anti-Muslim Scapegoating

In the mid-1800s, Catholic immigrants to the United States from places like Ireland and Italy were viewed with suspicion and treated with hostility. Newspaper cartoons dehumanized them as animals who would change America's Protestant culture. Catholic churches and convents were even set on fire. Politicians demonized Catholics as disloyal "papists" bent upon covertly taking over America, saying they were intent on subverting the Constitution and replacing it with canon law. This bigotry resurfaced prominently in the twentieth century during the presidential run of John F. Kennedy, who became the country's first Catholic president. Faced with charges that he would be more loyal to the pope than to his own country, Kennedy had to assure voters publicly that he would abide by the Constitution and put American law before that of the pontiff in Rome.

Once leveled against Catholics, these charges—of disloyalty, covert political infiltration, and eventual takeover and imposition of foreign religious law—have in our own time been recycled and applied to Muslims. When Ben Carson asserted during his presidential run in 2015 that a Muslim should not be president, he was echoing a parallel sentiment that had once been said about Kennedy and other potential Catholic politicians. This recycling is most evident in the hysteria generated over the purported threat of sharia law. In 2011, shortly after orchestrating the nationwide controversy around the Park51 Center in Manhattan and dubbing it the Ground Zero Mosque, activists in the Islamophobia network started heavily pushing a narrative that would grip the country for years.[56] Muslims, they claimed, were intent on imposing sharia, or Islamic law, which they cast as universally and uniquely "misogynistic, anti-Semitic, anti-infidel, anti-gay, anti-free speech,"[57] to quote anti-Muslim blogger-activist Pamela Geller. Conveniently, all of these supposed attributes of sharia line up with all the worst things people believe about Muslims—the well-entrenched stereotypes we have already explored.

This frightening picture does not match what sharia is or how it functions in Muslims' lives. In Arabic, sharia means "path" or "way."[58] It is not a single legal book of unchangeable statutes enacted in Muslim contexts everywhere, as we often imagine when we use the phrase "Islamic law." Rather, sharia is the "idea of God's law," as scholar Jonathan Brown puts it.[59] Muslims, like Christians and others, believe that God has a will for how they should live, and so they strive to discover and implement God's will.[60] From their diverse contexts and stations in life, Muslims have interpreted "God's law" in myriad ways, and Muslim legal scholars have often disagreed with one another on certain matters. These human interpretations of God's law are called *fiqh*, and there are numerous schools of jurisprudence that mutually recognize the validity of one another. Sharia concerns religious and ethical questions like, *How should one pray? What should one eat? How should one treat their neighbors? How should family relations be arranged?* In this way, sharia plays a similar role to *halacha* in the Jewish tradition, or even canon law among Catholics. Muslims appeal to the idea of sharia to justify the choices they make in their religious lives, sometimes conforming to existing norms or rulings in fiqh. I say more about sharia in chapter 6—particularly on its history and role in Muslim-majority countries—but suffice it to say here that both in content and function sharia does not resemble the monolithic, brutal legal system that its opponents decry. And contrary to the popular narrative, Muslims are not trying to impose it on the rest of Americans.[61]

Instead, fears about the threat of sharia have been manufactured by those seeking to benefit politically from the scapegoating of a despised group. Since 2011, in the run-up to midterm and presidential elections across the United States, politicians—the vast majority of them Republicans—have flooded state legislatures with "anti-sharia" or "anti–foreign law" bills.[62] They introduced these bills alongside vocal campaigns by anti-Muslim groups that spoke of the need to ban "Islamic law," which they claimed threatened to supplant the U.S. Constitution and upend the rights and freedoms it affords. The bills introduced were all inspired by (if not direct quotations from) model legislation authored by anti-Muslim activist and lawyer David Yerushalmi. Many other anti-Muslim activists already discussed in this book heavily promoted the supposed need for these laws, including Brigitte Gabriel and her group, ACT for America, which organized anti-sharia rallies and direct actions in local contexts around the United States.[63] On FOX News, anti-Muslim commentators like Frank Gaffney were invited on to push their narrative of "creeping sharia," as they called it.[64] Sharia became a buzzword of Republican politicians on the national presidential stage, too, especially during the 2016 race. Admirably, some Republicans resisted this sharia fearmongering, cognizant of the ways their own communities had been similarly targeted in the past based on religious or ethnic differences. For example, Mormon politicians and ordinary citizenry stood up to the anti-sharia hype when many others did not.[65]

This anti-sharia movement succeeded on at least two fronts. First, it generated fear of Muslims during politically expedient times.[66] As researchers at the Haas Institute at the University of California, Berkeley have written, the proposal and enactment of these bills "instigates an unfounded fear among the American society that Sharia will infiltrate the U.S. legal system."[67] When asked by journalists what sharia was, many Republican voters could not say, but they had no doubt it needed to go away and thus were supportive of the politicians and party who were advocating for its banning. Effectively, the anti-sharia movement manufactured a problem, convinced the public of its urgency, and then created a solution for it that they could benefit from politically or financially. Both the Trump campaign and Republican National Committee included leading questions in voter surveys, asking, "Are you concerned about sharia law?,"[68] further normalizing this false notion. If Muslims (and their supposed Democratic allies) were the problem, Republicans became the solution.

The Threat to Us All

If the anti-sharia movement's first success was in generating fear of Muslims on which the GOP politicians could capitalize, its second success was in undermining the actual rights and religious practice of Muslims and other religious communities in the United States. Dozens of anti-sharia bills—194 to be exact—have been introduced in thirty-nine of the fifty states across the union, and they have been enacted into law in twelve. The bills use the more generic language of banning "foreign law," since targeting Muslims specifically through the mention of "sharia" in the text of the bill would be struck down by the courts (as happened to one such law—the first—in Oklahoma). These bills stirred up anti-Muslim fervor that put Muslims physically at risk in their communities, undermining their basic rights. To compound that, when enacted, these laws can restrict the ability of Muslims and other groups to turn to religious arbitration in court settings. Jews, Christians, and Muslims (to a lesser extent) sometimes rely on the civil government to enforce intrareligious group contracts.[69] For example, a Muslim or Jewish couple might want to write out their marriage contract in such a way that comports with fiqh or halacha standards. This is a long-standing practice in the United States, and it gives religious groups relative autonomy to make decisions in civil (not criminal) matters in their communities.

Contrary to the impression left by the anti-sharia fearmongering, none of the decisions in these matters could conflict with U.S. constitutional or statutory law. This is why the sharia laws are unnecessary and redundant in the first place. There are already ample protections to prevent religious groups' preferences from winning out over existing legal rules. But these anti–foreign law bills have the potential to hinder this very legal religious arbitration. In a few cases, they already have, not just for Muslims but for other religious denominations, too.[70]

In this way, the targeting of Muslims in the United States is the start of the infringement on many other groups' rights to religious expression. Broad interpretations of laws banning "material support" to terrorist groups—which I discuss in the next chapter—have the potential to hinder the humanitarian work of Christian aid agencies in conflict zones in the Middle East.[71] CVE programs in the United States, originally focused on Muslims, under the Trump administration started targeting Native American activists.[72]

Another time that Islamophobia has an impact beyond the Muslim community is when non-Muslims are targeted precisely for standing alongside Muslims and working against the prejudice and discrimination that face them. In Portland, Oregon, in the summer of 2017, a man named Jeremy Christian boarded a public transit train car. He spotted two young women—Walia Mohamed, a Muslim teenager who wears a hijab, and her friend, Destinee Magnum, who is Black and was also wearing an article of clothing on her head. Christian immediately started berating the teenagers. "Get out of this country. . . . Burn. . . . Muslims should die. . . . Go back to Saudi Arabia," the young women recall him saying.[73] Frightened for their lives, Walia and Destinee tried to keep their distance. They received hardly any support from others standing nearby in the train car, though another man nodded approvingly as Jeremy Christian continued his anti-Muslim and racist tirade for several minutes. Eventually, at a stop, three other White men boarded the train and quickly realized something was very wrong. They stepped between Christian and the girls, confronting him and trying to get him to stop. Suddenly, the flash of a blade appeared, and Christian stabbed the three men with a knife. Micah Fletcher, badly wounded, survived, but Ricky Best and Taliesin Namkai-Meche did not. Christian, a known White supremacist with a history of harassing people of color and religious people,[74] was eventually arrested by police and convicted of murder and hate crimes.[75] Fletcher, Best, and Namkai-Meche, who stepped in to protect Walia and Desiree, were hailed as heroes, but they paid a heavy price for their solidarity.[76]

Conclusion:
What Solidarity Looks Like

Simran Jeet Singh is not Muslim—he is Sikh. But he's had more anti-Muslim slurs hurled at him in public than anyone I know. At San Antonio Spurs basketball games, while training for marathons in New York City, and while out with his family, Simran has been called a "terrorist," "f*cking Muslim,"[77] "f*cking Osama," and "Ali Baba."[78]

Faced with such dangerous hatred, it would be easy enough for Simran and his fellow Sikhs to direct their assailants elsewhere, and say, "Hey, I'm not Muslim!" But, as Simran said in an interview with *The Daily Show* corre-spondent Hasan Minhaj back in 2016, it is "not an option for us to throw another community under the bus. Even if it means things are harder for us, we believe it's the right thing to do."[79] Sikhs like Simran have worked tirelessly in recent years to combat Islamophobia in media, politics, and public life. The Sikh Coalition has been a key driver among activist groups pushing against discriminatory policies that primarily target Muslims, like CVE programs.[80]

This kind of solidarity is demonstrated by Sikhs, Jews, Christians, and so many others, whether religious or not. They do it not only because their community might be faced with the same bigotry or discrimination, but because they know that no matter who it targets, it is wrong.

5

Under the Surface

The Islamophobia We Don't See

Islamophobia operates in ways that are often invisible to us. In this chapter, I pull the curtain back on some of those hidden forms of Islamophobia, beginning with the impact of our own unconscious, unintentional biases, and some reasons why anti-Muslim hate crimes often go unreported. I also talk about more concerted efforts to marginalize Muslims, including government activities and programs that institutionalize Islamophobia in the United States. At the end of the chapter, I explore the connections between Islamophobic attitudes at home and U.S. foreign policy abroad, and the impact of the overwhelmingly negative media coverage of Muslims. These forms of Islamophobia remain under the surface of our public consciousness and only rarely appear in news reports. But while they may go unnoticed by us, these injustices are often top of mind for many Muslims, whom they affect deeply. Islamophobia can persist despite our best intentions, and its continued existence relies in large part on its being invisible to us. Islamophobia is embedded in institutions and societal norms—and also in our own minds—even if we wish it were not.

Deep Down:
The Reactions We Can't Control,
the Biases We Don't Recognize

In 2019, I was walking through the mall near my house in the Maryland suburbs of Washington, DC. The corridor was fairly crowded, as it typically is, with people milling in and out of stores. But one woman striding toward me caught my eye. She wore a long, flowing dress, and a black face veil, called a *niqab*. Her eyes peeked out, but I did not meet their gaze. As she approached and we quickly passed, I realized that my muscles had tensed up and my breath had quickened. It was startling to find my body reacting this way despite my wanting it not to. I knew in the moment that I should act no differently in this woman's presence than I would with any other person. But, for some reason, I couldn't help it.

This was by no means my first time being around women who wear face veils. When I lived in Amman, Jordan, I would pass women wearing niqabs on the sidewalk occasionally, and I spoke with women whose faces, save their eyes, were completely covered at conferences I attended. Even more often, I come across niqabi women in the Washington, DC, metro area where I live. I have never had a close friend who wears a face veil, but still, like most of my non-Muslim peers, I actively know that I should not assume something negative about Muslim women simply because they dress this way. Aware of the stereotypes that exist about Muslims, I know I should *not* assume that a woman in a face veil or billowy black clothing may be hiding something dangerous, or that she was forced to dress this way by her husband or an elder. Yet in moments like the one in the mall, it still made me uncomfortable.

This story now seems very ironic as I am writing this today, during the coronavirus pandemic in 2020, when covering one's face in public has actually become a social norm. And it seems even more irrational that seeing someone's covered face would illicit in me such a negative response given that this is exactly what I do every time I go to the grocery store these days—wear a mask, with only my eyes peeking out.

All of this is deeply unpleasant to share, but it is important to acknowledge because these biased behaviors and visceral reactions are not at all justified. They emerge out of untrue stereotypes that do not mirror reality. Yet it is not at all surprising that we have these reactions. In places like the United States and Europe, we have long been conditioned to have negative associations when we see images of people who are "visibly Muslim." Having been continually fed narratives about "Muslim violence and oppression," those associations seem second nature to us.

I am not alone in having these unfortunate physical and emotional responses. A few years back, my great-aunt Judy had a similar experience, which she graciously shared with me for this book:

> On a cross-country flight, I was seated next to a young Muslim man. We were waiting for the stewardess to close the door to the plane so we could depart. This gentleman kept glancing toward the front of the plane and then thumbing through the Qur'an, visibly becoming more agitated by the minute. The phrase: "If you see something, say something" started to run through my mind. What should I do? We heard the door shut. I had to make a decision. As we started to back away from the gate I heard him softly repeat certain words in Arabic several times. The stewardess was now coming down the aisle to do a

headcount. This was my chance. Just before she reached us, he turned to me and said, "I'm terrified of flying." There was a weak, apologetic smile on his face. Had he sensed my alarm? I consider myself to be a very open-minded person, yet I had immediately jumped to the worst possible conclusion about this person. If he had had a Bible in his hand instead of a Qur'an, I know the thought of terrorism would never have entered my mind. I'm ashamed. I learned that he was a college professor, of Turkish descent, newly engaged to be married. We talked for the rest of the flight. When we landed he thanked me and said our conversation kept his mind off the fact that he was thousands of feet in the air.

Many readers may have had similar, shame-inducing experiences. Well intentioned as we are, we may sometimes find ourselves making irrational assumptions about Muslims that we know are not valid. In Judy's case, she was operating out of a very common, post-9/11 anxiety: concern that Muslims will hijack commercial planes and cause carnage in the air and on the ground. Even my brother admitted to me his own, unbidden reaction to seeing men he presumed to be Muslim in an airport on the Fourth of July. Noticing their brown skin and dark beards, he found his mind wandering, *What if they are planning to launch some kind of attack, to send a message on this national holiday?* In his case, the "hijackers" association was paired with the stereotypes about Muslims "hating America" and hating "our freedoms," which are so often celebrated on July 4th in the United States.

What is crucial about Judy's and my brother's experiences is that they both recognized their active biases and knew that their emotional reactions and assumptions were wrong. There is no shame in admitting that they come up, and frankly it is healthy to do so. Having these visceral reactions does not make us bad people; in fact, they are natural human responses. The human mind has evolved to be wary of those who are different from us, of those who have long been portrayed to us as a threat—as Muslims have. Our moral character is not judged on whether we *have* stereotypical thoughts and unbidden reactions, but rather on what we *do* with them. Do we let them dictate our actions, or do we resist them, seeing them for what they are?

The trouble is this: what I have described above are only the biases of which we are actually aware. Much more damaging are the behaviors that come from the biases we don't recognize, of which we are not consciously aware. Social psychologists describe these as "implicit biases," the latent stereotypes we hold onto that are not accessible to our conscious mind. They live deeper, under the surface of our consciousness, and become ingrained as the result of absorbing negative associations about the "other" over the course of our lives. As scholars at the Kirwan Institute explain, "The implicit associations we hold do not necessarily align with our declared beliefs or even reflect stances we would explicitly endorse."[1] Even if we consciously hold the conviction that we should treat everyone equally, we may end up treating others differently without actually realizing it. These actions might include whom we select for a job interview, whom we allow to rent our apartment, or whom we might vote for in an election. Studies into human psychology and behavior reveal that unintentional prejudices often contribute more to our actions than our rational thoughts. In fact, psychologist John Bargh, who studies the unconscious mind, states, "The unconscious mind can lead us astray if we are not aware of its influence."[2]

Bargh's research supports the assertion that we can be purveyors of Islamophobia without meaning to be. Our mistreatment of people often occurs despite our best intentions and the beliefs we consciously hold. But Bargh gives us hope by noting that "when we actively integrate both the conscious and unconscious workings of the mind, and listen to and make good use of both, can we avoid the pitfalls of being blind to half the mind."[3] We may not be able to uproot our implicit biases altogether. But when we begin to admit to ourselves that we, despite our goodwill, have these implicit biases, we can begin to take actions to combat them and other more tangible forms of Islamophobia in our society.

Hate Crimes That Go Uncounted

Newlyweds in their early twenties, Deah Barakat and Yusor Abu-Salha were married only a few weeks before they were killed. Having bonded over basketball, community service, and prospective careers in dentistry, the young couple were leaders in their community and beloved by everyone who knew them. One evening in February 2015, they were having dinner in their Chapel Hill, North Carolina, apartment with Yusor's nineteen-year-old sister, Razan, when their neighbor came to their door, barged in, and shot all three of them at point-blank range. Deah, Yusor, and Razan were Arab American Muslims, and the two young women wore headscarves. The perpetrator, Craig Hicks, was a White man with strident views against religion and Islam, though he did not vocalize them that night.

The killings sent shock waves throughout the country and around the world. No other case of violence against Muslims in the United States has received more media attention nationwide than this one. No case was more exemplary of the rising American Islamophobia and its deadly impact. The Chapel Hill shooting occurred at the beginning of 2015, the year when hate crimes against Muslims had begun skyrocketing. Immediately after the shooting, many hate crimes against Muslims followed in quick succession, seemingly set off by this tragedy. But the murders of Deah, Yusor, and Razan were not listed among the official anti-Muslim hate crime statistics compiled by the FBI for that year. The reasons why are complicated, and they speak to the fact that the extent of Islamophobia is much more than what can be measured in statistics and confirmed in court.

In the immediate aftermath of the murders, Chapel Hill police interviewed Hicks, the perpetrator, who had turned himself in at the station. Hicks claimed that he had committed the heinous act because of a supposed dispute they had over parking spaces at the apartment complex—a story, of course, that in no way justified his actions. When the police filed their report and started talking to the media about the murders, they relied heavily on Hicks's framing, calling the crime the result of a "parking dispute."[4] They did not charge Hicks with a hate crime.

Up through his conviction and sentencing for the murders, Hicks denied that bias against religion or Islam had anything to do with his decision to take their lives. It was because of this lack of explicit anti-Muslim or anti-Arab intent during and after the murders that both local and federal law enforcement did not charge him with a hate crime. In the United States, for such an attack to be designated a hate crime against a protected group of people, there must be proof that the perpetrator targeted the victim due to their religious, ethnic, gender, or other identity. U.S. courts have a high standard of proof for determining intent, and it is understandable why—"proof beyond a reasonable doubt" is a hallmark of the American judicial system, and having a high bar when it comes to a defendant's thoughts serves as a protection against unjust and excessive incarceration.

But the fact that Hicks did not express explicit anti-Muslim bias does not mean Islamophobia didn't play a role in Hicks's gruesome crime, nor does it mean that the possibility of a hate-based motive should have been so quickly dismissed by law enforcement and journalists who covered the story. When Yusor and Razan's father, Mohammad Abu-Salha, heard the news of his daughters' killing, he immediately knew who the perpetrator was, without having to be told. Prior to Yusor marrying Deah and moving into his apartment, Deah and other residents at the apartment complex had been harangued by Hicks about supposedly violating parking rules. But Deah and his family noticed things worsen with Hicks when Yusor, who wears a headscarf, starting living there.[5] With their Muslim identities more clearly on display, Hicks's ire increased and he began to target her specifically.[6] Deah's family had even encouraged them to get a restraining order against Hicks shortly before the murders, because he had threatened them by showing them a gun on his belt.[7] They were not able to secure one in time.

Knowing all of this, the family was deeply disturbed that the police were framing this as a "parking dispute," and not a crime influenced by racial and religious bias. Islamophobic attacks were already on the rise that year, as the news was full of coverage of ISIS attacks, the Syrian refugee crisis, and political fearmongering about Muslims. Could this be why Hicks chose to unleash his rage on his Muslim neighbors? Even though Hicks denies this, scholars who study implicit bias point out that human beings often make decisions based on latent, underlying prejudices, not their conscious ideas. In an interview he gave about the Chapel Hill murders, law professor Joseph Kennedy used the metaphor of a fish swimming in water to explain this phenomenon.[8] Fully immersed in a climate saturated by Islamophobia, Hicks could be sucking in his environment without even knowing it. During the investigation and murder trial, new details came to light that pointed to the potential for implicit anti-Muslim bias shaping this crime. When he charged into their home, Hicks shot Yusor and Razan in the head through their hijabs, execution-style,[9] after he had sprayed Deah with bullets.[10]

The family pushed for the hate crime investigation and designation not because they wanted increased punishment—there was nothing that could bring their children back, and Hicks, who was pleading guilty, would receive multiple life sentences for the murder convictions.[11] What they wanted was the acknowledgment that Islamophobia indeed kills, and for this fact to hopefully help prevent other families from going through what they did. Though it may not have changed the outcome of the conviction, the police department now acknowledges that they were wrong in jumping to the "parking dispute" explanation and writing off so quickly the potential of a bigoted, Islamophobic motive. The police chief apologized to the family.[12]

The tragic story of Deah, Yusor, and Razan is just one of numerous cases like it. In recent years across the United States—not to mention Europe—many other Muslims have been killed in attacks that were never listed among anti-Muslim hate crime statistics but are nonetheless impossible to disentangle from the climate of Islamophobic hate and hostility that descended over the country. The killing of Nabra Hassanen, a seventeen-year-old girl from northern Virginia in the summer of 2017, is another example.[13] As she and her friends walked back to the local mosque from an IHOP restaurant, where they had eaten a pre-dawn meal before fasting for the day during Ramadan, a young man named Darwin Martinez-Torres chased after the girls with a baseball bat and abducted Nabra as they tried to run away. He was later charged with raping and murdering her. A bias charge was not brought in the case, but many felt the brutality of the attack meant that Nabra's faith and race could have played an implicit role. When people are dehumanized regularly in the media, as Muslims had been especially in the wake of Donald Trump's election, it can play into whether and to what extent they are mistreated in individual acts of violence.

Even when crimes with an explicit bias motivation are charged as a hate crime locally, they do not always make it into national FBI hate crime statistics. This happened in the case of Khalid Jabara, the Arab Christian who was killed by his neighbor who called him, among other slurs, a "Mooslum."[14] A number of problems lead to inaccuracies in national hate crime data collection: local law enforcement agencies are not all required to report their statistics to the FBI, many police officers are never trained in how to deal with hate crimes, some states prosecute different classes of hate crimes than others, and five states do not have hate crime statutes at all.[15] All of this inconsistency leads to skewed numbers and thus to skewed public perceptions about the extent of bias-motivated crimes. Khalid's family, along with the family of Heather Heyer—the young woman who was killed in a car-ramming by neo-Nazi James Fields in Charlottesville, Virginia, in 2017—have pushed legislation in Congress that would require this universal hate crime reporting.[16]

FBI hate crime statistics are only a broad and imperfect indication of the trends in interpersonal Islamophobia around the country.[17] Because they do not account for cases where Islamophobic sentiment may be an underlying factor but is not expressed, and because of issues with reporting and data collecting, these statistics do not give us a full picture. They are an outline of the wave of Islamophobia, but they do not account for what is under the surface.

"Traffic Congestion," "Parking Disputes," and "Road Rage"

One way to locate these more latent manifestations of Islamophobia is to look at the framing that has been used repeatedly to explain or justify supposedly bias-free incidents involving Muslims. The Chapel Hill shooting is not the only case where concerns over cars and parking have been cited as explanations (if not justification) for treating Muslims differently or inhumanely.[18]

Across the United States, numerous mosque construction projects have been stalled or halted due to the local community's concerns about increased traffic or excess cars in the area.[19] This is what happened in Carmel, Indiana, a well-to-do suburb of Indianapolis in 2018. As the local Muslim community was setting the plans to build a mosque for their growing congregation, they faced forceful pushback from local citizens, many of whom wrote letters of opposition that were published online. Few of the opponents were outright Islamophobic—though some were. Most, however, framed their opposition to the mosque as having to do with increased traffic in the area, congestion outside parking lots, and lowered property values.[20] Having grown up in the Indianapolis area, I followed the case closely, knowing some of the Muslim families who were part of the new congregation. As I read through the letters of opposition online, which were submitted ahead of the city meeting that would determine the fate of the building project, I found that I also knew personally one of the opponents—a family acquaintance and doctor who had treated me when I was a child. In his letter, he emphasized strongly that it was not bias against Muslims that informed his stance, but rather logistical concerns. His explanation was echoed over and over by many who wrote letters in opposition.

Another fact, however, challenges this well-meaning characterization. When large churches were built in residential areas of Carmel in years before the mosque project, they received little community pushback.[21] Aside from the religious affiliation of the congregations (Christian, instead of Muslim), the cases of the churches were not that different from the mosque case. The Christian houses of worship had large buildings and sizable parking areas. Some even had large gold domes as part of their roofing, like the proposed mosque would have. But only the mosque project received the heavy community backlash, nearly sidelining the whole endeavor. This fact calls into question the explanations given by the mosque's many opponents that their concerns were not rooted in any hesitations or negative sentiment about Muslims. This is not to say that the opponents were being insincere in what they shared. I take the doctor at his word that he does not consciously hold anti-Muslim beliefs. But, as we have already seen in the discussion of implicit bias, Islamophobia goes deeper than our consciously held beliefs. Negative stereotypes and sentiments are embedded down deep, so far that we do not realize they are there and informing our choices. Especially in the United States, where so much shame is associated with being considered a "racist" or a "bigot," we take great pains to explain our internal aversion to others who are different in ways that are more socially acceptable. Instead of interrogating and owning up to the possibility of our biases about those of religions or races different from our own, we often justify them through rational means, like complaints about cars and traffic. This dynamic was also on clear display during the opposition to a mosque in Sterling Heights, Michigan, in 2015. Outside a city planning meeting, over a hundred protesters derided the mosque plan, chanting, "God bless America!" When interviewed by a journalist, one woman paused her chanting to interject, "Traffic is going to be so bad!" Another woman standing beside her insisted animatedly, "We don't hate Muslim people! Never do we hate them, but we don't want a mosque here!"[22]

The fact that parking and road-related concerns[23] have been cited over and over again across the country[24] to oppose mosque construction is a signal that individuals' rationalized explanations should not be our main indicator of whether prejudice toward Muslims is involved in a particular situation. When it comes to Islamophobia and other forms of racism, the consciously held beliefs of the public tell us far less than these broader trends.

Another example of mischaracterized motivation is the numerous American Muslims who have been killed by other motorists during periods of heightened Islamophobic rhetoric nationwide. Many of these have been characterized as "road rage"[25] even when explicit bias was invoked, like when Robert Klimek killed Ziad Abu Naim after allegedly shouting at him, "Go back to Islam!"[26] in Texas, or when Dustin Passarelli followed motorist Mustafa Ayoubi in Indianapolis, and allegedly called him a number of anti-Muslim slurs before shooting and killing him.[27]

Spies and Soup Kitchens

In 2012, Asad Dandia was a college student in New York City, running a social service organization on the side while undertaking his studies. Animated by Islamic values of uplifting the poor, Asad's group delivered groceries to undocumented and working families, helped those experiencing homelessness, and raised funds for other charitable causes.

In March of that year, he received a Facebook message from a young man who wanted to get involved with the group and reinvigorate his Islamic faith. Asad started including him in the organization's meetings, which were held at a local mosque. He became involved in numerous community activities with Asad's circle of friends, like attending religious lectures with them at various college campuses, helping them raise money for Syrian refugees, and joining them in delivering food. He even slept over at Asad's house and got to know his family. Everything seemed normal.

But in October, the young man made it known that he had been paid to work as an informant for the New York Police Department (NYPD), who had tasked him with infiltrating the local Muslim community and reporting back on any suspicious activities.[28] Asad, his group, and the local mosque it operated out of felt betrayed and vulnerable. After this ordeal, how could they truly feel secure in their religious spaces? How could they be sure that their friends were not secretly spying on them? In an essay published online, Asad wrote,

> I still can't understand why people who are feeding the poor are being targeted by the NYPD. For me, Islam is about more than just praying at the mosque and fasting. Islam is about getting involved and engaging with the greater world. My friends and I do so by serving

our community through helping those less fortunate. The NYPD surveillance program has made it harder for me to practice my religion, even though I have done nothing wrong.[29]

Asad's organization was not alone in being targeted in this way. As revealed in an Associated Press investigation published the previous year, all across the city, the NYPD had instituted a broad program to spy on and "map" the Muslim community, sending in spies to pose as new members of mosques and Muslim student groups on college campuses, listening in to conversations among Muslims at cafés and restaurants, and tracking their comings and goings.[30] After the AP reports were released, the NYPD admitted that their "Muslim mapping" program—created after 9/11—had not yielded even one criminal lead or charge.[31] Despite the widespread outcry about the program, Michael Bloomberg (who was mayor of New York City during this time) defended the religious profiling of this program, even during his 2020 run for the Democratic presidential nomination.[32]

In the wake of his experience, Asad and other targeted New York Muslims filed a lawsuit against the NYPD, challenging the spying program on the basis of its blatantly Islamophobic premise that anyone who is Muslim is a potential threat. Asad and the others eventually won settlements leading to a litany of policy changes, among them being that the NYPD "agreed to actively prohibit investigations on the basis of race, ethnicity, religion or national origin, and to allow a civilian representative to monitor its compliance."[33]

But this positive step does not mean that law enforcement infiltration of Muslim communities no longer occurs. In fact, it is still common practice around the United States. In 2014, the Department of Justice promulgated guidance that allows for programs like the NYPD mapping program and other profiling measures.[34] Informants not only report back to their agencies what they see and hear, but are also often directed to lure the Muslims they "befriend" into committing crimes that will get them locked up on terrorism charges. Some of those who work as informants have been charged with crimes themselves, and the FBI offers to suspend their charges in exchange for them infiltrating a Muslim community.[35] Informants can also be offered large sums of money in compensation for their spying work. The targets of this infiltration are often recent converts to Islam, young people, or those suffering from mental illness—vulnerable individuals who are then goaded by informants into taking actions for which they can be charged.[36] In these undercover sting operations, the occasion for someone to commit an actionable offense does not arise organically, but it is rather meticulously and persistently set up by U.S. law enforcement.[37] A report published by the Institute for Social Policy and Understanding (ISPU), which analyzed cases of ideologically motivated violence (both plotted and carried out) from 2002 to 2015, found that in a majority of the cases involving Muslims "undercover law enforcement or an informant provided the means of the crime (such as a firearm or inert bomb)." According to another study, by George Washington University's Project on Extremism, 59 percent of those who were charged with offenses related to the Islamic State involved an informant or undercover agent.[38]

Despite these baiting tactics, the use of informants and undercover agents in terrorism prosecutions does not get much if any mainstream media attention. This very significant detail is often buried in news reports about terrorism cases, if it is mentioned at all. Many critics refer to this phenomenon as "entrapment," which occurs when law enforcement facilitates the occasion for a crime to be committed. The fact that so many terrorism prosecutions and convictions are obtained through the use of these tactics calls into question the extent of the domestic terrorism problem.

The Muslim communities into which informants embed themselves are typical religious and community spaces, where kids play in basketball tournaments and complete scouting projects, their parents put together holiday dinners, and preachers give sermons that inspire worshippers or sometimes put them to sleep. If and when a community does get wind of something concerning, they often report it,[39] as they did in California in 2006, when a new member of the mosque started talking a lot about wanting to commit a violent act. When his friends went to law enforcement to express concern, they learned that the man was in fact the FBI's own informant, tasked with spying on and stirring up trouble in their mosque.[40]

In the wake of the 9/11 attack in 2001, the U.S. government eroded civil protections by way of laws like the PATRIOT Act, leading American Muslims to become the targets of entrapment and other measures that critics call "preemptive prosecution."[41] Central to this is the PATRIOT Act's expansion of what legally constitutes "material support" to terrorist groups. By broadening the definition of "material support," the government opened the door to people being prosecuted as terrorists for engaging in nonviolent activities and even for innocuous ones that should be constitutionally protected, like "religious practice, humanitarian aid, speech, or association."[42] This has particularly impacted the realm of Muslim charitable giving. Making a donation to a foreign organization that *years later* would be blacklisted by the United States as a terror group could lead a person to be retroactively prosecuted for a charitable donation given with the best of intentions. Voicing a question that reveals the injustice of this situation, former U.S. government official Laila al-Marayati asks, "How can you punish me for giving today to an organization that is designated five years from now?"[43] With this possibility in mind, many Muslims have been fearful to give to overseas charities, concerned about how it might be used against them later.[44]

Since 9/11, there have been stunning disparities in the way the legal system treats cases of ideologically motivated violence, depending on whether the perpetrator (or would-be perpetrator) was identified as Muslim and perceived to be acting out of their faith. Based on data from 2002 to 2015, ISPU researchers found that Muslim perpetrators received far worse charges and far worse sentences than their non-Muslim counterparts.[45] A prison in Terre Haute, Indiana, has come to be colloquially referred to as "Guantánamo North" because of how many American Muslims have been imprisoned there in such cases.[46]

These trends give us a window into often-invisible forms of government-sanctioned Islamophobia in the United States, not to mention its manifestations in other countries.

The Dead We Don't Know

In the middle of night in September 2015, forces of the U.S.-led coalition fighting ISIS in Iraq dropped bombs on two buildings in the city of Mosul.[47] The next morning, they posted a video of the bombing online, claiming these structures were ISIS facilities used to make car bombs. But the buildings they destroyed were not car-bomb factories—they were civilian homes, targeted due to faulty U.S. intelligence. The blasts killed four people and injured two others—all of them family members. When his home was struck, Basim Razzo lost his wife, Mayada, and their daughter, Tuqa, and was severely injured himself. Basim's brother Mohannad, and nephew, Najib, who lived next door, were also killed. Azza, Mohannad's wife, miraculously survived after being flung from a second-story window.

The story got little news media attention anywhere, and the silence was especially deafening in the United States. Rarely if ever do murders of civilians at the hands of Western or U.S. military get news coverage, in part because the military itself often fails to acknowledge and document them. Until a *New York Times* investigation probed the matter, Mayada, Tuqa, Mohannad, and Najib were not counted among the civilians killed by coalition forces and were instead "placed in the 'ISIS' column."[48] The reporters found that "one in five of the coalition strikes we identified resulted in civilian death, a rate more than 31 times that acknowledged by the coalition."[49] Even when the killing of civilians by U.S. forces or their allies is acknowledged, it is often couched in vague terms like "casualties" or "collateral damage," which obscure the reality of loss of human life. Shortly after the bombing, American professor Zareena Grewal, who is a family relative of those killed in Mosul, wrote, "I desperately want the Islamic State to be defeated, but I wonder if our rage at it has made us blind to anyone we kill along the way, even those whose lives have been terrorized by the group."[50]

Since 1980, the U.S. military has bombed fourteen Muslim-majority countries, a staggering number that calls into question the conventional American narrative of Muslim aggression and U.S. victimhood.[51] Due to lack of coverage in mainstream news, many Americans do not realize that their military is involved in or responsible for so many deaths abroad. On top of that, stereotypes about Muslims as naturally violent help shield Americans from recognizing their own country's complicity in the violence and suffering that plague parts of the Middle East. The stereotypes also help to normalize and justify U.S. military incursions in Muslim-majority countries. In examining years of polling data on Americans' attitudes toward Muslims, my former colleagues and I at Georgetown University's Bridge Initiative found a curious trend that speaks to this. Seeking to measure across time Americans' association of Islam with violence, the data showed that during three distinct periods, more Americans than not agreed that Islam was "more likely to encourage violence" than other religions.[52] Contrary to what one might expect, these periods were not immediately after terrorist attacks carried out in the United States by Muslim individuals or groups. Instead, the spikes occurred during the lead-up to military incursions in Muslim-majority countries—the 2003 invasion of Iraq, the 2007 troop surge as the civil war there worsened, and in 2014 as the United States weighed getting involved in Syria and fighting ISIS in Iraq. As corporate media interests and government officials were drumming up the case for war, the American public came to see Islam as more violent—with the implication being that Muslims are a natural aggressor and thus a more worthy military opponent. These findings comport with the observation of scholar Kambiz GhaneaBassiri, who writes that "perceptions of an impending threat to national security drive negative attitudes towards Muslims."[53] Another study from 2018 found that, among Americans, having anti-Muslim stereotypes was a strong predictor of whether someone would support U.S. violence against Muslims abroad—in this case, the bombing of Iran.[54] The United States' own aggression can be downplayed or justified when the supposed violence of Muslims is alluded to over and over and over again.

These are just two examples of how Islamophobic sentiment in the United States is manufactured. It does not simply rise organically, but in large part because it serves U.S. interests, whether political, corporate, or military. Weapons manufacturers and military contractor companies receive massive profits from selling arms to the United States and its allies.[55] Some of these weapons companies themselves are donors to the anti-Muslim hate groups of the Islamophobia network.[56] Those groups, whose so-called experts generate and perpetuate dehumanizing narratives about Muslims, create a climate from which weapons manufacturers can ultimately profit.[57] The connection between dehumanizing rhetoric about Muslims at home and U.S. military interventions abroad is stronger than many realize. As scholar Stephen Sheehi writes, "The demonization of Muslims and Arabs is a process of deflection as much as justification, preventing many Americans from digesting the unfortunate realities of American Empire or at least preventing them from recognizing the humanity of those who are the victims of the Empire."[58] The dehumanization of Muslims creates these victims while also rendering them invisible to us.

Negative Coverage and
Subtle Stereotypes in Media

Another way that Islamophobia operates under the surface is through largely negative news coverage of Muslims and subtle stereotypes disseminated in Western media. We have already seen overt examples on FOX News, where programs give a wide platform for the Islamophobia network and where hosts echo their talking points. But even in media produced by well-intentioned journalists and entertainment professionals, disproportionate negativity abounds and stereotypical tropes are often employed. Numerous studies and research projects have borne this out. Scholars of media studies use a method called *sentiment analysis* to systematically analyze news stories from a range of outlets, spanning a large swath of time, to see the way they portray Muslims, Islam, and a host of other subjects and groups. One study, which examined 850,000 articles from major U.S. newspapers from 1996 to 2015, found that Muslims were portrayed far more negatively than Catholics, Jews, and Hindus, even when the study controlled for a range of other factors.[59] Another study, from 2015, examined the tone of media coverage about Islam in both American and European outlets, finding that the tone in stories about Muslims has increasingly worsened over time.[60] Those researchers also observed that, compared to other religious groups, mainstream Muslims were underrepresented in the media. In 2014, while Pope Francis was the public face in media stories about Catholics, the ISIS terrorist leader Abu Bakr al-Baghdadi was the face for Muslims. A study that looked at *New York Times* headlines found that Islam was portrayed more negatively than all other subjects it examined—not just other religions, but also drugs like cocaine.[61]

Other findings also reveal the way that violence committed by Muslims receives significantly more media attention than that committed by other individuals and groups. ISPU found that Muslims who committed acts of violence between 2002 and 2015 received twice as much coverage in the *New York Times* and *Washington Post* than non-Muslim perpetrators, and that "for 'foiled' plots, they received seven and a half times the media coverage as their counterparts."[62]

These findings, along with those of numerous other studies,[63] should not be taken to imply that journalists have the nefarious intention of portraying Muslims badly. Few, if any, do; they seek to be fair and honest in their work, upholding high journalistic standards. Yet journalists, like the rest of us, have both explicit and latent biases, which no doubt shape their work. As Islamophobia scholars Peter Gottschalk and Gabriel Greenberg have written, stereotypes become "expectations" that "shape how information about Muslims is interpreted," and lead to the public ignoring or overlooking stories that would buck those stereotypes.[64]

Like news media, entertainment media also contribute to and are products of Islamophobia. One project that tracks this is "the Riz Test," which was started by UK Muslims to measure how Muslims were portrayed in film and TV. Modeled off of the Bechdel Test, which looks at the portrayal of women in entertainment media, the Riz Test is named after the British Muslim actor Riz Ahmed, who has expressed his frustration at often being cast or considered for parts like the "Muslim terrorist" or the "oppressive Muslim male." The project's criteria for evaluating shows and movies are drawn from five common stereotypes about Muslims. It asks, is a Muslim character presented as:

1. "the victim of, or the perpetrator of terrorism"?
2. "irrationally angry"?
3. "superstitious, culturally backwards or anti-modern"?
4. "a threat to a Western way of life"?
5. "misogynistic" if male or "oppressed by her male counterparts" if female?[65]

If the answer to any of these five questions is yes, that piece of media "fails" the Riz test. And many, many do. Readers of this book may be hard-pressed to think of an example of a TV show or movie that passes this test.

The problem is not so much one single movie or show, which may portray a Muslim character as a terrorist, but more so all of them in aggregate. When Muslims are constantly and primarily portrayed in dehumanizing ways in the media, it has an impact beyond the particular episode or film, fueling both implicit and explicit biases that in turn affect the way Muslims are treated in society. The goal of the Riz Test is to draw attention to the pervasiveness of these stereotypes, and to push for more diverse representation of Muslims in entertainment, portrayals that more accurately reflect their lives and attitudes. Negative media portrayals of Muslims not only affect non-Muslims' perceptions, but they also take a toll on Muslims, especially children. When they see how Western media constantly send the message that Muslims are "bad guys," Muslim children can be made to feel unwelcome in the societies they call home.

Stopping the Spiral

Even when Islamophobia is not always overt or obvious, it remains a deep and pervasive problem that impacts the lives of many, and serves to uphold systems of power and privilege that benefit some and marginalize others. Islamophobia is a multifaceted phenomenon—one that is both private and public, both attitudinal and institutional, committed by individuals while also being state-driven. The different forms of Islamophobia are not walled off from each other but rather shape each other. Scholar Khaled Beydoun calls this "dialectical Islamophobia," an "ongoing dialogue between state and citizen that binds the private Islamophobia . . . to the war-on-terror policies enacted by Presidents George W. Bush, Obama, and Trump."[66] Disrupting this downward spiral of Islamophobia may seem like a massive undertaking, and indeed it is. But by learning and educating ourselves about these dynamics of Islamophobia, we have already begun the task.

6

WE SHOULD KNOW BETTER

Thinking Differently and Uprooting Stereotypes

The problem is not that we have doubts and fears. The problem is when they condition our way of thinking and acting to the point of making us intolerant, closed, and perhaps even—without realizing it—racist. In this way, fear deprives us of the desire and ability to encounter the other, the person different from myself; it deprives me of an opportunity to encounter the Lord.

—Pope Francis, Message for the 105th
World Day of Migrants and Refugees, 2019[1]

Amid the dust and debris of crumbling apartment buildings in a war-torn neighborhood of Damascus, Syria, men wearing protective helmets cried, "Allahu akbar!" The sound of bombs echoed in the distance as they clamored over the rubble. "Allahu akbar!," they yelled repeatedly.

These men were not launching the bombs but rescuing a child. As part of a civilian rescue team, they pulled out the little girl who had been buried under twisted wire and cinder blocks by a recent airstrike.[2] By the grace of God, the toddler was alive, and the men voiced their shock and relief with cheers of "God is greatest!," which is what "Allahu akbar" means in Arabic.

Most of us do not immediately associate this phrase with lifesaving rescues, but rather with war and jubilant disregard for life. In a 2013 interview, South Carolina senator Lindsey Graham said he associated the phrase with a "war chant."[3] His reaction is likely not dissimilar to our own. In news media coverage of the Iraq War and the conflict in Syria, many of us have only heard shouts of "Allahu akbar" accompanying images of successful rocket launches and the sound of gunfire. We rarely if ever hear it in the range of ordinary contexts that it is used—in prayer, in celebration, in excitement, and in moments of fear. Just as in English people say, "Oh my God!" or "Thank God!" in a range of scenarios, so do Arabic speakers with "Allahu akbar!" When a flash flood swept through the ordinarily dry walkways of Petra, the UNESCO World Heritage site known for its ancient buildings carved into red rock-faces in the Jordanian desert, a man filmed the rising water and expressed his panic and surprise through a repeated "Allahu akbar." Though fighters in a conflict may use the phrase "God is greatest," it is not solely their possession.

For Muslims around the world, many of whom are nonnative Arabic speakers, "Allahu akbar" is a phrase they use and encounter daily in the context of prayer. The phrase is the first and repeated line of the Islamic call to prayer, the *adhan* (pronounced "athan" or "azan"). It is a way of praising God, affirming God's greatness. Occasionally in news or entertainment media, we get to hear this "Allahu akbar" in the context of Islamic prayer. But even then, its ordinary meaning can be clouded by connotations of violence. We unconsciously import our association between "Allahu akbar" and violence into this prayerful picture, thus tainting the gestures and words of Islamic prayer with the stereotype that "Muslim equals violent." Or worse yet, images of Muslims praying and violence are explicitly linked in movies and television shows. Muttering Arabic prayers and bowing in prostration, Muslim perpetrators are portrayed as people whose motives can be easily explained by their apparent religiosity. Together, these layers upon layers of association—which equate violence with Arabic, Allah, and prayer—leave us with patterns of thinking that do not match reality and are hard to escape.

A New Heart, A New Head

We need to rethink what we've been taught. In the Christian tradition, we are constantly called to *metanoia*—conversion, repentance, change of heart. One of my teachers, the theologian Leo Lefebure, translates this Greek word in a literal way: *metanoia* is about "getting a new head." This is what we are called to, as Christians, when it comes to Islamophobia and our relationships with Muslims—to get a new perspective, a new heart, a new head.

Too frequently, the things we say about Muslims or the questions we ask about them are based on flawed logic or uncharitable sentiments. They emerge out of double standards, generalizations, or stereotypes that are usually unconsciously held but nonetheless serve to uphold unequal and harmful treatment of Muslims. These ideas and questions fuel Islamophobia or are the result of it. In previous chapters, we have already gotten a sense of some of the underlying political, economic, and even psychological reasons why stereotypes have come to define our collective thinking about Muslims. Here, I continue to shed light on these motives but also address the ideas themselves, debunking them and focusing on the conceptual problems that undergird them.

Unraveling Islamophobic ways of thinking also requires us to step back and critically consider the ways we think about religion and its place in people's lives. So often, the perpetuation of Islamophobia relies on unnuanced thinking about religion in general and about Islam specifically, approaches that we would rightly be resistant to if applied to our own religion. In this chapter, I also address issues in our vocabulary, looking at inconsistencies in the way we use English terms like *terrorism*, and how our usage of words and phrases like *sharia*, *jihad*, and *Allahu akbar* do not reflect what they typically mean when Muslims use them.

"Why Don't Muslims Condemn Terrorism?"

During a papal press conference in 2014, Pope Francis called on Muslims to condemn acts of terrorism committed by their co-religionists. "There needs to be international condemnation from Muslims across the world. It must be said, 'No, this is not what the Quran is about!'"[4] American political commentators and other Christian leaders have voiced this sentiment, too. In 2015, Cardinal Timothy Dolan, the archbishop of New York, wrote in the *New York Post*, "We encourage the majority of Islam to speak up and condemn these attacks ... and say, 'This is not Islam.'"[5]

This persistent refrain asking Muslims to condemn terrorism is almost always well intentioned; many of those voicing it have actively sought to combat untrue and unfair perceptions of Muslims. But this question is one we must let go of, for at least three reasons. First, Muslims all over the world are already condemning terrorism and violence—constantly. As Islamic studies professor Omid Safi said nearly twenty years ago, "I feel like I've lost my voice from speaking out."[6] Evidence of these condemnations is just a Google search away. If one types in "Muslim condemnations of terrorism," countless entries will come up, including extensive databases, statements signed by Muslim religious leaders of various denominations, news reports of massive demonstrations, and social media campaigns launched by ordinary believers.[7] Many often invoke their Islamic faith tradition to demonstrate why these acts are wrong. This was the approach taken in an open letter signed by dozens of prominent Islamic scholars,[8] who extensively cited precedents in their religious tradition to show how the atrocities committed by ISIS contradict both "the spirit and the letter" of Islam.[9] When news commentators, politicians, and major Christian leaders call on Muslims to condemn terrorism, it implies that Muslims are not already speaking out and it leaves the public with a false perception of Muslim silence. On my social media feeds, after acts of terrorism, I see countless posts from Muslim friends and colleagues expressing horror, heartbreak, condemnation, and anguish at the loss of life committed by those who would dare invoke their Islamic faith.

The second problem with this question is that, as Islamophobia scholar Todd Green puts it, it "assumes an inherent link between Islam and violence."[10] It implies that ordinary Muslims are somehow guilty of or implicated in the violence of groups like ISIS and Al-Qaeda. We can see how false and unfair this is when we apply this logic to ourselves. When a Christian group commits an act of violence and claims to do so out of Christian convictions, outsiders should not (and typically do not) assume that the rest of us would approve of that harmful behavior. We are not perceived and treated as if we bear responsibility, nor should we be. Of course, we often feel compelled to speak out against these vile acts committed by those who share our faith, just as Muslims do. So many of us want our religious communities to be more just, and we do what we can to shape them for the better, while speaking out and letting those beyond our fold know that the harm caused by some of us is not an accurate reflection of our faith's ideals and norms. Muslims, as we have seen, do the same.

To reiterate, when we demand that Muslims condemn terrorism, we are wrongly presuming that all Muslims are inherently linked to this violence. This notion stems from the racialized stereotype that Islam, at its core, is about violence. In other words, we assume that all Muslims are, by default, violent, unless they explicitly disavow it or actively demonstrate to us that they are not. But we should not presume all Muslims guilty in this way.[11] The vast majority of Muslims have no ties to this violence. The fact that they share a religious affiliation with the perpetrators does not mean they have some kind of intrinsic connection to the actions of terrorists or bear responsibility for them.

The third reason we should let go of the demand for Muslims to condemn terrorism is because, as Todd Green has also written, it serves as a distraction.[12] When we call on Muslims to condemn terrorism, we do it—perhaps unconsciously—to deflect attention away from our own failures and complicity. It sets up an us-versus-them scenario, in which *they* are the unique source of the world's violence and terrorism, and *we* are the innocent victims. This keeps us from examining the complex set of factors that play a role in the violence we see around the world—including our own country's and religious community's actions. As we have already seen, American and European imperial endeavors have been responsible for much suffering in the world, but that can be glossed over when the conversation is perpetually about Muslims and terrorism.

Instead of asking "Why don't Muslims condemn terrorism?," we should grapple with new questions:[13] Why hasn't the media highlighted these condemnations? Why have the rest of us assumed that Muslims wouldn't condemn terrorism? Why have we failed to take notice of their myriad condemnations of violence? It has been easier for us to wrongly blame Islam and Muslims wholesale, rather than look at the more complex reasons behind acts of violence.

Coded Language:
The Problem with "Terrorism"

Embedded in the question "Why don't Muslims condemn terrorism?" is another problematic assumption—that "only Muslims commit acts of terrorism." It's a refrain that I hear often, but this is false logic. Rather, the problem is the other way around. Most of the time, acts of violence only end up being labeled *terrorism* when they are committed by Muslims.[14] During the last two decades, the word *terrorism* in Western media has been used primarily to describe violence committed by Muslims—think about the implicit targets of the war on terror—while it has rarely been applied to violence committed by people identified differently.[15] When Stephen Paddock killed 58 civilians and wounded 413 others in a concert shooting in Las Vegas—the largest "mass shooting" ever in the Western Hemisphere[16]—government and law enforcement were quick to say it was not a case of terrorism after it came to light that the perpetrator was not Muslim.[17] In one study looking at American newspaper coverage of mass shootings from 1999 to 2018, the researcher found that the words "terrorism" and "terrorist" were "much more likely to appear" in news articles about Muslim shooters than White ones, despite the fact that all of these mass-casualty events were very similar.[18] Each shooting had seven or more casualties, and many were committed by perpetrators who espoused an ideology that was thought to motivate their attack. Yet only some of these were described with the label "terrorism."

In our public discourse terrorism has been reduced to a code word for "Muslim violence."[19] A White person could (and often does) commit the same act, with similarly unclear motives, and only the case of the Muslim perpetrator will be called terrorism. In recent years, especially in the wake of Dylann Roof's White nationalist–motivated massacre of nine Black people in their church in North Carolina in 2015, journalists and the public have begun to recognize the double standard in the way this "terrorist" descriptor has been applied to some forms of violence and not others. Many argue that we should begin using the term more evenly or consistently.

Yet the association between "terrorism" and Muslims is hard to shake. On a Friday night in 2019, I ate dinner with my television tuned to CNN, but muted, watching the ticker feed crawl across the bottom of the screen. The news channel was reporting on a terrorist attack that had taken place in New Zealand. I had already heard the tragic news when I woke up that morning— that an Australian White nationalist had killed more than fifty Muslims at two mosques in the city of Christchurch. But as I watched the coverage on CNN, with the sound turned down, I realized that many viewers might not be getting this picture of the events. Even if they knew that Muslims were the attack's victims, seeing the word "terrorism" (and no indication of the perpetrator or his motives) might lead viewers to believe that the massacre was committed by a Muslim, and was some sort of "Islamist" or "jihadist" attack. It appeared to me that CNN, in covering the attack as "terrorism," was attempting to use the term more fairly and evenly, responding to the criticism that the word had been applied in a lopsided way for too long. But as I watched, I was not convinced that the casual viewer would realize the subtlety in what CNN was trying to do. I'm sure many viewers—occasionally glancing at a screen headlined with the word "terrorism" while distracted by other things—came away from the TV thinking that a Muslim perpetrated the attack, when in reality it was something far different.

Because of the word *terrorism*'s sticky associations with Muslim-committed violence, I am skeptical that the term can adequately be rehabilitated, stripped of its implicit connotation, and redeployed in a more neutral way in public discourse and journalism. There is no universally accepted definition of the word among academics and journalists, and on top of that, the way that law enforcement labels and prosecutes terrorism contributes to the notion that only Muslims commit acts of terrorism.[20]

What is the solution to this problem? Rather than applying the term *terrorism* more liberally in our public discourse, we should instead focus on being more specific about the cases of violence we are describing. When we slap the label *terrorism* onto any act of violence committed by a Muslim, we ascribe a false sense of unity to these attacks implying wrongly that they are all cut from the same religiously motivated cloth, when in fact they might have very different motivations, contexts, and so on. Regardless of whatever shifts occur in our public discourse, it is important that we as consumers of media are cognizant of how "terrorism" tends to be employed and the impact it has in the way we think about and punish violence.

Other words in our public discourse are also often used as coded references to Muslims—words like *fanatic, fundamentalist,*[21] *extremism,*[22] and *radicalization*. Though the latter two terms have in recent years been more readily applied to White nationalist violence and motivations, the ease with which they are applied to Muslims (and the hesitancy that many have in applying them to others) is evident. When Ted Cruz and other Republican presidential candidates during the 2016 campaign constantly invoked the threat of "radical Islamic terrorism," they were not employing a technical term but lumping together three words that each on their own would be enough to prompt the image of scary Muslims in the minds of the American public.[23]

"Islam Says . . .":
Rethinking Religion

Religion is not like the Matrix. Believers don't "plug in" to
their sacred texts and download a program that automati-
cally makes them think and act in a certain way.

—Todd Green[24]

"I think Islam hates us." When he was running for president in 2016, then-candidate Donald Trump declared this in an interview with CNN anchor Anderson Cooper.[25] It was a revealing, if not totally coherent, turn of phrase. Never clarifying who "us" is—is it Americans, the West, or another collective?—he spoke as if Islam, a religious tradition of over a billion and a half individuals, was a person with opinions, or an agent that exerts its will over others. Despite the strangeness of talking about a religion in this way, Trump is not alone; it's a common way of talking about religion—especially Islam—in our society. We imagine religions as forces that, through a holy book or an authoritative body, impose a set of beliefs and required actions on people. In the case of Islam, it is seen as a monolithic religion that, at its essence, is about violence and domination, and that compels its adherents to carry out this singular and threatening mission.

Frequently, bloggers tell us that the Qur'an *mandates* persecution of non-Muslims, leaving out the fact that many Muslims read the Qur'an as commanding tolerance and hospitality. Best-selling books and op-ed headlines decry "Islam's oppression of women," ignoring aspects of the tradition that facilitate empowerment and equity, and the ways that Muslims have harnessed their religion to advocate for women's rights. Though these ways of speaking are quite commonplace, the above examples are evidence of flaws in how we think about religion, its relationship to other facets of society, and how it functions in people's lives. Religious traditions are vast and varied, and religious people have widely diverging viewpoints on what is true and ways of practicing their faith. People interpret sacred texts in diverse ways, and often disagree with one another about beliefs and how to go about daily living. This is true of Muslims, Islam, and the Qur'an, just as it is within the fold of Christianity, where there are vastly different perspectives on how to interpret the Bible, how to pray, and how to live.

In 2018, then–attorney general Jeff Sessions cited a passage of the Bible in an attempt to give a religious justification for separating migrant parents from their children along the U.S.-Mexico border.[26] He pointed to the thirteenth chapter of Paul's Letter to the Romans, in which Paul encourages Christians to follow the law of the land. Many Christians objected to his interpretation and application of this passage, noting the many ways that Jesus and his followers bucked the norms and laws of their society in order to protect the most vulnerable. The same internal disagreements occur among Muslims. If a militant group appeals to a passage of the Qur'an to try to explain its brutality, many more Muslims will interpret it differently, or will not even think about that passage in forming their self-understanding as Muslims.

We often imagine Muslims to be automatons who get clear and singular commands from the Qur'an that they then are forced to apply in their daily life. That's not how Islam, or religion more broadly, works. The words of scripture, whether it is the Bible or the Qur'an, do not have one and only one possible meaning. Christians and Muslims both have interpreted the passages from their respective scriptures in myriad ways, and both traditions recognize that scripture can have multiple layers of meaning—literal, allegorical, and so forth. Not only that, but people bring their own biases, ideas, goals, and cultural contexts to the texts they read, and these lenses factor heavily into the meanings that readers glean from a holy text.

We know from our experience as Christians that religion is complicated. It involves people interpreting and negotiating among scriptural commandments, religious norms, societal expectations, their own personal preferences, and perhaps even their own experience of God in prayer. Islam is no different. As a religious tradition with centuries of diverse views applied in many settings, and with no formal clergy or centralized churchlike institution, Islam does not simply "say" one thing.[27] Much less should Islam be equated with its worst interpretations. Just as we do not give Christianity's worst adherents the right to define the religion, we should not allow Muslims who interpret their religion in harmful ways—or anti-Muslim voices who cherry-pick the worst examples—to speak for Islam or Muslims as a whole.

Unfortunately, this is what often happens. Anti-Muslim activists (not to mention more well-meaning politicians, commentators, and journalists) overlook the range of manifestations of Islam, instead treating the religion as a monolith defined by its bad apples. They conveniently bring forth the worst interpretations, and often ones that comport with common stereotypes (violence, oppression, intolerance, etc.). Even if that interpretation is only held by some and not all Muslims, they deploy it to portray all Muslims as a singular bloc who are all supposed purveyors of their harmful religion. Rather than listening to these mal-intended or ill-informed voices, who present "a version of Islam that is foreign to its own adherents,"[28] we should seek to learn about Islam from our classmates, teachers, and neighbors. What role does it play in their lives? How do they interpret it? What are the core values many of them share? Where do they differ? In undertaking this exploration, we will see that Muslims are a diverse, complicated community not unlike our own. By and large they share the goals of all people of faith—

to live in a peaceful and prosperous world around family and friends who love them, and in service of God who calls for justice, peace, and love.

It is also important for us to recognize that the concept of "religion" as we now know it has not been around forever. This insight may be surprising since it is so taken for granted. But only within the last few centuries did we start using "-isms" (like Juda*ism* or Buddh*ism*) and begin talking of entities (Christian-*ity* and Islam), understanding them as systems of beliefs and practices that exert a unique power over people and are walled off from politics and other realms of society. These ideas about religion and religions were formulated by European thinkers during the Enlightenment, as Christians in Europe were breaking into more and more denominations during the Protestant Reformation; as the Church was losing power and governing authority;[29] and as much of Africa, Asia, and the Middle East—not to mention the Americas—were being colonized by European powers. The concept of religion helped Christians in Europe and beyond to make sense of these "others," and it was subsequently adopted globally as all people came into contact with difference and absorbed these European categories. All of this is not to say that people were not "religious" before this time. Of course, they were. People lived in accordance with beliefs about God and the world, carried out rituals in houses of worship and beyond, and identified as Christians, Muslims, and so on. But there was little to no talk of religions as if they were agents or persons, like we see today, nor was there the clear modern-day distinction we make between religious and secular spheres.

The boundary between what is "religious" and what isn't is not as clear as we often make it out to be. As journalist Jeffrey Goldberg wrote back in 1997, "Religious persecution seldom takes place in a vacuum. Countries like the Sudan, China and Cuba, all of which oppress Christians with vigor, regularly violate almost every recognizable human right. How, then, does one categorize a Catholic priest who is thrown in jail for attacking the government: as a religious martyr or a political prisoner—or both?"[30] His question highlights the fuzziness of the border between religion (itself a category forged only in recent centuries) and other realms of life. This fuzziness is another reason why it is not helpful to talk about religion as "motivating" violence, oppression of women, persecution, and so on without considering the other factors at play. Social and political factors usually explain more than theological convictions do. As Todd Green writes, "Otherwise, it makes no sense how the same religion can produce a terrorist organization [Al-Qaeda] and a Nobel Peace Prize winner [Malala Yousafzai]."[31]

This should make us more critical when we hear non-Muslims make statements like, "Islam says this," or "the Qur'an commands that." Muslims, as insiders to the tradition, can and should make normative statements about what is true or false in the eyes of God, and to make assertions about what they believe is God's will. But outsiders ought not play a role in these internal debates about what is "authentic" or "true" Islam, nor should they reduce the religion's essence to its worst manifestations. This is the kind of courtesy we expect when the roles are reversed. We do not want outsiders telling us what they think counts as "true Christianity." We also hope that they are willing to listen to our perspective seriously, rather than writing off our interpretations and instead preferring those of Christianity's main critics or worst representatives.

Instead of talking and thinking about religions as if they were persons—as Trump and so many of us often do—it may be more helpful to think of them as broad, living "traditions," chock-full of diverse aspects and shaped over time by the people and communities that claim them.

Shining a Light on Sharia

In chapter 4, we saw how anti-Muslim activists fan fears and sow misunderstanding about sharia, much in the same way that "papist" Catholics have been targeted. Anti-Muslim activists and their political allies portray sharia as a brutal legal code to which Muslims are universally adherent and that they seek to impose on everyone else. But this does not match reality. As scholars at the Bridge Initiative have summarized, "Muslims generally regard Sharia as an ethical and moral code to live by. It is not a book or a set of legal rulings; rather, it is considered divine guidance, which is interpreted by humans and laid out in a body of work called Fiqh."[32] In other words, sharia is the perfect ideal to which Muslims aspire, and fiqh is the human approximation or attempt to achieve that ideal.[33] In seeking to discern God's will for them, Muslims draw on a range of sources and methods, including the text of the Qur'an, sayings (*hadith*) and traditions of the Prophet Muhammad (or figures known as the Imams, in the case of Shi'a Muslims), analogical reasoning, communal consensus, and reason. As a human endeavor, fiqh is subject to change, and there are several different schools of thought that mutually recognize one another's legitimacy, leading to considerable diversity of opinion within fiqh.

The fourteenth-century Muslim jurist Ibn al-Qayyam wrote about the broad objectives associated with sharia:

> Shariah is based on wisdom and achieving people's welfare in this life and the afterlife. Shariah is all about justice, mercy, wisdom, and good. Thus, any ruling that replaces justice with injustice, mercy with its opposite, common good with mischief, or wisdom with nonsense, is a ruling that does not belong to the Shariah, even if it is claimed to be so according to some interpretation.[34]

Muslims have often disagreed about what constitutes justice, mercy, and goodness, and as individuals and as societies Muslims have not always lived up to these standards, enacting laws or instituting norms that have at times betrayed these ideals. But these ideals, which are shared broadly by religious and nonreligious communities, often guide Muslim discernment of God's will.

Contrary to the common assumption, sharia—or more accurately the fiqh rulings of scholars—was not simply adopted wholesale by pre-modern Muslim polities. Many aspects of sharia have nothing to do with courts or state enforcement, but are rather matters dealing with prayer, fasting, charitable giving, manners, and so on. These are the kinds of things most Muslims have in mind when they talk about sharia. As legal scholar Asifa Quraishi-Landes has written, something may be considered "a sin but not one that is the business of the state to punish."[35] Historically, some fiqh opinions have been considered and implemented in court settings, but sharia is not simply "the law of the land."[36] Nowadays, many governments with Muslim-majority populations have legal systems inspired and informed by fiqh rulings, but they are equally if not more influenced by European legal traditions. As we can see, sharia and Western concepts of law do not map exactly onto one another, but we would not know that from the way sharia is often framed as "Islamic law" in public discourse.

Though the word and idea of sharia are top of mind for many Christians and Westerners when they think about Islam, it is not always so for Muslims. A Muslim friend of mine, who grew up in Saudi Arabia, rarely encountered the phrase or concept until she came to the United States and was exposed to the Islamophobic discourse here. Even when Muslims do use the term, and say that it guides their life, their concept differs significantly from the common stereotypes about it.[37] And the stereotypical characterization of sharia is not innocuous. When politicians like Republican Newt Gingrich say—as he did in 2016—that they want to disenfranchise or deport Muslims who "believe in sharia," they are effectively targeting the entire Muslim community, while also ascribing to them views that most do not hold.[38]

"Islam Is Not a Religion"

Also common in the United States and Europe is the idea that "Islam is not a religion." This claim is made not only by pundits of the Islamophobia network, but also has become a kind of truism in the broader public discourse. When this idea is asserted, the implication is that Islam goes *beyond* what a typical religion entails; it extends beyond belief and private rituals into public life, and as such is a "totalitarian political ideology." Islam is seen to stand in contrast to Christianity and other religions, which supposedly stick to the private realm and do not verge into politics.

The assumptions baked into this claim are problematic, in that they emerge from the distinctly modern, post-Enlightenment notion of religion as a private affair. It relies on the questionable notion that religion and secular life are easily distinguishable realms. Yet, as we know, people who believe in God—including Catholics, Jews, and others—usually have related ideas about how the world should look beyond their house of worship or home life. Ironically, some Evangelical Christians who express concern about Islam in public life themselves often push for their religious beliefs to influence American governance.[39] The fact that the Islamic legal tradition of sharia and fiqh deal with questions that speak to the whole of one's life should not be taken as a threat, nor as something utterly different from what "we" do.

The claim that Muslims are trying to impose their "way of life" on the rest of us is a talking point used to scare the American and European publics, much in the same way that Catholics in the mid-1800s were cast as wanting to subject Americans to papal law. Most importantly for us to understand is the real harm this claim can cause to Muslims, the way it is used to "otherize" Muslims and how it can be invoked to take away Muslims' rights. In the United States and beyond, individuals and communities are afforded numerous rights from the state that are tied to the fact that their religiosity is recognized as such—as religion. When Islam is declared not to be a religion, it paves the way for all those protections to be stripped from Muslims. The claim that "Islam is not a religion" has been invoked to deny or hold up mosque construction in the United States, and it has been at the root of the anti-sharia hysteria in the United States.

Jihad: Mandate to Violence?

The trope that Islam is inherently violent is probably the most familiar one. The claim provides easy, albeit inaccurate, explanations for violent attacks on civilians committed by groups like ISIS and Al-Qaeda. This idea of Muslim violence is usually linked with the Arabic word *jihad*. The term's most general definition is "to strive" or "exert oneself," and to do so with God and God's will in mind. (The word is not the sole possession of Muslims though. You will find Arab Christians who bear this as a first name, and the verb form of the word is used in Arabic translations of Paul's New Testament writings when he talks about striving to please God.) Most of us know the term because it has also been used by violent groups like ISIS and Al-Qaeda in an attempt to legitimate their cruel actions, but this goes against how the vast majority of Muslims conceive of jihad. Historically, the term was used in the Islamic legal tradition to tease out the limits and extent of acceptable warfare with non-Muslim polities, in what some have called a Muslim version of Christian just war theory. Concerns about just cause, minimizing harm, and protecting noncombatants and even the houses of worship of non-Muslims, often factored into these Muslim theorists' ideas about jihad.[40] Though some jurists interpreted the Qur'an to permit military expansion, other scholars past and present have rejected this view, which they see as contravening Qur'anic prescriptions for non-aggression.[41] The norms of just war laid out by Muslim religious scholars throughout history were not always consulted or respected by the armies of Muslim polities, which nevertheless often cast their military actions as jihad. ISIS and similar groups today trample on these norms, as contemporary Muslim scholars noted in their open letter to the late ISIS leader, al-Baghdadi.

Beyond its usage in these contexts, for most Muslims around the world the only connection to jihad is its sense of personal striving, struggling to live a good life, faithful to God, despite hardships. Inspired by this idea, a former colleague of mine who is Muslim once told me that she would like to name a future son "Jihad." But she is hesitant to do so because of the misperceptions that many in the West have about the word.

In addition to concerns and misunderstandings about jihad, another factor that bolsters the trope of Muslim violence are bloated perceptions about how many Muslims are actually involved with violent groups. The "terrorists" we hear about are an infinitesimally small minority of all Muslims. Most Muslims go about their daily lives in ordinary ways. In fact, Muslims make up the greatest share of the victims of groups like ISIS.[42]

On top of being inaccurate, the stereotype of inherent Muslim violence has other negative consequences. As we have already seen, it allows us to ignore or write off the complex social, political, and psychological reasons that lead people to harm others, and it obscures the widespread violence carried out by the United States and other Western powers, both at home and abroad, in the past and present day. Additionally, the trope has been deployed to delegitimize many Muslim movements that seek to push against oppression at the hands of Western powers or secular governments in the Middle East and elsewhere. And finally, the stereotype of "Muslims as terrorists" has also served to justify "retaliation" against ordinary Muslims, who are perceived as connected to or responsible for the actions of militant groups and lone-wolf attackers who share their faith. This collective backlash against Muslims occurs both in the form of hate crimes in North America and Europe and military operations that result in civilian deaths in Muslim-majority countries.

"Aren't Muslim Women Oppressed?"

The trope of the oppressed Muslim woman is also an entrenched and lasting one. It evokes mental images of women in headscarves, long robes, and face veils. In popular Western culture, these are often taken to be symbols of their subjugation, whereas the uncovered hair and bare arms and legs of "our" women are perceived as symbols of liberation. But the reality for Muslim women—and for those in the West—is much more complicated than that reductive dichotomy.

While in some Muslim-majority countries women struggle to attain an education, in others they far outpace men in getting advanced degrees.[43] In some they may be barred from aspects of public life, but in numerous others Muslim women have become heads of state. When it comes to women's dress, there is a wide range in what Muslim women wear. In the country of Jordan alone, where I lived for a time, I knew Muslim women who wore headscarves and some who did not. At the university where I studied, there were girls who wore T-shirts and girls who wore full body coverings along with a face veil. Most often, the clothing choices Muslim women make—including whether to wear a headscarf—are guided by the norms of the society, her particular preference, or her personal religious convictions. Iran is the only country where, as of this writing, the government universally mandates women to wear a headscarf in public.[44]

It is often said that "Islam is oppressive to women." We have already seen why this "Islam says" language is not accurate or helpful, given the vast diversity in the tradition. In their religion, Muslim women often find sources of personal and collective empowerment and fuel for gender justice. Indeed, looking back at history, there were Muslim societies where women were afforded more rights and legal protections than women in Christian realms had. At the same time, there are ways that Muslim men have constructed or invoked the tradition to deny Muslim women equality or inhibit their full flourishing. Just as Christian women are working to dismantle misogyny and gender inequality in their religious communities and institutions, so are Muslim women in their own settings, and they often have very different opinions about what constitute justice and fairness between the sexes in the eyes of God.

The "Muslim World" versus "the West"

The fact that both [Bernard] Lewis and Osama bin Laden
spoke of an eternal clash between a united Muslim world
and a united West does not mean it is a reality.

—Cemil Aydin[45]

The phrase the "Muslim world" is one commonly used today in politics, media, and everyday conversation. Yet it is a fairly recent concept in world history.[46] Though the idea of external Muslim enemies was long present in European Christendom, the idea of a monolithic Muslim entity emerged during the time that European powers were colonizing what we now call the Middle East and North Africa, where Muslims constituted the majority of the population. In the late 1800s and early 1900s, as the Ottoman Empire was crumbling, European nations including Great Britain, France, Italy, and Spain exerted political control from Morocco in the west to Persia and the Indian subcontinent in the east.

Construing Muslims as a racial group wholly separate from (and inferior to) European Christians, colonizers could justify their subjugation of them. Historian Cemil Aydin writes that "by racializing their Muslim subjects with references to their religious identity, colonizers created the conceptual foundations of modern Muslim unity."[47] In reaction to being lumped together and colonized, Muslim thinkers also started to conceive of themselves in pan-Muslim terms.

This period also saw the formulation of the idea of "the West." The phrase "the West" conveys not only a geographic location—the "Western" continents of Europe, North America, and Australia are actually distant from one another on the map—but also a set of values (enlightenment, progressivism, tolerance) and identities (Whiteness, Christianity) that "the Muslim world" is assumed to lack.

Interestingly, this bifurcation between "the Muslim world" and "the West" was built on the racial theories that gained prominence in the nineteenth century. As Aydin writes, "European missionaries or colonial officers . . . favored [the term 'Muslim world'] as a shorthand to refer to all those between the 'yellow race' of East Asia and the black race in Africa."[48] As we have already seen, the racial ideas of this period also sought to contrast Semitic peoples (which included Muslims and also Jews) with Indo-European ones. Today, Jews are typically perceived to be part of the West, which we now often refer to as "Judeo-Christian."[49] But this characterization only emerged in the 1950s in the wake of the genocide against Jews across Europe, which—as we have already seen—was founded on racial ideas that cast Jews (and Muslims) as perpetual outsiders and inferior people.

Though the "Islam versus the West" framing was adopted by people on both sides of the imagined divide throughout the 1900s, the supposed civilizational conflict between Muslims and the West gained more even traction at the end of the twentieth century and into the early twenty-first century, fueled by events like the Iranian Revolution, the 9/11 attacks, and U.S. military incursions into Afghanistan and Iraq. This framing informed how people viewed these events, and the events themselves further cemented the idea of a Muslim-Western clash. American academics–turned–war-advocates like Bernard Lewis, and leaders of militant groups like Osama bin Laden, the head of Al-Qaeda, ensured that the flawed framing stuck.

The trouble with these phrases is that they treat both "the Muslim world" and "the West" as monolithic and mutually exclusive. They ignore the fact that extraordinary diversity exists within these two entities and erase histories of intra-Christian and intra-Muslim conflict and debate. The binary also obscures the reality that Muslims and Christians, as well as Jews, Hindus, Buddhists, and others, have lived among each other in many parts of the world throughout history. Some examples of this are explored in chapter 8.

The "Islam versus the West" framing grew out of unjust world events initiated in large part by imperial powers, and it has continued to uphold harmful ways of relating ever since. Excising this framing from our discourse may be nearly impossible to achieve, especially because people's identities have been forged from this binary over the last century and a half. What we can do is make sure that when we talk about Muslims (and when we talk about ourselves as Christians), we do not feed into the idea that they are an undifferentiated bloc, that they are all the same, and that our values are wholly different from theirs. Rather than aligning with one side or the other in this imagined competition, we need to reject the idea that there are two separate teams at all.

Warping Words:
How Arabic Terms Are Weaponized
to Scapegoat Muslims

Sharia. Jihad. Allahu akbar. In our public imagination, these words and other Arabic terms have come to have sinister connotations. As we have already seen, our perceptions of them do not match how Muslims typically invoke them, or the role they play in the Islamic tradition broadly. Why is there this mismatch? Ignorance and lack of information are only parts of the problem. For the last decade, anti-Muslim activists and commentators have drawn many of these Arabic words into their broader strategy to scapegoat Muslims, and their efforts have succeeded. They pluck an Arabic word out of relative obscurity and define it in the way that fits their narrative, attaching to it their own sinister meanings and interpretations. Because many non-Muslims are unfamiliar with these Arabic terms and how Muslims employ them, we do not know any better than to absorb the definitions offered by the commentators and writers we encounter in media.

There are additional examples beyond those we have already explored. Take *dawa*, which means "call" or "invitation," and is a rough equivalent for proselytism or evangelization in the Christian tradition. It's a word that Muslims know well but few non-Muslims had heard of, until a few years back when Ayaan Hirsi Ali started invoking it frequently, defining it as "indoctrination that poisons minds"[50] and claiming that the "ultimate goal of dawa is to destroy the political institutions of a free society and replace them with the rule of sharia law."[51] Ali's colleagues took a similar approach with *taqiyya*, a very obscure word, even to most Muslims. The word for "hat" in many Arabic dialects, it refers to a rare practice of hiding one's religion in settings of hostility or persecution.[52] But anti-Muslim activists have redefined it as Muslims' supposedly stealthy means of infiltrating American society and government in order to take it over. The notion that Barack Obama was secretly Muslim and practicing this taqiyya became widespread in online memes, and the talking point was even adopted by Republican politicians like Ben Carson, who said during his presidential run, "Taqiyya is a component of Sharia that allows, and even encourages you, to lie to achieve your goals."[53] Taqiyya was portrayed as "stealth jihad"—nonviolent means to realize the same brutal outcome of sharia. During the height of the Syrian refugee crisis, anti-Muslim groups also surfaced the word *hijra*, or "migration" in Arabic, which conveniently had resonances to the world event that was top of mind. These voices defined hijra as Muslims' intentional invasion of non-Muslim spaces, as part of a unified and concerted effort to indoctrinate the world and put it under Muslim rule.[54] They thus cast all Muslim refugees as a threat, and the narrative succeeded in shaping public opinion and policy. In numerous states, Republican governors (and one Democrat) vowed to ban the entry of Syrian refugees, most of whom would have been Muslims.[55]

Stepping outside these examples and details,[56] we can see how anti-Muslim groups have capitalized on the non-Muslim public's ignorance and used it to their advantage. By introducing and redefining these words, and putting them all into a new schema that seems coherent but bears no resemblance to how Muslims use the terms, they succeed in casting all Muslims as a threat worthy of discrimination.

Conclusion

The tropes and talking points I have discussed in this chapter often fuel both the consciously held beliefs we maintain about Muslims and the latent, unconscious biases we possess. Thus, the task of intentionally grappling with these stereotypes is an important step toward uprooting Islamophobia from our psyches and its tangible impact in the world. But this is a process. Old habits die hard, and these stereotypes and entrenched ways of thinking are indeed habitual for many of us.

Still, we are called to metanoia, getting a new head, a new heart. The spiritual writer Valerie Schultz says that metanoia—real conversion and repentance—"is more lasting than a momentary epiphany, more active than an intellectual revelation. Metanoia is a radical change of heart, forcing one to dig deeply. It is a prayer answered, but it requires a further response."[57] Unlearning the flawed conventional wisdom about Muslims and beginning to think differently will take time and work. But, as Christians, we know that much can be achieved if we let God aid us in our struggle. If we let down our barriers of fear and suspicion, we can welcome in with love and trust the many good things that God and our Muslim friends have to teach us.

Part II

ISLAMOPHOBIA AND CHRISTIANS, PAST AND PRESENT

7

"In Vain Do They Worship Me"

Islamophobia among Christians Today

"Why do you call me 'Lord, Lord,' and do not do what I tell you?"

—Jesus, in Luke 6:46

In the summer of 2017, a Muslim in Texas pulled up behind a pickup truck in the evening traffic. As the truck's brake lights flashed red, a message emblazoned on a bumper sticker became visible. "Kill a Muslim for Jesus," it declared.[1]

Just a few months earlier in London, a British man named David Moffatt walked into a local bookstore. The shop was run by Muslims and featured books on Islam and religion. Moffatt began threatening to "kill the Muslims" and to blow up the store.[2] Fortunately, Moffatt ended up leaving and the store-owners called the police. He was eventually apprehended by police and pleaded guilty in court a few months later to the crime of "religiously aggravated intentional harassment, alarm and distress." When police questioned him about what he had done, he told them, "I'm not anti-Muslim, I'm Catholic"—as if being anti-Muslim were a natural expression of his Christian faith.[3]

Having looked at Islamophobia broadly in Part I of this book, we now turn our gaze back upon our own Christian communities. This chapter focuses on contemporary Islamophobia among Christians (with particular emphasis on English speakers in the United States), both its manifestations in Christian settings and the ways that Christians have contributed to it in the public sphere. Oftentimes this occurs unintentionally, but there are also many ways that Christians—whether laypeople or clergy—have deliberately promoted or enacted anti-Muslim prejudice and discrimination, sometimes even couching it in Christian language. Christian media outlets and institutions have served as platforms for the activists of the Islamophobia industry, and pastors have disseminated anti-Muslim rhetoric from the pulpit. Many Christians have been involved with anti-Muslim hate groups and at the forefront of campaigns to prevent the construction of mosques.[4] A small fraction of Christians have even gone so far as to attack religious spaces and take Muslim lives in heinous acts of violence.[5]

Islamophobia among U.S. Evangelical Christians has received considerable attention in other publications on Islamophobia,[6] but the problem extends to other branches of Christianity as well, including other Protestants, Catholics, and Eastern Orthodox Christians. My own research has focused heavily on Catholic Islamophobia in the United States, so this chapter gives the most attention to that phenomenon. To be sure, Christians of all denominations have also worked hard to dismantle Islamophobia, both inside and outside their community spaces. Many do so as an expression of their faith, and I highlight many of those examples in the book's final two chapters.

Even though Islamophobia as a phenomenon received its form and function among Western Christians and it has a unique shape in Christian contexts, Islamophobia is by no means something inherent to Christianity, nor is it solely a Christian issue. Islamophobia is also a problem in other faith groups and nonfaith populations, as we have already seen.

"For the Bible Tells Me So"?
Anti-Muslim Acts in the Name of Christian Faith

As he pushed his cart through the grocery store, a Florida man turned to a woman he was passing and said, "Merry Christmas, buddy."[7] Ordinarily a friendly greeting, this one was offered ironically. The woman was Muslim, and as he said it, he tossed a package of pork bacon into her shopping cart. Muslims by and large do not eat pork, and those seeking to harass Muslims have used pork products in an attempt to "offend" them and desecrate their holy spaces.

In the United States alone in the last several years, numerous anti-Muslim acts have been committed by people citing their Christian faith, or who have branded their actions with Christian symbols. In Delaware, vandals damaged the signage and demolished the fencing at a mosque. From the pieces of broken wood, they forged a cross and hoisted it up on the property.[8] In New Mexico, someone vandalized a mosque shortly before Christmas, spray-painting the words "Happy Birthday Jesus, from a real Christian," also writing "Trump" across the entry doors.[9] In California, vandals spray-painted "Jesus is the way" at a mosque entrance; in New York, three people burned crosses on a mosque's lawn;[10] in Colorado, a man broke into a mosque, "overturned trash cans and chairs and left a Bible in the mosque's prayer room."[11]

In Twin Falls, Idaho, where anti-Muslim hate groups have been particularly active in smearing local Muslims, someone left a cross draped in bacon at a mosque.[12]

There have also been more high-profile cases where Christian faith has been invoked in anti-Muslim acts. In 2010, amid the manufactured fervor of the Ground Zero Mosque controversy, Florida pastor Terry Jones planned to hold a public burning of thousands of copies of the Qur'an on the ninth anniversary of the 9/11 attacks.[13] Author of a book called *Islam Is of the Devil*, Jones urged other Christians to hold their own Qur'an bonfires around the country, praying as the book burned. After the plan received international criticism, he cancelled the event, but in subsequent years burned copies of the Qur'an in reaction to acts of violence committed by Muslims abroad.

Evangelical Christians and the Islamophobia Network

Months before Donald Trump called for a Muslim ban during his election campaign, a well-known Protestant evangelist and humanitarian did the same. In the midst of the increasing anti-Muslim fervor of 2015, Franklin Graham called for Muslims to be barred from immigrating to the United States, and for American Muslims to be rounded up—not unlike how Japanese and German Americans were during World War II. His justification was that Muslims have "the potential to be radicalized" and want to kill to "honor their religion and Muhammad."[14]

Many Evangelical and born-again Christians in the United States share Graham's views. As a bloc, they have much more negative views of Muslims than other Christian denominations.[15] According to one 2018 poll, 72 percent of White Evangelicals supported the Trump administration's policy to ban Muslims, the highest of any religious demographic polled.[16] Surveys have also found that White Evangelicals strongly oppose refugee resettlement in America, perhaps because many refugees are Muslim.[17] In 2019, the Institute for Social Policy and Understanding polled Americans to see if and to what extent they agree with the main stereotypical claims about Muslims that are used to justify their mistreatment—that Muslims are more prone to violence than others, more likely to discriminate against women, are hostile to the United States, are less civilized, and are partially responsible for acts of violence carried out by other Muslims. White Evangelicals were the group to hold the most Islamophobic views, and they also were the group to have the most expressly negative view of Muslims (with twice as many saying they had "unfavorable" views toward Muslims as "favorable" ones).[18] One reason for this could be that many Evangelicals do not know personally anyone who is

Muslim—only one-third reported in 2019 that they did. For all Americans and religious groups, lack of personal familiarity with Muslims is correlated with having more negative views and buying into anti-Muslim stereotypes. Protestants of other denominations typically have moderately better views than their Evangelical counterparts, particularly Black Protestants who have much less negative views than White mainline Christians.[19] More of them know Muslims, too.

In part, the Islamophobia network has become so influential in American life because of the support it receives from Evangelical Christians and the religious right. Major Christian televangelists, like Baptist Pat Robertson of the Christian Broadcasting Network (CBN), have given anti-Muslim writers and activists a platform for over a decade. CBN has frequently featured Robert Spencer, Pamela Geller, and Brigitte Gabriel as "experts" to speak to their sizable audience about Islam, and hosts have replicated their talking points alongside sinister images that make Muslims out to be universally dangerous. Robertson himself has been one of the most strident anti-Muslim voices on American airwaves, calling Muslims "crazed fanatics," comparing Islam to Nazism, and describing the religion as "almost demonic."[20] The Islamophobia network has also benefited from existing connections and activism of the American religious right. The first executive director of the major anti-Muslim group, ACT! for America, was Guy Rodgers, who had previously served as the field director for Robertson's Christian Coalition, a grassroots political organization in the 1990s that significantly shaped GOP politics.[21] Taking a similar approach of orchestrating nationwide political action in local communities around the country, ACT has succeeded in influencing GOP (and national) rhetoric and policies regarding Muslims.[22] Other well-known Evangelicals, like John Hagee and Franklin Graham, have also served as mouthpieces for anti-Muslim rhetoric and policy ideas that have been funneled out of anti-Muslim groups,[23] and less prominent pastors have also absorbed these ideas.[24]

Surveys have also been conducted of American Protestant pastors, both from Evangelical and other denominations. Compared to the U.S. public, Protestant pastors have much more negative views of Muslims, which worsened considerably between 2010 and 2015, during the height of the Islamophobia network's activity in the United States.[25] One key finding shows that over 80 percent of pastors see Christianity and Islam as fundamentally at odds, with Evangelical/born-again pastors holding this view more than mainline ones. It is not clear what these pastors take to be the source of this fundamental dissimilarity. Does it have to do with doctrinal beliefs like the Trinity or divinity of Christ; views about the (perceived) relationship between religion and politics in the two traditions; or both? This finding is not necessarily evidence of Islamophobia per se, but the fact that many Christian leaders see a chasm between their religion and Muslims' is not irrelevant to questions of prejudice. Very often, Christians' appraisal of Islam as "wholly other" is based on a warped sense of what Muslims believe, what their practice is like, and how religion factors into their lives. Much of the time—but not usually on purpose—we compare the best of our tradition with the worst of theirs. And, as we've already seen, the othering of Muslims can verge on racialized animus.

Prejudice from the Pulpit and Pews: Islamophobia and U.S. Catholics

The Church holds Muslims in high regard.

—*Nostra aetate*, 3

On a Sunday in early 2020, Catholic priests across the United States were directed by the national bishops' conference to emphasize the importance of "welcoming the stranger" in their sermons. Instead, a priest in Minnesota took to the pulpit to give a homily that sowed fear and suspicion about Muslims. Calling Islam "the greatest threat" to Christianity and to America, the Rev. Nick VanDenBroeke argued that Muslim immigration to the United States should be curtailed.

"We do not need to pretend that everyone who seeks to enter into America should be treated the same," he said.[26]

After news of the homily spread, the local chapter of a Muslim civil rights group called upon the Catholic Church to repudiate the priest's remarks. Archbishop Bernard Hebda, who leads the diocese where VanDenBroeke ministers, released a statement conveying the Catholic Church's positive teaching on Muslims and indicating that he had spoken to the priest. VanDenBroeke then published his own brief statement: "My homily on immigration contained words that were hurtful to Muslims. I'm sorry for this. I realize now that my comments were not fully reflective of the Catholic Church's teaching on Islam."[27]

However sincere it may have been, VanDenBroeke's statement failed to acknowledge the fact that the views he expressed put Muslims at risk, and it did not indicate if the priest's own views had shifted and how he would seek to make amends. More than simply "hurtful," VanDenBroeke's comments were harmful. As a prime example of scapegoating, they contribute to an us-versus-them mentality and serve to rationalize discriminatory action against Muslims. The whole incident is reflective of a broader issue in U.S. Catholicism—

the discrepancy between the Church's official teaching on Muslims (quoted in the epigraph above and which I explore later in the book) and the Islamophobia that often permeates U.S. Catholic spaces.

Polling data suggest that many U.S. Catholics hold negative and stereotypical views of Muslims. According to a 2015 survey I commissioned as part of a Bridge Initiative report on Catholic perceptions of Islam, twice as many Catholics admitted to having negative views of Muslims than positive ones.[28] A 2019 ISPU study found that Catholics' self-declared views of Muslims have improved, but a majority still say they have "unfavorable" views or "no opinion" of Muslims, compared to less than 40 percent who say they view Muslims positively.[29]

This may have to do with the fact that, over time, more Catholics have developed personal relationships with Muslims. In the Bridge survey, Catholics were slightly less likely than the general American population to know a Muslim personally. Three in ten Catholics reported that they personally know someone who is Muslim, whereas at the time other polls found that closer to 40 percent of the general American public claimed to know a Muslim. As of 2019, twice as many Catholics said they personally knew a Muslim—61 percent—exceeding the also higher national figure of 53 percent. Each poll indeed showed that Catholics who did know a Muslim personally were more likely to report favorable views of the entire group.

Still, many Catholics hold Islamophobic views, including the stereotypical notions already explored.[30] Majorities of Catholics also lack basic knowledge of Islamic beliefs and practices, and hold views that can contribute to "us versus them" attitudes. For example, when asked in the Bridge survey what the strongest similarity is between Catholicism and Islam, half of Catholics said that they couldn't name one, or that there aren't any.[31] As for their views on political issues, a 2018 survey found that 60 percent of White Catholics favored the Trump administration's "travel ban," whereas only 34 percent of Hispanic Catholics did.[32]

These views are not the result of simple ignorance and unfamiliarity with Muslims. In addition to factors outside the Catholic sphere, church media outlets and publications have also played a role. The Bridge Initiative study I penned also examined the way Islam and Muslims were portrayed in a range of Catholic media outlets. An analysis of hundreds of articles dealing with Islam from 2014 to 2015 found that they had a negative and angry sentiment overall, with some of the most prominent subjects having to do with violent attacks and refugees. The Bridge Initiative poll found that Catholics who frequently read Catholic media outlets had more negative views of Muslims than Catholics who did not frequently consume Catholic media. As for books published about Islam for Catholic audiences, the characterization of Islam as a "threat" has been one of the most consistent themes—an idea that Fr. VanDenBroeke echoed in his homily in 2020. On top of this, Catholic institutions and media outlets have actively given a platform to voices who promote prejudice and fear, including key leaders in the Islamophobia network.

The Islamophobia Network and Catholics:
The Case of Robert Spencer

Sadly, in recent years, there has been a deliberate rejection of this call to engage in dialogue with our Muslim brothers and sisters by some in the Catholic Church and in other ecclesial families.[33]

—Statement of the U.S. Bishops' Committee for
Ecumenical and Interreligious Affairs in 2014

If you ask them, many U.S. Catholics remember the opposition to the so-called Ground Zero Mosque in 2010, as well as other anti-Muslim campaigns that garnered national attention over the last several years. But what most do not realize is that one of the principal organizers behind these moments of anti-Muslim hysteria—Robert Spencer—has also been a prominent voice on Islam in U.S. Catholic circles. Since the aftermath of the 9/11 attacks, Robert Spencer has capitalized on the curiosity and fear that many Americans have about Muslims. Pitching himself as an expert on Islam, he started the blog JihadWatch and, together with Pamela Geller, founded nonprofits that have been named "hate groups" by the Anti-Defamation League and the Southern Poverty Law Center. Despite that, his work and views have reached broad audiences from FOX News to CNN to CBN, and he does speaking tours around the country (sometimes to law enforcement agencies), spreading the view that Islam is an inherently violent religion. Most of his twenty-plus books, including two *New York Times* best sellers, have been written for broad audiences. But Spencer has also written books specifically aimed at Catholics, including the reductively titled *A Religion of Peace: Why Christianity Is and Islam Isn't*.[34] Between 2003 and 2013, he published three books on Islam with Catholic publishing companies, and these books (as well as his others) are sold at many Catholic religious bookstores around the United States and online.[35] Most notably, Spencer's books have been prominently featured and sold at the Basilica of the National Shrine of the Immaculate Conception, in Washington, D.C., the largest Catholic church in North America and a pilgrimage site that sees over one million visitors a year. There, the book has been a reliable seller.[36]

With no verifiable credentials in the academic study of Islam,[37] Spencer's early writing on Islam after 9/11 shows him to be a self-identified freelancer who had only recently begun publishing in Catholic outlets on Islam, a topic about which many Americans were curious and ill-informed. In a 2002 piece in the magazine *Lay Witness*, he seems to be interested in educating Catholics about Islam for the purpose of evangelizing Muslims.[38] Though reductionist claims about Islam are present, this more measured piece stands in contrast to his later work.

Nowadays, a consistent message permeates Spencer's blog posts, book pages, and broadcast interviews: Islam is an inherently violent religion, and its true followers are bent upon subduing nonbelievers or at least subjecting them to harsh and brutal laws. "Violence and terror are the fundamentals of Islam," he declared in his 2003 book for Catholics, *Inside Islam*.[39] He portrays Islam and Muslims in an almost exclusively negative light, with his blog JihadWatch serving as a kind of litany of Muslims' worst deeds, which he consistently interprets as having their basis in the core of Islam. In his most recent book for Catholics, *Not Peace but a Sword: The Great Chasm between Christianity and Islam*, Spencer explicitly discourages dialogue and cooperation between Catholics and Muslims. The book's sinister cover features a curved sword, with the name "Muhammad" inscribed in Arabic on the blade, piercing a red cross. He argues that Catholics and Muslims have virtually nothing in common, and claims that authentic Islam teaches that Christians should be persecuted. According to Spencer, Catholics put themselves in harm's way by engaging in dialogue. Not only do his views place him in defiance of the spirit and letter of the Catholic Church's teachings on dialogue and relations with Muslims, but it also reinforces the dangerous belief that Muslims as a group are a violent threat and should be avoided and at times even opposed. Spencer has also been an outspoken critic of Pope Francis[40] and other prominent Catholics who do not share his views, saying they "advocate a strategy of submission to the Islamic State."[41]

Amid the rise in anti-Muslim attacks and hate crimes across the United States, Spencer denied the existence of anti-Muslim discrimination, calling it a "false narrative that Muslims are treated unjustly in this country."[42] At a January 2015 rally outside a Muslim conference in Garland, Texas, the force and extent of his views were on display. Speaking to the raucous crowd, he said, "They're not going to kill us in America . . . yet!" "Yet!" the crowd echoed. Pointing to the conference venue, he declared that the "goal" of American Muslims there "is exactly the same" as that of Muslim attackers who killed journalists working for the French publication *Charlie Hebdo* earlier that year.[43] "What you have across the street is the soft side of the Charlie Hebdo massacre," he said, to which one protester shouted in reply, "The underbelly of the snake!"

Despite views like these, comments that verge on incitement, and his integral role as a "misinformation expert" within the Islamophobia network,[44] Spencer's work has been given a wide platform by prominent Catholic figures and institutions, who themselves have absorbed his message. In a review of *Not Peace but a Sword* in the widely read *National Catholic Register*, the late Father C. J. McCloskey, a well-known member of Opus Dei and founder of the Catholic Information Center in Washington, DC, wrote that Spencer is "perhaps the foremost Catholic expert on Islam in our country." In praising Spencer's writing, McCloskey affirmed the mistaken yet pervasive belief that "the Muslims hate us," and writes, "at its worst, Islam is diabolical; at its best, it is a Christian heresy—not unlike Mormonism without the violence."[45] Other Catholics—many of whom have authored their own books on Islam for a Catholic audience—have boosted or endorsed Spencer's work. They include the television personality Fr. Mitch Pacwa; well-known biblical scholar Scott Hahn; radio hosts Patrick Madrid and Al Kresta;[46] and writer Rod Dreher, a former Catholic who has since converted to Orthodox Christianity.[47] Spencer has written for or been cited as an expert in a range of Catholic outlets, both mainstream and fringe.[48] He has also been a frequent speaker at major conferences at the Franciscan University of Steubenville, and interview specials with him have run on the Catholic network, EWTN. These institutions do not make mention of Spencer's work with the Islamophobia network, nor his organization's designation as a hate group. Among Catholic circles, Spencer seems to minimize his connections to Geller and his role in activities like the Ground Zero Mosque controversy. Because he flies slightly more under the radar than Geller and portrays himself as more of an intellectual than an activist, he has been able to gain and maintain a credibility among many Catholics, even some who work in high-level positions within the Catholic hierarchy.[49]

There has been some pushback, albeit limited, among U.S. Catholics against Spencer's views and uncharitable approach. A few dioceses have cancelled talks he was scheduled to give to their men's groups,[50] and some Catholic commentators penned pieces expressing their concern about his being given a platform in Catholic spheres.[51] Though the U.S. bishops have not publicly denounced Spencer, the U.S. Conference of Catholic Bishops—according to him—pulled their representative from attending an event after it was announced that Spencer would be a keynote speaker.[52]

Spencer was a longtime member of the Melkite (or Greek Catholic) Church, which is in communion with the pope in Rome. In his writing for Catholics, his Catholic identity was on full display; he wrote as an insider to his fellow Catholics. However, in 2016, Spencer reverted to Greek Orthodoxy, the tradition into which he was born.[53] Writing about that decision, Spencer has said, "The Pope's decision to become an Islamic apologist led me to reexamine some of my premises, revisit some history and theology (Christian for once), and come to some conclusions that led me to make the decision to go."[54]

The Islamophobia Network's Catholic Wing

Spencer's exit from the Catholic fold has not meant that the influence of the Islamophobia network has disappeared, nor that his views left with him. Commentators Zuhdi Jasser and Walid Phares, who are key players in the Islamophobia network and give voice to conspiracy theories, have been frequently interviewed as experts on the Catholic television channel EWTN.[55] Steve Bannon, the former Breitbart executive and Trump administration official, is himself Catholic and has worked closely with the Islamophobia network. Since leaving the administration, he has worked with and been featured as a speaker by the Dignitatis Humanae Institute, a right-wing Catholic think-tank.[56] He sees an "existential war" between the West and Islam, which he has called "something much darker" than fascism and Nazism.[57]

In recent years, a key funder of the main Islamophobia network groups began investing in a Catholic-centric endeavor. The Shillman Foundation, which funds Geller's and Spencer's groups,[58] is a financial backer of the Turning Point Project,[59] which is "dedicated to educating Catholics ... about the threat from Islam by arming them with the information ... necessary to meet the challenge."[60] The project supports the writing of William Kilpatrick, who—though lacking credentials—publishes regularly on Islam in conservative Catholic outlets and reproduces the talking points of the Islamophobia network. With a consistent narrative about the dangers of Islam, Kilpatrick believes in a "civilizational struggle with Islam."[61] His book *Christianity, Islam and Atheism: The Struggle for the Soul of the West* is published by the prominent Catholic publishing company Ignatius Press, and in 2020 he published a new book about Islam for Catholics. Like Spencer, Kilpatrick has often criticized the Catholic Church's outreach to Muslims,[62] chastising them as "Catholic enablers of Islam" who "seem to have embraced" an "Islamic cultural invasion."[63]

Numerous others have taken up Spencer's mantle and served as mouthpieces for his ideas, publishing their own books and materials and offering public talks on Islam, including Scott Hahn and Al Kresta, mentioned above.[64] Because these individuals initially rose to prominence due to other apologetic work or academic expertise, their forays into writing about Islam have been met with less resistance than Spencer's—even though their views are sometimes identical to his. The late Jesuit political theorist James Schall, himself a fan of Spencer, blogged extensively on Islam for Catholic outlets. His book of these essays was also published by Ignatius Press and received many positive reviews, despite the fact that, as Islamic studies scholar David Rahimi has observed, the book "suffers from reductionist arguments, non-existent evidence, and historical ignorance."[65] Schall engages in cherry-picking and falls into many of the fallacies and problems in discussing Islam and religion that I discussed in chapter 6. Rahimi describes how Schall "makes strange statements like 'Islam learned . . . from 9/11' and 'Islam says of itself' as though Islam is a person" or as though has a formal magisterial body—which it does not.[66]

The Catholic apologist Steven Ray is even less qualified than Schall. During a major 2018 conference lecture on Islam at Steubenville it was evident that his knowledge was slim, and he acknowledged that his preparation for the lecture consisted largely of drawing from Hahn's and Spencer's materials. Despite his dearth of expertise, his video—entitled "Islam: What Every Infidel Should Know"—has been viewed over one million times on YouTube. In it he portrays Muslims as utterly different from Catholics, makes sweeping and false generalizations about Muslim beliefs, mocks Muslim practices, and makes declarations about Islam "wanting to have jihad terrorism and sharia law; they want to impose that on the world."[67] Even longtime supporters of Ray noted the "condescending tone" he used throughout the speech.[68] Other well-known Catholics have helped normalize Islamophobic ideas in the church and beyond, including George Weigel, who authored a book called *Faith, Reason, and the War against Jihadism.*

Though it may lack the intentional orchestration of the broader Islamophobia network, a de facto network of Catholic voices and institutions who spread fear and misinformation about Muslims has taken shape in recent years. These authors often cite and endorse one another, cross-post each other's writings online, and replicate the same anti-Muslim messages in their respective contexts, leading them to become conventional wisdom in Catholic circles. Much as FOX News, CBN, and Breitbart became platforms for the broader Islamophobia network to regularly disseminate their message, some Catholic sites and institutions have done the same for these voices.

When Leaders Let Us Down:
Islamophobia and the Catholic Hierarchy

While perusing the produce section at Costco a few years back, my husband and I ran into a priest from a parish we had formerly attended in Washington, DC. After we exchanged pleasantries, he asked me what I did for a living. At the time I was working at the Bridge Initiative. After I briefly explained that I did research on Islamophobia there, his friendly face contorted into a skeptical reaction. He insisted that Islam was a "dehumanizing" religion and that the bearers of "true Islam" were the fighters of ISIS. I listened quietly and patiently, while trying to provide a more nuanced view and politely challenge his assumptions, but to no apparent avail. I left the conversation disappointed and troubled, for two reasons. The first was that a priest, a faith leader with the ability to influence the thinking of so many people, held such views and feelings about Muslims. It was clear to me that his views did not come from knowing anyone who was Muslim personally or learning about Islam from them. Rather—and this was the second reason—he seemed to be getting his information from anti-Muslim sources that have proliferated extensively in Catholic circles in the United States. To my knowledge, no survey has been conducted of Catholic priests in the United States or elsewhere on their views of Islam and Muslims. But my years of research and anecdotal evidence indicate that anti-Muslim views—shaped by mainstream news and politics, as well as Catholic outlets—are fairly common among clergy.

Though Pope Francis and other bishops have actively resisted anti-Muslim fearmongering, the Vatican and episcopal hierarchy have had their own challenges with Islamophobia, which church leaders have sometimes normalized despite their good intentions and other positive work on Muslim-Christian relations. In 2012, Cardinal Peter Turkson of Ghana screened a short YouTube video for over two hundred bishops gathered in Rome for a major bishops' meeting.[69] It was the xenophobic *Muslim Demographics* video discussed in chapter 3, which uses shoddy statistics on Muslim birthrates to sow concern about Muslims upending Western culture and Christianity in Europe and North America. After the screening came to light, which the Vatican radio outlet characterized as "anti-Islamic propaganda,"[70] Turkson apologized and said he did not mean to offend or denigrate Muslims.[71] Turkson is not alone among Catholic cardinals in sowing fear about Muslims in Europe. In 2016, Austrian Cardinal Christoph Schönborn warned in a homily about Muslims' supposed intention to launch a "third attempt at an Islamic conquest of Europe."[72]

In 2006, Pope Benedict XVI spoke in Regensburg, Germany, on the topic of faith and reason. At one point in the speech, to make a point about the relationship between religion and violence in Islam, he quoted a fourteenth-century emperor, Manuel II Paeologus, who had said, "Show me just what Mohammed brought that was new, and there you will find things only evil and inhuman, such as his command to spread by the sword the faith he preached."[73] This reductive statement is not only a betrayal of the reality of history, but its inflammatory nature reflects the common tropes of Islam's inherent violence, barbarity, and evilness. Both Christians and Muslims globally were stunned that Pope Benedict had made such a remark, and a small number of Muslims in different places attacked churches and Christian indi-

viduals in retaliation. Benedict apologized for the statement and said that
the quotation did not reflect his personal views. Even so, he used the quotation with a purpose in his speech, as part of a section arguing that the Islamic
notion of God leads to violence among Muslim believers.

During his pontificate Pope Benedict undertook steps that marginalized
some of the Church's dialogue activities with Muslims.[74] One of Benedict's
advisers on Islam was the Egyptian Jesuit priest and scholar Samir Khalil
Samir, who himself has published a book for Catholics on Islam that is sold
widely in U.S. Catholic bookstores.[75] Like so many others whose ideas we
have already explored, Samir has expressed the view that Islam is inherently
prone to violence[76] and subscribes to other fallacies and stereotypes in his
assessment of Islam (many of which he claimed Pope Benedict shared).[77] In
a 2017 interview with *National Catholic Register*, Samir claimed that ISIS "is
applying Islam." In speaking of the wide condemnations that ISIS received
from Muslim leaders worldwide, Samir declared, "This is in fact a lie. It has
100% to do with Islam. . . . They're not doing anything against Islamic law."[78]
It is not only Pope Benedict who has drawn from and lifted up the views of
Samir;[79] so has Robert Spencer, who wrote that "Fr. Samir Khalil Samir stands
out among Catholic authorities in being unafraid to speak honestly about the
nature and magnitude of the jihad threat."[80] Samir himself lists three books by
Spencer in his own book, *111 Questions on Islam*.[81]

The American cardinal Raymond Burke has similar views. Though he no
longer holds the prominent Vatican position he occupied under Benedict, he
is a trusted figurehead for traditionalist Catholics who are unhappy with Pope
Francis on a range of issues (including Francis's less oppositional approach to
Muslims). Having absorbed many of the talking points and conspiracy theories advanced by the Islamophobia network, and allying himself with Steve
Bannon, Burke has made statements like, "If you really understand Islam, you
understand that the Church really should be afraid of it,"[82] and "When they
[Muslims] become the majority in any country they have the duty to submit
the whole population to Shariah."[83] Burke has also echoed the idea that Islam
is not a religion but fundamentally a political ideology bent on world domination, and thus that the United States should curb Muslim immigration, calling
it a "patriotic" action. In a quote that reveals the eventual discriminatory ends
of all these views, Burke has encouraged Catholics to be suspicious of every
Muslim:

> And while our experience with individual Muslims may be one of
> people who are gentle and kind and so forth, we have to understand
> that in the end what they believe most deeply, that to which they
> ascribe in their hearts, demands that they govern the world.[84]

Not only is this untrue and a dangerous case of scapegoating, but also, as we see in chapter 9, this kind of suspicious attitude toward Muslims stands in direct contradiction to teachings promulgated by the Catholic Church.

Whose Religious Freedom?
Prioritizing Christians at Muslims' Expense

Since the early years of the Obama administration, religious liberty has been a key priority and rallying cry for politically conservative American Christians, both Catholic and Protestant. Oftentimes, however, that concern was mainly for the religious freedom of their fellow Christians at home and abroad, and has not extended to Muslims in the United States or in other Western countries. Starting in 2012, the U.S. Conference of Catholic Bishops launched its annual religious freedom campaign for prayer, education, and political action for religious liberty issues.[85] It focused on conscience exemptions for religious institutions on issues related to contraception and same-sex marriage (an issue that mainly affected Catholic schools and hospitals). This focus on "the freedom to serve" was severely out of touch with the pressing challenges to religious liberty that Muslims were facing during those years, namely a rise in hate crimes, brutal assaults, and attacks on houses of worship. In 2016—the year that saw the highest rate of anti-Muslim hate crimes in over a decade—the only reference to Muslims in the materials on the USCCB's Fortnight webpage was in an article that spoke about "militant factions of Islam" that "kill Christian believers" in the Middle East. It took years and considerable pushing from myself and others for the USCCB to even give lip service to American Muslims' religious liberty during their annual religious freedom campaigns.

Additionally, in the United States, Christians' very real concern about the persecution of Christians has sometimes been framed through an Islamophobic lens. Christian persecution in Muslim-majority contexts is often portrayed or interpreted as an inherently religious problem, or as having a unique character when compared to other cases of Christians persecuted by other religious groups. This problem is reflected in how the organization Open Doors (whose data is widely cited in news media) classifies cases of Christian persecution. Open Doors puts cases of so-called Islamic oppression in a separate category from others they see as resulting from "religious nationalism." The former is vaguely defined as having anything to do with Muslim perpetrators, while the latter includes all other religious perpetrators "other than Islam" (Hindu, Buddhist, Jewish, etc.).[86] The choice to pull Muslims out into a separate category makes it seem that persecution of Christians is inherently different among Muslims and emerges more organically from the core of Islam than it does in other religions. This classification also obscures the other social and political factors that may play into these cases. A more objective approach would be to include cases of Muslim persecution of Christians in the broader religious nationalism category, or to break apart the religious nationalism category into the range of religions it encompasses.

On a related note, advocacy and political action for persecuted Christians in the Middle East often does not extend beyond those harmed by Muslims.[87] For example, Washington, DC-based advocates are often very quiet on the ways the Israeli state has persecuted Christians in Israel and the occupied Palestinian territories.[88] This imbalance, along with the public's lack of awareness of positive Muslim-Christian relations in the Middle East, leaves American Christians believing that Christian persecution is inherently an Islamic problem, further solidifying already-widespread anti-Muslim sentiment.

"Speaking the Truth in Love," or Sowing Stereotypes?

In the last couple of decades, numerous memoirs have been published telling the stories of Muslims who converted from their former faith to Christianity. Published by well-known Christian institutions in both Catholic and Protestant spheres, these stories often follow a similar pattern—a young man or woman is raised Muslim in a majority-Muslim country or community, moves away, and becomes Christian.[89] In some cases, these individuals claim to have been former terrorists or would-be extremists.[90] These accounts can be hard to verify, as authors often go by pseudonyms or change their names, claiming that they would be violently targeted if they were identified. Some of these books set up a stark contrast between a very negative experience of Islam and their positive experience of Christianity, a dichotomy that makes many Christian readers feel validated but is hardly a universal experience. These authors—as well as others with similar backstories who have not published memoirs but travel the United States giving speaking tours about Islam in churches[91]—embody a kind of "insider status" that few would challenge. Some of these individuals echo the anti-Muslim claims of the Islamophobia network,[92] and a few work with them directly. A self-described former terrorist, Walid Shoebat was a key player in the Islamophobia network before a CNN investigation seriously called into question the veracity of his story and credentials.[93]

The proliferation of these kind of narratives in the post-9/11, war-on-terror era is also evidence of the market for "us versus them," "Islam versus Christianity" narratives, which in turn can be harnessed for political purposes or foreign policy goals. In this context, at a time when Muslims in the United

States and elsewhere are already misunderstood and often scapegoated, allowing one's own Christian conversion to contribute to the demonization of Muslims is at odds with the gospel message to love our neighbor.

A cohort of Arab Christians who were born into the faith[94] and former Muslims who have not converted to Christianity[95] also play a significant role in sowing Islamophobia. Termed "validators" by the Center for American Progress report on the Islamophobia network, these include Brigitte Gabriel and Walid Phares, both of whom are Arab Christians from Lebanon. According to a *Mother Jones* investigation, during the Lebanese civil war, Phares was one of the "chief ideologists" for a Christian militia group that was involved with massacres against Muslims.[96] Today, Phares, a Maronite Catholic, makes frequent appearances on the Catholic news channel EWTN. Gabriel, who runs the anti-Muslim group ACT for America, cites her experience growing up during the Lebanese civil war as evidence of her knowledge of the threat of Islam, though historians and those who knew her during the war have cast doubt on her story and noted major inaccuracies in her portrayal of events.[97] Christians in the United States, however, do not recognize these problems, and by and large find Gabriel's supposed "insider" perspective convincing.

"Not Peace but a Sword": When Christians Advocate Violence

In a YouTube video seen thousands of times, a man with slicked-back black hair sits in a dark room, the light of the computer screen illuminating his face. He speaks to another man over a videoconference feed, and to his many viewers. "They must convert or be wiped off the face of the earth," he says.[98]

Contrary to stereotypical expectations, this video was not published online by a militant Muslim group, but by a Catholic writer in the United States. Taylor Marshall, who has a following of over eighty thousand on Twitter, posted the video as part of a conversation series he tapes with Timothy Gordon, also a Catholic.

"You can't have coexistence with Islam. Period," Marshall continued.

Gordon agreed. "There's no coexisting. It's like what Wyatt Earp's little brother tells him. 'They're bugs, Wyatt. There's no live and let live with bugs.'"

Marshall, who had also spoken of Catholics' duty to oppose this "evil," nodded.

This is an incredibly jarring exchange. Readers who have read about or studied the precursors to genocide will know that equating an entire group of people to insects is a common tactic in the dehumanization that often ends in mass violence.

This kind of incitement has been invoked by other Christians, too. In 2015, then Liberty University president and prominent Evangelical Jerry Falwell Jr. encouraged his student body to carry weapons to "end those Muslims."[99] In tragic cases, some of which we have already explored in this book, Christians have carried out these kinds of injunctions, targeting Muslims violently. In Kansas in 2016, after the election of Donald Trump, three men formed a group they called "the Crusaders" and plotted an attack against local Muslims.[100] They planned to detonate two large truck bombs outside an apartment complex where mainly Somali Muslim immigrants and other refugees lived. Fortunately, their plot was foiled by law enforcement, and they were arrested and convicted, though not on terrorism charges.[101]

Christian religious language has also been invoked in U.S. wars against Muslim opponents.[102] During 2010, it came to light that U.S. military personnel were using weapons in Iraq and Afghanistan that had biblical quotes inscribed on them.[103] The scopes of these guns featured coded references from the New Testament about Jesus.

Christian Zionism and the State of Israel

In Christian circles, especially among Evangelicals, Islamophobic sentiments and ideas are often tied to a particular political agenda for the state of Israel.[104] Holding to a theo-political ideology known as Christian Zionism,[105] they believe that, in order to usher in the second coming of Christ and the end times, there needs to be conflict in the Middle East and that all of the territory of biblical Israel needs to be held by the current Israeli state. As religion scholar Steven Fink writes,

> a fundamental Christian Zionist belief is that Jesus will take his true believers into heaven during the rapture and will subsequently return to earth, but only after Israel, especially Jerusalem, is completely under Jewish control and contains a majority Jewish population. Palestinians are the adversary, since their presence and influence in the region must be greatly diminished, if not obliterated, for the desired eschatological events to occur.[106]

In the same article, Fink later notes,

> Constructing Islam, the religion of most Palestinians, as essentially evil and violent, Christian Zionist leaders seek to make this choice extremely obvious, as if there was no need whatsoever to even

question the position that the United States should support Israel rather than its malignant Palestinian "enemies."[107]

In the eyes of Christians who hold these ideas, Islam is the Antichrist,[108] and Judeo-Christian conflict with Muslims in the Middle East is a necessity.[109]

Many American Christians accept this theological message and political agenda in part because of their ignorance about the gross injustices and inequality that persist in the Israeli state and the Palestinian territories over which Israel asserts control, including the way the Israeli government seizes Palestinians' homes and property, engages in systematic intimidation and humiliation of Palestinians, denies their freedom of movement, and often lets the killings of Palestinians by military personnel or vigilantes go unpunished—to name just a few of the present problems. To be sure, there has been Palestinian resistance to this state of affairs, and sometimes it has involved violence, including reprehensible attacks against Israeli civilians. This latter phenomenon is what most Christians hear about, but they are not aware of the violence exerted by the Israeli state on Palestinians, nor the history of dispossession and mass expulsion of Palestinians that has occurred for decades. Compounding this ignorance is the false perception that all Palestinians are Muslims. Many American Christians are unaware that Palestinian Christians, who have lived in the Holy Land since the earliest days of the Christian faith, also suffer from these injustices.

Groups that espouse Christian Zionist ideas, like John Hagee's Christians United for Israel (CUFI), are very politically active in the United States, and some proponents of this ideology are donors to anti-Muslim groups who themselves support Israeli Jewish dominance over Palestinians there.[110] By helping to normalize the public's perception of (Palestinian) Muslims as an existential threat to the United States and to Israel, the Islamophobia network is able to give cover to harmful policies in Israel, which are often supported by U.S. politicians on both sides of the political spectrum.

Sage Tea and Stereotypes: Islam on Christian TV in the Middle East

When I was an undergraduate student, I studied abroad just an hour's drive east of the border of Israel-Palestine, in the Jordanian capital of Amman. Every night, I would sit with my Arab Christian host family and watch TV, drinking steaming, sugary tea, scented with mint or sage leaves. If we were not watching the singing competition, *Arab Idol*, modeled on the U.S. show, the television was often tuned to Christian programming. In Jordan and around the Middle East, there are widely popular Christian television channels. Produced in Arabic and primarily featuring Arab person-alities, some channels provide programs for existing Christian communities, while others seek to call Muslim viewers to the Christian faith. Some of these Evangelical channels have entire programs dedicated to discussing Islam, and they reproduce many of the common anti-Muslim tropes and ideas that are common in the West. I returned to Amman to study this phenomenon on a Fulbright research grant after college, finding that rather than promoting understanding and coexistence, these programs sow fear and distrust between Christians and their Muslim neighbors.[111] Many of these channels are produced in Western countries, and some are funded by Christian minis-tries that espouse Christian Zionist views about conflict in the Middle East that will usher in the second coming of Christ. Two of the most well-known personalities on these channels are the Egyptian Coptic priest Zakaria Botros and ex-Muslim from Morocco Brother Rachid, whose programs on Islam have drawn criticism and condemnation from Muslims and Christian alike.[112] Both men are well known in the United States also, often serving as validators for Americans' anti-Muslim views.

On one occasion during my first stay in Amman, a Jordanian Christian asked me, "Have you ever heard of the writers Pamela Geller and Robert Spencer? You should read their books on Islam." Given my prior study of the Islamophobia network in the United States, I was well aware of these indi-viduals and their views. But up until then I had no idea how much influence they also had around the world and even in the Middle East. Robert Spencer and other players in the Islamophobia network, like Geert Wilders and Wafa Sultan, have appeared on at least one of these Arabic-language Christian channels to talk about Islam. Even when they are not featured, their views are echoed on the Islam-related programs of some of these channels.

How Islamophobia Unifies Christians

Those who say, "I love God," and hate their brothers or sisters,

are liars; for those who do not love a brother or sister whom they

have seen, cannot love God whom they have not seen.

—1 John 4:20

In a Vatican-approved publication in 2017, Italian Jesuit priest Antonio Spadaro and Argentine Presbyterian pastor Marcelo Figueroa lamented what they called an "ecumenism of hate" among some U.S. Catholics and Evan-gelical Protestants, who come together around a shared "xenophobic and Islamophobic vision that wants walls and purifying deportations."[113] In this chapter, we have seen numerous examples of the Islamophobia within these communities. Catholics and Evangelicals are not alone in this. Christians of other branches, including Eastern Orthodoxy and mainline Protestants, also contribute to Islamophobia. Though he sought in the late 2010s to forge an alliance between conservative Christians and Muslims,[114] the Orthodox Christian author of *The Benedict Option*, Rod Dreher, a decade earlier helped spread a now-popular anti-Muslim conspiracy theory about a covert Muslim Brotherhood takeover of the United States.[115]

Much of what has been discussed in this chapter stands in stark contradiction to the values we as Christians hold, and the way we believe we should treat others. People of other faiths, including Muslims, no doubt feel the same way when they see their religion trotted out in an attempt to rationalize attitudes or behaviors that harm others. These examples and trends demonstrate how any of our religious traditions or affiliations can be invoked for ill, and how so often human beings fail to live up to the ideals we claim to profess.

8

SAINTS AND SINNERS

The Roots of Contemporary Islamophobia in the History of Muslim-Christian Relations

There is another temptation which we must especially guard against:
the simplistic reductionism which sees only good or evil;
or, if you will, the righteous and sinners. . . . We know that
in the attempt to be freed of the enemy without, we can be tempted
to feed the enemy within. To imitate the hatred and violence of
tyrants and murderers is the best way to take their place.

—Pope Francis to the U.S. Congress in 2015[1]

On a beach on the cold coast of the Baltic Sea, a Catholic Polish woman clutched a white rosary.[2] Dozens of others stood along the sandy shoreline, as part of a day of prayer to Mary for the protection of Poland. On that October day in 2017, Poles nationwide assembled along the length of the country's outer limits for a unique event dubbed "Rosary to the Borders." Though organized by lay Catholics, it was endorsed by hundreds of Catholic churches and nearly two dozen dioceses. The event coincided with the anniversary of the Battle of Lepanto, when European Catholic forces defeated the Ottoman Muslims in a sea battle in 1571. Remembered as a key moment in preventing Muslims from taking over Europe, the victory was thought to be due to the miraculous apparition of Mary, who aided the Christians in this victory. In 2017, Polish Catholics turned to Mary again, asking for her intercession to repel the impending "Islamization" of their country. On another beach, a Polish man named Krzysztof Januszewski told a reporter, "In the past, there were raids by sultans and Turks and people of other faiths against us Christians. Today Islam is flooding us and we are afraid of this too."[3] A majority-Catholic country, Poland has a very small Muslim population, but in recent years Islamophobia has risen, both in interpersonal and institutional forms.[4]

The roots of contemporary Islamophobia—especially among Christians—are deep, extending back into the history of Muslim-Christian relations. Delving into this history will help us understand our current situation with more clarity, seeing the continuity between our time and that of earlier centuries.

This chapter highlights some of the different ways that Christians have viewed Muslims and their religion. Political factors and (lack of) proximity to Muslims played an important role in how Christians constructed their image of the "other." Christians who lived among Muslims in the Middle East, for example, often had different views from Christians who lived in Western Europe. These European conceptions of Islam, which were often inaccurate, have been carried forward into our present day, where they play into contemporary Islamophobia. Sadly, some of our most beloved historical figures—saints and scholars, reformers and role models—have contributed to the persistence of anti-Muslim attitudes and ideas in our Christian tradition. In other cases, the stories about Christian figures or historical events have been put at the service of an "us versus them" message. Christian identity has often been constructed over and against Muslims, as our own self-understanding has been worked out in contrast to a sometimes falsified or exaggerated picture of Muslims.

Many readers will have heard of historical examples of how Muslim powers have mistreated Christian communities or given them a subordinate status in some contexts. We have far less exposure, however, to the ways that *we* have mistreated Muslims (and other religious communities) in the past, as well as the ways that Christian religious discourse was used to justify prejudice and discrimination against Muslims and other groups. In this chapter, I shed light on some of these things that we would rather not know about ourselves, events that we would prefer to write out of the history we tell about ourselves.

Despite the fact that conflict and mutual mistreatment have plagued Muslim-Christian relations, that is not the full picture. The history has also been characterized by friendship, collaboration, and ordinary living, and I highlight some of those examples as well in this chapter. Though conflict is typically what gets recorded in the history books, Muslim-Christian coexistence was arguably more common—people living side by side, albeit in imperfect situations, but living together nonetheless.

Coexistence, Crusades, and Complex Relations:
Key Moments in Muslim-Christian History

Christians and Muslims have been in contact and relationship since the earliest days of Muhammad's community.[5] The Islamic tradition tells us that, faced with persecution in their hometown of Mecca, some of Muhammad's followers left to seek shelter and protection under the care of the Christian king in Ethiopia/Abyssinia. Christian communities also lived in regions of the Arabian Peninsula and Levant region that came under the rule of Muhammad and his successors, initially by negotiation and treaty and later by military conquest. Some historical reports note that many Christians fought with the Muslim armies against the Byzantine Christian Empire, which had persecuted some Christian sects. For the first few centuries of Islamic rule in the Middle East and beyond, Christians made up a majority of the population. Contrary to the notion that often circulates today, Christians as a bloc were not faced with the ultimatum to "convert or die."

The treatment and experiences of Christians in Muslim-ruled contexts varied widely in the pre-modern period, but by and large Christians were able to practice their faith freely and manage their own religious (and even civil) affairs, remaining sizable and vibrant communities in Muslim-ruled societies.[6] In many cases, however, social restrictions were imposed on Christian communities and individuals—things like wearing distinctive clothing, being barred from building new churches or repairing old ones, and not holding religious celebrations publicly.[7] By today's standards these are cases of religious persecution, and as this chapter shows, they were common practice in many pre-modern societies—whether Muslim or Christian, Middle Eastern or European.[8] Pogroms or state-sponsored killings of Christians occurred,[9] but infrequently and not as the result of long-standing state policy. Despite these harms and challenges, many Christians were able to hold high positions in Muslim court settings, scholarly circles, and commercial life. They collaborated with Muslims in spheres of religious learning, scientific inquiry, and artistic endeavor. These trends also reflect the experience of Jews, who, along with Christians, were considered *ahl al-dhimma*, a "protected" class within Muslim states who paid taxes in exchange for political, religious, and social rights and privileges.[10] This legal status was tied to Muslim interpretation of the Qur'an, the events of the Prophet Muhammad's life, and other early Islamic texts, which emphasized that these religious groups—as "people of divine scripture"—should have relative autonomy and be allowed to follow their own tradition's precepts.[11] (With the global transition to nation-states and the disintegration of Muslim political entities in the modern period, the *dhimma* status became obsolete, though some Muslim-majority countries today have laws that mirror some of the *dhimma* legal norms.)

Just as in Europe during the medieval period and later, there was not simply one Muslim empire. Muslim ruling entities held territory as far west as modern-day Spain and Portugal and extending east beyond the Indian Ocean, meaning that there was no single experience of Christian life under Muslim rule—something that is also true today. As we see later, Muslim rule was very often more hospitable to Christian and Jewish minority communities than Christendom was to Muslims (and Jews).

While many Christians lived in Muslim-ruled lands, those in Europe had far less exposure to Islam and Muslims. Though some Christian realms had Muslim populations, many did not, meaning that Muslims were largely perceived as "an enemy from without." A key moment in Western Christians' encounter with Muslims was the series of military campaigns and conflicts we now call the Crusades, which were launched by the Roman Catholic papacy and Christian leaders. European Christian armies sought to uproot Muslim rule in lands previously held by Christians, particularly in the places where Jesus had lived, died, and, in Christian belief, rose. Crusaders killed many civilians (Jewish, Muslim, and Eastern Christian[12]) in this "Holy Land," areas of which they succeeded in holding for a time. Crusaders also massacred non-Christians en route to the Middle East. As part of what is now called the People's Crusade, Christian fighters killed thousands of Jews in cities across what is now Germany.[13] This also occurred a few centuries later in France, where Jewish populations were decimated in 1320.[14]

To this day, the Crusades loom large in the minds of both Arab Muslims and Euro-American Christians when they think about the other, shaping their perceptions of present-day events. Christians sometimes view the Crusades as a justified war against Muslim aggression, with the noble goal of protecting local Christians and their holy sites in the Middle East. When the Crusades are taught in grade schools, the massacres are often brushed over or go unmentioned, though many educators do teach them in their fullness. Due to whitewashing of this history, the term *crusader* has also come to have positive or innocuous connotations for many Christians, being a popular name for sports teams of Christian schools. Crusader symbols have also been used by contemporary Christians to brand their anti-Muslim and White nationalist activities.[15] When vandals spray-painted the exterior of the Al-Farooq Mosque in Nashville, Tennessee, in 2010, they also included a version of a Crusader cross.[16] For Muslims, especially in the Arab world, the Crusades have a deeply negative connotation.[17] For them, the Crusades were an example of Western aggression against them that has been renewed in recent decades. When President George W. Bush declared that the U.S. war on terrorism would be a "crusade" in 2001, he only added to this impression.[18]

As we have already seen, European colonialism in the Middle East was also a major turning point in Muslim-Christian relations, as were 9/11, the wars that came in its wake, and the rise of groups like ISIS in the twenty-first century. In this chapter, we continue to explore the many other instances of Muslim-Christian encounter (both positive and negative, exceptional and ordinary) that shape our current state of affairs in important ways. Although in "the West" Muslim-Christian contact is sometimes framed as a new phenomenon, it has been a reality of history in many parts of the world since the mid-seventh century.

Imagined Islam:
Ideas about Muslims in Europe

In Europe, with little firsthand experience of Muslims, Christians' ideas about them were often influenced by older tropes about non-Christian outsiders. These secondhand associations ended up sticking long-term, even when more accurate information about Islam became available. Long before Muhammad lived and the Muslim community formed in Arabia, Christians in the Middle East had written about a people referred to as the Ishmaelites, Hagarenes, or Saracens.[19] These were names for nomadic, Arab peoples on the fringes of the Roman Empire, and who were considered by the settled Christian populations farther north to be a nuisance or threat. Accounts of these peoples reached European audiences through popular writings and sermons.[20] Thus, when those who called themselves followers of Muhammad began to push beyond the Arabian Peninsula and to conquer and settle in the Middle East and beyond in the seventh century, Christian theologians applied their existing terms and categories to these newcomers, assuming they were little different than the Saracens they had always known.

In the Christian mind, the Saracens were the descendants of the biblical character Hagar, the concubine of Abraham, and her son, Ishmael. Claiming to be the rightful descendants of Abraham, they masqueraded as being "of Sarah" (the possible origins of *Sara-cen*),[21] lawful wife of Abraham, whose descendants God had promised many blessings. The Saracens were thus viewed as untrustworthy and only deserving of God's punishment and wrath, while Christians instead were the rightful descendants of Abraham. These writings also associated Saracens with worshipping celestial bodies and the goddess Venus, leading Saracens to be cast as licentious, lacking sexual restraint.[22] As we have already seen, the idea of Muslims as violent, devious, and overzealous in matters of sex has persisted into our own time. Even the idea of Muslims worshipping celestial bodies has also been lasting. Thanks in part to Christian leaders like Pat Robertson, there remains a popular misconception among American Christians today that Allah is the "moon God of Mecca."[23]

In reaction to Muslims' beliefs and practices, Christians early on considered Islam a "heresy,"[24] acknowledging that Muslims shared some core features of the faith but were seriously wrong on others.[25] This designation had been applied by Christians to other groups, too, but in this case the label was first applied by John of Damascus, a Christian theologian and monk who was born in Umayyad-era Damascus and whose father and grandfather worked in the Muslim caliphal court. In the West, where Islamic faith was less understood, Muslims were sometimes considered nonbelieving pagan idolaters, despite their being monotheists. Sometimes called Mohametans, they were believed to worship the Prophet Muhammad,[26] a notion that still is held widely by Western Christians today.[27] In some European Christian texts written by nonexperts, Muhammad was portrayed as one of three of an idolatrous trinity, including others like Apollo and Jupiter.[28] The image of Islam in Europe, especially in the north and west, was often so distorted from what Muslims actually believed that it had little resemblance to Muslims' own ideas. Though some of the information about Islam was produced by learned scholars who did their best to accurately represent Muslims' faith, much of what the laity consumed in popular, vernacular literature was an imaginary Islam, presented to them by writers who were not educated on these matters and who recycled older stereotypes.[29] They often resembled the books and blogs of our own day, which present what readers want to hear but ultimately portray Islam inaccurately.

Thanks to John of Damascus and others, Muslims were also cast as the Antichrist or the sign of the apocalypse.[30] This association between Muslims and the devil was carried from the medieval period into the Protestant Reformation and beyond. Though his views of Islam were more nuanced than his assessments of Judaism and Catholicism, Martin Luther still interpreted Islam as the work of Satan,[31] a view that some scholars today continue to promote. The idea of Islam as a punishment from God was also common. When Muslim powers gained control in much of the former Byzantine Empire, Christians interpreted these events as a retribution from God for their own sinfulness.[32] As John Tolan writes in *Saracens*, "Muslim victories were punishments of Christians' sins but in no way reflected God's approval of Islam." As is a common tactic in "othering" writ large, Christians also depicted Muslims as barbaric, savage,[33] and unclean.[34] Christian writers cast the Prophet Muhammad as the direct opposite of what they saw themselves to be,[35] and Muhammad's supposedly abhorrent personal character has remained a staple of anti-Muslim discourse since. This was not only common in the West, but also in contexts where Christians had much more exposure to Muslims. When they had access to the details of the Islamic tradition, most read the Qur'an and stories of the Prophet's life in ways that, in their view, necessarily demonstrated the immorality and illegitimacy of Islam.[36]

Before the last 150 years or so, it was rare to see the word *Muslim* used in Christian texts about adherents of Islam.[37] In medieval Europe, *Saracen* was the most common term, and referred mainly to Arab Muslims from the Holy Land. *Moors* was the term used in Spain and elsewhere to refer to Iberian or North African Muslims, and *Turks* became prominent after the rise of the Ottoman Empire. "Saracen" and "Moor" were also bound up with notions of anti-Blackness.[38] Images of Saracens and Moors in European Christian art often depict them as dark-skinned people.[39]

The existence of these different terms reflects the times and context, and was shaped by whoever was the "foreign enemy" of Christian powers at the time. Rarely if ever did Christians use Muslims' own self-designations, and in English, derogatory terms like "Mahometan" only recently became supplanted with more accurate and respectful terms. But the shift to the use of "Muslim" is not only a reflection of increased respect for the global community. As we have already seen, the emergence of the racialized category of "the Muslim other" in the modern period has led to a flattening out of the diversity of Muslims and cast them as a unified foreign enemy.

Many prominent figures in Christian history held hostile views of Muslims or called for aggressive actions against them. Saints Bernard of Clairvaux[40] and Catherine of Siena,[41] both of whom are widely revered today for their mystical writings, wrote in support of crusades, which themselves were instigated and preached by the Church hierarchy. In proclaiming the Crusades, popes like Urban II and Innocent III promised Christian soldiers the immediate remission of their sins and salvation[42] if they died in the cause, as when Pope Urban II declared, "I, or rather the Lord, beseech you . . . to carry aid promptly to those Christians and to destroy that vile race from the lands of our friends."[43] He concluded his call to arms by declaring, "Deus vult!" or "God wills it!" The phrase has been resurrected in contemporary times by Christian nationalists and White supremacists, including those at the 2017 Unite the Right rally in Charlottesville, Virginia,[44] who used it as a code word to indicate their opposition to Muslims, Jews, and others.[45] Today, Catholics with anti-Muslim views cite past popes' own opposition to Muslims as justification for their own, as evidenced in a blog post titled "15 Popes Whose 'Islamophobia' Saved the Christian World from Muslim Takeover."[46]

In medieval Spain, the figure of Saint James, the apostle of Jesus, came to be known as Santiago Matamoros, or "James the Moorslayer." Though he died centuries earlier, he was believed to have appeared during a battle between Christians and Muslims in Spain in the 800s, killing scores of Muslim soldiers and achieving victory for the Christians. This legendary event shaped the national identity of Spain considerably, and later Saint James was named the patron saint of the nation. As Spain conquered and colonized the Americas, James was similarly invoked against the Indigenous populations. European colonizers viewed Indigenous people through their existing ideas about

Saracens, Moors, and Turks. As race and religion scholar Junaid Rana writes, "The Age of Discovery was on the heels of the defeat of the infidel Moor and their expulsion or conversion, along with the Jews, manifested in the Iberian Inquisition and Reconquista."[47] Thus, when colonizing the Americas, Europeans brought their ideas about Muslims with them, ascribing traits like "barbaric, depraved, immoral, and sexually deviant" to Indigenous populations, and then to enslaved Black people (some of whom were Muslim), other immigrant groups, and eventually immigrant Muslims.[48] Symbolic of the importation of European anti-Muslim attitudes to early America is the crest of John Smith, the British captain known for his interactions with the Native American woman Pocahontas. It depicted the heads of three Turkish soldiers whom he had supposedly killed.[49]

As John Tolan, a scholar of Western perceptions of Islam, writes, these European ideas about Muslims were "used to authorize and justify military action, legal segregation, and social repression of Muslims."[50] As we have already seen, the same remains true today.

Muslims (and Jews) in Christendom: The Histories We Don't Know

The Saracens and Jews were yoked together as intimate adversaries of Christendom, as twin threats to the flock.

—Leerom Medovoi[51]

The year Christopher Columbus sailed from the Iberian Peninsula to the Americas, the Catholic monarchs of the kingdom of Spain issued an Edict of Expulsion that initiated the forced deportation of tens of thousands of Spanish Jews.[52] Those who did not leave or convert to Christianity would be put to death. Many of those who fled settled in the Muslim-ruled territories of North Africa and the Ottoman Empire (present-day Turkey and the Middle East). This event was the pinnacle of a series of persecutions faced by Jews and Muslims at the hands of Spanish Catholics, not to mention elsewhere in Europe.[53]

In 1179, the Third Lateran Council of the Western Christian church prohibited Jews and Saracens from living with Christians or having Christian servants, since they "ought to be subject to Christians and to be supported by them on grounds of humanity alone."[54] As historian Andrew Jotischky writes, by that time, "Jews and Muslims were routinely considered in the same legal category in ecclesiastical law in Christendom as a whole."[55] In 1215, the Fourth Lateran Council declared that in Christian realms Jews and Muslims (then referred to as "Saracens") should be required to wear special dress, to distinguish them from Christians[56] and to "prevent unwanted interreligious sexual contact."[57]

A few years later in England, this injunction was put into effect, and Jews became required by law to wear identifying badges on their clothing. This was one of many laws that served to subjugate English Jews during the thirteenth century, which culminated in the mass expulsion of Jews in 1290.[58] In 1274, the Church at the Council of Lyon encouraged Catholic rulers who held power in areas with Muslim populations to ban the call to prayer and public extolling of the Prophet Muhammad: "They are to remove this offence altogether from their territories" and prohibit Muslim pilgrimages, calling them "the impious enemies of the Christian name, the blasphemous and faithless Saracens."[59]

Back in Spain, the lines between Muslim- and Christian-ruled lands were always shifting, as armies gained and lost ground. In the early eighth century, Muslim armies conquered southern Spain, establishing a foothold there for centuries. When the Catholics from the north gradually wrested control from the Muslim powers, Muslim populations came under their authority,[60] as did major mosques that were converted into churches. In the late 1400s and into the 1500s, these Muslims were pressured—sometimes on pain of death or expulsion—by the Christian authorities to convert to Christianity, and many were indeed baptized.[61] But their acceptance of the Christian faith was not deemed to be enough to make them true insiders.[62] Moriscos, as these Muslim converts and their ancestors were called, were still viewed with suspicion, as outsider "others" who could never be truly Christian. They were thought to still be Muslim at their core. It was a prime example of the racialization of religion. Concerned about crypto-Muslims and crypto-Jews (who had also been compelled to convert or face the sword), Christian authorities had an "obsession" with so-called *limpieza del sangre* or "blood purity."[63] They issued laws that distinguished between true Christians—who could prove that their genealogy reflected Christian heritage—and those who were converts and as such not "true" Christians.[64] Ultimately, in 1609, the Spanish king issued an expulsion order for the Moriscos, some of whom had indeed secretly retained aspects of their Muslim faith and practice.[65] About three hundred thousand were expelled from the kingdom and resettled in North Africa,[66] in what historians call "a significant instance of ethnic, religious and political cleansing,"[67] the result of the idea among Spanish Catholics that diversity was a danger to society and that only full assimilation was acceptable.[68]

Earlier, in the mid-fifteenth century, the pope authorized the king of Portugal to subject Saracens and nonbelievers to slavery and to seize non-Christian lands, writing that he granted the king approval "to invade, search out, capture, vanquish, and subdue all Saracens and pagans whatsoever, and other enemies of Christ wheresoever placed."[69] These moves served to sanctify the broader slave trade undertaken by Europeans as well as their conquests in the Americas.

Closer to our own time, there have been more examples of Christian-on-Muslim violence and discrimination. Between the early 1800s and the start of World War I, Christians in Eastern Europe committed numerous atrocities against Muslim civilian populations.[70] For example, as part of the Greek war of independence, Christians massacred thousands of Muslim civilians in Greece,[71] one of many episodes of Muslim-Christian violence during that fraught period of conflict between the Greeks and the Ottomans. Ultimately, after World War I, there were forced population swaps between Greece and Turkey, where Christians from Anatolia were relocated to Greece, and Muslims from Greece were moved to Turkey.

Conflict in the former Yugoslavia in the 1990s was also the site of tragic interreligious violence.[72] Srebrenica, a town in Bosnia that was supposed to be a safe haven for civilians, saw the worst atrocity in Europe since the genocide against Jews during the Holocaust. Besieging Serbian Christian forces killed eight thousand Bosnian Muslim men and boys there; others walked long distances to escape the slaughter.[73] The civil war in the Middle Eastern country of Lebanon in the 1980s involved multiple factions that often broke down across religious and sectarian lines, with the Israeli and Syrian militaries invading the country as well. Many Muslim and Christian civilians were killed, with one of the worst massacres taking place in the Beirut neighborhood of Sabra and Shatila, where Christian Phalangist militiamen supported by the Israeli military killed hundreds or thousands of mostly Muslim residents (many of whom were Palestinian in origin).[74]

Many readers of this book likely have not heard about these historical accounts. These troubling episodes are ones we rarely if ever learn in school textbooks, whether in public or parochial schools. For Christians today, this history about our forebears and co-religionists is passed over, forgotten, thus allowing us to maintain a rose-colored vision of ourselves and our history. It is indeed jarring and unsettling for those of us who are Christian to learn about the ways that those who claim to be acting in the name of our faith have persecuted and subjugated non-Christians. From the examples offered above, it should be obvious that none of these can be explained purely by "religion." Rather, a host of complex factors, including desire for power and domination over others, is involved.

What many Christians have heard of, however, are similar facts from Muslim history—massacres, mandates to wear distinguishable dress, or forced conversions or expulsions. We also know that there have been Muslims, both in the past and today, who have used their religious tradition to call for war and violence and who believe God approves of the harm they do to others. Looking at this history, our task is not to condone or explain away any of these condemnable actions, nor to play a game of who did worse, but rather to contemplate the question: why do we so often know the worst about *them*, while knowing so little of that in ourselves?

We should also know that there were many bright spots and ordinary moments in this history of pre-modern Europe, not to mention today. For example, in Polish territories since the 1300s, Tatar Muslims lived in the predominantly Christian country.[75] Though they did not always have the same full rights and privileges as Christians, they had the right to practice their religion and build mosques, and those who served in the military gained the social status and privileges held by Christians. The historian Brian Catlos has also charted the experiences of Muslim populations in Christendom in places like southern Italy and Hungary.[76] There, Christians and Muslims lived side by side as neighbors, business partners, and friends.

Mary:
Mother of Mercy or Patroness of War?

"Surely, from now on all generations will call me blessed."

—Mary in the Gospel of Luke 1:48

"O Mary! God has chosen you . . . above all women."

—Qur'an 3:42

In the seventeenth century, a German pamphlet was circulated to promote the Catholic feast day of Our Lady of the Rosary, an increasingly popular Catholic devotion. It featured a drawing of Mary, holding the infant Jesus. But this image of mother and child was quite different from the ones with which many of us are familiar. In this depiction, Mary is standing on top of the corpse of a defeated Turk. She has a sword and a rosary in hand, and Jesus is grasping the Turk's bloodied head, which his mother has just severed from his body.[77]

Most Catholics today think of Mary as nothing other than the benevolent and loving "Mother of God," but she has been invoked throughout history as a warrior against perceived enemies of the Church, including Muslims—her image sometimes emblazoned on Christian military banners in battles. This depiction with the headless Turk is illustrative of Catholics' particular and long-standing association of the rosary with wars against Muslims.[78] During and after the battle of Lepanto against the encroaching Ottoman navy in 1571, the Catholic armies saw Mary as the key to their success, and they continued to invoke her—and the newly popular rosary devotion—against Muslims as well as Protestants. Some still do so today, as we saw in the contemporary example from Poland at the beginning of this chapter. The annual Catholic feast day of Our Lady of the Rosary—originally Our Lady of Victory—celebrated on October 7, marks the Lepanto battle and Mary's miraculous intervention to secure the Christian victory. Though many are unaware of this, the event looms large in the minds of some contemporary Catholics who invoke the Blessed Mother to justify their hostility toward Muslims.[79]

Another of these much-invoked battles linked to Mary is the siege of Vienna in 1683, which is remembered as "the Islamic civilization's near-take-over of 'the West.'"[80] Today, it is often portrayed as a conflict split along clear lines of religion, with Christians on one side as victim and Muslims on the other as aggressor. Christian nationalists and White supremacists who have attacked Muslims and committed acts of mass violence in Europe have some-times had fixations on this portrayal of these battles,[81] which are often cast as a "clash of civilizations" online and are featured prominently in fascist, right-wing Great Replacement discourses.[82] In reality, the Battle of Vienna was much more complicated.[83] Rather than a religious clash, the Lutheran Prot-estant Hungarians sided with the Ottoman sultan's forces, and Muslim Lipka Tatars fought alongside the Catholic Habsburgs and Holy Roman Empire who held Vienna.[84] Historian Dag Herbjørnsrud writes, "If we examine the battle closely, we can understand it rather differently: as a battle based on inter-ethnic cooperation" with both sides being "multi-religious."[85]

The figure of Mary herself also has a multireligious quality, so to speak, and she has served as a bridge to bring Christians and Muslims together, both in the past and present day.[86] Mary (or *Maryam* in Arabic) is a prominent figure in the Islamic tradition, with stories about her told in the Qur'an. There, she is also the virgin mother of Jesus, who Muslims believe is a revered prophet like Muhammad. The story of the annunciation in Luke's Gospel, where Gabriel appears to Mary, is echoed in the Qur'an, which has an entire chapter named after her. Holy sites dedicated to Mary also serve as points of unity for Christians and Muslims. From Turkey to Jordan to Pakistan, pilgrims from both traditions visit these places to remember her and seek her intercession.

In Christian Europe, Mary and the idea of "the Muslim other" was caught up in Catholic-Protestant conflict and competition, too. When one side wanted to demonize the other, they would sometimes compare them to Muslims, who were already seen negatively. For example, Protestants, in charging Catholics with Mary worship, claimed that Catholics were "worse than the Saracens," who only honored her as Jesus's mother. Catholics would criticize Protestants with a reversal of this logic. They claimed that Protestants were worse than Muslims, charging that Protestants honored Mary even less than Muslims did.[87]

The Forgotten Story of Saint Francis and the Sultan al-Malik al-Kamil

Eight hundred years ago, in the midst of the Fifth Crusade, an Italian man named Francis crossed battle lines in Egypt to see a Muslim ruler. The leader of a new religious order, he was accompanying the European Crusaders, who were stationed on the Nile delta outside a city called Damietta. It was 1219, and his fellow Christians sought more war with the armies of the Egyptian sultanate, part of the Muslim-ruled Ayyubid dynasty. But the Italian—whom we now know as the beloved Saint Francis of Assisi—was there to seek peace.

On the other side of the battle lines, the sultan himself had sought to stave off more fighting. Al-Malik al-Kamil was a man well educated in his Muslim faith,[88] and had many previous encounters and personal relationships with Christians. Not only did he have Christian subjects in Egypt, but there were Arab Christians present in his court and he had negotiated commercial treaties with Italians in the past.[89] Al-Kamil was the nephew of Saladin (Salahiddin, in Arabic), the well-known Muslim leader and warrior who was remembered positively in many European sources for his generosity in his own dealings with Crusaders.[90] Al-Kamil had offered his European Christian opponents considerable territory in exchange for a truce, but to no avail.

To the surprise of people on both sides, Francis was brought peacefully into the encampment of al-Kamil, and he stayed there as a guest for several days, potentially even a few weeks.[91] Little if anything is known definitively about the encounter between these two men, but they spent time in one another's company, learning about each other and their respective faith traditions. Francis likely came seeking the sultan's conversion to Christianity; that, he thought, would achieve peace. The dialogue between Francis and the sultan did not end in al-Kamil's baptism, nor in Francis's conversion to Islam. The writings Saint Francis penned afterward give us clues as to how he was influenced by his time with al-Kamil. He wrote a prayer reminiscent of the Islamic litany of the "99 names for God," something al-Kamil might have exposed him to; he penned an open letter recommending that bells or a vocal call to prayer be used in Christian contexts, similar to the Islamic call to prayer he would have experienced in Egypt; and he encouraged his friars to go among Muslims in a ministry of presence, witnessing to their faith in word and deed but not with the goal of proselytizing.

This meeting between Saint Francis and al-Kamil was an important and positive moment amid a period of grave conflict between Christians and Muslims. It holds many lessons for Muslim-Christian relations today. Both men bucked the norms in their own communities to pursue peace and harmony, and they put themselves physically on the line to build a better world. Their encounter was also a model for what interreligious dialogue can be—a mutual sharing of self that results not in a changing of religious affiliation but in a joint conversion to God. But later biographers of Saint Francis left out these facets and implications of his encounter with the sultan, often instead opting for a depiction of Francis and Muslims that fit their own ideas of conflict and superiority.[92] Like other examples we have seen, accounts of Saint Francis's meeting with the sultan became more a reflection of the author's own views than a trustworthy account of what really occurred. Eventually, even the encounter itself was excised from many accounts of Saint Francis's life and ministry. In the Catholic community I grew up in, Saint Francis was universally recognized and beloved by many as the patron of animals and nature, and statues of him were common in the gardens and yards of Catholic families, including my own. And yet, despite his ubiquity, I never heard about Saint Francis's meeting with the sultan. It was not until college that a Franciscan priest who leads the order's outreach to Muslims introduced me to the story. In recent years, many have sought to resurrect the story for Catholics and recover elements of it that were previously not appreciated or were hidden away. Though some Catholics today still cling to versions of the story that pit Muslim versus Christian (and use those versions as inspiration for taking a more oppositional approach to Muslims today), many are recovering the story for the purpose of fostering more positive relations.

Forgetting, or Forging a New Path?

At the Second Vatican Council in the 1960s, an event we explore more in the coming chapter, the Catholic Church stated, "Over the centuries many quarrels and dissensions have arisen between Christians and Muslims. The sacred council now pleads with all to forget the past and urges that a sincere effort be made to achieve mutual understanding."[93] Christians and Muslims have indeed caused each other pain in the past, and we need to be able to move beyond it. But the council's encouragement to forget, while well intended, is not the best course of action. While these past events should not be treated as a reason for us to hold back on dialogue or positive collaboration today, it is important that each side is aware of how the other feels about these past or present-day examples of harm. Many Christians in the West have never learned the history of how our faith community has hurt Muslims, and without exposure to this information, we can be left with an inaccurate picture of Muslim-Christian relations. Learning about our own history, being realistic about what has been done to us, and recognizing that there is harm on both sides allow us all to move forward with humility and forgiveness, without being defensive, without blaming others, and without nurturing a puffed-up sense of our own superiority. Naming these unpleasant aspects of our history helps us guard against repeating those mistakes, those sins, in our own time.

The stories of our past, and the actions of our saints and religious role models, also pose a challenge to us. Faced with both the good and the ill they have wrought, we have a choice about which legacy to carry forward. What stories will we highlight and lift up? While not ignoring the past, what stories will we invoke to guide us today? Will we take the path of conflict or coexistence?

Part III

CRAFTING A CHRISTIAN RESPONSE TO ISLAMOPHOBIA

9

"There Is No Fear in Love"

How Our Christian Tradition Can Guide Us

Engaging Muslims is not just about Muslims.
It is about Christians becoming the people God desires us to be.

—Pastor Joshua Graves[1]

Loving my Muslim neighbors as myself is the highest
articulation of my Faith and its most convincing moment.

—Amanda Johnson-Lufborrow

All these years later, I still remember what it felt like. When the anti-Muslim chain email arrived in my inbox, having been passed around by so many in my parish community, a sinking feeling came over me.[2] I was distressed and disturbed by what the message said—how it cast Muslims as a universal danger and enemy. Yet what troubled me most was its implication about *us*, the disconnect it revealed. The decision of my fellow Catholics to send around the anti-Muslim message stood in stark contradiction to the message of that uplifting song we so often sang at Mass—about the love that Christians show to others. The email was a clear betrayal of the values of love and welcome that we professed every week at church. But, as I would come to understand, my fellow parishioners did not realize this inconsistency. They did not see it because, to them, Muslims were threatening and harmful; in their eyes, it was natural to oppose and be suspicious of Muslims. The email encapsulated the mismatch between, on the one hand, the utter wrongness of Islamophobia, and, on the other hand, the entirely good intentions of the Christians who sometimes perpetuate it.

As the previous two chapters demonstrated, there are countless examples throughout history and in our present day where Christians have failed to

145

recognize this disconnect or who have interpreted our tradition in ways that
sanction or justify anti-Muslim prejudice and discrimination. But there is
another way, another path we can choose to take. In this chapter, I shed light
on principles and teachings from our Christian faith that can be harnessed to
forge a more positive way forward in our personal and collective relationships
with Muslims. Whether parables from the Bible, the lives of Christian role
models past and present who give us examples to emulate, or the principles of
Catholic social teaching, there are ample theological resources in the Christian tradition to construct a response to Islamophobia that is rooted in our
faith. Because I am a Catholic Christian, I draw primarily on resources from
that tradition, while recognizing and highlighting the many fruitful contributions from other denominations as well.

The Good Samaritan Today

On a street lined with boarded-up shops and flanked by crumbling side-
walks, a thin man with salt-and-pepper scruff sits slumped on the pavement.
He is sickly and suffering, in dire need of help. There are few passersby. One
is a Catholic priest in his white collar, but he rushes along on his way to Mass,
lacking time to help the man. Eventually, another person comes by. She works
at the archdiocese and has an important meeting to get to.

But then, a car driving down the road stops alongside the poor man. A
women gets out, a long robe flowing about her ankles and a scarf pulled across
her face. A Muslim, she bends over to guide the man into her car, and promptly
takes him to a local hospital, where she ensures he gets the care he needs and
tells the medical staff that she will take care of any and all bills he has.

This re-telling of the Good Samaritan story was offered in 2019 by the
parish priest, Father Bob, at the church my parents attend in Indianapolis,
Indiana. It is a poignant contemporary version that—using characters and
categories that are familiar to American Catholics today—captures the
essence of the original in the Gospel of Luke. In that first-century version,
a "religious outsider," a Samaritan, helps a dying man on the side of the road
after members of Jesus's own Jewish faith community (a priest and a Levite)
fail to give him aid.[3]

When most Christians hear the Good Samaritan story, it is often
interpreted as an injunction to serve others, to be generous to the poor. In
common parlance, calling someone a "Good Samaritan" usually means the
person is a friendly, generous stranger, who gives a helping hand to others.
Sermons on the parable often end with a call for us to be Good Samaritans in our own lives. These are important lessons, but what often gets left
out of these interpretations is the parable's point about "religious others."

Fortunately, Fr. Bob's recasting of the story allows us to see this other angle. As Muslims are today, Samaritans were seen negatively by many of Jesus's peers. Perhaps thinking Samaritans incapable of doing good or fulfilling the demands of the faith, Jesus's Jewish followers would have found the story of the Good Samaritan jarring, just as Fr. Bob's version about the Good Muslim is jarring for many Christians today. Faced with the generosity of the Good Samaritan/Muslim, we are challenged to reevaluate our negative expectations of them. As Jewish New Testament scholar Amy-Jill Levine writes in her book *The Misunderstood Jew*, in these stories "outsiders who are not expected to show compassion do."[4]

What the Good Samaritan/Muslim story does so effectively is jerk us out of our usual "us versus them" mind-set. It knocks off the rose-colored glasses that we often use to view our own faith community, and it gives us no choice but to see religious others in that positive light. Evangelical Protestant pastor Joshua Graves, who applies the parable of the Good Samaritan to Muslim-Christian relations in his own book, writes, "Theologically, this paradigmatic text is not about belief or action. It is primarily about sight and vision. *How do you see?*"[5] Fr. Bob's retelling of the story allows us to see that Muslims can and often do embody the kind of life that Christ wants us all to live.

From Opposition to Esteem: Catholic Teaching about Muslims

Though many Christians throughout history have written and spoken positively of Muslims[6]—not to mention the countless unrecorded examples of Muslim-Christian friendship—it was not until the 1960s that the Catholic Church in a formal and institutional way spoke respectfully and fondly of Muslims.[7] It was also the first time that the Church referred to Muslims as "Muslims," rather than as "Turks" or "Saracens."

At the Second Vatican Council, held in Rome between 1962 and 1965, the Catholic Church had sought to reflect on its relationship to the modern world, including its relationship to other religious communities. Convened by Pope John XXIII and later Pope Paul VI, Catholic bishops from around the world gathered together, along with many academic theologians, to articulate the Church's vision moving forward, characterized by a more hopeful disposition. The council issued documents on topics including the liturgy, missionary activity, and priestly education, and the council proceeded to shape many aspects of Catholic life around the world. Arguably the council's biggest impact was on interreligious relations. It not only revolutionized Catholics' relationships to those of other faiths, but it jump-started other Christian denominations' interfaith engagement as well. Several council documents spoke about people of other faiths in a general way,[8] and Muslims were specifically mentioned in two documents.

One of these is *Nostra aetate*, a declaration on "the relation of the Church to non-Christian religions." There, the Church describes what it has in common with other religious communities and makes positive and affirming statements about aspects of their beliefs and practices. It opens with a reflection on the unity of all human beings, who have their origin in the Creator and whose destiny is also God: "Ever aware of its duty to foster unity and charity among individuals, and even among nations, [the Church] reflects ... on what people have in common and what tends to bring them together."[9] The document was initially intended to speak about Jews and grapple with the role of Christians in the Holocaust, which had occurred just two decades before the council convened. But eventually, the document evolved to address religious diversity more generally, seeking to foster improved relationships between people of different faiths as well as set the stage for "dialogue," which became a buzzword globally in subsequent decades and into our own time.

An entire extended paragraph of *Nostra aetate* is dedicated to Muslims. The paragraph begins with a declaration that the Church has "high regard" or "esteem" for Muslims, and it goes on to highlight our shared faith in God, whom we both affirm as one, merciful and creator, as well as Muslims' praiseworthy endeavor to submit themselves to God, their reverence for Jesus and Mary, and their commitment to prayer, fasting, and almsgiving—practices that Catholics also undertake. *Nostra aetate* did not comment on some core aspects of the Islamic religious traditions—like the Qur'an, which is the Word of God for Muslims, or the Prophet Muhammad—but it sought to be an impetus for dialogue and collaboration between Catholics and Muslims around the world.

The declaration acknowledges the "many quarrels and dissensions" that have occurred between Christians and Muslims throughout history. It urged that, moving forward, "a sincere effort be made to achieve mutual understanding; for the benefit of all, let them together [Christians and Muslims] preserve and promote peace, liberty, social justice and moral values."[10] *Nostra aetate* also encouraged Catholics to recognize all that is "true and holy" in other religions and to "preserve and encourage the spiritual and moral truths found among non-christians [*sic*], together with their social life and culture."[11]

The Catholic Church's statements about Muslims in *Nostra aetate* laid important groundwork for a Catholic—and even more broadly Christian—response to Islamophobia. First and foremost, it says that the Church's default attitude toward Muslims is one of positivity, esteem, and high regard. This is not simply because Muslims share much in common with Christians in the way of beliefs, practices, and values—including our shared devotion to the one

God—but more so because of the basic bond that connects us: being human beings created by God and loved by God.

The general conclusion of *Nostra aetate* is even more relevant to the question of Islamophobia than the specific section on Muslims. In strong terms, it makes clear that there is no basis for discrimination or persecution of people based on their religion, and it insists that our own personal relationship with God is intimately interwoven with how we treat others. *Nostra aetate* declares, "We cannot truly pray to God the Father of all if we treat any people as other than sisters and brothers, for all are created in God's image."[12]

The Subject of Salvation

The second Vatican II document that mentions Muslims is the "Dogmatic Constitution on the Church," more commonly known as *Lumen gentium*. There, Muslims are listed among the people who are included in God's "plan of salvation." Contrary to its earlier teaching and the view held by some other Christian denominations today, the Catholic Church no longer views Muslims (or any non-Catholic persons) as automatically damned if they do not convert. (Similarly, the Church does not assert that all professed Catholics are guaranteed salvation.[13]) This teaching comes as a surprise to many, including Catholics, due in part to the fact that it is not widely communicated, and because some other denominations have a more cut-and-dried position.

How do Catholics articulate this view of salvation as it pertains to people of other faiths? Countless books have been written grappling with the topic, but the following are some salient points. As eminently loving and merciful, God wills that all people be saved, and thus God harnesses all that is "true and holy" in people's lives (including their religious traditions) to help them achieve union with God. Ultimately, people are justified through God's grace—we cannot "save" ourselves. At the same time, in the Catholic tradition, our works are not meaningless and have an impact on our relationship with God. As we saw in the modern version of the Good Samaritan story, Muslims often live their lives in ways that fulfill Christ's commandment of loving God and loving neighbor. In fact, Jesus offers the parable of the Good Samaritan in response to someone's question, "What must I do to inherit eternal life?" In Jesus's reply, the model he points to is "the one who showed mercy"—the one who was "a neighbor" to the person in need. Even if Muslims and others do not profess Christian beliefs, they can live their lives in ways that fulfill the core commandments of love of God and love of neighbor.

Salvation is more than simply going to some heavenly realm after we die, but rather—as the apostle Paul spoke about almost two thousand years ago—

being "incorporated into the Body of Christ." When people experience and
enact the generous and humble love that Jesus himself embodied in his life
and death, we become whole, part of the "Paschal Mystery," joined to Christ,
even if we do not bear the name "Christian." All of this does not mean that
the Church takes the position that all religious traditions are equal or that
Christ is unimportant; the hierarchical Church and most Catholics attest to
the absolute centrality of Christ in the salvation of humanity (even if they
articulate Christ's salvific function in different ways). But it does mean that
Muslims should not be seen as written off with regard to salvation; indeed, it
is possible that the communion of saints is full of Muslims.

Not all Christians hold this view that Muslims, without converting
to Christianity, have hope of redemption. Regardless, the question of what
happens to any of us after death does not let Christians off the hook for
our responsibility to combat Islamophobia in the here and now. The social
message of the gospel, dealt with in the next section, implies that Christians
should do what we can to improve the lives of all God's children during our
time together on earth.

"A Light to Our Path":
Catholic Social Teaching and Islamophobia

*In every age, the church carries the responsibility of reading the signs
of the times and of interpreting them in the light of the Gospel.*

—*Gaudium et spes*[14]

Catholic social teaching (CST) is often jokingly called the Catholic
Church's "best kept secret." Emerging out of the scriptures and the Church's
tradition, CST is a rich and evolving framework for living the Christian faith
in public life. It "provides a compelling challenge for living responsibly and
building a just society,"[15] not just as isolated individual Christians, but as a
community of God. CST is not an "add-on" to the gospel, some additional set
of rules and commandments, but is a set of principles distilled from Christ's
message and mission and applied to the social challenges that we encounter
today.

This corpus of social teaching is made up of encyclicals and teachings
issued by popes, documents of the Second Vatican Council, and statements
made by bishops—all of which are indelibly shaped by the work, ideas, and
lived experiences of other ordained or lay Catholics. CST applies the Gospels
and church tradition to a broad array of human issues, from the economy
to human rights, from family and community relations to the environment,

from justice and peace to politics and government. From this broad body of texts, Catholic leaders and scholars have identified principles that undergird these teachings. There is not a single, universally agreed-upon list of principles, in large part because the core ideas are interrelated and overlapping. Still, some of the most widely recognized CST principles are: the inherent dignity of each human person and the protection of human life; concern for the common good; solidarity—the recognition that we are "our brother's keeper"; subsidiarity—the notion that we should solve problems at the most local level possible; and the "preferential option" for the poor—meaning that the needs of the poor and vulnerable should be prioritized. Other principles that are commonly mentioned are supporting family and community relationships, care for the environment, and support for workers and their rights.

The intention of the Church is that Christians—and indeed all people—can use this framework of principles to guide their daily private and public lives. Leaders of governments, businesses, nonprofits, religious organizations, and more can all find helpful guidance in CST. Unfortunately, as theologian Marcus Mescher has pointed out, "The great failure of Catholic social teaching . . . is that it exhorts people to adopt universal principles into their life without consistently describing how these ideas can be practiced by individuals and families or integrated into schools, parishes, and other institutions."[16]

Fortunately, many scholars have taken this next step and looked deeply at pressing contemporary issues through the lens of CST, including climate change, anti-Black racism,[17] and migration crises. To date, however, Islamophobia has escaped attention. Though Islamophobia has been addressed in Catholic interreligious dialogue settings, CST has not to my knowledge been applied in a concerted way to the problem of Islamophobia, at least in published works.[18] This is a missed opportunity, because of the many ways that CST can be a helpful aid in crafting a Christian response to Islamophobia. In the section that follows, I offer a reading of how "the Church's best kept secret" speaks powerfully to the problem of Islamophobia, and I suggest concrete applications that readers can carry into their own lives. I not only use CST as a framework to diagnose the ills of Islamophobia from a Christian perspective, but also to recommend remedies to this endemic problem.

Though the principles of CST emerge from the Catholic tradition, there is nothing that makes them exclusively Catholic. Many Christians of other denominations, not to mention those from other faiths or no faith, will share these guiding principles. Muslims themselves will recognize many of the CST principles as familiar; in many respects they mirror the *maqasid al-sharia*—"the aims or intentions of God's law." The twelfth-century Sunni Muslim scholar Abu Hamid Al-Ghazali understood God's revelatory law to be aimed at preserving human beings' well-being, and thus he defined the *maqasid* as protecting five core things: religion, life, intellect, offspring/lineage, and property.[19] In modern times, Muslim scholars have understood these objectives of sharia to be "justice, equality, freedom, dignity as well as social, economic, and political rights."[20]

Human Dignity and Protection of Human Life

The dignity of each human person—and the call to protect, respect, and encourage its flourishing—is the cornerstone of Catholic social teaching. Without it, the rest would crumble. This inherent and universal human dignity stems from the fact that all people are created in "God's image" (Gen 1:27), and it means we are entitled to "certain basic goods: life, knowledge, sociability, reason, religion, and such like."[21] Asserting that God has endowed humans with dignity also means that all are fundamentally equal, and inherently good. Mere toleration of each other does not do justice to God's love and plan for each person; rather, we are called to honor each person to the fullest, doing as much as we can to enable all people to flourish. When the Catholic Church, in *Nostra aetate*, declares that it "holds Muslims in high regard," it is not just because Catholics have similarities with them on the level of religion. More fundamentally, it is because they are human beings, each of whom is created in God's image and likeness. God loves each and every Muslim—all 1.8 billion of them—beyond measure.

Protecting human life is a core part of acknowledging human dignity. As we have seen throughout the book, Islamophobia can kill. It has resulted in tragic and unjust deaths around the world. Even when there is not loss of life, anti-Muslim prejudice and discrimination directly harm the well-being of Muslims. Physical hurt, psychological trauma, and persistent dehumanization are affronts to the human dignity of every person, including Muslims, whether they are carried out by individual actors, communal bodies, or governments.

The right to religious freedom is also a natural extension of the principle of human dignity. As an institution, the Catholic Church has not always affirmed the right of all people to have freedom of religion, but in the modern period the Church has asserted this universal human right staunchly. In the declaration *Dignitatus humanae*, promulgated by the Catholic bishops during Vatican II, the Church states that no persons should be "forced to act against their convictions nor . . . be restrained from acting in accordance with their convictions in religious matters in private or in public, alone or in association with others."[22] It goes on to discuss the importance of people enjoying "both psychological freedom and immunity from external coercion,"[23] meaning that people should be free to act in accord with their consciences in matters of religion, and that governments should not interfere in these matters.[24] Viewing

Islamophobia through this lens, many forms of Islamophobia are infringe-ments on Muslims' religious freedom. When Muslims are unable to assemble in safety at their houses of worship, when they are denied by governments the ability to dress in accordance with their religious convictions, when they are barred or expelled from countries because of their faith—all of these curtail Muslims' religious freedom. This is not just about government persecution but also forms of more subtle coercion and pressure from the broader society.

The principle of human dignity leads us to recognize not only the impor-tance of protecting people's *rights*, but also the fact that human beings also have *responsibilities* to each other. As *Dignitatis humanae* declares, it is the "common responsibility" of all people to ensure the right of religious freedom for all. Thus, it is not simply Muslims' job to push for that protection themselves, but it is also our responsibility, and vice versa. Fortunately, both groups are already doing this mutual defending—though more is surely necessary. In Marrakesh, Morocco, in 2015, Muslim politicians and scholars gathered to commit to the protection of religious minorities in their countries.[25] U.S. Christians of all backgrounds have been strong opponents of the Muslim ban. At the nonprofit Becket Fund for Religious Liberty, both Christian and Muslim lawyers have defended the rights of legal clients from the other faith tradition.

Additionally, the protection of rights allows people to fulfill their human responsibilities more successfully. The Catholic Church also recognizes that impingements on Muslims' religious freedom hampers their ability to live out their faith in ways that benefit the rest of society. *Dignitatis humanae* says that societies should work to "create conditions favorable to the fostering of reli-gious life so that . . . society itself may enjoy the benefits of justice and peace, which result from people's faithfulness to God and his holy will."[26] Thinking back to the example of Asad Dandia, whose Muslim charity group was spied on by the New York Police Department, we can see how this surveillance hampered the good work that Asad's group was doing for their community. Like Catholics (and others), Muslims ascribe to the idea that human beings have both rights and responsibilities/duties, and that God's will for the world is only achieved when both of those are upheld. As Asad wrote, "As a Muslim, I feel it is my duty to help the needy members of my community, Muslims and non-Muslims alike. In other words, my charity work is a central part of my religious practice."[27]

The Common Good

The Christian tradition, as well as our personal experiences, tell us that human beings are not isolated, solitary creatures, but rather interdependent and meant for relationship with one another. Our well-being is bound up with that of others, and we cannot truly flourish—or truly be in right relationship with God—unless all are cared for, unless all people's rights are respected, and until all people carry out the responsibilities they have to one another. This is what the Church means when it speaks of salvation as a corporate, rather than individual, event. As Pope Francis has written, "No one is saved alone, as an isolated individual. Rather God draws us to himself, taking into account the complex fabric of interpersonal relationships present in a human community."[28]

This is the notion that undergirds the CST principle related to "the common good," defined as "the sum total of social conditions which allow people, either as groups or individuals, to reach their fulfillment more fully and more easily."[29] Fixing our gaze on the common good means that we cannot resort to a cold individualism or a kind of religious supremacy that only shows concern for our own faith community. With the common good in mind, we will not be content if only the needs and well-being of our fellow Christians are met. Rather, we feel compelled to work for the flourishing of all. As Archbishop William Lori has written in applying CST to anti-Black racism, "When any group of people in society is hindered by bigotry and racial prejudice from attaining a healthy measure of fulfillment, the common good of the whole society is undermined."[30] Again, this means we are called to defend Muslims' rights just as much as we would defend our own.

It also means that we have a lot of work to do, and a long way to go. As Muslim educator and activist Namira Islam has written, "The work is not complete while Muslim men are still detained in Guantánamo Bay despite never being formally charged or when drones are still being dropped on civilians abroad or when Black Muslims are political prisoners for their work."[31] But the far-off realization of the common good should not be a deterrent to starting down the path to achieve it. For the Christian tradition also gives us frameworks and tools for treading that path with hope and effectiveness.

Solidarity

> *The joys and hopes, the grief and anguish of the people of our time . . . are the joys and hopes, the grief and anguish of the followers of Christ as well.*
>
> —*Gaudium et spes*[32]

In January 2017, Gérald Lacroix was in Rome for meetings at the Vatican. The cardinal and archbishop, who ministers in Quebec City, Canada, was shocked when he heard the news of a shooting at a mosque there, which left six Muslims dead and twenty injured. Pope Francis came to him, hugged him, and said, "Have courage. Go home—tell these people we are with them. . . . Bring them hope."[33] Just hours after arriving back in Quebec, Cardinal Lacroix held a press conference with one of the cofounders of the mosque where the massacre took place, Boufeldja Benabdallah. "We will respond to these hateful acts through our solidarity and pledge ourselves to continue building a society where social peace and respect for all cultures guide our daily lives," he said. Immediately after, local Catholics held a Mass in the Catholic church next to the mosque to express grief and solidarity.[34] Muslim congregants attended and Boufeldja spoke, thanking the local Catholics for their support. In a moving gesture, Lacroix offered the support of Pope Francis through a hug. "Whether we are Christians or not, an act of violence such as that experienced at the Great Mosque of Quebec touches us all," Lacroix said.[35]

"Solidarity" is a well-known buzzword today, but it has long and deep roots in the Catholic tradition. It is the principle that informs how we are to live when we recognize the reality of human dignity and the importance of serving the common good. It means that, even amid our differences with others, we stand with them. Solidarity assumes an equality between people— it is not an attitude of pity or condescension, but a recognition of others as equals. Solidarity can be enacted in myriad ways, and I give more examples in the next chapter, highlighting ways Christians are already standing with Muslims in the face of Islamophobia. But a few are worth mentioning here.

As Cardinal Lacroix and Pope Francis did, we can express our support during hard times. When anti-Muslim hate crimes occur in our local communities, we can reach out to Muslims and offer our help, whether it be tangible or emotional aid. In a TED Talk she gave in 2016, Suzanne Barakat spoke about the help that her friend Neal gave after her brother Deah was killed in the 2015 Chapel Hill shooting. Neal worked in journalism and offered to help the victims' families set up a press conference, something they would have struggled to do on their own. Suzanne asked her TED audience, "What resources and expertise do you bring to the table? Are you willing to step into your discomfort and speak up when you witness hateful bigotry? Will you be Neal?"[36]

Living in solidarity with Muslims does not mean just waiting until tragedy strikes. The Catholic Church, under the papacy of Pope Saint John Paul II, outlined four types of interreligious dialogue that it promotes: the dialogue of *theological exchange*, where scholars and laypeople discuss their beliefs; of *spiritual experience*, where people share and learn about the religious rituals and prayer lives of others; of *social action*, of working together to solve social problems; and—the final and most important type—*the dialogue of life*, in which people of different religions simply live alongside one another, "where people strive to live in an open and neighborly spirit, sharing their joys and sorrows, their human problems and preoccupations."[37] This is what solidarity is—relationships of mutuality, in which people support one another in good times and bad. Praying for each other is also an expression of solidarity. We can pray not only for the individual needs and concerns of our Muslim friends, but also for an end to Islamophobia and for our own strength and courage to address it in our own lives and communities.

Solidarity also involves standing up for Muslims in the public sphere, and working toward dismantling institutional and structural forms of Islamophobia. When Christians and those of other faiths protested against the Trump administration's Muslim ban at airports in 2017, it was not only a public gesture of solidarity that was meaningful to Muslims, but it sent a powerful message that politicians and the rest of the public could not ignore. This is why protests and other public actions of dissent are important ways of living out our solidarity.

The principle of solidarity also calls us to embrace a posture of hospitality toward Muslims who are recent immigrants or refugees, and who have so often been demonized in our public and political discourse. Fortunately, the world over, Catholic and other Christian charities have been at the forefront of caring for Muslims and others who have been displaced by violence and hardship in the Middle East, Africa, and Asia. After he was elected to the U.S. presidency, Donald Trump's administration drastically cut the numbers of refugees and asylum-seekers it would allow to settle in the United States—a move that disproportionately affected Muslim populations. Informed by the biblical commandment to love the stranger, Christians in the United States and beyond have pushed government officials to enact more robust and welcoming programs for immigrants, refugees, and asylees. We can also do more to support refugees who are already living in our communities.

This principle also informs the kinds of causes we support financially and how we vote. When we give to charities and political causes, and when we enter the ballot box, Muslims—like so many other people—should be on our minds. This does not mean we should be single-issue voters around the issue of Islamophobia; even if it did, our choice would not be clear, since Islamophobia is not limited to one political party or side of the spectrum. Rather, the principle of solidarity and our concern for the common good mean that we should consider Islamophobia among the many other issues that drive and inform our political activism and civic action. The human dignity of Muslims is not something that can be written off flippantly.

Subsidiarity

While solidarity is often a popular term among those on the left, the principle of subsidiarity is commonly touted by those on the right. Yet, when it comes to Islamophobia—and virtually all other social problems—both principles are eminently important. The principle of subsidiarity has to do with seeking solutions to problems at the most local, personal level possible. It rests on the recognition that there are unique challenges in different contexts, and that universal problems have different manifestations depending on their setting. As we have seen throughout this book, Islamophobia is such a problem. Thus, the principle of subsidiarity should empower us to take actions in our local communities to combat Islamophobia.

While drawing on resources and expertise from broad-based entities, local communities can effect great change by focusing their efforts close to home. When there are movements to block the building of a neighborhood mosque or to slander local Muslim political candidates, grassroots efforts can have a big impact in pushing back. The Islamophobia network may be a well-funded transnational industry, but we can work to stave off its influence in our own towns and cities. Oftentimes, local initiatives and success stories are not covered widely in the press, but their impact is tremendous. Two small towns that come to mind from my own personal experience are Winchester, Virginia, and St. Bonaventure, New York. There, Christians, Muslims, and others have worked hard to break down fear, correct misunderstanding, and build up a common life defined by respect and hospitality.[38] Applying the principle of subsidiarity to Islamophobia also may mean that people in different settings will take different approaches to combatting Islamophobia; there is not always a one-size-fits-all solution.

Additionally, the principle of subsidiarity acknowledges the importance of limiting undue government interference in people's lives. The theologian William Byron, SJ, writes that "oppressive governments are always in violation of the principle of subsidiarity."[39] Recognizing this is vitally important when it comes to addressing Islamophobia. As we have seen, Islamophobia is often enacted and perpetuated by government entities that spy on and unjustly incarcerate Muslims; infringe on their freedom of movement, dress, and worship; and invade and bomb foreign countries. Thus, prioritizing subsidiarity can be an important corrective for this abusive government treatment of Muslims.

Sometimes, the principles of solidarity and subsidiarity are mistakenly taken to be at odds. But if we think about them instead as being in a kind of creative tension, it opens up new possibilities for how we might address the challenges that Islamophobia poses in different contexts. Subsidiarity also helps ensure that our solidarity is not just for show. Marching at a protest is a worthwhile action, but so is pairing that with tangible work in one's community.

Preferential Option for the Poor and Vulnerable

> *Serving and accompanying . . . means taking the side of the*
> *weakest. How often do we raise our voice to depend our own rights,*
> *but how often we are indifferent to the rights of others!*

—Pope Francis[40]

Strongly tied to CST's focus on human dignity is the principle that the most vulnerable individuals and populations should be our foremost concern, as they were Jesus's. This principle puts emphasis both on those who are materially poor and those who are marginalized by society in other ways, including by racism and other oppressive systems. This principle can inform a Christian approach to Islamophobia in a few ways. First, it should help us discern how to prioritize advocacy around our own needs and concerns in relation to those that affect Muslims. For example, Catholic campaigns for religious liberty in the United States have focused heavily on securing our own "freedom to serve," while giving little to no attention to the basic issues of safety and freedom of worship for Muslims. In a context of heightened Islamophobia, foregrounding the principle of the preferential option for the vulnerable would mean that religious liberty campaigning does not ignore the fundamental religious freedom violations that Muslims experience. This principle also has implications for Christian approaches to refugee resettlement. Rather than prioritizing Christian refugees at the expense of Muslims and others, we should be concerned with providing hospitality and safety to whomever is in need of it.

The preferential option for the poor also calls to mind the fact that Islamophobia compounds other systems of oppression. In the United States, for example, Muslims who are Black, immigrants, or are lower-income often bear the brunt of Islamophobia more than others. Thus, work to combat Islamophobia should prioritize the needs of these communities, and should bleed into other anti-racist work and initiatives to solve other, albeit intersecting, problems.

This principle can also inform the kinds of causes that Christians and Muslims jointly take up together as a part of the "dialogue of social action," one of the four forms of interfaith dialogue the Church promotes. Keeping in mind the preferential option for the poor may mean that rather than allying with one another to take part in "culture war" issues, we should instead prioritize the upending of unjust systems that contribute to chronic poverty and inequality.

Family and Community Relations

Catholic social teaching, like much in the Islamic tradition, puts a large emphasis on the family unit. The family is valued as the cornerstone of society, and as such should be protected.[41] As this book has illustrated, Islamophobia harms families in indelible ways. Deadly hate crimes have ripped them apart, as have policies like the Muslim ban. Children have witnessed their parents assaulted in hate crimes, and parents have had to lay their children to rest, as Suzanne Barakat's parents were forced to do in Chapel Hill. Thus, when we curb Islamophobia, we are defending the cohesion and flourishing of Muslim families.

Turning to our own Christian families, they can be important places where we teach and learn about Islamophobia.[42] By bringing up children with a respect for people of other religions, and showing them how Christian convictions support this orientation, we do important work to combat Islamophobia. Even something as simple as exposing young ones to children's books with Muslim protagonists can help—both children and their parents—from forming untrue stereotypes and negative biases about Muslims. The work of educating about Islamophobia in families is not just about older people educating children. Younger people and children have much to teach adults or elders, too. Because of their youth, they are not as conditioned to the racism of the world and can help older people unlearn it. Their idealism and energy are helpful correctives to the burnout and cynicism of many adults. Additionally, because many young people have greater exposure to religious and cultural diversity than their parents and grandparents, they can bring their experiences home to share them with those with whom they live and interact.

Additional CST Insights for Islamophobia

The compendium of Catholic social teaching comments explicitly on the problem of collective blaming after terrorist attacks. After condemning terrorism as a clear affront to basic human dignity, the compendium reminds readers that entire religious communities should not be considered responsible for the actions of a few—a tendency that, as we have already seen, often underpins anti-Muslim discrimination. Quoting Pope Saint John Paul II, the document states that "criminal responsibility is always personal, and therefore cannot be extended to the religions, nations or ethnic groups to which the terrorists belong."[43] After affirming people's right to defend themselves from terrorism, it also encourages all to undertake "a courageous and lucid analysis of the reasons behind terrorist attacks," an alternative to jumping to collective blame and scapegoating.

Seeing through God's Eyes

By looking at Islamophobia through the lens of Catholic social thought, we can see that it is both a "social justice" issue and a "religious freedom" issue, and one that is not unrelated or tangential to our faith commitments as Christians. CST, with its fundamental concern with human dignity, can also help us see Muslims as God does. Fr. Christian de Chergé, the late Catholic priest and abbot of a Cistercian monastery in Algeria, wrote about this divine gaze—how he imagines God sees Muslims, and how he hopes to adopt that perspective, too:

> This is what I shall be able to do, God willing: immerse my gaze in that of the Father to contemplate with him His children of Islam just as He sees them, all shining with the glory of Christ, the fruit of His Passion, filled with the Gift of the Spirit whose secret joy will always be to establish communion and restore the likeness, playing with the differences.[44]

Shining a Light on Scapegoating

"Father, forgive them; for they do not know what they are doing."

—Jesus in Luke 23:34

As mentioned in chapter 1, Islamophobia can be understood as a form of scapegoating. The broader society, for the sake of expediency, blames someone or a group for the ills that have befallen them. Heaping the blame on the scapegoat and casting them (sometimes literally) from the society allows the society to ignore the perhaps more complicated rivalries and problems that led to this state of affairs. Scapegoating has occurred over and over in human history. We find examples of it in accounts of ethnic cleansing and communal violence, and even on a smaller scale in our own family and work dynamics. Islamophobia operates similarly; it serves as a distraction. Collectively blaming Muslims is an "easy fix" to our problems, and it allows us to ignore or paper over our own personal or collective complicity in larger issues. It is much easier to blame Islam for terrorism than to consider the material, geopolitical, and psychological conditions from which individual acts of terrorism arise. Scapegoating can only succeed if those doing the scapegoating do not realize what they are doing. It only works if they see no issue in their practice of heaping collective blame—in this case, on Muslims. Because of this, shining a light on Islamophobic scapegoating is of vital importance.

In his reading of the Gospels, the prominent theorist of scapegoating, René Girard,[45] saw Christ as a scapegoat. Jesus was targeted by religious and political authorities, and put to death unjustly. By refusing to respond to that persecution with violence, Jesus resisted the scapegoating of his society. By his death and resurrection, Christ shone a light on the scapegoat mechanism at play. In the Gospels, episodes of Jesus's ministry depict him as one who highlights and criticizes the scapegoating and "othering" that those around him are undertaking.

Just as Christ shone a light on the scapegoating that characterized his society, so too must we in our own time. As pastor Joshua Graves writes, "Part of Jesus' intent on earth was to show . . . how not to kill Samaritans. Or isolate . . . or hate . . . or deem as inferior . . . or engage in *othering*. . . . Jesus didn't stand for any of these options."[46] Neither should we. Just like the One at the center of our faith, we must disrupt the cycle of violence and scapegoating, no matter whom it targets. Many people around us, including our fellow Christians, are unaware of the scapegoating going on (or that they—and we—are complicit in it). We can help others realize what is occurring; we can bring the scapegoating into the light.

Naming Our Sins

It's on us to confess how . . . Christians have contributed to Islamo-

phobia and transform our repentance into collective action.

—Catherine Orsborn[47]

In addition to pushing for positive change, Christians should be more straightforward in naming anti-Muslim prejudice and discrimination for what it is—a sin. This is not a novel idea, even if it has not often been put in these precise terms. The Catholic Church, in its *Catechism*, teaches that "every form of social or cultural discrimination . . . on the grounds of sex, race, color, social conditions, language, or religion must be curbed and eradicated as incompatible with God's design."[48] In the Church's Compendium of Social Doctrine, it states that "any theory or form whatsoever of racism and racial discrimination is morally unacceptable."[49] As we have seen throughout this book, Islamophobia can be understood as a form of racism, in which religion is turned into a racial category and people are mistreated on that basis. In the United States, the bishops have declared that racism is a particularly devastating form of sin. In a 1979 document called *Brothers and Sisters to Us*, they wrote, "racism is not merely one sin among many, it is a radical evil dividing the human family."[50]

In this way, Islamophobia not only harms Muslims, but it also hurts us. Sin, at its core, is about a broken relationship between us and God, and between the members of the human family. When we fail to treat others as the dignified "image of God" that they are, our own relationship with God is put in jeopardy. Shortly after he became the Catholic pontiff, Pope Francis spoke of the need to improve Muslim-Christian relations, and he drew a connection between our relationship with God and our relationship with the Muslims in our midst: "It is not possible to establish true links with God while ignoring other people."[51] Later in 2018, he wrote on Twitter: "If we fail to suffer with those who suffer, even those of different religions, languages or cultures, we need to question our own humanity."[52]

Fortunately, repentance and reconciliation are possible. As individuals and communities, we can repair our relationships with God and others, making things more right between ourselves and Muslims. We may not be able to excise ourselves from webs of social sin and structural forms of racism, but we can go about our lives with the awareness of that fact, and do what we can do to build a better world.

Beyond "the Golden Rule"

None of you truly believes until he loves for his
brother that which he loves for himself.

—The Prophet Muhammad[53]

"Do unto others as you would have them do unto you." This line from Luke 6:31 is one of the most repeated quotes of the Gospels, and versions of it exist across religious traditions, including Islam. When in doubt, the Golden Rule is a good yardstick for evaluating our approach to Muslims, or any other group, for that matter. The rule can be applied at the higher level of political activism and government policy, but it also remains salient for our daily living. For example, when we are tempted to let the actions of terrorists color our view of Muslims as a whole, we can call to mind the fact that we as Christians do not want to be judged based on the actions of abusive priests, bigoted pastors, or violent Christian nationalists. And in our daily interactions, we should treat Muslims how we would treat anyone else.

While eminently useful, the Golden Rule, on its own, is not a particularly high bar. As Christians, like people of goodwill no matter their religious affiliation, we do good for others not because we expect reciprocation, but because it is right. We do it because it is what it means to love as Christ did—to love, to sacrifice, to care for others, right until the end. As Saint Ignatius once said, we are called to give, and not to count the cost. We are also to remember Jesus's instruction that what ultimately matters in God's eyes is how we serve and accompany the most vulnerable (Mt 25:31–40). As the United Church of Christ declared in its statement against religious bigotry from 2019, "When we regard our neighbors, with the right eyes and heart, we can see God, and are therefore called to interact with other people as we would with God."[54] Indeed, when we do good for others, it is as if we are doing it for Christ; it is an opportunity for encounter with God.

10

LIVING OUT "LOVE OF NEIGHBOR"

What Christians Can Do about Islamophobia

For this command that I enjoin on you today is not too mysterious

and remote for you. . . . No, it is something very near to you, already

in your mouths and in your hearts; you have only to carry it out.

Deut 30:11, 14

After a mosque in Lynnwood, Washington, was defaced with black paint and targeted with threatening phone calls on September 11, 2001, two pastors of a nearby Christian congregation knew they had to do something. They gathered their own community together to respond. The next Friday, over one hundred churchgoers accompanied their pastors to the mosque during the *jumu'ah* prayer time to express their support for their Muslim neighbors. The mosque's congregants were so moved by the gesture of solidarity that, on the following Sunday, a number of Muslims paid the church a visit, bringing with them a bouquet of flowers. They also visited a Catholic church whose leaders had also shown support.[1] A week that began with violence and black paint ended with a bouquet of flowers and a warm embrace.[2]

The bulk of this book has recounted many tragic instances of anti-Muslim discrimination and has traced the trends of the systemic injustice that is Islamophobia. We have also seen the harm that many Christians have caused and the ways we have contributed to this injustice. But many Christians all around the world are already living out the teachings and principles that we discussed in the last chapter. Many have been doing so for a long time, and more are treading the path every day. To conclude this book, which began with spray-painted hate, we end with signs of hope—flowers, friendship, and the fierce and faith-filled courage it will take to build the world God wants for all of us.

I also offer a road map—or at least the start of one—for what we as Christians can do about Islamophobia—how we can respond in our own lives and practically implement the broader vision of solidarity from the previous chapter. What should we do when we are faced with prejudicial, untrue, or unkind comments made about Muslims? How should we go about educating our friends and peers about Islamophobia? How might we begin to dismantle more institutionalized forms of Islamophobia, in addition to its implicit and interpersonal forms? There are many positive examples we can emulate, particularly in the United States. I also provide insights that I have learned over time from a range of experts, as well as through my own mistakes and successes. I hope the ideas and tools I share can be helpful for Christian individuals and congregations who seek to live out "love of neighbor" in their own lives, as well as Christian journalists, educators, and activists, for whom many of these lessons will be relevant.

A Surge of Support for Muslims: Christians Speak Out

On the steps of the National Cathedral in Washington, DC, religious leaders stood side by side, forming a sea of heads topped with knit yarmulkes, colorful scarves, ribbed turbans, and necks wrapped with priestly collars and crosses.[3] Jewish, Catholic, Protestant, Orthodox, Muslim, Sikh, and other religious leaders were gathered for a press conference, pledging to protect one another's freedom of religious expression in ways big and small. They were convened on that fall morning in 2015 by Shoulder to Shoulder, a national campaign founded in 2010 to push back against rising Islamophobia. Since its creation, Shoulder to Shoulder has succeeded in equipping local faith communities to address Islamophobia in their own contexts and mobilizing those communities to engage in advocacy on behalf of Muslims in the public square.

During this period, numerous Christian denominations and organizations released public statements against Islamophobia—some speaking publicly on the issue for the first time.[4] Existing Christian advocacy groups like Sojourners, Faith in Public Life, and the New Evangelical Alliance for Common Good also focused much of their efforts on addressing Islamophobia in the form of media and ad campaigns.[5] As a counterweight to anti-Muslim ads that Pamela Geller had put up in public transit stations, Sojourners bought ad space for billboards that read "Love your Muslim Neighbor."[6] New groups also began to form, including Neighborly Faith, which aims to bring Evangelical Christians and Muslims together, and Bridges Not Walls, created by Catholics in Spokane, Washington, to address Islamophobia locally. Christian leaders, including Shoulder to Shoulder executive director Catherine Orsborn and Catholic activist Sister Simone Campbell,[7] have written op-eds in national news outlets, as did many more Christians on the local level.

Embodied Solidarity:
Using Our Bodies to Stand Up

In Phoenix, Arizona, in 2015, individuals wearing shirts that said "F*ck Islam" and toting automatic weapons assembled in crowds outside a mosque. It was just one of numerous anti-Muslim events that were held outside mosques across the country during that time, with organizers dubbing them "Freedom of Speech rallies." When Adam Estle, an Evangelical Christian, heard about the event, he called Usama Shami, his friend and the head of the mosque, which neighbored Adam's own congregation, Orangewood Nazarene Church.[8] They decided that Adam would help organize his fellow Christians to form a counterprotest, sharing messages of love and solidarity to counteract the hateful messages and threatening posture of the others. Putting their bodies between the armed, hostile protesters and the mosque, they held up signs reading "Love Your Neighbor."

Meaningful solidarity with Muslims can indeed be expressed through words, but sometimes solidarity requires us to use our physical bodies. This is what Larycia Hawkins did, when Islamophobia was at a fever pitch in the United States at the end of 2015. A Black professor of political science at Wheaton College, a prominent Evangelical liberal arts school, she donned a hijab during the Christian holy season of Advent, ahead of Christmas, to express solidarity with Muslim women who were facing increased hate crimes and harassment at the time. On her Facebook page, she posted a picture of herself—her face wrapped in a purple scarf—and wrote about Christians and Muslims worshipping the same God. The post went viral, and something that was meant as a small gesture of solidarity turned into a nationwide controversy. Wheaton suspended Dr. Hawkins from her post, claiming that she had violated their statement of faith that all teachers affirm before taking up posts as Wheaton. Eventually, she and the college broke ties, and she lost her position as the first tenured Black professor at the school. But Dr. Hawkins does not regret doing what she did. "Being with people requires sacrificing our bodies," she said as her gesture made headlines. "I won't turn back on that."[9]

Sometimes standing for what is right comes with a cost and with strong opposition from some in our own Christian community. Many Christian academics and activists who seek to combat Islamophobia in their work have faced both in-person and online harassment from fellow Christians. I have experienced this directly, as have many of my friends and colleagues. Name-calling like "Muslim apologist," "Christian traitor," "bloodsoaked betrayer," and worse become familiar ones in Twitter replies or the comments section of our publications. Anonymous accounts encourage others to "send us bombs," say we "should be beheaded," and make grotesque sexualized comments. Sometimes they even target our family members with insults or threats. Though this harassment is disconcerting, it does not at all amount to what many of our Muslim colleagues experience, not to mention the kind of physical harm and general uncertainty that Muslim friends of mine have faced in their daily lives.

In 2020, a young Muslim American woman, Somaia Harrati, was taking public transit when a group of young men verbally assaulted her, called her "bin Laden" (the name of Al-Qaeda's former leader). They roughed her up, pulling on her clothes, and threw things at her, including urine. She was left crying and shaken, and no one came to her defense.[10] "If you ever see this happen to someone," she said in a video posted online, "please stand up for them."[11]

We can help mitigate this kind of anti-Muslim harassment and violence in our own communities. White people in particular can capitalize on the privilege we have in public spaces to disrupt potentially violent Islamophobic incidents. Experts and activists who work on interpersonal conflict and harassment have found tried-and-true techniques for de-escalating tensions and keeping both you and the person being victimized safe in the process.[12] Let me give an example to demonstrate what you could do in such a situation.

Say you're on the subway in Washington, DC. From your seat a few rows back, you notice that a middle-age woman is eyeing a younger woman who is wearing a headscarf who is sitting alone. Eventually, the first woman starts making hostile, derogatory comments to the woman in the hijab: "If you want to wear that on your head, you should go back where you came from! We don't want you here. Mark my words—we'll send you back." Instead of confronting the harasser, you get up from your seat and go to greet the woman in the headscarf.[13] "Hey!" you say gently, plopping down next to her in the empty seat, with your back angled away from the harasser, "Is this seat taken?" Doing your best to keep calm and collected, you then engage the Muslim woman in friendly conversation about movies or the weather—"Aren't the cherry blossoms beautiful this time of year?" All the while, you're ignoring the harasser and focusing on your diversionary conversation. Though the harasser continues with her negative, hostile comments, you are creating as best as you can a safe bubble for the victim and yourself. Failing to get a reaction from you, the harasser may stop or leave the vicinity. If she doesn't, at the next stop you and your new acquaintance step off the train and out of the situation. Once you're safe, check in with her to make sure she's okay, but don't be overbearing. When you've both collected yourselves, you can be on your way, unless she feels the need to contact authorities. These techniques can be applied in a range of other settings, say, in a grocery store or in a parking lot.

In these settings, where you have to walk into a situation, you could pretend to know the person being harassed, saying, "Hi there, it's great to see you!"

Though it might feel wrong or cowardly not to confront the bigoted aggressor directly, it is the safest thing both for you and the target of the harassment. Let the harasser keep talking. De-escalation experts warn that when aggressors are prevented from verbally venting out their bigoted anger, it can come out as physical violence, as it did in Portland, Oregon, when three men confronted an anti-Muslim bigot directly and were stabbed. As offensive and hurtful as verbal abuse and tirades may be, letting it continue to flow helps maintain the physical safety of those being targeted (as well as ourselves) until we can get away to a secure space. What is important is that we no longer remain bystanders to hate. Our silence and inactivity give others a license for Islamophobia to persist.[14]

In Good Times and in Bad:
Solidarity beyond Crisis

In the woods of southern Indiana, at a Catholic youth summer camp, teenagers prepared themselves to pray after a day of canoeing and rope courses. But these young people were not Catholics; they were Muslims. In the summer of 2018, the Catholic Camp Rancho Framasa opened its cabins and mess hall to Muslim campers for a week. It was an act of hospitality that emerged from the camp's Catholic identity and faith.

Each year during Ramadan, the holy month of prayer and fasting the Muslims observe, Saint Stephen and the Incarnation Episcopal Church in Washington, DC, offers its sanctuary space to local Muslims for their nightly *taraweeh* prayers. Other Christian institutions support Muslims' religious observances with more permanent spaces. At Benedictine University, a Catholic school in Illinois, there is a *wudu* station for Muslim students to be able to perform the proper ablutions before praying, and at Georgetown University, a Catholic school in Washington, DC, there is a permanent prayer hall for Muslim students, as well as a worship space for Jewish students. These gestures, whether onetime or long-standing, are deeply impactful. In a general climate of Islamophobia, they send a message of hospitality and support, and the positive connections that these initiatives foster between Christian and Muslim communities can be drawn on when there are moments of crisis.

Another increasingly common gesture are the open letters that Christian individuals and institutions write to Muslims to wish them a blessed Ramadan. The Vatican's Pontifical Council for Interreligious Dialogue has done this for years, and a few times in recent years Pope Francis has authored the letter himself. The Franciscan friars, the Catholic order founded by Saint

Francis of Assisi, also publish a letter each year during Ramadan, and some individual Catholic bishops do as well.[15] This not only sends a message of fraternity to Muslims around the world, but it also signals to Catholics the stance of the Church—that it holds Muslims in high esteem. A similar intent was behind the foundation of the joint Document on Human Fraternity, which was issued by Pope Francis and Imam Ahmed al-Tayeb, the head of a prominent Islamic educational institution in Egypt, after years of building a professional relationship and friendship. In it, they charted their faith communities' common values and commitments to one another.

Long before the joint statement of Pope Francis and Imam Ahmed al-Tayeb, Catholics and Muslims in Rochester, New York, were forging that path. In 2003, in the wake of 9/11 and as the U.S. war in Iraq was ramping up, the Roman Catholic Diocese there and the Council of Masajid (Mosques) entered into a formal Agreement of Understanding and Cooperation.[16] The leaders of these two institutions committed to work together on social issues, to stand up for one another, and to help correct misunderstandings about the other in their own communities.[17] Today, nearly two decades later, the alliance still persists. Every month, the alliance and its members gather together to plan events, but also to connect as friends.[18] This long-standing bond has allowed the two communities to support and accompany one another in good and bad times.

Harness Your Privilege and "Insider Status"

Eliminate every form of closed-mindedness and disrespect,
and drive out every form of violence and discrimination.

—Pope Francis[19]

When Republican governors across the United States announced that they would be blocking Syrian refugee resettlement to their states, Indianapolis archbishop Joseph Tobin got in touch with then-Indiana governor Mike Pence. It was during the height of the anti-Muslim fearmongering ahead of the 2016 election campaign, and fear about the mostly Muslim refugees coming to the United States from countries like Syria had become deeply politicized. In a closed-door meeting, Tobin made his case for why the future vice president should reverse his policy and allow the local branch of Catholic Charities to go forward with their plan of welcoming a mother, father, and their two children to Indianapolis. Pence also asked Tobin to reconsider his position, and not resettle the family. After "prayerfully considering his request," Tobin defied Pence's order and Catholic Charities welcomed the Syrian family anyway.[20] Ultimately, because of Tobin's actions, Pence announced he would not enforce his call to bar the resettlement of Syrian refugees, and around 150 Syrians were resettled across Indiana in the wake of the encounter.[21]

In his own unique context, Cardinal Tobin did what so many of us can also do: harness our privilege and use it to push for change. As a prominent archbishop, Tobin could draw on his social capital, and the pressure he applied—and the heavy media attention the affair garnered—no doubt shaped the outcome of the events. Tobin could also appeal to Pence from a place of shared values and religious identity. He knew that Mike Pence grew up Catholic and remains today a Christian, and so he could appeal to their shared faith and the biblical injunctions to welcome strangers. In these settings, we, like Tobin, can also remind or educate our fellow Christians about the teachings and theological resources we have in our tradition that compel us to live in ways that resist Islamophobia.

These are also techniques we can use to hold our religious leaders, government officials, media outlets, and each other accountable. We can harness whatever privilege or insider status we have when we write letters to the editor, speak to our pastors after church services if they speak in uncharitable ways, kindly call people out on Twitter, and educate those around us about the Islamophobia network and its impact. We can use our platforms and power to oppose Islamophobic legislation, to push for more protections for Muslims in workplaces and public settings, and to resist wars abroad and unjust imprisonment. As mentioned in the last chapter, the ballot box and pocketbook are also tools we have to exert influence on behalf of Muslims' rights.

Show and Tell:
Creating a "New Normal"

"Now go and do likewise."

–Jesus in Luke 10:37

The year is 2016. Kneeling down over a wide basin, Pope Francis guides the feet of those sitting before him into the cool water. As part of the Holy Thursday ritual called "the washing of the feet," Pope Francis made sure that those whose feet he washed and wiped dry were not his fellow priests, as is common, but those who more accurately represented the wide array of humanity, including Muslim refugees.[22] It was just one gesture that set the tone for a papacy defined in part by his welcoming and affirming stance toward Muslims. Pope Francis is the master of the gesture, showing people how to act, not just telling them how they should think and behave. There is something to be learned from his approach.

Though Islamophobia is a widespread problem in Christian communities, every day more and more people are dedicating themselves to building up a culture of love and welcome. In our individual lives and in our community work to address Islamophobia, it is important that we not only follow these examples, but also that we lift up and publicize these positive steps and trends. Drawing attention to these good things, rather than simply lamenting how bad things are, can have a significant impact and allow us to actually move the needle when it comes to dismantling implicit and interpersonal forms of Islamophobia in our Christian communities.

In recent decades, scholars from a range of academic fields have developed what is called the "social norms approach"[23] to changing people's views and behavior. They have found that rather than guilting people into acting differently, a better approach is to show them how many of their peers are already thinking and acting in this way. Most people do not respond well to being told they *should* do something, but if they see everyone else doing something they will often follow suit. If our fellow Christians perceive that Islamophobia is tolerated and promoted in our Christian communities, they will be less likely to resist it. But if they see that their peers and especially their leaders are opting for an attitude of love and hospitality toward Muslims, they are more likely to conform to that positive norm. Lifting up biblical stories and teachings from our Christian tradition can also be an effective way of normalizing a new, more charitable—and more Christian—approach to Muslims.

Taking this positive, social norms approach does not mean we should ignore or downplay bad examples and negative trends. Indeed, this approach can only go so far. If we are not honest about the ills that exist, particularly about forms of institutionalized Islamophobia and the Islamophobia network, they will remain unchallenged. As we saw in chapter 5, these forms of Islamophobia often go unnoticed, and it is our collective ignorance that allows them to persist. If we have any hope of breaking them down, we must shine a light on them. Discerning when and where to employ each of these approaches (positive social norming or shining a light on what is wrong) depends on the goal: to improve social norms or to galvanize people to push for institutional change.

The Importance of Personal Encounters

A group of pastors and imams go hunting, fishing, and skeet shooting in Texas. It sounds like the first line of a bad religion joke. But it is what actually happens on a retreat for Christian and Muslim leaders organized by Dr. Bob Roberts, a Southern Baptist pastor who heads Northwood Church in Keller, Texas. Struck by the findings of surveys that showed Evangelical pastors had far more negative views of Muslims than their flocks or the broader U.S.

population, he set out to remedy this problem. As he told me during an interview we conducted for a Bridge Initiative podcast in 2016,[24] Dr. Roberts himself had been transformed by personal encounters with Muslim leaders he met during trips to Pakistan and Afghanistan. He now declares, without hesitation, that "Islamophobia is a rejection of the Gospel of Jesus Christ." His retreats bring together American leaders from both faiths who are skeptical of the encounter, rather than those who are already active in interfaith affairs. The goal is for them to get to know one another on a human level—as parents, spouses, and ministers.

Numerous public opinion polls and studies have found that knowing someone who is Muslim leads to having a more positive view of Muslims as a group, as well as being more apt to reject policies that would harm Muslims. This is not only true of Muslim-Christian relations, but intergroup relations in general. Increased familiarity with one person correlates to more positive feelings toward the entire group. This is why opportunities for Christians to get to know Muslims are eminently important for breaking down Islamophobia in its range of forms. Like Dr. Roberts, many of us may have had such an experience; getting to know a Muslim person helped break down our misconceptions, because we got to meet a real human being, as opposed to a one-dimensional caricature on TV. Sharing about these experiences with others who have not had such an opportunity also makes an impact. Our experiences of dialogue and friendship can have ripple effects beyond our own one-on-one relationships.

Personal friendships also help make us more resistant to the false and dehumanizing narratives that we read and hear about Muslims. When theologian and spiritual director Mallory Wyckoff saw an anti-Muslim ad in a Tennessee newspaper, she knew that its characterization of Muslims was wrong. Rather than buying into that narrative, she writes,

> I knew that Mariam would be organizing another food drive for people hit hard economically by the COVID-19 pandemic, providing thousands of food boxes. I knew that Sadia would be caring for her newborn baby. I knew that Furrukh would be working tirelessly to treat patients amidst COVID-19 concerns. I knew that Haroon would be meeting online with his Jewish friends to share a meal. I knew that Abdou would be collecting thousands of masks for children and educators in preparation for the school year. I knew that Basma would be serving on the board of a Muslim anti-racism collaborative.[25]

Mallory's friendships with Muslims helped her more fully recognize how wrong-headed this portrayal of Muslims was.

While acknowledging the necessary and transformational impact of interpersonal bonds, we also need to recognize the burden this can put on our Muslim friends and neighbors. In the United States, Muslims only make up around 1 percent of the total population. Though many Christians don't know any Muslims, most Muslims know someone who is Christian. In this way, many of them are involved in interreligious encounters every day, as a part of their normal lives. Expecting them to take additional time out of their lives for us to get to know them is a lot for us to ask. At its worst, this expectation turns Muslims into a tool for our own self-betterment. Though many Muslims do indeed feel called to participate in dialogue and anti-Islamophobia initiatives in Christian spaces, we should not put the onus on Muslims to "humanize" or explain themselves and their religion to us, as if they must prove their worthiness to not be discriminated against. As the Reverend Jen Bailey, a minister in the African Methodist Episcopal Church, has said, when we ask Muslims to be involved in "bridging" work, we need to be cognizant of the reasons why we are doing so and the burden we are imposing, especially when we are asking them to be in the same room with people who might view them with hostility or who do not acknowledge their full human dignity.[26]

While we should work closely with Muslims and actively draw on the expertise of those who are harmed by Islamophobia, ultimately, it is not Muslims' job to put themselves on the line to combat the Islamophobia in our communities and to help our Christian communities to realize that Muslims deserve care and protection just like anyone else. We (Christians) must take up that mantle. One of the ways we can creatively harness the benefits of personal encounter is by drawing on the many books, podcasts, videos, and other forms of personal expression that Muslims have produced. Social media also offer worthwhile forums for exposure to new individuals and ideas. Even if someone cannot meet a Muslim in person, following diverse accounts on social media can provide a virtual introduction.

Another problem with focusing exclusively on relationship-building as a remedy to Islamophobia is the assumption that Islamophobia is solely the result of lack of personal familiarity. Fear and ignorance are not the sole drivers of Islamophobia, but rather, the nefarious interests that capitalize on this fear and ignorance. Because of this, we cannot rely only on familiarity and friendship to solve the problem of Islamophobia.

The Limits of "Islam 101"

As readers will have surely noticed, this book has not been an Islam 101 book. That may have been disappointing to many, who perhaps expected that approach. Though I have sought to introduce readers to Muslims and the

Islamic tradition at different points throughout the book, I have not endeavored to provide a thorough overview of Islam as a religious tradition.

There are a few reasons for this approach—of explaining Islamophobia itself, rather than only educating about Islam—and they are important for us to have in mind as each of us crafts responses to Islamophobia in our own lives as Christians. This first reason is that, as we have seen throughout this book, ignorance of Islam is only one contributing factor to Islamophobia. Ignorance of another's religion does not necessarily mean that we hold negative views of its adherents. For example, you might know very little about Buddhism, yet still have generally positive views of Buddhists. Simple ignorance alone does not yield hostility or bigotry.

Islamophobia exists in part because people think they *do* know something about Islam—and that something is bad. Because of this, there is a dire need to "set the record straight," to debunk misconceptions that so often circulate about Muslims and that contribute to negative feelings and poor treatment of Muslims. The problem is that this incremental education about Islam is so often not enough. In my work on Islamophobia, I have often encountered a phenomenon I call the "'What about . . . ?' spiral," which typically works like this: A person asks an educator or expert, "Don't Muslims believe X?" When that person is provided with an answer that should settle his query, he continues, "Well, what about Y?" When he receives an answer to that, he asks yet another question, "What about Z? Doesn't Islam say that?" To me, this series of ever-shifting questions reveals that the person's persistence in maintaining their original misgivings about Muslims is far stronger than any desire to actually learn about Islam and Muslims. And it demonstrates that the person's misgivings are likely not rooted in any perceived facts in the first place, but rather in oppositional attitudes and emotions. Recognizing this, we have to find a way to head off or interrupt this line of questioning, and instead address the source of the underlying negative sentiment.

One way is to instead help people understand the problem of Islamophobia in the first place—how it works, who benefits from it, and how similar tropes have been used to scapegoat other populations. If we simply focus on disproving claims made about Muslims, we are left playing an endless game of defense; once one claim has been refuted, another arises, demanding our attention. Rather than taking twice the time to explain what sharia is, in response to the claim that Muslims want to impose it on the rest of us, we can point out the fact that many of the generalizations leveled at Muslims in the United States today were once used to smear Catholics and others, and that politicians capitalize on fear of recent immigrants to score political points. We can also inform people about the Islamophobia network, the fact that there is an entire industry dedicated to maligning Muslims for financial and personal benefit.

Similarly, rather than trying to answer questions with a flawed premise—like some of the ones we examined in our discussion of religion in chapter 6—we should shed light on that flawed premise, rather than getting into the weeds.

To give a parallel example about the limits of the "teaching about religion to combat Islamophobia" approach, it would be misguided for us to think that reading the Torah or learning about Jewish traditions would be the main avenue for understanding or upending anti-Semitism. To many this will seem obvious, as we know that anti-Semitism is not a result of what Judaism supposedly teaches; instead, it is a warrantless scapegoating. In the same way, it would be wrong for us to rest our anti-Islamophobia efforts on having people read the Qur'an.

All of this being said, there is still great value in exposing our fellow Christians to the vast religious tradition that is Islam. I myself have given Islam 101 presentations to Catholic audiences. In my view, this approach has two critical functions: (1) it upends some of the misinformation that contributes to people's negative feelings, and (2) it challenges those negative feelings themselves (feelings that often lead people to be susceptible to anti-Muslim narratives and claims). When we discover similarities, or are exposed to beautiful aspects of something that is new to us, positive feelings and sympathy often follow. When we are made aware of the many inspiring and ordinary ways that Muslims worship and live, we are less likely to buy into the stereotyping and monolithic image of Islam that is often presented to us elsewhere. So, while education on Islam is not the "be all, end all" for combatting Islamophobia, it can have an important role.

Tilling Soil and Planting Seeds: A Guide for One-on-One Conversations

When I ran into the Catholic priest in the Costco produce section several years ago, as described earlier in the book, I had tried to gently push back against his uncharitable and untrue claims about Muslims. But each time he heard my responses, he would pull his head backward with a swift motion and shake it vigorously, seemingly unable to consider or accept an alternative view. My informed and measured responses did nothing to sway him. In reflecting back on that disappointing interaction, it has become clearer to me that the priest's reaction was a visceral, physical one, not at all based in rationality or learning new information. This dynamic is something we need to keep in mind as we seek to respond to Islamophobic ideas in conversations. It means that we need to adjust our expectations about what we can achieve in a conversation like this. Our goal should not necessarily be the immediate or total conversion of our interlocutor's ideas.

Instead, to use a metaphor from gardening, we can think of the conversation as an opportunity to plant seeds that might come to fruition long after our conversation has concluded. We can do this by reflecting their assumptions back to them, asking them to clarify their view; by letting them know that we see the topic in a different way; and by offering a perspective they have not considered. These seeds may germinate later, as our interlocutor ponders what we have shared in the quiet and comfort of their own mind and heart, rather than in the more vulnerable space of a difficult conversation. When people are in a defensive state, they cannot have a change of heart or be argued with rationally. This is also why, in such conversations, it is important not to attack, not to shut people down, not to shame them. To use another garden metaphor, we want to till soil, fertilize it, keep it loose and open. We do not want it to dry up, crust over, and be impermeable to the potential flowers that could bloom later. Thus, we should remember that a successful conversation about Islamophobia—one that will have lasting positive effects in the long run—may *not* entail you getting the person to reach your conclusion during the course of your discussion. Focus on facilitating the right feelings, more than on providing all the facts.

All this being said, there are of course many times and places for blatantly calling out bigotry, especially in public settings where it is clear that someone has made a conscious decision to remain rooted in prejudice. When we take this alternative approach, we show others how wrong-headed this is and we create a climate where bigotry does not go unchallenged.[27] In one-on-one conversations, if someone makes an unfair or truly harmful comment, we can let them know in a straightforward way, with responses like "That's not fair" or "That's really not okay."

Fear among Friends and Family

Oh you who believe! Stand firmly for justice, as witnesses to God,

even though it may be against yourselves, or your parents, or your

close relatives. . . . Follow not your prejudice, so as not to abandon

justice—if you do, truly God is well-acquainted with what you do.

—Qur'an 4:135

Receiving the anti-Muslim chain email that passed around my Catholic community was a critical moment in my life, a vocation-clarifying moment. It has informed so much of what I have done in the many years since—my studies, my career, and more. Yet, on that afternoon, and in the months and years that followed, I failed to respond directly to the message. This is partly because, at the time, I was not sure how to respond. I knew that what the email said was wrong, but not how to adequately and effectively counter its message. I also wondered if it was my place to respond. The woman who forwarded the message was much older than me, and I felt too intimidated to voice my dissent and opposition to a close family friend. I was afraid it would damage my family's relationship with her and those in our circle.

That feeling of paralysis, of not knowing what to do or say, of not wanting to disrupt important relationships, has arisen in me in the years since when similar situations have occurred. One summer, while at a family gathering at my grandparents' house outside Indianapolis, someone briefly brought up something about the Middle East—the exact topic or comment now escapes me. But, all of a sudden, one of my uncles bellowed, "Loo-loo-loo-loo-loo!," mocking the exclamations of celebration or sorrow sometimes used by women in the Middle East and North Africa.

I was stunned that this reaction had come out of his mouth so naturally. It was a degrading, dehumanizing thing to do—and it strangely seemed to be a way for him to assert how "civilized" he felt in comparison to people who express themselves like that. But the shock of the moment left me stuck. I didn't say anything, though it should have been so easy to say, "That is really not okay." This incident happened during a period of time in my undergraduate studies when I was very involved with the Muslim student group on campus, learning about Islam and Islamophobia. Yet I could not manage to translate even a little of that experience into some sort of response. Instead I let my uncle's Islamophobia pass by unchallenged.

Reflecting back later, I vowed to be more prepared next time something like this happened. But in more than one moment since then, I have found myself in a similar situation, frozen and unable to do what I know is right and necessary. Despite my years of study and work on Islamophobia, there have been too many moments like this when I have let myself—and my Muslim friends—down, by letting Islamophobia slide by.

I share these stories to acknowledge the real difficulty of these situations, and to be frank about the fact that few if any of us can perfectly live out the solidarity that we are called to by God and our faith. Suzanne Barakat, the sister of Deah, who was killed in Chapel Hill, said in her TED Talk, "We can all agree that bigotry is unacceptable, but when we see it, we're silent, because it makes us uncomfortable."[28] This discomfort arises particularly among friends and family. For me at least, it is much easier to address Islamophobia in the abstract and in situations where I am not personally invested. It is much harder to confront this bigotry, I have found, when it surfaces among those I love. But Suzanne encourages us to step into that discomfort, to do the right thing. We can do so with the charity and courage that our faith demands of us.

Admitting Your Bias, Naming Your Fears

Be courageous!

—Pope Francis[29]

As human beings, we are often blind to our own biases, or are in denial about them, especially when it comes to forms of racism like Islamophobia. These tendencies hamper our efforts to challenge Islamophobia, and they are reasons why Islamophobia so easily persists. But one thing we can do that will help spark change around us is admitting our own biases when we do recognize them. When we come clean about our own biases and fears— or talk about our changes of heart and mind—we give others license to do the same. We show them that having prejudice does not imply that we are a "bad person." We demonstrate that changing one's position, while perhaps unsettling and destabilizing for a time, can also be very freeing. As I shared in chapter 5, we can also acknowledge how fear remains lodged in our bodies long after we have consciously unlearned flawed ways of thinking about Muslims. Even when we know the stereotypes are wrong, sometimes we can still be shaped by them. Talking about this struggle, though, gives them less power over us. Confessing these things among our Christian peers in the right setting can help both us and them to become aware of the webs of Islamophobic thinking and feeling that often trap us.

A number of times, after I have given talks to Christian audiences, attendees have come up afterward and told me about their own changes of heart when it came to Muslims. A college student in Seattle, Washington, once said to me, "I realized I hold onto a lot of negative views of Muslims, and I'm working on that." It was a simple admission, but a powerful and important one. Rather than remaining in denial about her feelings toward Muslims, she could face them without shame and begin to work on dismantling them in herself. Sometime later, a young man in Los Angeles, California told me, "I have Muslim friends, but I've been viewing them as 'being in a different box' than other people. I shouldn't do that." This kind of honesty—with ourselves if not with others—may be difficult, but it allows us to move forward.

The commitment of these young people reminds me of the wise words of anti-racism activist Ijeoma Oluo, who wrote on Twitter in 2020, "The beauty of anti-racism is that you don't have to pretend to be free of racism to be an anti-racist. Anti-racism is the commitment to fight racism wherever you find it, including in yourself. And it's the only way forward."[30]

The Significance of Similarities

We are all living, dying, mating, yearning, hoping, feeling,
striving, wondering, doubting, believing humans.

—Kenneth Cragg[31]

Whether on the level of our shared humanity or on the level of our faith traditions, there are many similarities between Christians and Muslims. Discovering and drawing attention to these can be an effective antidote to much of Christians' fear and aversion toward Muslims. Catholics, for example, are often pleasantly surprised to learn that Mary, mother of Jesus, is important for Muslims, too. For others, similar lifestyle choices may serve as a bond—say, among those Christians and Muslims who refrain from alcohol in accordance with religious convictions. As human beings, it is easier for us to sympathize with those with whom we feel we have more in common.

There are times, however, where focusing on similarities can go too far, when it leads to the erasing of the unique qualities of Muslims as a community. Christians should be cognizant of the perils of homogenizing all religious traditions and assuming everyone else thinks about God, religion, and life just like us. We should also refrain from assuming that other religions operate just like Christianity, with elements that can be easily mapped onto the same conceptual framework we have. For example, we should not jump immediately to the assumption that the Qur'an functions just like the Bible, or that Muhammad is the Muslim version of Jesus. Rather, we should let Muslims present their tradition without trying to force it into the conceptual boxes we have. Along the way, we will likely discover similarities we did not expect, and unique aspects of their faith that inspire fascination and perhaps even appreciation.

Another way we can draw out similarities in a helpful way is to highlight the points of overlap and intersection between Islamophobia and other forms of bigotry—perhaps even ones that we have experienced.[32] Calling attention to the universal qualities that define diverse forms of racism, while also being cognizant of what makes them dissimilar, can inspire solidarity that will motivate action on behalf of all marginalized people.

Can We Be "Us" without "Them"?

In a declaration on interfaith relations adopted by the Evangelical Lutheran Church in 2019, the church wrote, "Lutherans have a responsibility to overcome stereotypes and misunderstandings of Muslims and Jews and to seek fuller understanding and cooperation. Doing so may well involve rethinking aspects of Christian self-understanding."[33]

Too often, our collective conception of ourselves as Christians is built on idealized pictures of ourselves and a warped, negative picture of religious others. Sometimes we cast Muslims negatively in ways that make us feel better about ourselves.[34] Even in contexts where religious others are not explicitly spoken of, talk of *we* and *us* still reflects our conceptions of *them*. We sometimes declare that "*Our* God is a loving God" or "Christianity is all about X," as if others do not live or believe in these ways. Implicit and unspoken is a contrast between *us* and *them* that rests on a picture of "the other" that likely is not wholly accurate. This is not innocuous. Those who study the way societal discourse leads to eventual intercommunal violence have observed that how we talk about *us* is just as important (and just as potentially damaging) as how we talk about *them*.[35] When we frame ourselves as good, we are implicitly contrasting ourselves with those who are not this way, or implying that they are bad. There are echoes of this in that song I would sing at Mass growing up: "And they'll know we are Christians by our love!," which seems to imply that non-Christians are not as loving as we are.

All of this requires us to ask and wrestle with the following questions: Can we create a sense of community without exclusion, scapegoating, or othering? What makes us "Christian"? Does our identity hinge on otherness? These are questions for every faith community to ask themselves, and we as Christians have a responsibility to do so as well.

"Already, but Not Yet": Building the Kingdom of God

"The coming of the kingdom of God cannot be observed,
and no one will announce, 'Look, here it is,' or, 'There it is.'
For behold, the kingdom of God is among you."

—Jesus in Luke 17:20–21

In the Christian tradition, we talk often about the "kingdom of God." Every time we say the Lord's Prayer, which Jesus himself taught his disciples, we invoke God's kingdom, declaring, praying, and hoping: "Thy kingdom come, thy will be done, on earth as it is in heaven." God's reign is not only something that we look forward to at the end of time, nor is it a place in the sky that we will someday reach. It is also something that we can experience here, even if only in glimpses, and work to build now.

This is what Christians mean when we say that the kingdom is both "already, but not yet." We live in a world marred by sin, suffering, and separation from God and neighbor. We are nowhere near what God desires for us as a human and earthly community. In this book, we have seen that clearly. The suffering that Islamophobia has wrought is a stain on the conscience of humanity and of Christians. The pain and hurt that Muslims have experienced as a result is evidence of the fact that we, as a human family, have not lived up to our obligations to each other.

And yet, Jesus tells us repeatedly in the Gospels that, even amid our brokenness, the kingdom is "close at hand." It is not only something about to occur, but rather something that is already breaking forth. As Jesus says, the kingdom is "among you," within our hearts, in our communities. We experience the kingdom whenever we choose to live as if the justice, peace, and love of God's reign are already present. Whenever we love our neighbor, give of ourselves to honor their dignity, or put ourselves on the line for their sake, the kingdom is in our midst. When we stand with Muslims, when we advocate for their rights and their human flourishing, when we push our Christian communities to live up to our fundamental values, we enact the kingdom. It may not be present in its fullness, and we may not see the fruits of our labor, but this experience of the kingdom is very real nonetheless.

This is our task as Christians, to occupy the space in between "already" and "not yet." It is a holy and blessed endeavor. Just moments before he was killed for standing with the poor of El Salvador, Saint Óscar Romero told his congregation, "We know that every effort to better a society, especially one that is so enmeshed in injustice and in sin, is an effort that God blesses, that God desires, that God demands of us."[36] As Texan pastor Steve Bezner has said, "The guiding principle for Christians is: How would I live my life if this was heaven today? I'd love my Muslim neighbor."[37]

Let us take up that work: to live the kingdom into being, alongside our Muslim friends.

ENDNOTES

Notes to Readers

[1] "The Changing Global Religious Landscape," Pew Research Center's Religion & Public Life Project, April 5, 2017, https://www.pewforum.org.

[2] Cindy Wooden, "Global Catholic Population Tops 1.28 Billion; Half Are in 10 Countries," *National Catholic Reporter*, April 8, 2017, https://www.ncronline.org.

[3] "Projected Changes in the Global Muslim Population," Pew Research Center's Religion & Public Life Project, April 2, 2015, https://www.pewforum.org.

[4] Edward E. Curtis IV, "The Black Muslim Scare of the Twentieth Century: The History of State Islamophobia and Its Post-9/11 Variations," in *Islamophobia in America: The Anatomy of Intolerance*, ed. Carl W. Ernst (New York: Palgrave Macmillan, 2013), 78.

[5] Sylviane Diouf, "African Muslims in the Caribbean," *Wadabagei* 11, no. 1 (2008): 83.

[6] Besheer Mohamed, "A New Estimate of U.S. Muslim Population," Pew Research Center, January 3, 2018, https://www.pewresearch.org.

[7] Some of these identities overlap as well—there are many Muslims in the United States and around the world who are Afro- or Black Arabs.

[8] Iman Ghosh, "Ranked: The 100 Most Spoken Languages around the World," Visual Capitalist, February 15, 2020, https://www.visualcapitalist.com.

[9] Prior to the last few decades, the spelling "Moslem" was used, but today that is considered derogatory.

Introduction

[1] Lauri Lebo, "Did TV 'News' Spark Anti-Islam Vandalism?," *Religion Dispatches*, February 15, 2010, https://religiondispatches.org; Amanda Terkel, "Tennessee Mosque Vandalized after Local TV Station Airs Irresponsible Report on 'Homegrown Jihad,'" ThinkProgress, February 12, 2010, https://archive.thinkprogress.org.

[2] Lebo, "Did TV 'News' Spark Anti-Islam Vandalism?"

[3] "They Are Home: Nashville Supports Its Muslim Community," *Not in Our Town*, February 18, 2010, https://www.niot.org.

[4] As we will see in chapter 4, Christians are sometimes targeted by Islamophobic bigotry by those who mistake them for Muslims.

[5] Second Vatican Council, "Dogmatic Constitution on the Church, *Nostra aetate*, 28 October 1965," in *Vatican Council II: The Conciliar and Post-Conciliar Documents*, ed. Austin Flannery (Collegeville, MN: Liturgical Press, 1975), sec. 14 (hereafter cited as *NA*).

[6] Ibid., sec. 5.

[7] Islamophobia is not solely an interpersonal, "non-Muslim on Muslim" problem. Rather, it is a problem of systemic injustice and inequality, and as such, Muslim individuals and entities can contribute to it.

[8] Todd Green has argued the same point in "Rethinking Our Response to Islamophobia," February 4, 2019, https://religica.org/.

[9] I provide some examples of this later in this introduction and in chapter 8.

[10] In recent years, a few books by American Christian theologians have been published that address negative views and treatment of Muslims by Christians in the West and offer a Christian theology that can underpin new ways of relating to Muslims. These books offer valuable contributions in the Protestant Christian contexts for which they are written. They do not, however, treat Islamophobia comprehensively. See Matthew Kaemingk, *Christian Hospitality and Muslim Immigration in an Age of Fear* (Grand Rapids: Eerdmans, 2018); Joshua Graves, *How Not to Kill a Muslim: A Manifesto of Hope for Christianity and Islam in North America* (Eugene, OR: Cascade Books, 2015).

[11] *NA*, sec. 5.

[12] The young girl's name was not released to the media, in order to protect her privacy and ensure her safety. Travis Anderson, "Community Responds after Muslim Girl, 10, Receives Hateful Letters at School," *Boston Globe*, November 14, 2018, https://www.bostonglobe.com; Charlene Arsenault, "Hateful Notes Targeting Muslim Student Found in Framingham School," *Patch*, November 14, 2018, https://patch.com/massachusetts/framingham/; "A Letter from Dr. Tremblay | Response to Hemenway Incident," Framingham Public Schools, https://www.framingham.k12.ma.us/.

[13] Christine Clarridge, "Kenmore Clerk's Killer Gets 24 Years, Apologizes," *Seattle Times*, May 26, 2007, https://www.seattletimes.com.

[14] Jack Herrera, "Most Terrorist Victims Are Muslim," *Pacific Standard*, March 18, 2019, https://psmag.com; "Majority of ISIS Victims Are Muslim—CNN Video," July 14, 2016, https://www.cnn.com.

[15] Ruth Maclean and Eric Schmitt, "ISIS Affiliate in Nigeria Releases a Video Showing 11 Executions," *New York Times*, December 27, 2019, https://www.nytimes.com; Ruth Michaelson, "Egypt: Isis Claims Responsibility for Coptic Church Bombings," *The Guardian*, April 9, 2017, https://www.theguardian.com; "Sri Lanka Marks Easter Sunday Attack Anniversary," *BBC News*, April 21, 2020, https://www.bbc.com.

[16] "Letter to Baghdadi," Open Letter to Baghdadi, http://www.lettertobaghdadi.com/.

[17] Bukola Adebayo, "Muslim Cleric Who Hid Christians during Attacks Honored in the U.S.," *CNN*, July 18, 2019, https://www.cnn.com.

[18] U.S. in Nigeria, "Chatting with a Hero—Imam Abdulahi," YouTube video, at 14:32, August 17, 2018, https://www.youtube.com.

[19] Dooshima Abu, "The Nigerian Imam Who Saved Christians from Muslim Gunmen," July 1, 2018, *BBC*, https://www.bbc.com.

[20] U.S. in Nigeria, "Chatting with a Hero."

[21] Dale Gavlak, "Christians, Muslims Hope Mosul Project Helps Rebuild Trust," *National Catholic Reporter*, June 3, 2020, https://www.ncronline.org.

[22] "Muslim Community Helps Rebuild Catholic Church in Pakistan," *UCA News*, February 14, 2020, https://www.ucanews.com.

[23] Umer Nangiana, "Need of the Hour: Interfaith Action," *Gulf Times,* June 29, 2015, https://www.gulf-times.com.

[24] Susan Hayward, "Understanding and Extending the Marrakesh Declaration in Policy and Practice," United States Institute of Peace, September 30, 2016, https://www.usip.org.

[25] See Fadi Daou and Nayla Tabbara, *Divine Hospitality: A Christian-Muslim Conversation* (Geneva: World Council of Churches Publications, 2017).

[26] Gina Ciliberto, "This Easter, a Group of Muslims in Australia Will Attend Mass—As They Have for the Past 13 years," *Sojourners*, March 28, 2018, https://sojo.net.

[27] This alliterative list takes Nathan Lean's concept of the "three I's of Islamophobia" as its start. To his "imperialism, institutionalization, and industry," I add *interpersonal* and *implicit*. Just as Lean says about his own list, there are no doubt additional ways Islamophobia operates and manifests, but these five cover a large swath. See Nathan Lean, "Islamophobia in the United States: A Case of the Three 'I's," Oxford Islamic Studies Online—*Focus On* blog, http://www.oxfordislamicstudies.com.

1. More Than Fear

[1] The women's real name was not reported by the news media, but I have given her a pseudonym here to make the narrative flow more naturally.

[2] An investigation into the crime found that the perpetrator had been severely intoxicated during the attack. Appalled by his own actions, he later said that his actions did not represent his views and he did not intend to commit a crime based in anti-Muslim bias, leading prosecutors to not file hate crime charges against him. Nevertheless, the perpetrator held latent views that led him to attack a visibly Muslim woman, particularly targeting the symbol of her faith and identity. See Laura Lane, "Former IU Student Charged in Attack on Muslim Woman Gets 1 Year on Probation," *Hoosier Times*, January 24, 2017, https://www.hoosiertimes.com.

[3] The word *Islamophobia* has proved to be a controversial one. On one side, those skeptical that anti-Muslim bigotry even exists warp the term into "Islamo*faux*bia" in an attempt to claim that everything it describes is made up. On the other side, among academics and activists who dedicate their time and energy to addressing Islamophobia, there are endless debates about whether the word is adequate to describe a wide-ranging and entrenched form of racism.

[4] This definition has much in common with the definition issued by the All Party Parliamentary Group on British Muslims in the United Kingdom in 2018. It also shares much with a previous definition issued by the Georgetown University–based Bridge Initiative.

[5] In both academic and activist circles, the task of defining Islamophobia has occupied much time and generated considerable debate, resulting in dozens of scholarly definitions. This body of work has been exceedingly helpful in my own conceptualization of Islamophobia, but often it is full of academic jargon that does not make sense for practical application in everyday life. While not necessarily precluding other definitions, I hope my above definition of Islamophobia encapsulates the best of these academic definitions and formulates it in a way that can be widely understood.

[6] Peter Gottschalk and Gabriel Greenberg, "Common Heritage, Uncommon Fear: Islamophobia in the United States and British India, 1687–1947," in *Islamophobia in America: The Anatomy of Intolerance*, ed. Carl Ernst (New York: Palgrave Macmillan, 2013), 23.

[7] Here I use the word *race* as it is popularly understood in common parlance, as something biological and fixed. But I agree with scholar of racism Geraldine Heng that race, in fact, "is a structural relationship for the articulation and management of human differences,

rather than a substantive content." Geraldine Heng, "The Invention of Race in the European Middle Ages I: Race Studies, Modernity, and the Middle Ages 1: Invention of Race in the European Middle Ages I," *Literature Compass* 8, no. 5 (May 2011): 319.

⁸ Junaid Rana also makes this point, writing, "Without a doubt, the diversity of the Islamic world in terms of nationality, language, ethnicity, culture, and other markers of difference, would negate popular notions of racism against Muslims as a singular racial group." Junaid Rana, "The Story of Islamophobia," *Souls* 9, no. 2 (June 6, 2007): 149.

⁹ As Namira Islam writes, "Islamophobes often ask how their rhetoric could be racist if 'Muslim' refers to those who follow a faith tradition and not to those who are of a certain racial background. In the same breath, however, many Islamophobes stereotype all Arabs as Muslims and all Muslims as Arabs." Namira Islam, "Soft Islamophobia," *Religions* 9, no. 280 (September 15, 2018): 2.

¹⁰ I am indebted to Ilyse Morgenstein Fuerst for her succinct and cogent discussion of the racialization of Islam in a 2019 podcast published by the Alwaleed Center for Muslim-Christian Understanding at Georgetown University. She states, "Racialization is a process by which groups are made to be one cogent whole. . . . It's not just about defining groups as a whole but those definitions become inheritable and prognostic and intrinsic. So you get them from your parents and your community and they are a part of you regardless of whether or not you convert to another religion. And they're prognostic. We can imagine that a seven-year-old Muslim boy is at risk of becoming a jihadi because of these intrinsic and inherited qualities." Ilyse Morgenstein Fuerst, "Building Bridges—Dr. Ilyse Morgenstein Fuerst," interview by Andrew Condon, 2019, audio, 40:54, https://soundcloud.com/acmcu.

¹¹ Andrea Smith, *Unreconciled: From Racial Reconciliation to Racial Justice in Christian Evangelicalism* (Durham, NC: Duke University Press, 2019), 142.

¹² I appreciate Carlos A. Hoyt Jr.'s discussion of racialization in this video, particularly his explanation of essentialization and the permanence of racialized qualities. Oxford Academic (Oxford University Press), "The Racialization Process," YouTube video, 2:09, April 6, 2016, https://www.youtube.com.

¹³ Steve Garner and Saher Selod, "The Racialization of Muslims: Empirical Studies of Islamophobia," *Critical Sociology* 41, no. 1 (January 2015): 3.

¹⁴ This kind of racialized logic has also been applied to many other individuals and groups. In the summer of 2018, as the Trump administration began its practice of separating families who had crossed the U.S.-Mexico border without legal documentation, some media personalities cast these children, who were held in chain-link cages, as threats. Fox News host Laura Ingraham called these Latinx children "fresh recruits" for the gang MS-13 as a way to justify their imprisonment. Jack Holmes, "Watch Laura Ingraham's Soul Leave Her Body as She Describes Border Facilities as 'Summer Camps,'" *Esquire*, June 19, 2018, https://www.esquire.com.

¹⁵ Miqdaad Versi, "Concerns on Prevent," Muslim Council of Britain, 2015, https://www.mcb.org.uk.

¹⁶ Enes Bayrakli and Farid Hafez, eds., *European Islamophobia Report 2016* (Ankara: SETA: Foundation for Political, Economic, and Social Research, 2017), 8.

¹⁷ Leerom Medovoi, "Dogma-Line Racism: Islamophobia and the Second Axis of Race," *Social Text* 30, no. 2 (2012): 44.

¹⁸ This understanding draws on Howard Winant's definition of *racism* as "the routinized outcome of practices that create or reproduce hierarchical social structures based

on essentialized racial categories." Howard Winant, *Racial Conditions: Politics, Theory, Comparisons* (Minneapolis: University of Minnesota Press, 1994), 126.

[19] My definition, with its reliance on the concept of the racialization of Islam, comports with this one by Steve Garner and Saher Selod: "Islamophobia as a set of ideas and practices that amalgamate all Muslims into one group and the characteristics associated with Muslims (violence, misogyny, political allegiance/disloyalty, incompatibility with Western values, etc.) are treated as if they are innate." Garner and Selod, "The Racialization of Muslims," 5.

[20] I am indebted to the editors of the *Journal of Africana Religions* for this insight. As they write in a special issue dedicated to Islamophobia, "the very term 'Islamophobia' has come under rigorous scrutiny, as it can be interpreted to denote *fear* instead of the conflicts over social and political *power* that have inspired anti-Muslim behavior." Sylvester A. Johnson, Edward E. Curtis IV, Kristian Petersen, Michael Brandon McCormack et al., "Africana Perspectives on Islamophobia," *Journal of Africana Religions* 7 no. 1 (2019): 139.

[21] I generally do not use the word "Islamophobe," a term that scholars and others sometimes employ to label those who work for anti-Muslim groups, or politicians or prominent figures who contribute to Islamophobia and hold anti-Muslim views. I prefer not to employ the word because I have found it to be an unhelpful label on a psychological level. Name-calling does not help people lose their prejudiced positions, nor does it appeal to those who sympathize with them. Just as happens when someone gets called a "racist," calling people "Islamophobes" makes most of them defensive, causing them to dig in their heels and have little hope for critically examining their feelings or positions. Another reason I generally do not employ the term is that it is unclear where the line between an Islamophobe and someone who is not begins or ends. Because Islamophobia is a systemic issue, we all are to a certain extent implicated in it. Many of us have implicit biases about Muslims or contribute to discrimination in small and unseen ways. In that way, we all are Islamophobes, making the term meaningless. Instead, I prefer to point to the specific ways that persons contribute to Islamophobia. Some run anti-Muslim groups; others are pundits or politicians or talk-show hosts who hold or promote anti-Muslim views.

[22] Bridge Initiative Team, "Islamophobia: The Right Word for a Real Problem," *Bridge Initiative*, April 26, 2015, https://web.archive.org/web/20160913211817/http://bridge.georgetown.edu/islamophobia-the-right-word-for-a-real-problem/.

[23] It should be noted that the word *anti-Semitism* was originally coined and deployed by people who were proudly and openly anti-Jewish. As James Renton and Ben Gidley write in the introduction to their edited volume on Islamophobia and anti-Semitism in Europe, this political movement used the word in the name of their group, the Antisemiten-Liga of Berlin. See *Antisemitism and Islamophobia in Europe: A Shared Story?* (London: Palgrave Macmillan, 2017), 7.

[24] For a brief history of the word, see Bridge Initiative Team, "Islamophobia: The Right Word for a Real Problem."

[25] Ibid.

[26] In 1985, the author of the famous book *Orientalism*, Edward Said, made mention of the word, and in 1997 a report about Muslims in the United Kingdom used the term in its title. Gordon Conway, "Islamophobia: A Challenge for Us All" (The Runnymeade Trust, 1997).

[27] Bobby Ghosh, "Is America Islamophobic?," *Time*, August 30, 2010.

[28] Jordan Denari Duffner and the Bridge Initiative Team, "As Islamophobia Increases, So Does Use of the Word," *Bridge Initiative*, May 11, 2016, https://bridge.georgetown.edu.

[29] Ibid.

[30] See, for example: Eileen F. Toplansky, "Hiding behind 'Islamophobia,'" Campus Watch, June 3, 2019, https://www.meforum.org/campus-watch; Philip Carl Salzman, "'Islamophobia' Invention Has Served Its Purpose Spectacularly Well," Middle East Forum, January 15, 2019, https://www.meforum.org; Robert Spencer, "Did the Muslim Brotherhood Invent the Term 'Islamophobia'?," Jihad Watch, August 27, 2012, https://www.jihadwatch.org; Tarek Fatah (@tarekfatah), "The Word 'Islamophobia' Was Created by #Islamists @OmarAlghabra to Silence Muslims Who Want to Cleanse Islam of Polygamy, Arab Supremacy, FGM, Ayatullahs, Kings, Sharia Law, & Mullahs Who Pray in Mosque Sermons for Defeat of Kafirs (Hindus Jews Christians) at the Hands of Muslims," Twitter, February 2, 2018, 2:22 a.m., https://twitter.com/TarekFatah; Justin Tyler Clark, "How Political Correctness Led to Islamophobia," *Boston Globe*, August 5, 2017, https://www.bostonglobe.com.

[31] This important point is emphasized by scholars like Zareena Grewal and the authors of the #IslamophobiaIsRacism syllabus. Increasingly, this has become the new premise of much anti-Islamophobia activism and education. See Su'ad Khabeer, Arshad Ali, Evelyn Alsultany et al., eds., "#IslamophobiaIsRacismSyllabus," https://islamophobiaisracism.wordpress.com/; Islam, "Soft Islamophobia"; and Alison Kysia, "Challenge Islamophobia: A Project of Teaching for Change," Challenge Islamophobia, https://www.challengeislamophobia.org.

[32] The notion and practice of scapegoating have their origins in the Hebrew Bible. In Leviticus 16, the people of Israel are instructed to sacrifice or send away a goat, by whom the sins of the community are symbolically carried. This practice achieves atonement between the community and God. I am grateful to Fr. Patrick Rogers, SJ, for his suggestion of framing Islamophobia as a manifestation of the scapegoat mechanism, as theorized by René Girard.

[33] James Aho, "Scapegoating," in *Encyclopedia of Global Religions*, ed. Wade Roof and Mark Juergensmeyer (Thousand Oaks, CA: Sage Publications, 2011).

[34] René Girard, *Violence and the Sacred* (Baltimore, MD: Johns Hopkins University Press, 1979).

[35] René Girard, "On War and Apocalypse," *First Things: A Monthly Journal of Religion and Public Life* 195 (2009): 19.

[36] Ibid.

[37] Samir Khalaf, "Protestant Images of Islam: Disparaging Stereotypes Reconfirmed," *Islam and Christian–Muslim Relations* 8, no. 2 (July 1, 1997): 211–29, at 217.

[38] Peter Gottschalk and Gabriel Greenberg define *stereotypes* as "descriptions of a group by outsiders using characteristics understood both to be shared by all members and to define them as different from 'normal' society." Peter Gottschalk and Gabriel Greenberg, *Islamophobia: Making Muslims the Enemy* (Lanham, MD: Rowman & Littlefield, 2008), 63.

[39] Bridge Initiative Team, "Factsheet: Common Anti-Muslim Tropes," *Bridge Initiative*, December 4, 2018, https://bridge.georgetown.edu/research/factsheet-common-anti-muslim-tropes-2/. Kambiz GhaneaBassiri has pointed out the "tyrannical" stereotype, in "Islamophobia and American History: Religious Stereotyping and Out-Grouping of Muslims in the United States," in Ernst, *Islamophobia in America*, 53–74.

[40] Khalaf, "Protestant Images of Islam."

[41] Ibid., 220.

[42] One event that had a particular impact on the early American imagination were the stories of White Americans imprisoned or enslaved at the hands of Muslim Barbary pirates in North Africa. See David L. Johnston, "American Evangelical Islamophobia: A History of Continuity with a Hope for Change," *Journal of Ecumenical Studies* 51, no. 2 (2016): 224–35.

[43] Melanie McAlister writes that during this period, the distinctions between these cases and peoples were not made clear to Americans, leaving Islam to be the factor that defined these different problems and thus unified then. "It didn't matter that Iran was not Iraq (nor that they'd recently ended their own war). It did not matter that one was largely Shi'i and the other largely Sunni, nor that Persian was mainly spoken in one and Arabic in the other. In the minds of Americans, Islam had come to define them both, making it hard to distinguish one from the other." Melani McAlister, "Iran, Islam, and the Terrorist Threat, 1979–1989," in *Epic Encounters: Culture, Media, and U.S. Interests in the Middle East since 1945*, Updated Edition with a Post-9/11 Chapter (Berkeley: University of California Press, 2005), 233–34.

[44] Kambiz GhaneaBassiri writes that these stereotypes were present, though latent, during this period. GhaneaBassiri, "Islamophobia and American History," 53.

[45] Edward E. Curtis IV, "The Black Muslim Scare of the Twentieth Century," in Ernst, *Islamophobia in America*, 76.

[46] Peter Gottschalk, *American Heretics: Catholics, Jews, Muslims, and the History of Religious Intolerance* (New York: St. Martin's Press, 2013).

[47] "Dangerous Speech: A Practical Guide," Dangerous Speech Project, https://dangerousspeech.org/guide/.

[48] Donald Trump, Executive Order 13780, Protecting the Nation from Foreign Terrorist Entry into the United States, 82 Fed. Reg. 13209 (March 6, 2017).

2. The Not-So-Recent History of Islamophobia in the United States

[1] Yasmin Amer, "20 Years after a White Supremacist Almost Killed Him, He's Dedicated His Life to Changing Hearts," NPR/WBUR, November 26, 2019, https://www.wbur.org/kindworld.

[2] For reasons discussed in more depth elsewhere in this book, it is not accurate to blame Islam as a religion for acts of violence committed by terrorist groups. In the case of 9/11, the leader of Al-Qaeda, Osama bin Laden, released a public letter to the United States outlining his reasons for orchestrating the attack. Though he framed his views in Islamic religious language, the reasons he cited were largely political ones, including grievances about U.S. military involvement in the Middle East and American support for the region's oppressive governments. See "Full Text: Bin Laden's 'Letter to America,'" *The Guardian*, November 24, 2002, https://www.theguardian.com.

[3] Readers can find a graph depicting the FBI's hate crime data at jordandenari.com and on the website associated with this book.

[4] As discussed in chapter 5, FBI hate crime data does not give us a full picture or accounting of the extent of anti-Muslim incidents or crimes that occur across the United States. Due to poor reporting, the high standards for hate crime charges and convictions,

and the way unconscious biases shape perpetrators' actions, many Islamophobic crimes go uncounted.

⁵ N. R. Kleinfield, "Rider Asks If Cabby Is Muslim, Then Stabs Him," *New York Times*, August 25, 2010, www.nytimes.com.

⁶ Lorenzo Ferrigno, "New York Man Gets Nearly 10 Years for Hate Crime against Cabbie," *CNN*, June 26, 2013, https://www.cnn.com.

⁷ Robert Spencer is not to be confused with Richard Spencer, the more well-known leader of an alt-right, neo-Nazi group.

⁸ CNN Wire Staff, "Protesters Descend on Ground Zero for Anti-Mosque Demonstration—CNN.Com," *CNN*, June 7, 2010, http://www.cnn.com; "CNN: Anderson Cooper 360 on Ground Zero Mosque: It's Geller's Fault!," YouTube video, 17:08, August 17, 2018, https://www.youtube.com; "Sean Hannity Discusses the Ground Zero Mosque with Robert Spencer," YouTube video, 4:25, August 8, 2010, https://www.youtube.com.

⁹ Anne Barnard and Alan Feuer, "Pamela Geller—Blogger, Provocateur, Lightning Rod," *New York Times*, October 8, 2010, https://www.nytimes.com.

¹⁰ Azmat Khan, "Pamela Geller: 'This Is a Clash of Civilizations,'" *PBS Frontline*, September 27, 2011, https://www.pbs.org/wgbh; "New York Mosque Controversy Fires Up National Campaign," *FOX News*, August 2, 2010, https://www.foxnews.com.

¹¹ Sheryl Gay Stolberg, "Obama Strongly Backs Islam Center near 9/11 Site," *New York Times*, August 13, 2010, www.nytimes.com; Ken Rudin, "Harry Reid, the GOP, and the Politics of the 'Ground Zero Mosque,'" NPR/WNYC, August 18, 2010, https://www.npr.org.

¹² Alex Altman, "TIME Poll: Majority Oppose Mosque, Many Distrust Muslims," *Time*, August 19, 2010.

¹³ According to a *Time* magazine poll from August 2010, only 44 percent of Americans responded having "very" or "somewhat favorable" views of Muslims, compared to other religious groups who received large majorities of "favorable" ratings from the American public: Jews (75 percent), Protestants (74 percent), Catholics (73 percent), and Mormons (57 percent). Americans also expressed more negative attitudes toward Muslims than other groups; 43 percent admitted to having "somewhat" or "very unfavorable" views of Muslims, compared to only 13 percent feeling this way toward Jews and Protestants. See "TIME Poll Results: Americans' Views on the Campaign, Religion and the Mosque Controversy," *Time*, August 18, 2010.

¹⁴ Greg Sargent, "The Plum Line—GOP Senate Candidates Drag Obama's Mosque Speech into Their Races," *Washington Post*, August 16, 2010, http://voices.washingtonpost.com; Bobby Ghosh, "Islamophobia: Does America Have a Muslim Problem?," *Time*, August 19, 2010, http://www.time.com.

¹⁵ Bloomberg has since run for the U.S. presidency as a Democrat, but at the time he served as the mayor of New York City, having run as a Republican. See "New York Mosque Controversy Fires Up National Campaign," FOX News.

¹⁶ Travis Loller, "Tenn. Candidate Denounces Mosque Proposal," Highbeam Research, June 25, 2010, www.highbeam.com.

¹⁷ Rudin, "Harry Reid, the GOP, and the Politics of the 'Ground Zero Mosque;'" Carl Hulse, "G.O.P. Seizes on Mosque Issue Ahead of Elections," *New York Times*, August 16, 2010, www.nytimes.com.

¹⁸ *Sharia* is often transliterated into English in a range of ways, but for consistency's sake I spell it this way throughout this book (except in quotations in which it appears differently).

[19] Arjun Singh Sethi, "Calling the Muslim Brotherhood a Terrorist Group Would Hurt All American Muslims," *Washington Post*, February 8, 2017, https://www.washingtonpost.com.

[20] Sharia is discussed at length, as well as these campaigns to ban it, later in the book.

[21] William Spindler, "2015: The Year of Europe's Refugee Crisis," UNHCR, December 8, 2015, https://www.unhcr.org.

[22] Richard Winton, "We May Never Know Why the San Bernardino Terrorists Targeted a Christmas Party. Here's What We Do Know," *Los Angeles Times*, December 2, 2016, https://www.latimes.com.

[23] Ehab Zahriyeh, "Incidents Targeting US Mosques Triple in 2015, Report Says," *Al-Jazeera*, December 18, 2015, http://america.aljazeera.com.

[24] Kayatoun Kishi, "Assaults against Muslims in U.S. Surpass 2001 Level," *Pew Research Center—FactTank* (blog), November 15, 2017, https://www.pewresearch.org.

[25] As educator Alison Kysia notes, in recent years anti-Sikh and anti-Arab hate crimes have been counted separately from anti-Muslim attacks, and are thus not included in these numbers. Those incidents are, however, connected to Islamophobia, since Arabs (regardless of their religion) and those of the Sikh faith are often mistaken for Muslims. Alison Kysia, "Who Benefits from Islamophobia? Investigating the Profit Motive behind Bigotry and Discrimination," Teaching for Change (July 2019), 6.

[26] Nancy Coleman, "On Average, 9 Mosques Have Been Targeted Every Month This Year," *CNN*, August 7, 2017, https://cnn.com.

[27] Shannon Murray, "Police: Vandals Tore Apart, Dumped Feces on Quran at Mosque," *The Tennessean*, November 16, 2015, https://www.tennessean.com.

[28] Christopher Mathias, "There Were a Lot of Alleged Anti-Muslim Crimes during This Year's Ramadan | HuffPost," *HuffPost*, July 15, 2016, https://www.huffpost.com.

[29] Talal Ansari, "Suspect in the Beating of Two Youths outside of a Brooklyn Mosque Has Been Arrested," *BuzzFeed News*, July 3, 2016, https://www.buzzfeednews.com.

[30] Rachael Pells, "Muslim Doctor 'Shot and Stabbed' outside Mosque in Texas," *The Independent*, July 3, 2016, https://www.independent.co.uk.

[31] Aysha Khan, "Indianapolis Muslims Call for Hate Crime Investigation into Mosque Shooting on Eid," Religion News Service, May 28, 2020, https://religionnews.com.

[32] Ibrahim Hooper, "CAIR-LA Concerned about Suspicious Package Found at Mosque Following Harassment of Worshipers," Council on American-Islamic Relations, July 15, 2019, https://www.cair.com/press_releases/; Massarah Mikati, "Houston Mosque Threatened for Second Time in Online Forum," *Houston Chronicle*, June 14, 2019, https://www.houstonchronicle.com.

[33] Kristine Phillips, "'It's a Sickness': Letters Calling for Genocide of Muslims Sent to Mosques across the Country," *Washington Post*, November 29, 2016, www.washingtonpost.com.

[34] Corey Peel and Kent Justice, "Authorities: Man, 69, Planned Mass Shooting at Islamic Center in Jacksonville," WJCT, December 4, 2017, https://news.wjct.org.

[35] James Fanelli, "Muslim Biz Gal Beaten," *New York Post*, September 16, 2007, https://web.archive.org/web/20160628065545/http://nypost.com/2007/09/16/muslim-biz-gal-beaten/.

[36] "California Woman Videotaped Throwing Coffee on Muslim Man Charged with Hate Crime," *Times Record*, December 17, 2015, https://www.swtimes.com.

[37] Hilary Hanson, "Woman Allegedly Attacks Muslim Mums and Babies in Hate Crime," *HuffPost Australia*, November 9, 2016, https://www.huffingtonpost.com.au.

[38] Alaa Elassar, "Muslim Woman Files Discrimination Charge after She Says a Target Starbucks Barista Wrote 'ISIS' on Her Cup," *CNN*, July 8, 2020, https://www.cnn.com.

[39] "Islamophobia: Understanding Anti-Muslim Sentiment in the West," Gallup.com, December 12, 2011, https://news.gallup.com.

[40] Azka Mahmood and Dalia Mogahed, "American Muslim Poll 2019: Predicting and Preventing Islamophobia," ISPU, April 15, 2019, https://www.ispu.org/ .

[41] CAIR California, "Singled Out: Islamophobia in the Classroom and the Impact of Discrimination on Muslim Students" (San Francisco, California, November 2019), https://ca.cair.com.

[42] Scott Gleeson, "Muslim Student Disqualified for Wearing Hijab in Cross-Country Race," *USA Today*, October 25, 2019, https://www.usatoday.com.

[43] Carma Hassan and Catherine Shoichet, "Arabic-Speaking Student Kicked Off Southwest Flight," *CNN*, April 18, 2016, https://www.cnn.com; Khaled A. Beydoun and Arun Kundnani, "Professor Removed from a Southwest Flight Is Symbolic of a Pattern of Airline Islamophobia," *Truthout*, October 22, 2017, https://truthout.org.

[44] Omid Safi, "You Know You're An Immigrant When . . . —The On Being Project," *On Being*, November 1, 2017, https://onbeing.org/blog.

[45] Jack Jenkins, "American Muslim Family's Home Attacked in the Middle of the Night," *ThinkProgress*, March 17, 2015, https://archive.thinkprogress.org.

[46] FOX 4 News-Dallas-Fort Worth, "Plano Muslim Family's Home Vandalized," YouTube video, 3:29, December 10, 2015, https://www.youtube.com.

[47] Shachar Peled, "Muslim Family's Home Vandalized; Quran Torn, Green Cards Stolen," *CNN*, March 29, 2017, https://www.cnn.com/.

[48] Tim Ghianni, "Tennessee Man Sentenced over Plot to Attack Muslim Community," *Reuters*, June 15, 2017, https://in.reuters.com.

[49] John Cardinale, "Muslim Leader Assaulted in Bloomington," CBS3Duluth, August 8, 2020, http://cbs3duluth.com.

[50] Rebecca Clay, "Muslims in America, Post 9/11," *American Psychological Association* 42, no. 8 (September 2011): 72.

[51] "U.S. Muslims Concerned about Their Place in Society, but Continue to Believe in the American Dream," *Pew Research Center's Religion & Public Life Project*, July 26, 2017, https://www.pewforum.org.

[52] Safiyya Hosein, "Muslim Grief and Identity after Christchurch," *The Nib*, April 3, 2019, https://thenib.com.

[53] Samira Sadeque, "After Christchurch, US Mosques Bulk Up Security during Ramadan," *Al-Jazeera*, May 24, 2019, https://www.aljazeera.com.

[54] Eman Bare, "Islamophobia Has Become So Bad That Some Muslim Girls Are Afraid to Wear Their Hijabs," *Teen Vogue*, February 25, 2016, https://www.teenvogue.com.

[55] Theodore Schleifer, "Donald Trump Doesn't Challenge Anti-Muslim Questioner," *CNN*, September 18, 2015, https://www.cnn.com/2015/09/17/politics/donald-trump-obama-muslim-new-hampshire/index.html.

[56] Ibid.

[57] He later stood by the statement, and his campaign manager even acknowledged that the vast majority of Republican voters were in agreement. Peter Beinart, "The Muted GOP Response to Roy Moore's Anti-Muslim Prejudice," *The Atlantic*, September 28, 2017; https://www.theatlantic.com. In attempting to walk back his statement later, he said that only Muslim politicians who were secular and "subjugated" their beliefs would be fit to

serve in office. Bridge Initiative Team, "Islamophobia and the 2016 Elections," *Bridge Initiative*, January 29, 2017, https://web.archive.org/web/20170129095400/https:/bridge.georgetown.edu/islamophobia-and-the-2016-elections/.

[58] Kyle Cheney, "No, Clinton Didn't Start the Birther Thing. This Guy Did," *Politico*, September 16, 2016, https://www.politico.com.

[59] Chris Moody and Kristen Holmes, "Trump's History of Suggesting Obama Is a Muslim," *CNN*, September 18, 2015, https://www.cnn.com.

[60] Ibid.

[61] Ibid.

[62] The idea that Obama is Muslim still persists and is spread through memes to this day. As I was writing this book, Reuters had to issue a fact-check article to combat the viral meme claiming that Obama, unlike other presidents, insisted on standing in front of a "Muslim prayer curtain" instead of the U.S. flag during speeches. There is no such thing as a Muslim prayer curtain. "Fact Check: Obama Not Standing in Front of 'Muslim Prayer Curtain' in White House," *Reuters*, June 25, 2020, https://www.reuters.com.

[63] Moody and Holmes, "Trump's History of Suggesting Obama Is a Muslim."

[64] Edward E. Curtis IV, "The Black Muslim Scare of the Twentieth Century," in *Islamophobia in America: The Anatomy of Intolerance*, ed. Carl W. Ernst (New York: Palgrave Macmillan U.S., 2013), 76.

[65] Bridge Initiative Team, "Islamophobia and the 2016 Elections."

[66] David Shariatmadari, "Britain First May Be Fringe, but Its Anti-Islam Views Aren't—Opinion," *The Guardian*, November 30, 2017, https://www.theguardian.com.

[67] Abby Ohlheiser and Lindsey Bever, "Analysis: How an Old, Far-Right Meme about Muslim 'Prayer Rugs' at the Border Became a Trump Tweet," *Washington Post*, January 18, 2019, www.washingtonpost.com. The claim about prayer rugs at the border could not be verified, but journalists and movie critics pointed out that this happens to be a plot point from a movie as well as a rumor that had previously circulated in right-wing media. See Andrew Whalen, "Was Trump's Prayer Rugs Tweet Really From 'Sicario 2'?," *Newsweek*, January 18, 2019, https://www.newsweek.com.

[68] Karsten Müller and Carlo Schwarz, "From Hashtag to Hate Crime: Twitter and Anti-Minority Sentiment," SSRN, July 24, 2020, www.ssrn.com.

[69] Jeremy Diamond, "Cruz: Police Need to 'Patrol' Muslim Neighborhoods," *CNN*, March 22, 2016, https://www.cnn.com.

[70] Bridge Initiative Team, "Islamophobia and the 2016 Elections."

[71] Massod Farivar, "Attacks Against US Muslims Growing in Frequency, Violence," *VOA News*, August 17, 2016, https://www.voanews.com.

[72] Bridge Initiative Team, "Islamophobia and the 2016 Elections."

[73] Jordan Denari Duffner, "What's Wrong with Rubio Comparing Muslims to Members of the Nazi Party," *HuffPost*, November 17, 2016, https://www.huffpost.com.

[74] Max Fisher, "Marco Rubio's Comments about Muslims Are Getting to Be Almost as Frightening as Trump's," *Vox*, February 4, 2016, https://www.vox.com.

[75] Christopher Mathias, "Front-Runner for U.S. Senate Seat in Alabama Calls Islam a 'False Religion,'" *HuffPost*, July 25, 2017, https://www.huffpost.com.

[76] Beinart, "The Muted GOP Response to Roy Moore's Anti-Muslim Prejudice."

[77] Chris Riotta, "Rudy Giuliani Promotes Long-Debunked Image of Ilhan Omar 'at al-Qaeda Training Camp,'" *Yahoo*, July 22, 2020, https://news.yahoo.com.

[78] William Cummings, "Ilhan Omar Tied to 9/11 Attack in Poster in West Virginia Capitol," *USA Today*, March 1, 2019, https://www.usatoday.com; Arsalan Iftikhar, "Islamophobia: A Bipartisan Xenophobia in American Politics," *Religion and Politics*, October 8, 2019, https://religionandpolitics.org.

[79] Mehdi Hasan, "When Ilhan Omar Is Accused of Anti-Semitism, It's News. When a Republican Smears Muslims, There's Silence," *The Intercept* (blog), August 28, 2019, https://theintercept.com.

[80] Scott Keyes, "EXCLUSIVE: Herman Cain Tells ThinkProgress 'I Will Not' Appoint a Muslim in My Administration," *ThinkProgress*, March 26, 2011, https://web.archive.org/web/20170325052039/https:/thinkprogress.org/exclusive-herman-cain-tells-thinkprogress-i-will-not-appoint-a-muslim-in-my-administration-158c8bead223.

[81] Igor Volsky, "Bachmann Stands by Widely Condemned Islamophobic Attack, Finds Ally in Glenn Beck," *ThinkProgress*, July 19, 2012, https://archive.thinkprogress.org.

[82] Matthew Duss et al., "Fear, Inc. 2.0: The Islamophobia Network's Efforts to Manufacture Hate in America" (Washington, DC: Center for American Progress, February 2015), 12.

[83] "Allen West," Council on American-Islamic Relations, October 5, 2017, http://www.islamophobia.org.

[84] Jessica Taylor, "Trump Calls for 'Total and Complete Shutdown of Muslims Entering' U.S.," NPR, December 7, 2015, https://www.npr.org. Trump reiterated and doubled down on this proposed ban during much of his campaign. See CNN, "Trump Again Calls for Ban on Muslim Immigrants," YouTube video, 2:38, June 3, 2016.

[85] Nick Gass, "Poll: 6 in 10 GOP Voters Back Trump's Muslim Ban," *Politico*, December 14, 2015, https://www.politico.com.

[86] Bridge Initiative Team, "Infographic: Muslims Not Welcome: Vast Majority of GOP Voters Agree with Trump," *Bridge Initiative*, March 23, 2016, https://bridge.georgetown.edu.

[87] Josh Barro, "How Unpopular Is Trump's Muslim Ban? Depends How You Ask," *New York Times, The Upshot* (blog), December 15, 2015, https://www.nytimes.com.

[88] *CNN*, "Trump Supporters React to His Plan to Ban Muslims," YouTube video, 2:22, December 7, 2015, https://www.youtube.com.

[89] "Gun Store Owner: We're a Muslim-Free Zone—CNN Video," *CNN*, July 21, 2015, https://www.cnn.com; Jennifer Hassan, "'Punish a Muslim Day' Generates Anger, Fear and Solidarity in Britain," *Washington Post*, April 3, 2018, https://www.washingtonpost.com.

[90] One example of this is Robert Spencer's *Confessions of an Islamophobe* (New York: Bombardier Books, 2017).

[91] Maryam Saleh, "U.S. Courts Have Been Treating Muslims Differently for a Very Long Time," *The Intercept* (blog), December 7, 2017, https://theintercept.com.

[92] Abigail Hauslohner and Abby Phillips, "Trump Continues to Sow Confusion over His Plan for Muslims Entering the Country," *Washington Post*, December 22, 2016, https://www.washingtonpost.com.

[93] Kevin Liptak and Shachar Peled, "Obama Administration Ending Program Once Used to Track Mostly Arab and Muslim Men," *CNN*, December 22, 2016, https://www.cnn.com.

[94] Rebecca Savransky, "Giuliani: Trump Asked Me How to Do a Muslim Ban 'Legally,'" *The Hill*, January 29, 2017, https://thehill.com.

[95] A comparison of versions of the policy shows how U.S. economic and geopolitical factors also played into the changes; at one point, Trump considered letting in Muslims who were wealthy and who would thus contribute positively to the U.S. economy. Hauslohner and Phillips, "Trump Continues to Sow Confusion."

[96] Bridge Initiative Team, "The Muslim and African Bans: By the Numbers," *Bridge Initiative*, June 23, 2020, https://bridge.georgetown.edu.

[97] Beeta Baghoolizadeh, "The #MuslimBan Primer: Key Terms and a Timeline of Events," *Ajam Media Collective* (blog), February 6, 2017, https://ajammc.com.

[98] Greg Toppo, "New Travel Ban Adds North Korea, Venezuela," *USA Today*, September 24, 2017, https://www.usatoday.com.

[99] Pema Levy, "The Question for the Supreme Court: Is Trump's Latest Travel Ban Still the Same Old Muslim Ban?," *Mother Jones*, October 9, 2017, https://www.motherjones.com.

[100] This is reflected in the way that the news media and politicians spoke of the executive order. They adopted the Trump administration's more euphemistic characterization, calling it a "travel ban." A ban on travel makes it sound like it is only a luxury that is being taken away, not people's ability to flee war, reunite with family, and make a dignified life in the United States.

[101] Jessica Lussenhop, "US Residents in Legal Limbo at Airport," *BBC News*, January 29, 2017, https://www.bbc.com.

[102] "Executive Order Protecting the Nation from Foreign Terrorist Entry into the United States," The White House, January 27, 2017, https://www.whitehouse.gov.

[103] "Executive Order Protecting the Nation from Foreign Terrorist Entry into the United States," The White House, March 6, 2017, https://www.whitehouse.gov.

[104] This is a pseudonym, because the student wished to remain anonymous.

[105] Bridge Initiative Team, "The Muslim and African Bans."

[106] Ibid.

[107] Keegan Hamilton, "Trump Has Banned Muslim Refugees. These Numbers Prove It," *VICE News*, April 25, 2018, https://www.vice.com.

[108] Bridge Initiative Team, "The Muslim and African Bans"; Phillip Connor and Jens Manuel Krogstad, "Muslim Refugees Admitted to US Down Sharply in Fiscal 2018," *Pew Research Center* (blog), May 3, 2018, https://www.pewresearch.org/fact-tank.

[109] Bridge Initiative Team, "The Muslim and African Bans."

[110] Ishaan Tharoor, "Stephen Miller's Far-Right Agenda," *Washington Post*, Today's Worldview, November 25, 2019, https://www.washingtonpost.com.

[111] Curtis, "The Black Muslim Scare of the Twentieth Century," 99.

[112] Wajahat Ali et al., "Fear, Inc.: The Roots of the Islamophobia Network in America" (Washington, DC: Center for American Progress, August 26, 2011), https://www.americanprogress.org; Nathan Lean, *The Islamophobia Industry: How the Right Manufactures Fear of Muslims* (London: Pluto Press, 2012).

[113] See Lean, *The Islamophobia Industry*.

[114] "Hijacked by Hate: American Philanthropy and the Islamophobia Network" (Washington, DC: CAIR, 2019), http://www.islamophobia.org; Kysia, "Who Benefits from Islamophobia?"

[115] The Bridge Initiative, "Have You Ever Heard Someone Say This about Muslims?," YouTube video, 3:52, July 28, 2017, https://www.youtube.com.

[116] Mobashra Tazamal, "Is ACT for America Really a Grassroots Organization?," *Bridge Initiative*, September 10, 2018, https://bridge.georgetown.edu.

[117] Other individuals include Daniel Pipes, Steve Emerson, David Horowitz, Zuhdi Jasser, David Yerushalmi, and Nonie Darwish. Center for American Progress, "The Islamophobia Network," https://islamophobianetwork.com/.

[118] Ibid.

[119] Christopher Bail, "Fringe Benefits: How Anti-Muslim Organizations Became Mainstream," in *Terrified: How Anti-Muslim Fringe Organizations Became Mainstream* (Princeton, NJ: Princeton University Press, 2015), 67–86.

[120] "Anti-Muslim Hate Groups," Southern Poverty Law Center, https://www.splcenter.org/fighting-hate/extremist-files/ideology/anti-muslim.

[121] Tazamal, "Is ACT for America Really a Grassroots Organization?"

[122] Mobashra Tazamal, "FOX News: A Megaphone for Anti-Muslim Hatred," *Bridge Initiative*, March 18, 2019, https://bridge.georgetown.edu.

[123] Bridge Initiative Team, "Trump Calls for Ban on Muslims, Cites Deeply Flawed Poll," *Bridge Initiative*, December 9, 2015, https://bridge.georgetown.edu.

[124] Zack Beauchamp, "How John Bolton and Mike Pompeo Mainstreamed Islamophobia," *Vox*, March 27, 2018, https://www.vox.com; see also Bridge Initiative factsheets on these individuals.

[125] Bridge Initiative Team, "Factsheet: Steve Bannon," *Bridge Initiative*, September 16, 2016, https://bridge.georgetown.edu.

[126] One example is Mark Kevin Lloyd, who was appointed the religious freedom adviser for the U.S. Agency for International Development (USAID) by Trump in 2020. See Bridge Initiative Team, "Factsheet: Mark Kevin Lloyd," *Bridge Initiative*, June 25, 2020, https://bridge.georgetown.edu.

[127] David Noriega, "Brigitte Gabriel Wants You to Fight Islam," *Buzzfeed News*, September 27, 2016, https://www.buzzfeednews.com/; Peter Beinart, "America's Most Prominent Anti-Muslim Activist Is Welcome at the White House," *The Atlantic*, March 21, 2017, https://www.theatlantic.com.

[128] Hannah Allam and Talal Ansari, "State and Local Republican Officials Have Been Bashing Muslims. We Counted," *BuzzFeed News*, April 10, 2018, https://www.buzzfeednews.com/.

[129] Rachel Slajda, "Just before Hearings, King Will Appear on Anti-Muslim Group's TV," *Talking Points Memo*, January 20, 2011, https://talkingpointsmemo.com.

[130] Namira Islam, "Soft Islamophobia," *Religions* 9, no. 280 (September 15, 2018): 5.

[131] "Can't We Talk About This? More Anti-Muslim Propaganda from Pamela Geller," Southern Poverty Law Center, October 2, 2017, https://www.splcenter.org; Ali et al., "Fear, Inc."

[132] Michael Powell, "In Police Training, a Dark Film on U.S. Muslims," *New York Times*, January 23, 2012, https://www.nytimes.com.

[133] Nathan Lean, "Islamophobia in the United States: A Case of the Three 'I's," Oxford Islamic Studies Online—*Focus On* blog, http://www.oxfordislamicstudies.com; Ali et al., "Fear, Inc."

[134] Tim Lister and Clare Sebastian, "Stoking Islamophobia and Secession in Texas—From an Office in Russia," *CNN*, October 6, 2017, https://www.cnn.com.

[135] Aisha Ghani and Tom Phillips, "Inaccurate or Misleading News Stories about Muslims Have Been Shared Hundreds of Thousands of Times This Year," *BuzzFeed News*, August 16, 2017, https://www.buzzfeed.com.

[136] Nathan Lean and Jordan Denari, "The Super Survey: Two Decades of Americans' Views on Islam & Muslims" (Washington, DC: Bridge Initiative, 2015), 31.

[137] Shibley Telhami, "Analysis | How Trump Changed Americans' View of Islam—for the Better," *Washington Post*, January 25, 2017, https://www.washingtonpost.com.

[138] Ibid.

[139] "How the U.S. General Public Views Muslims and Islam," *Pew Research Center's Religion & Public Life Project* (blog), July 26, 2017, https://www.pewforum.org.

[140] Gallup Inc., "Perceptions of Muslims in the United States: A Review," *Gallup.com*, December 11, 2015, https://news.gallup.com.

[141] Brian Levin, "Explaining the Rise in Hate Crimes against Muslims in the US," *Salon*, July 31, 2017, https://www.salon.com/.

[142] Jason Lemon, "Less Than 40 Percent of Republicans Would Vote for a Muslim for President: Poll," *Newsweek*, May 13, 2019, https://www.newsweek.com.

[143] Mahmood and Mogahed, "American Muslim Poll 2019."

[144] Amer, "20 Years after a White Supremacist Almost Killed Him."

[145] The Secret Lives of Muslims team, "This Muslim American Was Shot after 9/11. Then He Fought to Save His Attacker's Life," *Vox*, November 28, 2016, https://www.vox.com/videos.

3. Both Sides

[1] These are not pseudonyms. I received permission from Asima Silva to recount their story in this book.

[2] Abdul Malik Mujahid, "How the Muslim Ban Legalized Islamophobia," *HuffPost*, July 21, 2017, https://www.huffpost.com.

[3] As Edward E. Curtis IV points out, the fact that Islamophobic sentiment exists on the left and that anti-Muslim discrimination occurs under Democratic administrations is not accidental. In fact, he writes, Islamophobia is "constitutive" of liberalism, which spans both the right and left of the political spectrum in the United States and elsewhere. Edward E. Curtis IV (@JAfricanaRelig), "Islamophobia is a constituent element of rather than an exception to U.S. liberalism," Twitter, June 23, 2020, 3:40pm, http://twitter.com.

[4] "Text: President Bush Visits Islamic Center," *Washington Post*, September 17, 2001, https://www.washingtonpost.com.

[5] I am grateful to Imam Yahya Hendi, who was present with President Bush that day, for sharing his experiences with me.

[6] "Text: President Bush Addresses the Nation," *Washington Post*, September 20, 2001, https://www.washingtonpost.com.

[7] "President: Today We Mourned, Tomorrow We Work," The White House: President George W. Bush, September 16, 2001, https://georgewbush-whitehouse.archives.gov.

[8] Tara Golshan, "Joe Biden's Iraq Problem," *Vox*, October 15, 2019, https://www.vox.com.

[9] ACLU, "Surveillance under the USA/Patriot Act," https://www.aclu.org/other/surveillance-under-usapatriot-act.

[10] Heena Musabji and Christina Abraham, "The Threat to Civil Liberties and Its Effect on Muslims in America," *DePaul Journal for Social Justice* 1, no. 1 (2016): 31.

[11] Dara Lind, "Everyone's Heard of the Patriot Act. Here's What It Actually Does," *Vox*, June 2, 2015, https://www.vox.com/.

¹² Rights Working Group, "The NSEERS Effect: A Decade of Racial Profiling, Fear, and Secrecy," *Center for Immigrants' Rights Clinic Publications* (Penn State Law, May 2012), https://pennstatelaw.psu.edu. NSEERS, which stands for National Security Entry-Exit Registration System, was also called INS Special Registration.

¹³ Chantal Da Silva, "Court Ruling Branding U.S. Terror Watchlist Unconstitutional Celebrated as 'Tremendous Victory' for Muslim-Americans 'Unjustly Profiled by the Government,'" *Newsweek*, September 5, 2019, https://www.newsweek.com.

¹⁴ "Body Count: Casualty Figures after 10 Years of the 'War on Terror'—Iraq, Afghanistan, Pakistan" (Physicians for Social Responsibility, 2015), https://www.psr.org/wp-content/uploads/2018/05/body-count.pdf.

¹⁵ "Casualty Status" (U.S. Department of Defense, August 31, 2020), https://www.defense.gov/casualty.pdf.

¹⁶ Bridge Initiative Team, "Factsheet: The Human Cost of Guantánamo Bay Detention Camp," *Bridge Initiative*, July 18, 2020, https://bridge.georgetown.edu.

¹⁷ CNN Editorial Research Team, "Iraq Prison Abuse Scandal Fast Facts," *CNN*, March 22, 2020, https://www.cnn.com.

¹⁸ Bridge Initiative Team, "Factsheet: The Human Cost of Guantánamo Bay."

¹⁹ Mohamedou Ould Slahi, *Guantánamo Diary*, ed. Larry Siems (New York: Little, Brown and Company, 2015); a revised edition was published in 2017 by Back Bay Books. See also http://guantanamodiary.com.

²⁰ Bridge Initiative Team, "Factsheet: Torture at Guantánamo Bay Detention Camp," *Bridge Initiative*, July 19, 2020, https://bridge.georgetown.edu.

²¹ Bridge Initiative Team, "Factsheet: The Human Cost of Guantánamo Bay."

²² Jon Greenberg, "PolitiFact | Lizza Says Obama Has Bombed More Nations Than Bush," *Politifact*, September 25, 2014, https://www.politifact.com/factchecks.

²³ "Powell's Muslim Question—The Top 10 Everything of 2008," *Time*, November 3, 2008, http://content.time.com.

²⁴ See "Watch John McCain Strongly Defend Barack Obama during the 2008 Campaign," www.time.com.

²⁵ Dan Nowicki, "In Rebuke of Donald Trump, Religious Intolerance, Sen. Jeff Flake Talks Solidarity at Scottsdale Mosque," *AZCentral*, December 11, 2015, https://www.azcentral.com.

²⁶ Amber Phillips, "That Time Paul Ryan Gave a Succinct, Near-Perfect Response to Trump's Call to Ban Muslims," *Washington Post*, January 28, 2017, https://www.washingtonpost.com.

²⁷ See, for example, the statements made by Republicans that are quoted in Zeke Miller and Tessa Berenson, "Republican Rivals Condemn Donald Trump's Proposed Muslim Entry Ban," *TIME*, December 7, 2015, https://time.com. See also Deirdre Walsh, Jeremy Diamond, and Ted Barrett, "Priebus, Ryan and McConnell Rip Trump Anti-Muslim Proposal," December 8, 2015, *CNN*, https://www.cnn.com. See also "Donald Trump's Muslim US Ban Call Roundly Condemned," *BBC News*, December 8, 2015, https://www.bbc.com.

²⁸ Paul Kane, "Ted Cruz Rejects Trump's Muslim Ban Policy, but Stands by Trump Himself," *Washington Post*, December 8, 2015; https://www.washingtonpost.com.

²⁹ Nick Gass, "Poll: 6 in 10 GOP Voters Back Trump's Muslim Ban," *Politico*, December 14, 2015, https://www.politico.com.

³⁰ David A. Graham, "Donald Trump, George W. Bush, and How the Republican

Party Won and Lost the Muslim Vote," *The Atlantic*, December 9, 2015, https://www.theatlantic.com.

[31] David A. Graham, "Hillary Clinton's Careful Courtship of Muslim Voters," *The Atlantic*, October 24, 2016, https://www.theatlantic.com.

[32] Dalia Mogahed and Azka Mahmood, "American Muslim Poll 2019: Predicting and Preventing Islamophobia," Institute for Social Policy and Understanding (ISPU), April 15, 2019, https://www.ispu.org.

[33] Talal Ansari and Hannah Allam, "Trump's Anti-Islam Rhetoric Convinced These Muslims They Should Run for Office," *BuzzFeed News*, October 31, 2017, https://www.buzzfeednews.com.

[34] "Remarks by the President at Islamic Society of Baltimore," The White House, February 3, 2016, https://obamawhitehouse.archives.gov.

[35] Andrew Rafferty, "Trump Calls for 'Complete Shutdown' of Muslims Entering the U.S.," NBC News, December 7, 2015, https://www.nbcnews.com; Ryan Teague Beckwith, "Muslim Ban: Hillary Clinton Speech Criticizes Donald Trump," *Time*, June 14, 2016, https://time.com.

[36] Jordan Denari and the Bridge Initiative Team, "As Islamophobia Increases, So Does Use of the Word," *Bridge Initiative*, May 11, 2016, https://bridge.georgetown.edu/research/as-islamophobia-increases-so-does-use-of-the-word/. Even Trump was compelled to hesitantly use the word and acknowledge that Islamophobia exists in a town hall debate with Hillary Clinton. President Obama, however, never uttered the word as president, even at the height of the anti-Muslim election rhetoric.

[37] Niraj Warikoo, "Democrat O'Malley Slams Anti-Islam Hate in Dearborn Talk," *Detroit Free Press*, October 23, 2015, https://www.freep.com; Bridge Initiative Team, "Islamophobia and the 2016 Elections," *Bridge Initiative*, January 29, 2017, https://web.archive.org/web/20170129095400/https:/bridge.georgetown.edu/islamophobia-and-the-2016-elections/.

[38] C-SPAN, "Khizr Khan Full Remarks at Democratic National Convention," YouTube video, 9:41, July 28, 2016, https://www.youtube.com.

[39] Shibley Telhami, "Analysis | How Trump Changed Americans' View of Islam—for the Better," *Washington Post*, January 25, 2017, https://www.washingtonpost.com.

[40] Hanna Trudo, "DNC Favors Republicans over Muslim and Latinx Dems, Activists Say," *The Daily Beast*, August 15, 2020, https://www.thedailybeast.com.

[41] Asma Khalid, "Presidential Nominees Rarely Speak to Muslim Audiences. Biden Did Monday," NPR, July 20, 2020, https://www.npr.org.

[42] Khaled A. Beydoun, *American Islamophobia: Understanding the Roots and Rise of Fear* (Oakland: University of California Press, 2018), 31.

[43] Tuqa Nusairat, "Bill Clinton's Loyalty Test for Muslim Americans," *Foreign Policy*, July 28, 2016, https://foreignpolicy.com.

[44] Ismat Sarah Mangla, "Hillary Clinton Has an Unfortunate Way of Talking about American Muslims," *Quartz*, October 20, 2016, https://qz.com.

[45] Namira Islam, "Soft Islamophobia," *Religions* 9, no. 280 (September 15, 2018): 6.

[46] Mangla, "Hillary Clinton Has an Unfortunate Way of Talking about American Muslims."

[47] Beckwith, "Muslim Ban: Hillary Clinton Speech."

[48] Max Fisher, "Marco Rubio's Comments about Muslims Are Getting to Be Almost as Frightening as Trump's," *Vox*, February 4, 2016, https://www.vox.com; German Lopez,

"Marco Rubio Stood Up to Donald Trump's Islamophobia—In the Worst Possible Way," *Vox*, March 10, 2016, https://www.vox.com.

[49] Islam, "Soft Islamophobia," 6.

[50] Ben Smith, "Muslims Barred from Picture at Obama Event," *Politico*, June 18, 2008, https://www.politico.com.

[51] Sheryl Gay Stolberg, "Obama Says Mosque Upholds Principle of Equal Treatment," *New York Times*, August 14, 2010, https://www.nytimes.com.

[52] Ken Rudin, "Harry Reid, the GOP, and the Politics of the 'Ground Zero Mosque,'" *NPR*, August 18, 2010, https://www.npr.org.

[53] Narzanin Massoumi, Tom Mills, and David Miller, eds., *What Is Islamophobia? Racism, Social Movements, and the State* (London: Pluto Press, 2017), 42.

[54] Kevin Liptak and Shachar Peled, "Obama Administration Ending Program Once Used to Track Mostly Arab and Muslim Men," *CNN*, December 22, 2016, https://www.cnn.com.

[55] Jack Serle, "Obama Drone Casualty Numbers a Fraction of Those Recorded by the Bureau," *Bureau of Investigative Journalism*, July 1, 2016, https://www.thebureauinvesti-gates.com.

[56] Glenn Greenwald, "Obama Killed a 16-Year-Old American in Yemen. Trump Just Killed His 8-Year-Old Sister," *The Intercept*, January 30, 2017, https://theintercept.com.

[57] Ibid.

[58] Bridge Initiative Team, "Factsheet: Countering Violent Extremism," *Bridge Initiative*, December 4, 2018, https://bridge.georgetown.edu.

[59] Faiza Patel, "The Trump Administration Provides One More Reason to Discontinue CVE," Brennan Center for Justice, July 12, 2017, https://www.brennancenter.org.

[60] J. Wesley Boyd, "The Dangers of Countering Violent Extremism (CVE) Programs," *Psychology Today*, July 19, 2016, https://www.psychologytoday.com.

[61] Faiza Patel and Meghan Koushik, "Countering Violent Extremism," Brennan Center for Justice (2017), https://www.brennancenter.org.

[62] Emmanuel Mauleón, "Worst Suspicions Confirmed: Government Reports Show Domestic Anti-Terrorism Efforts Target Minorities," Just Security, October 3, 2018, https://www.justsecurity.org.

[63] Patel and Koushik, "Countering Violent Extremism."

[64] Nabiha Maqbool, "Defunding Police Must Include Ending Surveillance of Muslims," *The Intercept*, June 25, 2020, https://theintercept.com.

[65] Patel, "The Trump Administration Provides One More Reason."

[66] Eric Rosand and Stevan Weine, "On CVE, the Trump Administration Could Have Been Worse," *Brookings* (blog), April 7, 2020, https://www.brookings.edu; Alex Ruppenthal and Asraa Mustufa, "As Trump Relaunches Countering Violent Extremism, Records on Past Illinois Program Reveal Links to FBI, Law Enforcement," *Chicago Reporter*, August 14, 2020, https://www.chicagoreporter.com.

[67] Tom Gjleten, "Trump Reportedly Plans to Refocus Violent Extremism Initiative on Muslims," *NPR*, February 10, 2017, https://www.npr.org.

[68] Ian Schwartz, "Maher: No One Has Talked about Islamic Culture against Gays, Women as Cause for Orlando Massacre," *RealClearPolitics*, June 18, 2016, https://www.realclearpolitics.com.

[69] Maher has claimed, "The kooks and the terrorists in the Christian and the Jewish world are truly just a little fringe. And in the Muslim world they draw from a vast pool of support, which is not in any other religion." Hamid Dabashi, "When It Comes to

Islamophobia, We Need to Name Names," *Al-Jazeera*, March 31, 2019, https://www.aljazeera.com. See also Bridge Initiative Team, "Factsheet: Bill Maher," *Bridge Initiative*, December 8, 2017, https://bridge.georgetown.edu, and Raya Jalabi, "A History of the Bill Maher's 'Not Bigoted' Remarks on Islam," *The Guardian*, October 7, 2014, http://www.theguardian.com.

[70] "Transcript: *CNN American Morning with Paula Zahn*: Talk with Bill Maher," *CNN*, December 16, 2002, http://transcripts.cnn.com.

[71] Bridge Initiative Team, "Factsheet: Bill Maher."

[72] Jalabi, "A History of the Bill Maher's 'Not Bigoted' Remarks on Islam."

[73] Ibid.

[74] Bridge Initiative Team, "Factsheet: Bill Maher."

[75] Jalabi, "A History of the Bill Maher's 'Not Bigoted' Remarks on Islam."

[76] Ibid.

[77] Ibid.

[78] "Bill Maher: I'm Not Anti-Muslim, I'm Anti-Misogyny—I Thought Feminism Was a Thing with Liberals," *Haaretz*, October 7, 2018, https://www.haaretz.com.

[79] Lila Abu-Lughod, "Do Muslim Women Really Need Saving? Anthropological Reflections on Cultural Relativism and Its Others," *American Anthropologist* 104, no. 3 (2002): 783–90.

[80] "At stake, the prospects for peace in this conflict-racked nation, but also at stake progress for women there who, when ruled by the Taliban, could not work, study or even leave the house without a male escort." Jane Ferguson, "As Taliban Peace Talks Resume, What's at Stake for Afghan Women?" *PBS NewsHour*, November 29, 2019, https://www.pbs.org/newshour.

[81] "The Cover of the August 9, 2010, issue of *Time* Magazine, Depicting Bibi Aisha," *Time*, July 8, 2020.

[82] Chris Stedman, "Stop Trying to Split Gays and Muslims," *Salon*, April 2, 2013, https://www.salon.com.

[83] In an interview with Khizr Khan, *PBS NewsHour*'s Judy Woodruff echoed false data and stereotypical claims about Muslims and sharia, despite her notable pushback to Islamophobia in other areas of her reporting. See "Khizr Khan: As Candidate for the Highest Office, Trump Needs Tolerance for Criticism," *PBS NewsHour*, August 1, 2016, https://www.pbs.org/newshour, and "WATCH: Full Interview with 2020 Candidate Michael Bloomberg," *PBS NewsHour*, February 27, 2020, https://www.pbs.org/newshour. In 2006, MSNBC's Joy Reid published a range of anti-LGBTQ and anti-Muslim posts to her blog, and when they came to light in 2017–8, she disavowed the former but not the latter. See Jessica Kwong, "Joy Reid's Blog Called Islam 'Incompatible' with Free Speech," *Newsweek*, April 27, 2018, https://www.newsweek.com, and MSNBC, "Joy Reid Apologizes to LGBT Community for Tweets, Posts" YouTube video, 20:15, April 28, 2018, https://www.youtube.com.

[84] Rafia Zakaria writes, "The confluence of the liberal agenda of saving Muslim women from Muslim men with the conservative agenda of keeping Muslims out altogether so as to protect white women is a growing phenomenon throughout Europe as well as in the United States." Rafia Zakaria, "Why Donald Trump Needs Muslim Women," *The Nation*, August 11, 2017, https://www.thenation.com.

[85] Laurie Penny, "This Isn't 'Feminism.' It's Islamophobia," *The Guardian*, December 22, 2013, http://www.theguardian.com; Moustafa Bayoumi, "How the 'Homophobic

Muslim' Became a Populist Bogeyman," *The Guardian*, August 7, 2017, https://www.theguardian.com.

[86] Bridge Initiative Team, "Factsheet: Ayaan Hirsi Ali," *Bridge Initiative*, June 16, 2017, https://bridge.georgetown.edu.

[87] Ayaan Hirsi Ali, "Islam Is a Religion of Violence," *Foreign Policy* (blog), November 9, 2015, https://foreignpolicy.com.

[88] Center for American Progress, "Ayaan Hirsi Ali," Islamophobia Network, https://islamophobianetwork.com.

[89] Writing of Ali and her colleague Asra Nomani, Rafia Zakaria sheds light on the underlying motives of this approach: "Talking about honor killings, then, has very little to do with honor killings and far more to do with justifying neoliberal military interventions and legitimizing conservative xenophobia—all of the meddling and all of the hate purified by the noble ruse of protecting gender equality." Zakaria, "Why Donald Trump Needs Muslim Women."

[90] She has been featured in viral videos that convey misinformation about Islam, produced by PragerU. Bridge Initiative Team, "Factsheet: PragerU," *Bridge Initiative*, https://bridge.georgetown.edu.

[91] Robert Spencer, "'No One Has Upset Islamophobia Cabal More Than Spencer. He Knows More about Islam Than They Do.'—Ayaan Hirsi Ali," *JihadWatch* (blog), September 14, 2017, https://www.jihadwatch.org/.

[92] Robert Spencer, "Search Results for 'Ayaan Hirsi Ali,'" *Jihad Watch*, https://www.jihadwatch.org.

[93] Center for American Progress, "Ayaan Hirsi Ali."

[94] Enes Bayrakli and Farid Hafez, eds., *European Islamophobia Report 2019* (Ankara: SETA—Foundation for Political, Economic, and Social Research, 2020), https://www.islamophobiaeurope.com.

[95] "Mosque in Germany Attacked with Molotov Bombs," *Al-Jazeera*, March 20, 2018, https://www.aljazeera.com.

[96] Mobashra Tazamal, "Erasing Muslims from the 'West': Islamophobic Campaigns across Europe and the US," *Bridge Initiative*, February 14, 2018, https://bridge.georgetown.edu.

[97] Samirah Majumdar, "Emergency Laws Restricted Religious Freedom of Muslims More Than Others in 2016," Pew Research Center, *FactTank* (blog), November 7, 2018, https://www.pewresearch.org.

[98] Government of Canada, "The Daily—Police-Reported Hate Crime, 2017," Statistics Canada, November 29, 2018, https://www150.statcan.gc.ca.

[99] Les Perreaux, "Quebec Mosque Shooter Told Police He Was Motivated by Canada's Immigration Policies," *Globe and Mail*, April 13, 2018, https://www.theglobeandmail.com.

[100] Vikram Dodd and Kevin Rawlinson, "Finsbury Park Attack: Man 'Brainwashed by Anti-Muslim Propaganda' Convicted," *The Guardian*, February 1, 2018, https://www.theguardian.com.

[101] Henrik Pryser Libell and Megan Specia, "Norway Mosque Attacker Gets 21-Year Sentence," *New York Times*, June 11, 2020, https://www.nytimes.com.

[102] Mobashra Tazamal, "Christchurch, Immigration & the Fear Mongering That Incites Hate," *Bridge Initiative*, April 10, 2019, https://bridge.georgetown.edu; Murtaza Hussain, "New Zealand Suspect's Actions Are Logical Conclusion of Calling Immigrants 'Invaders,'" *The Intercept*, March 18, 2019, https://theintercept.com.

103 Lizzie Dearden, "Cologne Victims Speak," *The Independent*, February 19, 2016, https://www.independent.co.uk.

104 Ayesha Chaudhry, "Systemic Racism Encourages Half of Canadians to Fear Islam and Muslims," *Vancouver Sun*, October 13, 2017, https://vancouversun.com.

105 Richard Wike et al., "Views on Minority Groups across Europe," Pew Research Center—Global Attitudes & Trends, October 14, 2019, https://www.pewresearch.org.

106 Conrad Hackett, "5 Facts about the Muslim Population in Europe," *Pew Research Center-FactTank* (blog), November 29, 2017, https://www.pewresearch.org.

107 Eric Kelsey, "Germans More Negative towards Muslims Than Others," *Reuters*, December 2, 2010, https://uk.reuters.com.

108 Wike et al., "Views on Minority Groups across Europe."

109 Tazamal, "Erasing Muslims from the 'West.'"

110 Bridge Initiative Team, "Factsheet: Geert Wilders," *Bridge Initiative*, August 24, 2018, https://bridge.georgetown.edu.

111 Chloe Farand, "Marine Le Pen Launches Presidential Campaign with Hardline Speech," *The Independent*, February 5, 2017, https://www.independent.co.uk; Bridge Initiative Team, "Factsheet: National Rally (Rassemblement National, Previously Front National or National Front), *Bridge Initiative*, February 22, 2020, https://bridge.georgetown.edu.

112 Farid Hafez, "The Role of Islamophobia in the Upcoming German Federal Election," *Bridge Initiative*, September 22, 2017, https://bridge.georgetown.edu; Bridge Initiative Team, "Factsheet: Alternative for Germany (Alternative für Deutschland/AfD)," *Bridge Initiative*, April 7, 2020, https://bridge.georgetown.edu.

113 Robert Booth, "Britain First: Anti-Islam Group That Bills Itself as a Patriotic Movement," *The Guardian*, November 29, 2017, https://www.theguardian.com/.

114 Lizzie Dearden, "Ukip Being Turned into 'Anti-Islamic Party' That Could Soon Have Tommy Robinson as Leader, Defectors Say," *The Independent*, December 3, 2018, https://www.independent.co.uk.

115 H. A. Hellyer, "Ukip Might Not Get Votes—but Its Anti-Islamic Voices Have a Platform," *The National*, August 20, 2019, https://www.thenational.ae.

116 "Anti-Islam Movement PEGIDA Stages Protests across Europe," *Reuters*, February 6, 2016, https://www.reuters.com.

117 Pamela Duncan, "Europeans Greatly Overestimate Muslim Population, Poll Shows," *The Guardian*, December 13, 2016, https://www.theguardian.com.

118 Ibid.

119 Jasmin Zine, "Islamophobia and Hate Crimes Continue to Rise in Canada," *The Conversation*, January 28, 2019, https://theconversation.com.

120 Nick Cumming-Bruce and Steven Erlander, "Swiss Ban Building of Minarets on Mosques," *New York Times*, November 29, 2009, https://www.nytimes.com.

121 Vasiliki Fouka and Aala Abdelgadir, "How Will Austria's New Headscarf Ban Affect Muslims?," *Washington Post, Monkey Cage*, June 3, 2019, https://www.washingtonpost.com.

122 "Attitudes of Christians in Western Europe," *Pew Research Center's Religion & Public Life Project* (blog), May 29, 2018, https://www.pewforum.org.

123 Fouka and Abdelgadir, "How Will Austria's New Headscarf Ban Affect Muslims?"

124 Ibid.

125 Jason Silverstein, "France Will Still Ban Islamic Face Coverings Even after Making Masks Mandatory," CBS News, May 12, 2020, https://www.cbsnews.com; James McAuley,

"France Mandates Masks to Control the Coronavirus. Burqas Remain Banned," *Washington Post*, May 10, 2020, https://www.washingtonpost.com.

[126] Farid Hafez, "Hijab Ban: As the Far Right Targets Muslims, Austria's Response Is an Ugly, Complicit Silence," *Haaretz*, April 26, 2018, https://www.haaretz.com.

[127] Dan Bilefsky, "Quebec Bans Religious Symbols in Some Public Sector Jobs," *New York Times*, June 17, 2019, https://www.nytimes.com.

[128] Nora Loreto, "Opinion | A Quebec Bill to Ban Some from Wearing 'Religious Symbols' Is Fueled by Islamophobia," *Washington Post*, June 13, 2019, https://www.washingtonpost.com; Jason Madger, "A New Poll Shows Support for Bill 21 Is Built on Anti-Islam Sentiment," *Montreal Gazette*, May 18, 2019, https://montrealgazette.com.

[129] Dan Bilefsky and Nasuna Stuart-Ulin, "A Quebec Ban on Religious Symbols Upends Lives and Careers," *New York Times*, March 7, 2020, https://www.nytimes.com.

[130] Madger, "A New Poll Shows Support for Bill 21 Is Built on Anti-Islam Sentiment."

[131] Majumdar, "Emergency Laws Restricted Religious Freedom."

[132] Eleanor Beardsley, "France Ends State of Emergency after Nearly 2 Years," *NPR*, December 28, 2017, https://www.npr.org.

[133] Myriam François, "France's Treatment of Its Muslim Citizens Is the True Measure of Its Republican Values," *Time*, December 8, 2020, https://time.com; Adam Nossiter, "Macron's Rightward Tilt, Seen in New Laws, Sows Wider Alarm in France," *New York Times*, November 25, 2020, https://nytimes.com; Mira Kamdar, "France Is About to Become Less Free," *The Atlantic*, November 24, 2020, https://theatlantic.com.

[134] Edward Keenan, "When Stephen Harper Refers to 'Barbaric Culture,' He Means Islam—An Anti-Muslim Alarm That's Ugly and Effective Because It Gets Votes," *The Star*, December 2, 2017, https://www.thestar.com.

[135] Davide Mastracci, "OPINION: Canada's Misguided Women's Rights Campaign," *Al-Jazeera America*, October 12, 2015, http://america.aljazeera.com.

[136] Bridge Initiative Team, "Canada's 'Barbaric Practices' Law Mirrors American Campaigns to Ban Sharia," *Bridge Initiative*, June 24, 2015, https://bridge.georgetown.edu.

[137] "Muslim Demographics," YouTube video, 7:30, "friendofmuslim," March 30, 2009, https://www.youtube.com.

[138] "The number of tweets mentioning the theory nearly tripling in four years from just over 120,000 in 2014 to just over 330,000 in 2018." See Jacob Davey and Julia Ebner, "The 'Great Replacement': The Violent Consequences of Mainstreamed Extremism" (London: Institute for Strategic Dialogue, 2019), https://www.isdglobal.org; Eleanor Penny, "The Deadly Myth of the 'Great Replacement,'" *New Statesman*, August 9, 2019, https://www.newstatesman.com.

[139] Andrew Brown, "The Myth of Eurabia: How a Far-Right Conspiracy Theory Went Mainstream," *The Guardian*, August 16, 2019, https://www.theguardian.com/.

[140] Ibid.

[141] Homa Khaleeli, "'You Worry They Could Take Your Kids': Is the Prevent Strategy in Schools Demonising Muslim Children?," *The Guardian*, September 23, 2015, https://www.theguardian.com.

[142] Bridge Initiative Team, "Factsheet: Prevent," *Bridge Initiative*, March 25, 2019, https://bridge.georgetown.edu.

[143] Khaleeli, "'You Worry They Could Take Your Kids.'"

[144] Josh Halliday, "Prevent Scheme 'Fosters Fear and Censorship at Universities,'" *The Guardian*, August 28, 2017, https://www.theguardian.com.

[145] Scott Shane, "Killings in Norway Spotlight Anti-Muslim Thought in U.S.," *New York Times*, July 24, 2011, https://www.nytimes.com.

[146] Bridge Initiative Team, "Factsheet: Counter Jihad Movement," *Bridge Initiative*, September 17, 2020, https://bridge.georgetown.edu.

[147] Bridge Initiative Team, "Factsheet: Geert Wilders."

[148] Bridge Initiative Team, "Factsheet: Steve King," *Bridge Initiative*, October 10, 2019, https://bridge.georgetown.edu.

[149] Bridge Initiative Team, "Factsheet: Louie Gohmert," *Bridge Initiative*, July 16, 2020, https://bridge.georgetown.edu.

[150] Mobashra Tazamal, "Chinese Islamophobia Was Made in the West," *Al-Jazeera*, October 10, 2019, https://www.aljazeera.com.

[151] Mobashra Tazamal, "How 9/11 Spawned an Anti-Muslim Playbook Being Weaponised in India," *The New Arab*, March 5, 2020, https://english.alaraby.co.uk.

[152] Sigal Samuel, "China Holds a Million Uighur Muslims in Camps, UN Told," *The Atlantic*, August 28, 2018, https://www.theatlantic.com.

[153] Editorial Board, "Opinion | How China Corralled 1 Million People into Concentration," *Washington Post*, February 29, 2020, https://www.washingtonpost.com.

[154] Tazamal, "How 9/11 Spawned an Anti-Muslim Playbook Being Weaponised in India."

[155] Sigal Samuel, "India Passes a Citizenship Bill That Excludes Muslims," *Vox*, December 12, 2019, https://www.vox.com.

[156] Tazamal, "How 9/11 Spawned an Anti-Muslim Playbook."

[157] Lily Kuo, "In China, They're Closing Churches, Jailing Pastors—and Even Rewriting Scripture," *The Guardian*, January 13, 2019, https://www.theguardian.com.

[158] Joe Wallen, "Narendra Modi's Hindu Nationalism Gives Rise to Vigilante Attacks on Christians," *The Telegraph*, February 16, 2020, https://www.telegraph.co.uk; Aysha Khan, "Opposition to Modi Isn't Just about Anti-Muslim Violence, Indian Christians Say," *Religion News Service*, October 9, 2019, https://religionnews.com.

[159] Matthew Bowser, "Origins of an Atrocity," *Perspectives on History: A Newsmagazine of the American Historical Association*, June 25, 2018, https://www.historians.org.

[160] Bridge Initiative Team, "Caught in the Crosshairs of Hate: The Rohingya," *Bridge Initiative*, January 17, 2019, https://bridge.georgetown.edu.

[161] Sarah Kaplan, "The Serene-Looking Buddhist Monk Accused of Inciting Burma's Sectarian Violence," *Washington Post*, May 27, 2015, https://www.washingtonpost.com; Marella Oppenheim, "'It Only Takes One Terrorist': The Buddhist Monk Who Reviles Myanmar's Muslims," *The Guardian*, May 12, 2017, https://www.theguardian.com.

[162] Bowser, "Origins of an Atrocity."

[163] Derek Cai, "Aung San Suu Kyi Defends Policies toward Rohingya Muslims," *FOX News*, August 21, 2018, https://www.foxnews.com.

[164] Enes Bayraklı and Farid Hafez, eds., *Islamophobia in Muslim-Majority Societies* (Abingdon: Routledge, 2018).

4. More Than Muslims

[1] Moustafa Bayoumi, "Did Islamophobia Fuel the Oak Creek Massacre?," *The Nation*, August 10, 2012, https://www.thenation.com.

² Macy Jenkins, "Suspect Tells Police He 'Hates Muslims' after Attacking Sikh Clerk," *CBS Sacramento*, February 15, 2019, https://sacramento.cbslocal.com.

³ Rana Sodhi and Harjit Sodhi, "Remembering Balbir Singh Sodhi, Sikh Man Killed in Post-9/11 Hate Crime," *Storycorps*, September 14, 2018, https://storycorps.org.

⁴ Alex Orlando and Erin Sullivan, "Victim in Pasco Hate Crime Had Gun, Decided Not to Use It," *Tampa Bay Times*, January 4, 2013, https://www.tampabay.com.

⁵ Ibid.

⁶ Christopher Mathias, "The Killing of Khalid Jabara Is an American Tragedy," *HuffPost*, August 23, 2016, https://www.huffpost.com.

⁷ The term "intersectionality" was coined by Kimberle Crenshaw in "Demarginalizing the Intersection of Race and Sex: A Black Feminist Critique of Antidiscrimination Doctrine, Feminist Theory and Antiracist Politics," *University of Chicago Legal Forum* 1 (1989): article 8.

⁸ In many parts of the world, and in many historical contexts, Christian women—especially in the Middle East—have covered their hair with scarves in public, as many Muslim women do.

⁹ In the early 1990s, when asked what they associated with the religion of Islam, most could not come up with an answer, but about a fifth of Americans said "Mideast" or "Arab." See Kambiz GhaneaBassiri, "Islamophobia and American History: Religious Stereotyping and Out-Grouping of Muslims in the United States," in *Islamophobia in America: The Anatomy of Intolerance*, ed. Carl Ernst (New York: Palgrave Macmillan, 2013), 153.

¹⁰ Steve Garner and Saher Selod, "The Racialization of Muslims: Empirical Studies of Islamophobia," *Critical Sociology* 41, no. 1 (January 2015): 3.

¹¹ Christopher Mathias, "Uber Driver Says Passenger Mistook Him for a Muslim, Threatened to Kill Him," *HuffPost*, November 18, 2015, https://www.huffpost.com.

¹² "Mistaken as Middle Eastern, Indian Slain in Kansas as Hate Crimes Surge," *Middle East Eye*, February 25, 2017, https://www.middleeasteye.net.

¹³ "Research on Racism and the Experiences and Responses of American Muslims," Institute for Social Policy and Understanding, June 2, 2020, https://www.ispu.org.

¹⁴ Akinyi Ochieng, "Black Muslims Face Double Jeopardy, Anxiety in the Heartland: Code Switch," *NPR*, February 25, 2017, https://www.npr.org.

¹⁵ Kayla Renée Wheeler, "On Centering Black Muslim Women in Critical Race Theory," *Maydan*, February 5, 2020, https://themaydan.com.

¹⁶ Kevin Rawlinson, "Man Jailed for Life after Running over Muslim Woman in Leicester," *The Guardian*, March 27, 2018, https://www.theguardian.com.

¹⁷ Ochieng, "Black Muslims Face Double Jeopardy."

¹⁸ Max Londberg, "'Allah Scum': KC Muslim Family Leaves New Home after Hateful Slurs, Arson Ruin It," *Kansas City Star*, May 11, 2018, https://www.kansascity.com.

¹⁹ Ryan J. Kelly, "Feds: Small-Town Police Chief Said Black People Were 'Like ISIS' and Wished He Could 'Mow 'Em Down,'" *HuffPost*, November 1, 2017, https://www.huffpost.com; Melanie Burney, "Judge Postpones Sentencing, 2nd Hate-Crime Assault Trial of Former South Jersey Police Chief," *Philadelphia Inquirer*, March 6, 2020, https://www.inquirer.com.

²⁰ Edward E. Curtis IV, "The Black Muslim Scare of the Twentieth Century: The History of State Islamophobia and Its Post-9/11 Variations," in Ernst, *Islamophobia in America*, 99.

²¹ Ibid., 98.

[22] Ibid., 95.

[23] Ibid., 98.

[24] Will Caldwell, "'A Sword of Wrath, the Executor of Sinister Adventures': Domestic Islamophobia and International Black Muslim Solidarities during the Cold War," *Journal of Africana Religions* 7, no. 1 (January 30, 2019): 172–73.

[25] Curtis, "The Black Muslim Scare," 99.

[26] Ibid., 100.

[27] Khaled A. Beydoun and Justin Hansford, "Opinion | The F.B.I.'s Dangerous Crackdown on 'Black Identity Extremists,'" *New York Times*, November 15, 2017, https://www.nytimes.com.

[28] See, for example, M. Zuhdi Jasser, "The World's Red-Green Axis Has Come to Our Streets," Center for Security Policy, July 24, 2020, https://www.centerforsecuritypolicy.org; Lee Kaplan, "Hamas and Black Lives Matter: A Marriage Made in Hell," Center for Security Policy, September 23, 2016, https://www.centerforsecuritypolicy.org.

[29] Geneva Sands, "Trump Administration Expands Travel Ban to Include Six New Countries," *CNN*, February 22, 2020, https://www.cnn.com.

[30] Jeannine Hill Fletcher, *The Sin of White Supremacy: Christianity, Racism, and Religious Diversity in America* (Maryknoll, NY: Orbis Books, 2017).

[31] "Colonial Virginia Laws Related to Slavery," *Teaching American History*, https://teachingamericanhistory.org/.

[32] Khaled Beydoun, "America Banned Muslims Long before Donald Trump," *Washington Post*, August 18, 2016, https://www.washingtonpost.com.

[33] For more on this topic, see James Renton and Ben Gidley, eds., *Antisemitism and Islamophobia in Europe: A Shared Story?* (London: Palgrave Macmillan, 2017).

[34] Islam, despite being a diverse religious tradition that spans the globe, was reduced in the minds of these scholars to an Arab, Middle Eastern, Semitic phenomenon—a stereotype that sticks with us today.

[35] See Tomoko Masuzawa, *The Invention of World Religions: Or, How European Universalism Was Preserved in the Language of Pluralism* (Chicago: University of Chicago Press, 2005), and Theodore Vial, *Modern Religion, Modern Race* (Oxford: Oxford University Press, 2016).

[36] 2008 Pew Global Attitudes Project: Unfavorable Views of Jews and Muslims on the Increase in Europe, Washington, DC: Pew Research Center. Summary available from: http://pewglobal.org/reports.

[37] Alan Waring, "The Similarities in Far-Right Islamophobia and Anti-Semitism," *Rantt Media* (blog), July 15, 2020, https://rantt.com.

[38] Lizzie Dearden, "Neo-Nazis Telling Followers to 'Deliberately Infect' Jews and Muslims with Coronavirus, Report Warns," *The Independent*, July 9, 2020, https://www.independent.co.uk.

[39] Yonat Shimron, "FBI Report: Jews the Target of Overwhelming Number of Religious-Based Hate Crimes," *Religion News Service*, November 12, 2019, https://religionnews.com.

[40] Lois Beckett, "Pittsburgh Shooting: Suspect Railed against Jews and Muslims on Site Used by 'Alt-Right,'" *The Guardian*, October 27, 2018, https://www.theguardian.com.

[41] Associated Press, "Poway Synagogue Killer Was Inspired by New Zealand Attack, Court Papers Show," *Times of Israel*, August 1, 2019, https://www.timesofisrael.com.

⁴² "Muslims Unite for Pittsburgh Synagogue," LaunchGood, https://www.launchgood.com.

⁴³ Mary Emily O'Hara, "Muslims Ask for Help to Repair Jewish Cemetery. The Response Was Tremendous," *NBC News*, February 22, 2017, https://www.nbcnews.com.

⁴⁴ Peter Beinart has been an outspoken voice on behalf of American Muslims, writing frequently about Islamophobia in *The Atlantic*. Jewish organizations like Tru'ah: The Rabbinic Call for Human Rights, Jewish Voice for Peace, and Rabbis for Human Rights–North America have also done awareness and advocacy work around Islamophobia. See also Rachel Gartner, "An Antidote for Islamophobia," *HuffPost*, May 29, 2014, https://www.huffpost.com.

⁴⁵ Dalia Mogahed and Azka Mahmood, "American Muslim Poll 2019: Predicting and Preventing Islamophobia," *ISPU*, April 15, 2019, https://www.ispu.org; "How Americans Feel about Different Religious Groups," *Pew Research Center's Religion & Public Life Project* (blog), February 15, 2017, https://www.pewforum.org.

⁴⁶ Farah Akbar, "NYU Asks Students to Help Report Harassment Targeting Muslim Community," *NBC News*, December 9, 2015, https://www.nbcnews.com.

⁴⁷ Kate Dubinski, "Man in Southwestern Ontario Charged after Family Attacked with Bat amid Shouts of 'ISIS,'" *CBC*, December 8, 2017, https://www.cbc.ca/.

⁴⁸ Tim Arango, Nicholas Bogel-Burroughs, and Katie Benner, "Minutes before El Paso Killing, Hate-Filled Manifesto Appears Online," *New York Times*, August 3, 2019, https://www.nytimes.com.

⁴⁹ Harold D. Morales, *Latino and Muslim in America: Race, Religion, and the Making of a New Minority* (Oxford: Oxford University Press, 2018), 7.

⁵⁰ Scott Bomboy, "Did the Supreme Court Just Overrule the Korematsu Decision?," *Constitution Daily - National Constitution Center*, June 26, 2018, https://constitutioncenter.org/blog/did-the-supreme-court-just-overrule-the-korematsu-decision.

⁵¹ See, for example, John Hayward, "Frank Gaffney: 'We Have a 5th Column, Sharia Muslim Community,'" *Breitbart*, June 29, 2016, https://www.breitbart.com.

⁵² The Bridge Initiative, "Have You Ever Heard Someone Say This about Muslims?," YouTube video, 3:52, July 28, 2017, https://www.youtube.com.

⁵³ Arjun Singh Sethi, "Calling the Muslim Brotherhood a Terrorist Group Would Hurt All American Muslims," *Washington Post*, February 8, 2017, https://www.washingtonpost.com.

⁵⁴ Jonah Engel Bromwich, "Trump Camp's Talk of Registry and Japanese Internment Raises Muslims' Fears," *New York Times*, November 17, 2016, https://www.nytimes.com

⁵⁵ Mike Honda, "Muslim Hearings Recall My Life in Internment Camp," *CNN*, June 15, 2011, http://www.cnn.com.

⁵⁶ Anti-Muslim groups had been sowing concerns about sharia for years before this, and their views were normalized with the help of media personalities like Glenn Beck and politicians like Newt Gingrich. See Philip Bump, "How Sharia Law Became Embedded in Our Political Debate," *Washington Post*, July 15, 2016, https://www.washingtonpost.com.

⁵⁷ Hayward, "Frank Gaffney."

⁵⁸ Bridge Initiative Team, "Factsheet: Sharia," *Bridge Initiative*, December 5, 2018, https://bridge.georgetown.edu.

⁵⁹ Jonathan Brown, "Stoning and Hand Cutting—Understanding the Hudud and the Shariah in Islam," Yaqeen Institute for Islamic Research, January 12, 2017, https://yaqeeninstitute.org.

60 Asifa Quraishi-Landes, "How Anti-Shariah Marches Mistake Muslim Concepts of State and Religious Law (Commentary)," *Religion News Service*, June 8, 2017, https://religionnews.com. Arabic-speaking Christians sometimes use the word to speak about "God's law," too. For example, I heard it used in a prayer during Catholic Mass in Amman, Jordan, in 2013.

61 Asifa Quraishi-Landes, "Sharia and Diversity: Why Some Americans Are Missing the Point" (Washington, DC: Institute for Social Policy and Understanding, September 2013), https://www.ispu.org.

62 Anti-sharia bills were introduced in thirty-nine states across the union. See Elsadig Elsheikh, Basima Sisemore, and Natalia Ramirez Lee, "Legalizing Othering: The United States of Islamophobia" (Haas Institute for a Fair and Inclusive Society, September 2017), http://haasinstitute.berkeley.edu.

63 Bridge Initiative Team, "Factsheet: Sharia."

64 See, for example, Securefreedom, "Glenn Beck: Shariah, the Muslim Brotherhood & the Threat to America," YouTube video, 32:36, February 2, 2016, https://www.youtube.com.

65 Asma Uddin, "Opinion | What Islamophobic Politicians Can Learn from Mormons," *New York Times*, May 22, 2018, https://www.nytimes.com.

66 Abdul Malik Mujahid, "Sharia and the Lives of Muslim Americans," *HuffPost*, June 26, 2011, https://www.huffpost.com.

67 Elsheikh et al., "Legalizing Othering," 40.

68 David Smith, "'Are You Concerned by Sharia Law?': Trump Canvasses Supporters for 2020," *The Guardian*, March 2018, https://www.theguardian.com.

69 Asma T. Uddin, *When Islam Is Not a Religion* (New York: Simon and Schuster, 2019), 193–99.

70 Ibid., 198–99.

71 Legal scholar Arjun Singh Sethi has noted a hesitancy among the Catholic Church and other Christian institutions to engage in humanitarian aid in war-torn areas of Iraq and Syria, out of a concern that those on the receiving end of their charitable work could presently or down the road be named a terrorist organization. ACMCU, "'The Civil Rights of Muslim Americans: A Casualty of the War on Terror' with Arjun Singh Sethi," YouTube video, 35:29, December 13, 2016, https://www.youtube.com.

72 Emmanuel Mauleón, "Worst Suspicions Confirmed: Government Reports Show Domestic Anti-Terrorism Efforts Target Minorities," *Just Security*, October 3, 2018, https://www.justsecurity.org.

73 Arjun Singh Sethi, "Portland Train Attack Survivors Destinee Mangum and Walia Mohamed Speak Out," *Literary Hub* (blog), August 13, 2018, https://lithub.com.

74 Aaron Mesh, "Video Shows Alleged Portland Killer Ranting on a MAX Train against Religion and Antifa, and Threatening to Stab Anybody Who Tried to Stop Him," *Willamette Week*, May 28, 2017, https://www.wweek.com.

75 Meerah Powell, "Portland MAX Stabbing Victims Call Out Racist System during Sentencing Hearing," *OPB*, June 23, 2020, https://www.opb.org

76 Emanuella Grinberg, Traci Tamura, and Paul Vercammen, "Portland Stabbings: Remembering a 'Superhero,'" *CNN*, June 6, 2017, https://www.cnn.com

77 Elaine Ayala, "Racist Insult after Spurs Game a Sad Example of Hate in America," *Express News*, April 2, 2017, https://www.expressnews.com.

78 Arun Venugopal, "One Man Called Another a Racial Slur. Then They Shook Hands," *WNYC*, June 29, 2017, https://www.wnyc.org/story.

[79] The Daily Show with Trevor Noah, "Confused Islamophobes Target American Sikhs," YouTube video, 5:34, April 26, 2016, https://www.youtube.com.

[80] "Sikh Coalition Urges Trump to Reconsider CVE Strategy," *The Sikh Coalition* (blog), February 2, 2017, https://www.sikhcoalition.org.

5. Under the Surface

[1] Kirwan Institute, "Understanding Implicit Bias," http://kirwaninstitute.osu.edu.

[2] John Bargh, *Before You Know It: The Unconscious Reasons We Do What We Do* (New York: Simon and Schuster, 2017), 17.

[3] Ibid.

[4] There is no doubt that Hicks was obsessive about parking at the complex, but the day he killed the three residents, none of their cars were parked in the spots allotted to Hicks and his wife.

[5] Margaret Talbot, "The Story of a Hate Crime," *New Yorker*, June 15, 2015, https://www.newyorker.com.

[6] Ibid.

[7] Ibid.

[8] "Anatomy of Hate: It Was a Triple-Murder Fueled by Rage. But Was It a Hate Crime?," *The Marshall Project*, February 18, 2020, https://www.themarshallproject.org.

[9] Talbot, "The Story of a Hate Crime."

[10] Lily Puckett, "Chapel Hill Shooting: Prosecutors Played Video of Attack as Man Who Killed Three Muslim Students Pleads Guilty," *The Independent*, June 12, 2019, https://www.independent.co.uk.

[11] Talbot, "The Story of a Hate Crime."

[12] Tal Axelrod, "North Carolina Police Chief Apologizes for Saying Killing of 3 Muslim Students Was over a Parking Dispute," *The Hill*, June 12, 2019, https://thehill.com.

[13] Stephanie Ramirez, "Nabra Hassanen: New Charges Say She Was Raped," *USA Today*, October 17, 2017, https://www.usatoday.com.

[14] Christopher Mathias, "The Killing of Khalid Jabara Is an American Tragedy," *Huff-Post*, August 23, 2016, https://www.huffpost.com.

[15] A. C. Schwencke, Rohan Naik, and Ken Schwencke, "Hate Crime Training for Police Is Often Inadequate, Sometimes Nonexistent," ProPublica, November 29, 2017, https://www.propublica.org.

[16] Susan Bro and Haifa Jabara, "Opinion | Hate Crimes Are Slipping through the Cracks," *New York Times*, August 12, 2019, https://www.nytimes.com.

[17] Kristin Garrity, "Does Islamophobia Impact the Underreporting of FBI Hate Crime Data?," *Bridge Initiative*, December 14, 2017, https://bridge.georgetown.edu.

[18] Nathan Lean, "The Chapel Hill Shooting Was Anything but a Dispute over Parking," *Mic*, February 17, 2015, https://www.mic.com.

[19] American Civil Liberties Union, "Nationwide Anti-Mosque Activity," https://www.aclu.org.

[20] Chris Sikich, "Carmel Mosque Decision Is Delayed after Public Packs Zoning Meeting," *Indianapolis Star*, January 22, 2018, https://www.indystar.com.

[21] Brenna Donnelly, "Judge Puts Carmel Mosque Plans on Hold until May," *WISH-TV | Indianapolis News | Indiana Weather | Indiana Traffic* (blog), April 9, 2018, https://www.wishtv.com.

22 "Sterling Heights Mosque Voted Down," *WXYZ-TV Detroit*, September 10, 2015, https://www.youtube.com/watch?v=ME1pf_7NgFc

23 In Virginia Beach, Virginia, some mosque opponents originally said their view was based on the fact that the road wasn't good enough and couldn't handle the new traffic. When a journalist asked them if they would be okay with it if the city widened or improved the road, some fell quiet and others shifted their complaint to say that they wanted to keep the area "rural." CAIRtv, "Anti-Muslim Hate Spewed at Hearing on Va. Mosque," YouTube video, 2:03, September 5, 2013, https://www.youtube.com.

24 American Civil Liberties Union, "Nationwide Anti-Mosque Activity."

25 "Louisville Mourns 'Family Man' Shot after School Drop-Off," *NBC News*, February 27, 2015, https://www.nbcnews.com; Claire Galofaro, "Wife Recounts Shooting Victim's Last Farewell," *Courier-Journal*, February 26, 2015, https://www.courier-journal.com.

26 Aaron Morrison, "Texas Muslim Road Rage Hate Crime: Civil Rights Group Asks for FBI Probe of 'Go Back to Islam' Killing in Houston," *International Business Times*, June 30, 2015, https://www.ibtimes.com; Brian Rogers, "Jury Declines to Indict Man in Deadly Road Rage Shooting," *SFGate*, September 23, 2015, https://www.sfgate.com; CAIRtv, "Video: Texas Muslim Road Rage Victim Dies, Suspect Makes Bail, CAIR Seeks Hate Crime Probe," YouTube video, 1:29, June 29, 2015, https://www.youtube.com.

27 Rowaida Abdelaziz, "His Family Calls His Killing a Hate Crime—But Indiana Law Won't See It That Way," *HuffPost*, February 21, 2019, https://www.huffpost.com; Vic Ryckaert, "Road Rage Shooting: Sister of Muslim Man Calls It a Hate Crime," *Indy Star*, February 22, 2019, https://www.indystar.com.

28 Asad Dandia, "My Life under NYPD Surveillance: A Brooklyn Student and Charity Leader on Fear and Mistrust," American Civil Liberties Union, June 18, 2013, https://www.aclu.org; Asad Dandia, "I Was a Muslim Teen under NYPD Surveillance. But Now I Have More Hope Than Ever," American Civil Liberties Union, March 7, 2017, https://www.aclu.org.

29 Dandia, "My Life under NYPD Surveillance"; Chris Hawley, "NYPD Monitored Muslim Students All over Northeast," *Associated Press*, February 18, 2012, https://www.ap.org; Adam Goldman and Matt Apuzzo, "With Cameras, Informants, NYPD Eyed Mosques," *Associated Press*, February 23, 2012, https://www.ap.org.

30 Hawley, "NYPD Monitored Muslim Students All over Northeast"; Goldman and Apuzzo, "With Cameras, Informants, NYPD Eyed Mosques."

31 Adam Goldman and Matt Apuzzo, "NYPD Muslim Spying Led to No Leads, Terror Cases," Associated Press, August 21, 2012, https://www.ap.org; David Crary, "AP Series about NYPD Surveillance Wins Pulitzer," *Associated Press*, April 16, 2012, https://www.ap.org.

32 Yasmeen Alamiri, "WATCH: 'Of Course We Were Supposed to Do That,' Bloomberg Says of Surveillance of American Muslim Community Post 9/11," *PBS NewsHour*, February 27, 2020, https://www.pbs.org/newshour.

33 Abigail Hauslohner, "NYPD Settles Third Lawsuit over Surveillance of Muslims," *Washington Post*, April 5, 2018, https://www.washingtonpost.com.

34 According to legal scholar Arjun Singh Sethi, this Department of Homeland Security (DHS) guidance allows the Transportation Security Administration (TSA) and Customs and Border Patrol (CPB) to profile on the basis of faith, race, gender identity, or other protected categories. It also allows the use of informants, even "without any evidence of wrongdoing," and allows for programs like the NYPD mapping program. It also did not

ban profiling nationwide, even though some local jurisdictions may ban it themselves. See Arjun Sethi, "The Civil Rights of Muslim Americans: A Casualty of the War on Terror," YouTube video, 35:29, December 13, 2016, https://www.youtube.com.

[35] This was the case with the informant who infiltrated Asad Dandia's group, who says he was directed to "bait" Muslims into making statements that would get them in trouble. See Adam Goldman and Matt Apuzzo, "Informant NYPD Paid Me to 'Bait' Muslims," *Associated Press*, October 23, 2012, https://www.ap.org.

[36] Peter Aldhous, "How the FBI Invents Terror Plots to Catch Wannabe Jihadis," *BuzzFeed News*, November 17, 2015, https://www.buzzfeednews.com; Trevor Aaronson, "The Sting: How the FBI Created a Terrorist," *The Intercept*, March 16, 2015, https://theintercept.com.

[37] Glenn Greenwald, "The FBI's Anticipatory Prosecution of Muslims to Criminalize Speech," *The Guardian*, March 19, 2013, http://www.theguardian.com.

[38] Keonna Thomas, Adam Raishani, and Maalik Alim Jones, "Legal Proceedings (IS & Other Groups)" (Washington, DC: Program on Extremism at George Washington University), https://extremism.gwu.edu.

[39] A 2011 study found that since 9/11, tips from the American Muslim community constituted the biggest source of information on potential terrorism suspects, along with ongoing government investigations. See Charles Kurzman, David Schnazer, and Ebrahim Moosa, "Muslim American Terrorism since 9/11: Why So Rare?," *Muslim World* 101 (2011): 467.

[40] *This American Life*, "The Convert," August 10, 2012, https://www.thisamericanlife.org; "Trial and Terror (Rebroadcast)," *Reveal*, December 1, 2018, https://www.revealnews.org.

[41] Kevin Gosztola, "'Inventing Terrorists' Study Offers Critical Examination of Government's Use of Preemptive Prosecutions," *Shadowproof*, June 9, 2014, https://shadowproof.com/.

[42] "Blocking Faith, Freezing Charity: Chilling Muslim Charitable Giving in 'The War on Terror Financing'" (New York: ACLU, June 2009), https://www.aclu.org, 26.

[43] Ibid., 32.

[44] Ibid., 89.

[45] Kumar Rao and Carey Shenkman, *Equal Treatment? Measuring the Legal and Media Responses to Ideologically Motivated Violence in the US* (Washington, DC: Institute for Social Policy and Understanding, 2018), https://www.imv-report.org.

[46] Sara Jayyousi, "What I Lost (and Can Never Get Back) When My Father Was in Guantánamo North," *Common Dreams*, May 10, 2019, https://www.commondreams.org; Carrie Johnson and Margot Williams, "'Guantanamo North': Inside Secretive U.S. Prisons," *NPR*, March 3, 2011, https://www.npr.org.

[47] Daniel Boffey, "Mosul Civilian First to Be Compensated for Mistaken Coalition Bombing," *The Guardian*, September 9, 2020, https://www.theguardian.com.

[48] Azmat Khan and Anand Gopal, "The Uncounted," *New York Times*, November 16, 2017, https://www.nytimes.com/interactive/2017/11/16/magazine/uncounted-civilian-casualties-iraq-airstrikes.html.

[49] Ibid.

[50] Zareena Grewal, "Opinion | When War Comes Close to Home," *New York Times*, October 4, 2015, https://www.nytimes.com.

⁵¹ Glenn Greenwald, "How Many Muslim Countries Has the U.S. Bombed or Occupied since 1980?," *The Intercept*, November 6, 2014, https://theintercept.com.

⁵² Nathan Lean and Jordan Denari, "The Super Survey: Two Decades of Americans' Views on Islam & Muslims" (Washington, DC: Bridge Initiative, 2015), https://bridge.georgetown.edu, 62–65.

⁵³ Kambiz GhaneaBassiri, "Islamophobia and American History: Religious Stereotyping and Out-Grouping of Muslims in the United States," in *Islamophobia in America: The Anatomy of Intolerance*, ed. Carl Ernst (New York: Palgrave Macmillan, 2013), 55. He bases his comments off of a study that looked at anti-Muslim attitudes across the United States and a number of European countries. See Richard Wike and Brian F. Grim, "Western Views toward Muslims: Evidence from a 2006 Cross-National Survey," *International Journal of Public Opinion Research*, 22, no. 1 (2010).

⁵⁴ Sean McElwee, "Anti-Muslim Stereotypes Are Associated with Support for Bombing Iran," Data for Progress, April 2, 2018, https://www.dataforprogress.org.

⁵⁵ Samuel Stebbens and Evan Comen, "Military Spending: 20 Companies Profiting the Most from War," *USA Today*, February 21, 2019, https://www.usatoday.com.

⁵⁶ Eli Clifton, "Far-Right Birther's Secret Funders: Look Who's Backing Islamophobe Frank Gaffney," *Salon*, October 1, 2014, https://salon.com; Alison Kysia, "Who Benefits from Islamophobia? Investigating the Profit Motive behind Bigotry and Discrimination" (Teaching for Change); William D. Hartung, *Prophets of War: Lockheed Martin and the Making of the Military-Industrial Complex* (New York: Nation Books, 2011), 198.

⁵⁷ Kysia, "Who Benefits from Islamophobia?"

⁵⁸ Stephen Sheehi, *Islamophobia: The Ideological Campaign against Muslims* (Atlanta: Clarity Press, 2011), 38.

⁵⁹ Erik Bleich and A. Maurits van der Veen, "Media Portrayals of Muslims: A Comparative Sentiment Analysis of American Newspapers, 1996–2015," *Politics, Groups, and Identities* (November 8, 2018): 1–20.

⁶⁰ Bridge Initiative Team, "New Study Analyzes Media Coverage of Islam over Time," *Bridge Initiative*, April 24, 2015, https://bridge.georgetown.edu.

⁶¹ Dorghum Abusalim, "Study: 'NYT' Portrays Islam More Negatively Than Alcohol, Cancer, and Cocaine," *Mondoweiss*, March 5, 2016, https://mondoweiss.net.

⁶² Kumar Rao and Carey Shenkman, "Equal Treatment? Measuring the Legal and Media Responses to Ideologically Motivated Violence in the US" (Washington, DC: Institute for Social Policy and Understanding, 2018), https://www.imv-report.org/

⁶³ Arsalan Iftikhar, "Report: Muslims Most Negatively Portrayed Minority in US Media," *Bridge Initiative*, September 18, 2019, https://bridge.georgetown.edu; Muhammad Mussa, "Most UK Media Coverage of Muslims Is Negative: Study," Anadolu Agency, September 7, 2019, https://www.aa.com.tr.

⁶⁴ Peter Gottschalk and Gabriel Greenberg, "Common Heritage, Uncommon Fear: Islamophobia in the United States and British India, 1687–1947," in Ernst, *Islamophobia in America*, 21.

⁶⁵ The Riz Test, "About the Riz Test," https://www.riztest.com.

⁶⁶ Khaled A. Beydoun, *American Islamophobia: Understanding the Roots and Rise of Fear* (Oakland: University of California Press, 2018), 29.

6. We Should Know Better

[1] "Pope's Message for 2019 World Day of Migrants and Refugees," *Vatican News*, May 27, 2019, https://www.vaticannews.va.

[2] Helen Hoddinott, "White Helmets Rescue Little Girl after She Was Buried Alive by an Airstrike," *The Independent*, February 20, 2017, https://www.independent.co.uk.

[3] Paige Lavendar, "Lindsey Graham: I Associate 'Allahu Akbar' with a War Chant, and 'I Duck,'" *HuffPost*, September 23, 2013, https://www.huffpost.com.

[4] Rome Reports in English, "Pope to Muslim Leaders: We Must Condemn Violence Based on Religious Justification," YouTube video, 2:37, November 28, 2014, https://www.youtube.com/watch?v=5NUgIlCBi5E.

[5] Timothy Cardinal Dolan, "Cardinal Dolan: Civilization Is Threatened by Evils of ISIS," *New York Post* (blog), February 17, 2015, https://nypost.com.

[6] Speaking of Faith / On Being, "Hearing Muslim Voices Since 9/11," American Public Media, 2012, https://web.archive.org/web/20120210022636/http://being.publicradio.org/programs/hearingmuslims/particulars.shtml.

[7] Arwa Mahdawi, "The 712-Page Google Doc That Proves Muslims Do Condemn Terrorism," *The Guardian*, March 26, 2017, http://www.theguardian.com; "Islamic Statements against Terrorism," *Charles Kurzman* (blog), August 1, 2018, https://kurzman.unc.edu.

[8] "Letter to Baghdadi," http://www.lettertobaghdadi.com/.

[9] Omid Safi, "Is All Morality Gone? Condemning ISIS, and Beyond, in a World of Suffering," *On Being Project*, October 6, 2014, https://onbeing.org.

[10] Todd Green, "3 Reasons Christians Shouldn't Ask Muslims to Condemn Terrorism," *Sojourners*, July 20, 2015, https://sojo.net.

[11] Here I draw on the title and thesis of Todd Green's book *Presumed Guilty: Why We Should Not Ask Muslims to Condemn Terrorism* (Minneapolis: Fortress Press, 2018).

[12] This third insight comes from Todd Green, "3 Reasons Christians Shouldn't Ask Muslims to Condemn Terrorism," *Sojourners*.

[13] Green emphasizes that we must "ask better questions" of our Muslim friends. He also offers his own alternative questions: "The real question we should ask is why do some Muslims and Christians find inspiration to carry out despicable acts of violence from their scriptures, while many others find inspiration to work for peace and justice from the same scriptures? How can Islamic texts inspire ISIS to behead its enemies and also inspire Malala Yousafzai to fight for girls' education? How could slaveholders in nineteenth-century America find justification for slavery in the Bible while abolitionists found justification for eliminating slavery from the same book?" Green, "3 Reasons Christians Shouldn't Ask Muslims to Condemn Terrorism."

[14] In recent years, we have started to see some exceptions to this. When Dylann Roof killed several congregants at a Black church in 2015, many commentators and news outlets pushed for this to be called a terrorist attack. Authorities and news media also referred to the anti-Muslim massacre at two Christchurch, New Zealand, mosques as terrorism.

[15] A 2020 study comparing the portrayal of the perpetrator of the 2016 Orlando shooting (who was Muslim) and the 2017 Las Vegas shooter (who was not) found that "the examined newspapers were more likely to employ a 'terrorism' frame in their coverage of the Orlando shooting than in their coverage of the Las Vegas shooting; link the Orlando mass shooting with the global war on terrorism; and to humanize Stephen Paddock, the

White perpetrator of the Las Vegas shooting." Mohamad Hamas Elmasry and Mohammed el-Nawawy, "Can a Non-Muslim Mass Shooter Be a 'Terrorist'?: A Comparative Content Analysis of the Las Vegas and Orlando Shootings," *Journalism Practice* 14, no. 7 (2020): 863–79.

[16] CNN Editorial Research Team, "Mass Shootings in the US Fast Facts," *CNN*, May 3, 2020, https://edition.cnn.com.

[17] Todd Green, "It's Time to Abandon the Word 'Terrorism,'" *HuffPost*, October 10, 2017, https://www.huffpost.com.

[18] According to the Media Portrayals of Minorities Project, "57% of articles mentioning Muslims compared to only 14% of articles related to whites contain these words. More tellingly, they appear in only 26% of articles discussing ideologically motivated white shooters, who are individuals openly affiliated with white-supremacist or alt-right ideologies. Similarly, words like 'extremist,' 'radicalism,' 'militant,' and 'fanaticism,' appeared in 41% of articles about Muslim perpetrators, in only 13% of articles about white perpetrators, and in 26% of articles mentioning ideologically motivated white shooters." "Can White Shooters Be Terrorists?," Media Portrayals of Minorities Project, March 18, 2019, https://www.mediaandminorities.org/MassShooters/.

[19] Green, "It's Time to Abandon the Word 'Terrorism.'"

[20] Since 1997, the U.S. government has maintained a list of foreign terrorist organizations (FTOs) that shapes terrorism prosecution. A majority of the militant groups on the FTO list are ones that have Muslim membership or a declared motive framed in Islamic terms. It is not a group's use of militancy or their ideology that so much warrants inclusion on that list. Rather, the primary factors that play into the United States' decisions on FTO designations are the United States' own geopolitical interests and whether a group's activities oppose or align with U.S. foreign policy goals. The State Department describes its criteria as relating to "national defense, foreign relations, or the economic interests." "Foreign Terrorist Organizations," United States Department of State, https://www.state.gov/foreign-terrorist-organizations/. Some militant groups using Islamic framing are not considered FTOs (including the Taliban in Afghanistan) because the United States sees them as allies or wants to be able to cooperate with them if need be. When it comes to terrorism convictions in the United States, if a perpetrator of violence can be demonstrated to have some kind of connection to one of these groups, then they will be charged and convicted with "terrorism," a label that often leads to harsher outcomes in court. There is no U.S. statute for domestic terrorism, meaning that non-Muslim (would-be) perpetrators are often charged and sentenced less harshly than Muslims. See Sameer Ahmed, "Is History Repeating Itself? Sentencing Young American Muslims in the War on Terror," *Yale Law Journal* (2017): 1527; Seamus Hughes and Jon Lewis, "Perspective | Why the FBI Had to Pretend Hamas Wanted to Plot with 'Boogaloo Boys,'" *Washington Post*, September 9, 2020, https://www.washingtonpost.com.

[21] This term was initially coined to refer to Christians, but in recent decades it has been used more readily to talk about Muslims.

[22] A study by the American Friends Service Committee, which examined a wide swath of media coverage from 2015, found that the word *extremism* was used far more often to describe Muslims, in such a way that made extremism seem endemic to Islam and that justified military responses. Beth Hallowell, "Mixed Messages: How the Media Covers 'Violent Extremism' and What You Can Do about It" (Washington, DC: American Friends Service Committee, March 2016), https://afsc.org.

[23] Kenan Malik, "'Radicalisation' Has Become a Redundant Concept," *The Guardian*, February 4, 2018, https://www.theguardian.com.

[24] Green, "3 Reasons Christians Shouldn't Ask Muslims to Condemn Terrorism."

[25] Theodore Schleifer, "Donald Trump: 'I Think Islam Hates Us,'" *CNN*, March 10, 2016, https://www.cnn.com/2016/03/09/politics/donald-trump-islam-hates-us/index.html.

[26] Colleen Long, "Sessions Cites Bible to Defend Separating Immigrant Families," *AP News*, June 14, 2018, https://apnews.com.

[27] Of course, Muslims, as insiders to their religion, will have their own take on what is true or valid among the many divergent perspectives that their co-religionists hold. But it is not for us, as outsiders to the religion, to say what Islam's "true" teachings are.

[28] Shine Hawramani, Facebook Post, https://www.facebook.com/shine.hawramani/posts/10154536522590303.

[29] Leerom Medovoi, "Dogma-Line Racism: Islamophobia and the Second Axis of Race," *Social Text* 30, no. 2 (2012): 61.

[30] Jeffrey Goldberg, "Washington Discovers Christian Persecution," *New York Times*, December 21, 1997, https://www.nytimes.com.

[31] Green, "3 Reasons Christians Shouldn't Ask Muslims to Condemn Terrorism."

[32] Mobashra Tazamal, "Fox News: A Megaphone for Anti-Muslim Hatred," *Bridge Initiative*, March 18, 2019, https://bridge.georgetown.edu.

[33] Thank you to Asad Dandia for helping me formulate this idea.

[34] Jasser Auda, *Maqasid Al-Shariah as Philosophy of Islamic Law: A Systems Approach* (Herndon: International Institute of Islamic Thought [IIIT], 2008), xxi–xxii.

[35] Asifa Quraishi-Landes, "Five Myths about Sharia," *Washington Post*, June 24, 2016, https://www.washingtonpost.com.

[36] For more on sharia and its relation to the pre-modern Muslim state, see Wael B. Hallaq, *Sharīʿa: Theory, Practice, Transformations* (Cambridge: Cambridge University Press, 2009).

[37] Asifa Quraishi-Landes, "Sharia and Diversity: Why Some Americans Are Missing the Point" (Washington, DC: Institute for Social Policy and Understanding, September 2013), https://www.ispu.org.

[38] Cristiano Lima, "Gingrich Calls for Deportation Tests of Everyone with a 'Muslim Background,'" *Politico*, July 14, 2016, https://www.politico.com/.

[39] *Fresh Air with Terri Gross*, "The Evangelicals Engaged in Spiritual Warfare," *NPR*, August 19, 2011, https://www.npr.org.

[40] See Hallaq, "Jihād," in Sharīʿa, 326–41.

[41] Asma Afsaruddin, "Reconceptualizing the Military Jihad on the Basis of Non-Legal Literature," Maydan, June 28, 2018. https://themaydan.com/2018/06/reconceptualizing-military-jihad-basis-non-legal-literature/.

[42] "Majority of ISIS Victims Are Muslim—CNN Video," *CNN,* July 14, 2016, https://www.cnn.com.

[43] "QRF Factsheet: Gender and Education in Jordan" (Amman, Jordan: Queen Rania Foundation, May 2018), https://www.qrf.org.

[44] Fatemah Aman, "Iran's Headscarf Politics," Middle East Institute, November 3, 2014, https://www.mei.edu. In 2018 and 2019, Saudi Arabia also began relaxing its mandate on headscarves and long robes for women in public. See "Coverings for Women 'Not Mandatory,' Says Saudi Crown Prince Ahead of US Charm Offensive," *New Arab*,

March 20, 2018, https://english.alaraby.co.uk; and Zainab Fattah, Vivian Nerein, and Sarah Algethami, "Saudi Arabia Drops Dress Code for Foreign Women in Tourism Push," *Bloomberg News*, September 26, 2019, https://www.bloomberg.com. In some Muslim-majority countries, the wearing of headscarves and face veils has been banned. In the 1930s, the Iranian regime banned headscarves in public, a policy that was reversed after the 1979 Islamic Revolution there. For a time in Tunisia, headscarves were not allowed in many public settings, and only in recent years Turkey and Syria have lifted their ban on headscarves or face veils in certain public settings. See Swati Sharma, "MAP: Where Islamic Veils Are Banned—And Where They Are Mandatory," *Washington Post*, March 1, 2011, https://www.washingtonpost.com.

[45] Cemil Aydin, "The Idea of 'a Muslim World' Is Both Modern and Misleading," *Aeon*, August 1, 2018, https://aeon.co.

[46] See Cemil Aydin, *The Idea of the Muslim World: A Global Intellectual History* (Cambridge, MA: Harvard University Press, 2017). See also Asma Afsaruddin, "The Myth of the Muslim World," *Chronicle of Higher Education*, May 14, 2017, https://www.chronicle.com.

[47] Aydin, "The Idea of 'a Muslim World.'"

[48] Ibid.

[49] Jeremy Salkin, "What Is 'Judeo-Christian,' Anyway?," *Religion News Service*, October 16, 2017, https://religionnews.com; Gene Zubovich, "The Strange, Short Career of Judeo-Christianity," *Aeon*, March 22, 2016, https://aeon.co.

[50] Ayaan Hirsi Ali (@ayaan), "What this scumbag did today is called Jihad. How he got there is through dawa: the process of indoctrination that poisons minds," Twitter, October 31, 2017, https://web.archive.org/web/20171101005454/https:/twitter.com/Ayaan/status/925494192804999168.

[51] Ayaan Hirsi Ali, "The Challenge of Dawa: Political Islam as Ideology and Movement and How to Counter It," Hoover Institution, March 21, 2017, https://www.hoover.org.

[52] Ishmael N. Daro, "'Taqiyya': How an Obscure Islamic Concept Became an Obsession of Anti-Muslim Activists," *BuzzFeed News*, April 12, 2018, https://www.buzzfeednews.com.

[53] Ibid.

[54] For example, see Ann Corcoran, *Refugee Resettlement and the Hijra to America* (Washington, DC: Center for Security Policy Press, 2015).

[55] Ashley Fantz and Ben Brumfield, "Syrian Refugees Not Welcome in 31 U.S. States," *CNN*, November 19, 2015, https://www.cnn.com.

[56] Another example is how far-right Catholic commentator Timothy Gordon defines *intifada*, a term meaning "uprising," as meaning "basically breeding out the host organism." Franklin Strong, "The Webs Connecting 'Traditionalist' Catholics and White Nationalists," *Sojourners*, July 29, 2019, https://sojo.net.

[57] Valerie Schultz, "Metanoia," *America*, December 8, 2003, https://www.america-magazine.org.

7. "In Vain Do They Worship Me"

[1] Omar Suleiman, "'Kill a Muslim for Jesus.' Sigh. Come on Texas," Facebook Post, August 2, 2017, https://www.facebook.com/imamomarsuleiman/posts/1595804083772960.

[2] "Man Threatens to Blow Up Islamic Bookshop and 'Kill the Muslims,'" *The Independent*, August 3, 2017, http://www.independent.co.uk.

[3] Ibid.

[4] Laurie Goodstein, "Across Nation, Mosque Projects Meet Opposition," *New York Times*, August 7, 2010, https://www.nytimes.com.

[5] One example is Alexandre Bissonnette, who killed six Muslims and wounded many others in a mosque massacre in Quebec in 2017.

[6] Wajahat Ali et al., "Fear, Inc.: The Roots of the Islamophobia Network in America," Center for American Progress, August 26, 2011, https://www.americanprogress.org.

[7] Kelly Humphrey, "Story of Anti-Muslim Insult at Local Store Prompts Facebook Firestorm," *Northwest Florida Daily News*, December 21, 2015, https://www.nwfdaily-news.com.

[8] CAIRtv, "Vandals Hit Delaware Mosque and School, String Up Cross," YouTube video, 2:01, October 26, 2013, https://www.youtube.com.

[9] "New Mexico Mosque Vandalized by 'a Real Christian,'" *KRQE News 13 Albuquerque–Santa Fe* (blog), December 19, 2017, https://www.krqe.com.

[10] "Video: 3 People Appear in Court for Cross Burning at NY Mosque, CAIR Urges Repudiation of Hate," YouTube video, 1:44, September 8, 2015, https://www.youtube.com.

[11] "Nationwide Anti-Mosque Activity," American Civil Liberties Union, July 2020, https://www.aclu.org.

[12] Julie Wootton-Green, "Update: Police Say Cross Left Draped in Pig Parts at Twin Falls Mosque Was Hate Crime," *Twin Falls Times-News*, October 30, 2017, https://magicvalley.com.

[13] Russell Goldman, "Who Is Terry Jones? Pastor behind 'Burn a Koran Day,'" *ABC News*, September 7, 2010, https://abcnews.go.com.

[14] Jonathan Merritt, "Franklin Graham's Turn toward Intolerance," *The Atlantic*, July 19, 2015, https://www.theatlantic.com.

[15] Shibley Telhami, "2015-Full-Poll-Findings-Final.Pdf" (Washington, DC: Brookings Institution, 2016), https://www.brookings.edu; "Americans Uneasy about Islamic Threat to Religious Freedom," *LifeWay Research* (blog), June 25, 2015, https://lifewayresearch.com.

[16] Alex Vandermaas-Peeler et al., "Partisan Polarization Dominates Trump Era: Findings from the 2018 American Values Survey," PRRI, October 29, 2018, https://www.prri.org.

[17] Tara Isabella Burton, "68% of White Evangelicals Think America Shouldn't House Refugees," *Vox*, May 29, 2018, https://www.vox.com.

[18] Azka Mahmood and Dalia Mogahed, "American Muslim Poll 2019: Predicting and Preventing Islamophobia," ISPU, April 15, 2019, https://www.ispu.org.

[19] Vandermaas-Peeler et al., "Partisan Polarization Dominates Trump Era."

[20] "Robertson: Radical Muslims 'Satanic,'" *NBC News*, March 14, 2006, http://www.nbcnews.com.

[21] Ali et al., "Fear, Inc.," 67.

[22] For more on ACT! for America and how it operates, see Mobashra Tazamal, "Is ACT for America Really a Grassroots Organization?," *Bridge Initiative* (blog), September 10, 2018, https://bridge.georgetown.edu.

[23] Ali et al., "Fear, Inc."

[24] Matthew Duss et al., "Fear, Inc. 2.0: The Islamophobia Network's Efforts to Manufacture Hate in America" (Washington, DC: Center for American Progress, February 2015), https://cdn.americanprogress.org.

[25] "Pastors Grow More Polarized on Islam," LifeWay Research, October 22, 2015, https://lifewayresearch.com.

[26] Dan Browning, "Rice County Priest Apologizes for Criticizing Islam in Sermon," *Star Tribune*, January 30, 2020, https://www.startribune.com.

[27] "Immigration Sunday Homily Apology from Father Nicholas VanDenBroeke," *Archdiocese of Saint Paul and Minneapolis*, January 29, 2020, https://www.archspm.org.

[28] Jordan Denari Duffner, "Danger & Dialogue: American Catholic Public Opinion and Portrayals of Islam | Report" (Washington, DC: Bridge Initiative, September 2016), https://bridge.georgetown.edu.

[29] Mogahed, "American Muslim Poll 2019: Predicting and Preventing Islamophobia."

[30] Ibid.

[31] Duffner, "Danger & Dialogue."

[32] Vandermaas-Peeler et al, "Partisan Polarization Dominates Trump Era."

[33] "Dialogue with Muslims: Statement of the Committee for Ecumenical and Inter-religious Affairs," United States Conference of Catholic Bishops, 2014, http://www.usccb.org.

[34] See Robert Spencer, *A Religion of Peace? Why Christianity Is and Islam Isn't* (Washington, DC: Regnery, 2007).

[35] The Bridge Initiative report "Danger and Dialogue," which I authored in 2016, details where Spencer's books are sold in the Washington, DC, area. See Duffner, "Danger & Dialogue." Colleagues and other Catholics have also told me anecdotally that Spencer's books are sold in Catholic bookstores across the United States.

[36] Duffner, "Danger and Dialogue."

[37] Spencer holds a master's degree in religious studies from the University of North Carolina–Chapel Hill and wrote his thesis on Catholic history. Robert Bruce Spencer, "Master's Thesis," UNC University Libraries, March 1, 2017, https://web.archive.org/web/20170301144945/http://webcat.lib.unc.edu/record=b2172870~S1.

[38] Robert Spencer, "What Every Catholic Should Know about Islam," *Lay Witness | Catholics United for the Faith*, August 2002, https://web.archive.org/web/20160816051409/http://www.cuf.org/2002/07/what-every-catholic-should-know-about-islam/.

[39] Daniel Ali and Robert Spencer, *Inside Islam: A Guide for Catholics* (Exton, PA: Ascension Press, 2003), 22.

[40] JihadWatchVideo, "Robert Spencer: Pope Francis, the Pope of Islam," YouTube video, 6:14, October 26, 2017, https://www.youtube.com.

[41] Robert Spencer, "Roman Catholic Bishop Robert Barron Advocates Strategy of Submission to the Islamic State," *JihadWatch*, November 24, 2015, https://www.jihad-watch.org.

[42] Bridge Initiative Team, "Factsheet: Robert Spencer," *Bridge Initiative*, December 5, 2018, https://bridge.georgetown.edu.

[43] Robert Spencer, "Video: Pamela Geller and Robert Spencer Speak at Free Speech Rally, Garland, Texas, January 17, 2015," *JihadWatch*, January 19, 2015, https://www.jihad-watch.org.

[44] Ali et al., "Fear, Inc."

[45] C. J. McCloskey, "The Christian-Muslim Gulf," *National Catholic Register*, July 6, 2013, https://www.ncregister.com.

[46] Duffner, "Danger and Dialogue."

[47] Rod Dreher, "Not Peace-Loving, After All (Book Review: Islam Unveiled)," *Free Republic*, September 23, 2002, http://www.freerepublic.com.

[48] These include *Our Sunday Visitor*, *Catholic Answers*, *Zenit*, *Catholic World Report*, and *Crisis* magazine. See Duffner, "Danger and Dialogue."

[49] Several years back, I met an individual who holds a prominent position in Catholic interreligious dialogue work. This person recommended that I read the work of Robert Spencer for educational purposes. I have reason to believe that their views have since changed, but the exchange demonstrates how mainstream Spencer was considered at the centers of U.S. Catholic institutional life.

[50] Isabelle Dills, "Location Moved after Bishop Cancels Appearance of Jihad Watch Blogger," *Napa Valley Register*, July 3, 2013, https://napavalleyregister.com; "Massachusetts Diocese Cancels Appearance by Robert Spencer, Writer on Islam," CatholicCulture.org, January 31, 2013, https://www.catholicculture.org.

[51] Michael Sean Winters, "Who Should Be Barred from Catholic Forums?," *National Catholic Reporter*, August 8, 2013, https://www.ncronline.org.

[52] "Robert Spencer, PJM: U.S. Conference of Catholic Bishops: Bring Us More Jihadis," *JihadWatch*, October 16, 2015, https://www.jihadwatch.org.

[53] Jeffrey Rubin, "Robert Spencer and the Religion of Terror," *Crisis Magazine*, October 25, 2018, https://www.crisismagazine.com.

[54] Robert Spencer (@jihadwatchRS), Twitter, April 1, 2019, 8:00pm, https://twitter.com.

[55] Duffner, "Danger and Dialogue," 98.

[56] J. Lester Feder, "This Is How Steve Bannon Sees the Entire World," *BuzzFeed News*, November 15, 2016, https://www.buzzfeednews.com.

[57] Bridge Initiative Team, "Factsheet: Steve Bannon," *Bridge Initiative*, September 16, 2016, https://bridge.georgetown.edu.

[58] Mark Hosenball and Tim McLaughlin, "Meet Robert Shillman, the Tech Mogul Who Funds Pamela Geller's Anti-Islam Push," *The Forward*, May 9, 2015, https://forward.com.

[59] William Kilpatrick, "On the Civilizational Struggle with Islam," *Crisis Magazine*, April 4, 2017, https://www.crisismagazine.com.

[60] "Turning Point Project | Educating Catholics about the Threat from Islam," http://turningpointproject.com/.

[61] Kilpatrick, "On the Civilizational Struggle with Islam."

[62] William Kilpatrick, "Solidarity with Islam?," *Crisis Magazine*, January 26, 2016, https://www.crisismagazine.com.

[63] William Kilpatrick, "Catholic Enablers of Islam," *Crisis Magazine*, April 10, 2017, https://www.crisismagazine.com.

[64] Duffner, "Danger and Dialogue."

[65] For a critique of Schall's book from an Islamic studies scholar, see David A. Rahimi, "*On Islam* Fails to Enlighten," *Public Discourse: The Journal of the Witherspoon Institute*, August 29, 2018, https://www.thepublicdiscourse.com.

[66] Ibid.

[67] Steubenville Conferences, "Steve Ray—Islam: What Every Infidel Should Know—2018 Defending the Faith Conference," YouTube, 54:54, September 18, 2018, https://www.youtube.com.

[68] Allan Ruhl, "Why Is Steve Ray Talking about Islam?," *Allan Ruhl* (blog), November 2, 2018, https://allanruhl.com.

[69] Naomi O'Leary, "Cardinal Causes Uproar with 'Muslim Scare' Video at Vatican," *Reuters*, October 15, 2012, https://www.reuters.com.

[70] Tim Kington, "Vatican Tries to Create Distance from Row over Muslim Demographics Video," *The Guardian*, October 16, 2012, http://www.theguardian.com/world/2012/oct/16/vatican-distance-muslim-demographics-video.

[71] "Cardinal Turkson Apologizes for Video, Denies Anti-Islam Bias," *CatholicCulture*, October 17, 2012, https://www.catholicculture.org.

[72] The cardinal later sought to clarify his statements, but they still ended up casting Muslims as an enemy of Europe's character and "Christian legacy." Josephine McKenna, "Austrian Cardinal Clarifies: It's Not 'Islamic Conquest' but Christian Surrender," *Religion News Service*, September 16, 2016, https://religionnews.com.

[73] Benedict XVI, "Faith, Reason and the University Memories and Reflections" (Regensburg, Germany, September 12, 2006), http://www.vatican.va.

[74] Jane Kramer, "The Pope and Islam," *The New Yorker*, April 2, 2007, https://www.newyorker.com.

[75] Samir Khalil Samir, S.J., Giorgio Paolucci, and Camille Eid, *111 Questions on Islam: Samir Khalil Samir, S.J. on Islam and the West* (San Francisco: Ignatius Press, 2008).

[76] Samir Khalil Samir, "For Al-Baghdadi, Islam Is a Religion of War, a Shrewd Message According to Father Samir," *AsiaNews.it*, May 15, 2015, http://www.asianews.it/.

[77] Samir Khalil Samir, "Middle East Transparent—When Civilizations Meet: How Joseph Ratzinger Sees Islam," *METransparent*, May 26, 2006, https://www.metransparent.com.

[78] Edward Pentin, "Father Samir: Egypt's Palm Sunday Terror Reflects a Sickness within Islam," *National Catholic Register*, April 13, 2017, https://www.ncregister.com.

[79] Jeff Israely, "The Jesuit Who Inspired the Pope's Ideas on Islam," *TIME*, March 4, 2009, http://content.time.com.

[80] Robert Spencer, "Catholic Scholar: 'Equality Is Foreign to Islam . . . under Islamic Law, Someone Who Is an "Infidel" Could Be Put to Death,'" *JihadWatch*, July 25, 2015, http://www.jihadwatch.org.

[81] Samir et al., *111 Questions on Islam*.

[82] "Cardinal Burke: The Church 'Really Should Be Afraid' of Islam," *LifeSiteNews*, July 22, 2016, https://www.lifesitenews.com.

[83] David Gibson, "US Cardinal Says 'Christian Nations' in West Must Counter Islamic Influx," *Religion News Service*, July 21, 2016, https://religionnews.com.

[84] John Allen, "Why Muslims Need to Hear Both Pope Francis and Cardinal Burke," *Crux*, September 1, 2016, https://cruxnow.com.

[85] Originally two weeks and known as the "Fortnight for Freedom," the USCCB reduced the campaign to one week in 2018. Many Catholics, especially on the political left, have criticized these religious freedom campaigns for their apparently partisan concerns. See Pat Perillo, "We Are Having Another Fortnight for Freedom, but We Shouldn't," *National Catholic Reporter*, June 27, 2017, https://www.ncronline.org.

[86] Open Doors USA, "Christian Persecution World Watch List: How the Scoring Works / About the Ranking," Open Doors USA, https://www.opendoorsusa.org.

[87] Dale Sprusansky, "Dr. James Zogby Slams Religious Freedom Commission for Ignoring Israeli Violations," *Washington Report on Middle East Affairs*, https://www.wrmea.org.

[88] James J. Zogby, "James J. Zogby Column: When It Comes to Religious Freedom, Palestinians Are Left Out of the Discussion," *Richmond Times-Dispatch*, May 20, 2017,

https://richmond.com. Also see, for example, In defense of Christians' lack of information on issues of persecution in Israel: "Countries," In Defense of Christians, https://indefenseofchristians.org/.

[89] A few examples include books by Nabeel Qureshi, Daniel Ali, and Derya Little.

[90] These include Walid Shoebat, Mosab Hassan Yousef, and Hesham Shehab.

[91] One example is Shahram Hadian of Truth in Love Ministry.

[92] See, for example, Nabeel Qureshi, "The Quran's Deadly Role in Inspiring Belgian Slaughter: Column," *USA Today*, March 22, 2016, https://www.usatoday.com.

[93] CNN, "CNN: Terror Training Fraud?," YouTube video, 7:29, July 13, 2011, https://www.youtube.com.

[94] One example is Usama Dakdok. See Bridge Initiative Team, "As Islamophobia Surges, Anti-Muslim Speakers Exploit Fears," *Bridge Initiative*, June 29, 2016, https://bridge.georgetown.edu.

[95] Ayaan Hirsi Ali, Wafa Sultan, and Tawfik Hamid are a few examples. Those who still identify with the Islamic faith have also served as validators for Islamophobic ideas, including Zuhdi Jasser, Maajid Nawaz, Shireen Qudosi, and Asra Nomani. See also Nesrine Malik, "Islam's New 'Native Informants,'" *New York Review of Books*, June 7, 2018, https://www.nybooks.com.

[96] Adam Serwer, "Top Romney Adviser Tied to Militia That Massacred," *Mother Jones*, October 27, 2011, https://www.motherjones.com.

[97] David Noriega, "Brigitte Gabriel Wants You to Fight Islam," *Buzzfeed News*, September 27, 2016, https://www.buzzfeednews.com.

[98] Franklin Strong, "The Webs Connecting 'Traditionalist' Catholics and White Nationalists," *Sojourners*, July 29, 2019, https://sojo.net/articles/webs-connecting-traditionalist-catholics-and-white-nationalists. (The original video and audio have been taken offline, but I downloaded them before their removal.)

[99] Associated Press, "Liberty University President Urges: 'End Those Muslims' via Concealed Gun Carry," *The Guardian*, December 5, 2015, https://www.theguardian.com.

[100] Ted Genoways, "'The Only Good Muslim Is a Dead Muslim,'" *New Republic*, May 15, 2017, https://newrepublic.com.

[101] Associated Press, "3 Men Convicted in Kansas Plot to Bomb Somali Refugees," *WBEN*, April 18, 2018, https://wben.radio.com.

[102] Paul Vallely, "The Fifth Crusade: George Bush and the Christianisation of the War in Iraq," in *Re-Imagining Security*, ed. Alastair Crooke et al. (London: British Council, 2004), 42–68.

[103] Joseph Rhee, Tahman Bradley, and Bryan Ross, "U.S. Military Weapons Inscribed with Secret 'Jesus' Bible Codes," *ABC News*, January 15, 2010, https://abcnews.go.com/.

[104] Chrissy Stroop, "America's Islamophobia Is Forged at the Pulpit," *Foreign Policy*, March 26, 2019, https://foreignpolicy.com.

[105] For more on Christian Zionism, see *Comprehending Christian Zionism: Perspectives in Comparison*, ed. Gunner Göran and Robert O. Smith (Minneapolis: Augsburg Fortress Publishers, 2014), 61–84.

[106] Steven Fink, "Fear under Construction: Islamophobia within American Christian Zionism," *Islamophobia Studies Journal* 2, no. 2 (Spring 2014): 27.

[107] Ibid., 35–36.

[108] Ibid., 29.

[109] A 2015 Brookings Institution survey of Christians found that this view is widely held by Evangelical Christians. Shibley Telhami, "2015-Full-Poll-Findings-Final.Pdf" (Washington, DC: Brookings Institution, 2016), https://www.brookings.edu. Televangelist Pat Robertson has advocated for conflict over peace in the Middle East and in Israel: See "Pat Robertson: Why Evangelicals Support Israel," *CBN News*, May 23, 2017, https://www1.cbn.com; see also Duss et al., "Fear, Inc. 2.0," 17.

[110] Duss et al., "Fear, Inc 2.0."

[111] "Televangelizing Muslims: Christian Satellite Television and Its Impact on Muslim-Christian Relations in Jordan," in Tamara Sonn, ed., *Overcoming Orientalism: Festschrift in Honor of John L. Esposito* (New York: Oxford University Press, 2021).

[112] Ibid.

[113] Antonio Spadaro and Marcelo Figueroa, "Evangelical Fundamentalism and Catholic Integralism: A Surprising Ecumenism," *La Civiltà Cattolica*, July 13, 2017, https://www.laciviltacattolica.it.

[114] Rod Dreher, "A Muslim Benedict Option," *The American Conservative*, April 18, 2018, https://www.theamericanconservative.com.

[115] Rod Dreher, "Reporting the Muslim Brotherhood," *Hudson Institute*, February 1, 2008, https://www.hudson.org; Rod Dreher, "Yes Mosque, No MAS," BeliefNet—*Crunchy Cons* (blog), 2020, https://www.beliefnet.com; Steven Emerson and Rachel Milton, documentary, *Jihad in America: The Grand Deception*, 2012; Scott Johnson, "What the Muslim Brotherhood Means for the U.S.," Power Line, September 14, 2007, https://www.powerlineblog.com/archives; Rod Dreher, "Not Peace-Loving, After All (Book Review: Islam Unveiled)," *Free Republic*, September 23, 2002, http://www.freerepublic.com. I thank Jeremy McLellan for pointing me to Dreher's writings and views on Islam.

8. Saints and Sinners

[1] "Transcript: Pope Francis's Speech to Congress," *Washington Post*, September 24, 2015, https://www.washingtonpost.com.

[2] Vanessa Gera and Karel Janicek, "Poles Pray En Masse at Border; Some See Anti-Muslim Agenda," *AP News*, October 7, 2017, https://apnews.com.

[3] Ibid.

[4] "Poland, New Player in Islamophobia Game—European Islamophobia," *European Islamophobia Report | SETA* (blog), https://www.islamophobiaeurope.com.

[5] For an in-depth but accessible treatment of the history of Muslim-Christian relations, see Hugh Goddard, *A History of Christian-Muslim Relations*, 2nd ed. (Edinburgh: Edinburgh University Press, 2020).

[6] Rachel M. Scott, "Dhimmīs," *The Oxford Encyclopedia of Islam and Law* (Oxford Islamic Studies Online), http://www.oxfordislamicstudies.com.

[7] There were also places where rules like these were not enacted or enforced. Ronald L. Nettler, "Dhimmī," *The Oxford Encyclopedia of the Modern Islamic World*, ed. John L. Esposito (Oxford Islamic Studies Online), http://www.oxfordislamicstudies.com.

[8] As John Tolan writes, "One was born into a religious community, and one's community determined one's legal status: Jews, Christians and Muslims had separate legal and judicial systems, whether they lived in Baghdad or Barcelona." John Victor Tolan, *Saracens: Islam in the Medieval European Imagination* (New York: Columbia University Press, 2002), xv.

[9] One prominent example is the execution of nearly fifty Christians in Cordoba, who—with the goal of being martyred—publicly insulted the Prophet Muhammad or preached their faith publicly, both of which were illicit activities under the Muslim regime. Goddard, *A History of Christian-Muslim Relations*, 83.

[10] Muslims also had to pay a tax. Those with dhimmi status were exempted from military service and could partake in some activities from which Muslims were legally barred (like consuming alcohol or pork). *Ahl al-dhimma* status extended to Hindus and other religious groups in contexts where they were a significant portion of the population.

[11] Scott, "Dhimmīs."

[12] Though the Crusades were billed as an endeavor to preserve Christians and Christian land, Arab Christians in the Levant were seen as lesser than their European counterparts, often no different from their Muslim neighbors. Some Arab Christians were treated as a subordinate class (along with Muslims) in the Crusader states that European powers (known as the Franks) established in the Levant. Andrew Jotischky, "Ethnic and Religious Categories in the Treatment of Jews and Muslims in the Crusader States," in *Antisemitism and Islamophobia in Europe: A Shared Story?*, ed. James Renton and Ben Gidley (London: Palgrave Macmillan, 2017).

[13] Ibid., 25.

[14] Geraldine Heng, "The Invention of Race in the European Middle Ages I: Race Studies, Modernity, and the Middle Ages 1: Invention of Race in the European Middle Ages I," *Literature Compass* 8, no. 5 (May 2011): 315.

[15] Washington Post Staff, "Deconstructing the Symbols and Slogans Spotted in Charlottesville," *Washington Post*, August 18, 2017, https://www.washingtonpost.com.

[16] Jeff Woods, "After Sensationalized TV Report, Vandals Strike Nashville Mosque," *Nashville Scene*, February 10, 2010, https://www.nashvillescene.com.

[17] Amin Maalouf and Pamela Toler, "The Crusades through Arab Eyes," in *The Literature of Propaganda*, ed. Thomas Riggs (Detroit: Gale, 2013).

[18] "President: Today We Mourned, Tomorrow We Work," The White House: President George W. Bush, September 16, 2001, https://georgewbush-whitehouse.archives.gov.

[19] The first two terms are biblical, but Saracen is not. See Katharine Scarfe Beckett, *Anglo-Saxon Perceptions of the Islamic World* (Cambridge: Cambridge University Press, 2003).

[20] The influential translator of the Vulgate, Saint Jerome, characterized the Saracens in these ways, and his ideas traveled all the way through Europe to England by the sixth century. See ibid.

[21] Later writers believed the term indicated that they were "without Sarah." See Geert H. M. Claassens, "Jacob van Maerlant on Muhammad and Islam," in *Medieval Christian Perceptions of Islam: A Book of Essays*, ed. John Victor Tolan (New York: Garland Publishing, 1996), 211–42.

[22] Beckett, *Anglo-Saxon Perceptions of the Islamic World*.

[23] John Kearney, "Opinion | My God Is Your God," *New York Times*, January 28, 2004, https://www.nytimes.com; Beckett, *Anglo-Saxon Perceptions of the Islamic World*, 107 and 216.

[24] As Talal Asad points out, the label "heresy" in Christian discourse "at first designated all kinds of errors, including errors 'unconsciously' involved in some activity." It "acquired its specific modern meaning (the verbal formulation of denial or doubt of any defined doctrine of the Catholic Church) only in the course of the methodological

controversies of the sixteenth century." Talal Asad, "The Construction of Religion as an Anthropological Category," in *Genealogies of Religion: Discipline and Reasons of Power in Christianity and Islam* (Baltimore: Johns Hopkins University Press, 1993), 39.

[25] Thanks to this characterization, Christians have falsely ascribed Arianism to Muslim Christologies and Pelagianism to Muslim anthropologies.

[26] To give just one example: they "adore the infidel Mahomet." "Council of Vienne 1311–1312 A.D.," Papal Encyclicals, https://www.papalencyclicals.net.

[27] Jordan Denari Duffner, "Danger & Dialogue: American Catholic Public Opinion and Portrayals of Islam" (Washington, DC: Bridge Initiative), September 2016, https://bridge.georgetown.edu.

[28] Claassens, "Jacob van Maerlant on Muhammad and Islam," 213.

[29] John Victor Tolan, "Introduction," in Tolan, *Medieval Christian Perceptions of Islam*, xvii; Tolan, *Saracens*, xix.

[30] Tolan, *Saracens*, xxi.

[31] Adam S. Francisco, *Martin Luther and Islam: A Study in Sixteenth-Century Polemics and Apologetics* (Boston: Brill, 2007), 233.

[32] Claassens, "Jacob van Maerlant," 211.

[33] "Romanus Pontifex—January 8, 1455," Papal Encyclicals, June 16, 2017, https://www.papalencyclicals.net.

[34] "... unclean Saracens, faithless enemies of the Christian name." "Council of Vienne 1311–1312 A.D.," Papal Encyclicals.

[35] See Kecia Ali, *The Lives of Muhammad* (Cambridge, MA: Harvard University Press, 2016).

[36] Kenneth Baxter Wolf, "The Earliest Latin Lives of Muhammad: Texts and Contexts," https://www.academia.edu.

[37] The same is true of the word *Islam*. Back then, they would have used the phrase, "the law of the Saracens." This is because, as we have seen, the modern category of religion was not yet in use. Different religious communities were by and large differentiated by reference to the "law" they followed. See Tolan, *Saracens*.

[38] Junaid Rana, "The Story of Islamophobia," *Souls* 9, no. 2 (June 6, 2007): 154.

[39] Sophia Rose Arjana, *Muslims in the Western Imagination* (Oxford: Oxford University Press, 2014).

[40] "Why Another Crusade? By Saint Bernard of Clairvaux," Bartleby, https://www.bartleby.com.

[41] Franciscan Media, "Saint Catherine of Siena," *Franciscan Media*, https://www.franciscanmedia.org.

[42] Rome Editor, "Pope Innocent III, Quia Maior," *Franciscanum*, August 25, 2014, https://franciscanum.wordpress.com.

[43] "Medieval Sourcebook: Urban II: Speech at Council of Clermont, 1095, According to Fulcher of Chartres," *Internet History Sourcebooks Project*, https://sourcebooks.fordham.edu.

[44] Neda Ulaby, "Scholars Say White Supremacists Chanting 'Deus Vult' Got History Wrong," NPR.org, September 4, 2017, https://www.npr.org.

[45] Washington Post Staff, "Deconstructing the Symbols and Slogans Spotted in Charlottesville."

[46] Mario Alexis Portella, "Popes Whose 'Islamophobia' Saved the Christian World from Muslims," Thomas More Law Center, November 6, 2019, https://www.thomasmore.

org. The Thomas More Law Center has worked closely with anti-Muslim hate groups on anti-sharia legislation and other anti-Muslim campaigns.

47 Rana, "The Story of Islamophobia," 153.

48 Ibid., 154.

49 Meredith Hindley, "Soldier of Fortune: John Smith before Jamestown," National Endowment for the Humanities (NEH), February 2007, https://www.neh.gov.

50 Tolan, *Saracens*, xviii.

51 Leerom Medovoi, "Dogma-Line Racism: Islamophobia and the Second Axis of Race," *Social Text* 30, no. 2 (2012): 53–54.

52 Elizabeth A. Barre, "Expulsion of Jews from Spain and Portugal," in *World History: A Comprehensive Reference Set*, 2016, https://search.credoreference.com/content/entry/fofworld/expulsion_of_jews_from_spain_and_portugal/0?institutionId=702.

53 Rana, "The Story of Islamophobia," 153.

54 "Third Lateran Council–1179 A.D.," *Papal Encyclicals* (blog), March 5, 1179, https://www.papalencyclicals.net.

55 Jotischky, "Ethnic and Religious Categories," 29.

56 "Fourth Lateran Council: 1215 Council Fathers," *Papal Encyclicals* (blog), November 11, 1215, https://www.papalencyclicals.net.

57 Medovoi, "Dogma-Line Racism," 55.

58 Heng, "The Invention of Race," 323.

59 "Second Council of Lyons–1274," *Papal Encyclicals* (blog), May 7, 1274, https://www.papalencyclicals.net.

60 Goddard, *A History of Christian-Muslim Relations,* 98.

61 G. A. Wiegers, "Moriscos," *Encyclopaedia of Islam,* 2nd ed., April 24, 2012, https://referenceworks-brillonline-com.

62 Rana, "The Story of Islamophobia," 152.

63 Ibid., 153.

64 Rachel L. Burk, "Salus Erat in Sanguine: Limpieza De Sangre and Other Discourses of Blood in Early Modern Spain" (publicly accessible Penn Dissertations 1550), 2010, https://repository.upenn.edu.

65 Matthew Carr, "Spain's Moriscos: A 400-Year-Old Muslim Tragedy Is a Story for Today," *The Guardian*, March 14, 2017, http://www.theguardian.com.

66 Már Jónsson, "The Expulsion of the Moriscos from Spain in 1609–1614: The Destruction of an Islamic Periphery," *Journal of Global History* 2, no. 2 (July 2007): 195–212.

67 Mercedes Garcia-Arenal Rodriquez and Gerard A. Wiegers, *The Expulsion of the Moriscos from Spain: A Mediterranean Diaspora* (Leiden: Brill, 2014), 3.

68 Ibid.

69 Indigenous Values, "Dum Diversas," Doctrine of Discovery, July 23, 2018, https://doctrineofdiscovery.org.

70 For a narrative treatment of these atrocities, see "The Exchange" in Louis de Bernières, *Birds without Wings* (New York: Vintage International, 2004), 256–59.

71 Martin Moll, "Greek War of Independence," in *World History: A Comprehensive Reference Set*, 2016.

72 Associated Press, "Scenes from Hell: 1995 Srebrenica Genocide in Photos," July 10, 2020, https://apnews.com.

73 Seema Jilani, "Srebrenica Revisited," *New York Times*, July 10, 2015, https://www.nytimes.com.

[74] Leila Shahid, "The Sabra and Shatila Massacres: Eye-Witness Reports," *Journal of Palestine Studies* 32, no. 1 (2002): 36–58.

[75] Agata S. Nalborczyk and Paweł Borecki, "Relations between Islam and the State in Poland: The Legal Position of Polish Muslims," *Islam and Christian–Muslim Relations* 22, no. 3 (July 1, 2011): 343–59.

[76] Brian A. Catlos, *Muslims of Medieval Latin Christendom, c. 1050–1614* (Cambridge: Cambridge University Press, 2014).

[77] The image in reproduced in Rita George-Tvrtković, *Christians, Muslims, and Mary: A History* (Mahwah, NJ: Paulist Press, 2018), 79.

[78] Ibid., 161.

[79] One prominent example is Cardinal Raymond Burke. See David Gibson, "US Cardinal Says 'Christian Nations' in West Must Counter Islamic Influx," *Religion News Service*, July 21, 2016, https://religionnews.com.

[80] Cemil Aydin, "The Idea of 'a Muslim World' Is both Modern and Misleading," *Aeon*, August 1, 2018, https://aeon.co.

[81] Georgi Kantchev, Mike Bird, Drew Hinshaw and Lucy Craymer, "Mosque Shooter's Radical Views Fed by Trips to Christian-Muslim Battlegrounds," *Wall Street Journal*, March 19, 2019, https://www.wsj.com.

[82] Dag Herbjørnsrud, "The Battle of Vienna Was Not a Fight between Cross and Crescent," *Aeon*, July 24, 2018, https://aeon.co.

[83] Ibid.

[84] Ibid. For numerous other examples of Christian and Muslim powers supporting one another, see Edward E. Curtis IV, "The Forgotten History behind Anti-Muslim Terrorism," Edward E. Curtis IV (blog), March 27, 2019, https://edward-curtis.com.

[85] Herbjørnsrud, "The Battle of Vienna."

[86] See many examples of this in George-Tvrtković, *Christians, Muslims, and Mary*.

[87] Ibid., 81–89.

[88] Michael D. Calabria, OFM, "Introducing the Sultan Al-Malik al-Kamil," in *St. Francis and the Sultan, 1219–2019: A Commemorative Booklet* (Cincinnati, OH: Franciscan Media, 2019), 46.

[89] Ibid., 44.

[90] "Why Does Saladin Have Such Good PR in the Medieval West?," *Medievalists*, September 1, 2014, https://www.medievalists.net.

[91] Michael F. Cusato, OFM, "Healing the Violence of the Contemporary World: A Franciscan Paradigm for Dialogue with Islam," in *St. Francis and the Sultan*, 26.

[92] Ibid., 16.

[93] Second Vatican Council, "Declaration on the Relation of the Church to Non-Christian Religions," *Nostra aetate*, November 1964, in *Vatican Council II: The Conciliar and Post-Conciliar Documents*, ed. Austin Flannery (Collegeville, MN: Liturgical Press, 1975), sec. 3.

9. "There Is No Fear in Love"

[1] Joshua Graves, *How Not to Kill a Muslim: A Manifesto of Hope for Christianity and Islam in North America* (Eugene, OR: Cascade Books, 2015), 70.

[2] I describe this incident in more detail in the introduction.

³ In her book *The Misunderstood Jew*, New Testament scholar Amy-Jill Levine, who is Jewish, encourages this kind of reimagining of the Good Samaritan story so that audiences grasp its core message: "To recognize the shock and possibility of the parable in practical, political, and pastoral terms, we might translate its first-century geographical and religious concerns into our modern idiom." Amy-Jill Levine, *The Misunderstood Jew: The Church and the Scandal of the Jewish Jesus* (New York: HarperOne, 2007), 49.

⁴ Ibid., 146.

⁵ Graves, *How Not to Kill a Muslim*, 39. In his chapter "The Paradigm Is a Parable," 30–41, Graves gives an extended treatment of the Good Samaritan story, and how its different levels of interpretation can be applied to Christians' engagement with Muslims today. His writing contributed much to my own reflection.

⁶ One notable example is Pope Gregory VII who in 1076 wrote to Al-Nasir, the Muslim Ruler of Bijaya, present-day Algeria: "Almighty God, who wishes that all should be saved and none lost, approves nothing in so much as that after loving Him one should love his fellow man, and that one should not do to others, what one does not want done to oneself. You and we owe this charity to ourselves especially because we believe in and confess one God, admittedly, in a different way, and daily praise and venerate him, the creator of the world and ruler of this world." John Borelli, "Christian-Muslim Relations in the United States," U.S. Conference of Catholic Bishops, December 23, 2003, https://www.usccb.org.

⁷ Contrary to popular assumptions, declarations of Church councils are considered the most authoritative teaching issued by the Catholic Church. Papal infallibility as a concept was only articulated in the nineteenth century, and has only been invoked on two occasions (related to doctrines about Mary, the mother of Jesus).

⁸ See Second Vatican Council, "Decree on the Church's Missionary Activity, *Ad gentes*, 7 December, 1965," in *Vatican II Council: Constitutions, Decrees, Declarations*, ed. Austin Flannery, OP (Northport, NY: Costello, 1996), sec. 3; "Pastoral Constitution on the Church in the Modern World, *Gaudium et spes*, 7 December, 1965," sec 25 (hereafter cited as *GS*); "Dogmatic Constitution on the Church, *Lumen gentium*, 21 November 1964, sec. 16–17 (hereafter cited as *LG*); "Declaration on the Relation of the Church to Non-Christian Religions, *Nostra aetate*, 28 October, 1965," sec. 1–5 (hereafter cited as *NA*).

⁹ *NA*, sec. 1.

¹⁰ *NA*, sec. 3.

¹¹ *NA*, sec. 2.

¹² *NA*, sec. 5.

¹³ "A person who does not persevere in charity, however, is not saved, even though incorporated into the church. . . . If they fail to respond in thought, word and deed to that grace, not only will they not be saved, they will be the more severely judged" (*LG*, sec. 14).

¹⁴ *GS*, sec. 4.

¹⁵ "Catholic Social Teaching," Catholic Community Services and Catholic Housing Services of Western Washington, https://ccsww.org.

¹⁶ Marcus Mescher, *The Ethics of Encounter: Christian Neighbor Love as a Practice of Solidarity* (Maryknoll, NY: Orbis Books, 2020).

¹⁷ See, for example, Bryan N. Massingale, *Racial Justice and the Catholic Church* (Maryknoll, NY: Orbis Books, 2010).

¹⁸ University courses have touched on this intersection, however. At Catholic Theological Union, Scott Alexander teaches a course on Islamophobia that looks to craft a

Catholic response "in light of Catholic social teaching, theology of interreligious dialogue, and the longstanding praxis of Catholic-Muslim dialogue in the U.S." "Course Descriptions—2020," Catholic Theological Union, https://ctu.edu/.

[19] Felicitas Opwis, "Maqāṣid al-Sharīʿah," in *The Oxford Encyclopedia of Islam and Law*, Oxford Islamic Studies Online, http://www.oxfordislamicstudies.com.

[20] Ibid.

[21] Andrew Kim, *An Introduction to Catholic Ethics since Vatican II* (New York: Cambridge University Press, 2015), 120.

[22] Second Vatican Council, "Declaration on Religious Liberty, *Dignitatis humanae*, 7 December, 1965," in *Vatican II Council: Constitutions, Decrees, Declarations*, ed. Austin Flannery, OP (Northport, NY: Costello, 1996), sec. 2 (hereafter cited as *DH*).

[23] *DH*, sec. 2.

[24] *DH*, secs. 3–4.

[25] Susan Hayward, "Understanding and Extending the Marrakesh Declaration in Policy and Practice" (Washington, DC: United States Institute of Peace, September 30, 2016), https://www.usip.org.

[26] *DH*, sec 6.

[27] Asad Dandia, "My Life under NYPD Surveillance: A Brooklyn Student and Charity Leader on Fear and Mistrust," American Civil Liberties Union, June 18, 2013, https://www.aclu.org/blog/national-security/discriminatory-profiling/my-life-under-nypd-surveillance-brooklyn-student-and.

[28] Francis, *Gaudete et exsultate*, Vatican.va, sec. 6.

[29] *Catechism of the Catholic Church*, 2nd ed. (New York: Doubleday, 1995), 1906.

[30] Archbishop William Lori, "Archbishop Lori: How Church Teaching Can Help Explain Why 'Black Lives Matter,'" *America Magazine*, July 27, 2020, https://www.americamagazine.org.

[31] Namira Islam, "Soft Islamophobia," *Religions* 9, no. 280 (September 15, 2018): 11.

[32] *GS*, sec. 1.

[33] Sebastian Gomes, *The Francis Impact | Quebec Teaser* (Salt+Light Media, 2019), https://vimeo.com/325737692.

[34] "Quebec Cardinal Pledges Solidarity, Prayer for Victims of Mosque Attack," *Catholic News Agency*, January 30, 2017, https://www.catholicnewsagency.com.

[35] Ibid.

[36] Suzanne Barakat, "Islamophobia Killed My Brother. Let's End the Hate," TED Talk, 2016, https://www.ted.com.

[37] Pontifical Council for Interreligious Dialogue, "Dialogue and Proclamation: Reflection and Orientations on Interreligious Dialogue and the Proclamation of the Gospel of Jesus Christ," May 19, 1991, https://www.vatican.va.

[38] These observations come from my own visits to these towns and meeting with local educators and community leaders there.

[39] William Byron, SJ, "The 10 Building Blocks of Catholic Social Teaching," *America Magazine*, October 31, 1998, https://www.americamagazine.org.

[40] Pope Francis, *The Church of Mercy: A Vision for the Church* (Chicago: Loyola Press, 2014), 107.

[41] Though many Catholics invoke this principle to oppose same-sex unions and other "nontraditional" family dynamics, Catholics as a whole hold widely diverse ideas of what it means to value and protect family life.

⁴² Inspired by Archbishop Lori making this important point regarding anti-Black racism, I have adapted it to the case of Islamophobia.

⁴³ Pontifical Council for Justice and Peace, *Compendium of the Social Doctrine of the Church* (Washington, DC: USCCB Publishing, 2004), 514.

⁴⁴ James Martin, SJ, "Brother Christian's Testament," *America Magazine*, November 14, 2015, https://www.americamagazine.org.

⁴⁵ Despite his deep insights on the mechanism of scapegoating, Girard himself fell into scapegoating Muslims toward the end of his career. In interviews he gave in the years after September 11, 2001, he made comments like, "The fight is really between Christianity and Islam." Robert Doran and René Girard, "Apocalyptic Thinking after 9/11: An Interview with René Girard," *SubStance* 37, no. 1 (2008): 29.

⁴⁶ Graves, *How Not to Kill a Muslim*, 62.

⁴⁷ In its entirety, this quote focuses on "White Christians," among whom anti-Muslim views are more prevalent. However, Islamophobia is a problem that goes beyond White people, thus the adjustment to the quotation. Catherine Orsborn, "Christians, Islamophobia Is Our Problem," *Sojourners*, March 20, 2019, https://sojo.net.

⁴⁸ *Catechism of the Catholic Church* (United States Catholic Conference, 1994), no. 1935, quoting Vatican II, *GS*, sec, 29.

⁴⁹ Pontifical Council for Justice and Peace, *Compendium of the Social Doctrine of the Church* (United States Conference of Catholic Bishops, 2007), no. 433.

⁵⁰ United States Catholic Bishops, *Brothers and Sisters to Us*, 1979, no. 39.

⁵¹ Francis, "Address of Pope Francis to the Diplomatic Corps Accredited to the Holy See," March 22, 2013, http://www.vatican.va.

⁵² Pope Francis (@pontifex), Twitter, 7:30a.m., January 11, 2018, https://twitter.com.

⁵³ "40 Hadith Nawawi 13," Sunnah.com, https://sunnah.com.

⁵⁴ United Church of Christ Board, "Reaffirming the United Church of Christ's Commitment to Interreligious Relations and Deploring Religious Bigotry: A Resolution of Witness," United Church of Christ, April 2019, http://ucceverywhere.org.

10. Living Out "Love of Neighbor"

¹ Interview with Nazir Harb Michel.

² "Flowers and Good Wishes Shower Lynnwood Mosque," *HeraldNet*, September 13, 2001, https://www.heraldnet.com.

³ *Religion & Ethics NewsWeekly*, "'Shoulder to Shoulder' at Washington National Cathedral," YouTube video, 1:03, October 26, 2015, https://www.youtube.com/watch?v=_eSXv5EStTg.

⁴ See, for example, "UCC DOC Statement on Vilification of Muslims," Global Ministries, December 9, 2015, https://www.globalministries.org; Press Release, "The Hate That Hatred Produced: AME Church Statement on the Murder of Muslim Worshipers in New Zealand," *United Methodist Insight*, March 19, 2019, https://um-insight.net.

⁵ Matthew Duss et al., "Fear, Inc. 2.0: The Islamophobia Network's Efforts to Manufacture Hate in America" (Washington, DC: Center for American Progress, February 2015), https://cdn.americanprogress.org, 24.

⁶ Ibid.

⁷ Simone Campbell, "As Supreme Court Considers Trump's Travel Ban, Remember Pope's Words," *National Catholic Reporter*, April 25, 2018, https://www.ncronline.org.

[8] Maria Baer, "Christians at Phoenix Protest Stand between Muslims and Anti-Islam Crowd," *World*, June 2, 2015, https://world.wng.org.

[9] "Dr. Larycia Hawkins Speaks about Her Recent Suspension from Wheaton College," YouTube video, 0:54, December 16, 2015, https://www.youtube.com/watch?v=gtXmryT32oc.

[10] Aaya Al-Shamahi, "American-Moroccan Muslim Woman Targeted in Islamophobic Attack," *Middle East Eye*, August 13, 2020, https://www.middleeasteye.net.

[11] Ibid.

[12] "Bystander Intervention," American Friends Service Committee, https://www.afsc.org/bystanderintervention; "SPLC on Campus: A Guide to Bystander Intervention," Southern Poverty Law Center, October 5, 2017, https://www.splcenter.org.

[13] I adapted my example from this one: Camila Domonoske, "Boston Launches Anti-Islamophobia Poster Campaign," *NPR*, July 18, 2017, https://www.npr.org.

[14] "Bystander Intervention," American Friends Service Committee.

[15] Michael D. Calabria, OFM, "Message for the Month of Ramadan 2019," *Ordo Fratrum Minorum* (blog), May 5, 2019, https://ofm.org.

[16] "Muslim Catholic Alliance Fifth Anniversary," *Roman Catholic Diocese of Rochester* (blog), April 8, 2008, https://www.dor.org.

[17] "Muslim Catholic Alliance (MCA): Agreement of Understanding and Cooperation," April 9, 2003, https://www2.naz.edu.

[18] Jeff Witherow, "Interfaith Presentation Introduces Catholics to Basics of Islam," *Catholic Courier*, February 25, 2019, https://catholiccourier.com.

[19] Pope Francis, "*Misericordiae Vultus*—Bull of Indiction of the Extraordinary Jubilee of Mercy," April 11, 2015, http://w2.vatican.va.

[20] Michael O'Loughlin, "Defying the Governor, Indianapolis Archbishop Takes in Syrian Refugees," *Crux*, December 8, 2015, https://cruxnow.com.

[21] Associated Press, "Indianapolis Archbishop Joe Tobin, Who Defied Pence on Refugees, Named a Cardinal," *Indianapolis Star*, October 9, 2016, https://www.indystar.com.

[22] Rome Reports in English, "Pope Washes the Feet of Muslim Refugees: We Are Brothers, We All Want to Live in Peace," YouTube video, 4:00, March 24, 2016, https://www.youtube.com.

[23] "Social Norms Approach," National Social Norms Center at the Michigan State University, http://socialnorms.org/social-norms-approach/.

[24] Bridge Initiative Team, "These Evangelical Christians Are Standing with Muslims," *Bridge Initiative*, April 4, 2017, https://bridge.georgetown.edu.

[25] Mallory Wyckoff, "We Must Put Forth the Effort to Get to Know Our Muslim Neighbors | Opinion," *The Tennessean*, August 5, 2020, https://www.tennessean.com.

[26] Shoulder to Shoulder Campaign, "Reflecting and Re-Imagining with Rev. Jen Bailey," video recording, August 4, 2020, https://www.facebook.com.

[27] These ideas are informed by Todd Green, who has written and spoken about his own discernment of which approach to take.

[28] Suzanne Barakat, "Islamophobia Killed My Brother. Let's End the Hate," TED Talk, 2016, https://www.ted.com.

[29] Lauren Effron, "Pope Francis Tells Americans 'Be Courageous' during ABC News Virtual Audience," *ABC News*, September 4, 2015, https://abcnews.go.com.

[30] Ijeoma Oluo (@ijeomaoluo), Twitter, 8:38 pm, Jul 14, 2019, https://twitter.com.

[31] Kenneth Cragg, *Muhammad and the Christian: A Question of Response* (London: Oneworld, 1984), 64.

[32] Josh Zeitz, "When America Hated Catholics," *Politico*, September 23, 2015, https://www.politico.com.

[33] Inter-Religious Task Force, "A Declaration of Inter-Religious Commitment: A Policy Statement of the Evangelical Lutheran Church in America," August 9, 2019, http://download.elca.org.

[34] Examples of this are the following headlines: Kathryn Jean Lopez, "Could Islam Learn from Jesus—And Pope Francis?," *Crux*, April 11, 2017, https://cruxnow.com; John Allen, "Why Muslims Need to Hear from Both Pope Francis and Cardinal Burke," *Crux*, September 1, 2016.

[35] "Dangerous Speech: A Practical Guide," Dangerous Speech Project, August 4, 2020, https://dangerousspeech.org/guide/.

[36] Óscar Romero, "This Is the Homily Óscar Romero Was Delivering When He Was Killed," *America Magazine*, October 12, 2018, https://www.americamagazine.org.

[37] Michelle Boorstein, "Evangelical and Muslim Clerics Meet to Find Common Ground," *Valley News*, February 8, 2018, https://www.vnews.com.

Index

Abedin, Huma, 24
Abu Ghraib prison, 37–38
Abu Naim, Ziad, 78
Abukaram, Noor, 21
Abu-Salha, Mohammad, 74
Abu-Salha, Razan, 73–75
Abu-Salha, Yusor, 73–75
ACT! for America, 29, 30, 110, 122
Afghanistan, 16, 37, 172
  Afghan women, misperceptions of, 47
  drone attacks on, 44
  US militarism and, 38, 100, 123
Ahmed, Riz, 84
airport profiling, 21, 37
Al-Baghdadi, Abu Bakr, 83
alcohol consumption, 179
Al-Ghazali, Abu Hamid, 151–52
Ali, Ayaan Hirsi, 29, 47–48, 101–2
Ali, Muhammad, 60
Al-Kamil, Al-Malik, Sultan, 139–40
Allahu akbar phrase, 86–87, 88, 101
Al-Marayati, Laila, 80
Al-Tayeb, Ahmed, 169
Amazon.com book reviews, 31
Antichrist, Muslims cast as, 124, 132
anti-Muslim activism, 8, 25, 28, 30,
    35, 93
  American influence on, 52–53
  Christian faith, done in the name of,
    108–9
  scapegoating of Muslims, 101–2

sharia, misunderstanding, 66, 95
anti-Muslim dog whistles, 27
anti-Semitism, 7, 55, 62–63, 65, 175
apparel, 4, 21, 50, 70–71, 99, 153, 157.
  See also headscarves and hijabs;
  turbans
Arab peoples, 7, 37, 40, 59, 61, 130
  Arab Christians, 55, 61, 76, 122,
    124–25, 139
  Arabic language, Western
    discomfort with, 71, 86–87, 97,
    101–2
  demonization of, 73–74, 83
  Muslim, conflating with Arab, 4, 15,
    56, 63
Asian Exclusion Act of 1924, 61
Aydin, Cemil, 100
Ayoubi, Mustafa, 78

Bachmann, Michele, 24
Bailey, Jen, 173
Bannon, Steve, 29, 116, 119
Barakat, Deah, 73–75, 155
Barakat, Suzanne, 155, 159, 177
Bargh, John, 73
Battle of Lepanto, 127, 137, 138
Battle of Vienna, 138
Bayrakli, Enes, 6
beards, 4, 16, 45, 56, 63, 72
Becket Fund for Reli-
  gious Liberty, 153

233